Ghost Dances and Identity

The publisher gratefully acknowledges the generous contribution to this book provided by the General Endowment Fund of the University of California Press Foundation.

Ghost Dances and Identity

Prophetic Religion and
American Indian Ethnogenesis
in the Nineteenth Century

Gregory E. Smoak

UNIVERSITY OF CALIFORNIA PRESS
Berkeley · Los Angeles · London

University of California Press, one of the most
distinguished university presses in the United States,
enriches lives around the world by advancing scholarship in the humanities, social sciences, and natural
sciences. Its activities are supported by the UC Press
Foundation and by philanthropic contributions from
individuals and institutions. For more information,
visit www.ucpress.edu.

University of California Press
Berkeley and Los Angeles, California

University of California Press, Ltd.
London, England

Library of Congress Cataloging-in-Publication Data
Smoak, Gregory E., 1962–
Ghost dances and identity : prophetic religion and
American Indian ethnogenesis in the nineteenth century
/ Gregory E. Smoak.
        p.   cm.
Includes bibliographical references and index.
ISBN 0-520-24658-6 (cloth : alk. paper)
   1. Ghost dance—History—19th century.   2. Shoshoni
Indians—Rites and ceremonies.   3. Shoshoni Indians—
Religion.   4. Shoshoni Indians—Ethnic identity.
5. Bannock Indians—Rites and ceremonies.
6. Bannock Indians—Religion.   7. Bannock
Indians—Ethnic identity.   I. Title.
E99.S4S64   2005
299.7'98'09034—dc22   2005011962

Printed and bound in Canada

15   14   13   12   11   10   09   08   07   06
10   9   8   7   6   5   4   3   2   1

This book is printed on New Leaf EcoBook 60, contain-
ing 60% post-consumer waste, processed chlorine free;
30% de-inked recycled fiber, elemental chlorine free;
and 10% FSC-certified virgin fiber, totally chlorine free.
EcoBook 60 is acid-free and meets the minimum
requirements of ANSI/ASTM D5634-01 (Permanence
of Paper).

For Janet M. Everts Smoak
and Floyd A. O'Neil

Contents

Maps

Acknowledgments

During the time it took to write this book, I ran up a debt to many fine people and institutions. The Department of History at the University of Utah provided generous support through many of those years. The University's Tanner Humanities Center awarded me a year-long graduate student fellowship, and the Graduate School supported my research and writing with a University Research Fellowship and the Steffensen Cannon Scholarship. The American Philosophical Society awarded me a Phillips Fund Grant for Native American Research. I spent nearly three months in Washington, D.C., on a graduate-student fellowship from the Smithsonian Institution. During that time the staff of the National Anthropological Archives and the National Archives greatly assisted my work. Likewise, the good people at the Idaho State Historical Society, the Nevada State Historical Society, the Special Collections Department at Idaho State University, and the Special Collections and Western Americana Departments at the University of Utah's Marriott Library deserve a hearty thank-you. I am also grateful to my colleagues in the history departments at the University of Minnesota and Colorado State University.

   This book would have been impossible were it not for the time I spent at the American West Center of the University of Utah. It is a special place that entrusts young scholars (although that label no longer applies to me) with very important work. As other center alumni can attest, Floyd O'Neil, Pat Albers, and Dan McCool have kept the center a vibrant (not to mention fun) place to work. Thanks to my center colleagues Sharon Austin, Winston Erickson, Judy Hurst, Jennifer Lowry, and Jennifer Robinson.

A scholar is lucky to find one true mentor during an academic career. I have been fortunate to find three. Richard White was a demanding but understanding dissertation director. Just as important, he remained generous with his advice and support through the long process of turning that dissertation into this book. I have known Pat Albers not only as a teacher but also as a colleague and friend during her tenure as the director of the American West Center. I had the good fortune to spend another year in her company during a sojourn at the University of Minnesota. Finally, Floyd A. O'Neil, director emeritus of the American West Center, has been a constant source of inspiration (and bad jokes) who has meant more to me than words can describe.

The members of the Shoshone-Bannock Tribes and the staff of the tribal attorney's office with whom I have had the privilege of working during the last decade have also been a source of inspiration, especially Candy Jackson, Gail Martin, and Louise Dixey. Several tribal members, including Lionel Boyer, Gail Martin, and Ardith Peyope, read the manuscript. I have done my best to address their questions and concerns. Even so, this history is not officially sanctioned or approved by the Shoshone-Bannock Tribes or by any individual tribal member. All errors of omission or interpretation are mine.

Many friends and colleagues offered helpful suggestions for revisions. Pat Albers, Ruth Alexander, Mark Fiege, Kirsten Fischer, Bob Goldberg, Richard Hart, Eric Hinderaker, Rebecca Horn, David Jenkins, Floyd O'Neil, Jeff Ostler, and Richard White read the entire manuscript in one form or another. I inflicted it on Mark, Pat, and Richard more than once. I truly appreciate their feedback. Members of the faculty research seminar at Colorado State University commented on several chapters. Will Bagley kept a sharp eye out for sources, as only he can. Raymond J. DeMallie read the manuscript for the University of California Press. I am grateful for his advice and support throughout this process. Drusilla Gould and Christopher Loether of Idaho State University helped correct my understanding and spelling of Shoshone words.

I would also like to acknowledge my friends and family for their support. My brother Chris, sister-in-law Emily, and my twin nieces Hannah and Emma (who perhaps will read this book when they are a little older), thank you. My mom is no longer with us, but she left our family with a love of travel, history, and the American West. Chris Hopkins and

Christy McCowan make me part of their family when I visit Salt Lake City, as do Fiona Smith and Jamie Gill. Janet Ore, Mark Fiege, and Alexandra Fiege-Ore have become my family in Fort Collins. Cycling in the big hills with Ruth Alexander helps to keep me sane. Ann Little and Chris Moore keep their door open for me. Mark Fiege, Matt Klingle, Mike Lansing, David Rich Lewis, and Jay Taylor keep history fun! And, finally, thanks to Janet M. Everts Smoak, who, although she lives far away, is always close to my heart.

Introduction

Endings and Beginnings

> Your people have seen with their own eyes what we are doing
> out here in the west. We still have all our old customs. . . . We
> understand that in your country all the old Indian games and
> customs are abolished. We fail to see the humanity and justice
> in abolishing all our time immemorial pastimes and forms of
> worship.
>
> James Ballard and Joe Wheeler (Shoshone-Bannock)
> to the "Sioux Chiefs," 1894

Just after 9:30 on the morning of 29 December 1890, the shooting began.
The previous afternoon, soldiers of the United States Seventh Cavalry
had intercepted Bigfoot's Minneconjou Lakotas and forced them to camp
along Wounded Knee Creek in the new state of South Dakota. Like many
other Lakotas, Bigfoot's people had adopted a religion that had emerged
from the Walker River Reservation, in western Nevada, nearly two years
earlier. There, the Northern Paiute prophet Wovoka told the faithful that,
if they practiced the prescribed rituals and led honest, peaceful lives, they
would soon be reunited with their deceased friends and loved ones on a
reborn earth. Contemporary white observers labeled it the Ghost Dance
religion, or, more commonly, they derisively referred to the faith simply
as the "Messiah Craze." Among the Lakotas the dance had become a
religion of resistance. Many dancers wore "ghost shirts," which they
believed rendered them bulletproof. The religious excitement frightened
local whites and drew the attention of the military. At Standing Rock—a
Lakota reservation that straddles the border between North and South
Dakota west of the Missouri River—the agent James McLaughlin used
the unrest as a pretext to remove his great political foe, Sitting Bull, from
the reservation. News of the renowned Lakota leader's assassination during the attempted arrest spread like wildfire across the Dakota prairie.

Red Cloud Cheos
Pine Ridge

Fearing the soldiers would come for his people, Bigfoot fled the Cheyenne River Reservation in South Dakota, hoping to find sanctuary at Pine Ridge with Red Cloud. The Minneconjous never made it. As the soldiers attempted to disarm them, the shaman Yellow Bird told the warriors wearing the sacred shirts not to fear the soldiers' bullets. By Lakota accounts, a deaf young man refused to give up the rifle for which he had paid so much money, and in a struggle with the soldiers the weapon discharged. The Seventh Cavalry then opened fire into the camp. When the rifles and Hotchkiss cannons finally fell silent, well over 150 Lakotas and twenty-five soldiers were dead.[1]

The Wounded Knee Massacre, one of the most horrifying and iconic moments in American Indian history, has exerted a profound influence over historical interpretations of the Ghost Dance. As Wounded Knee became a marker for the end of the Indian wars and, indeed, for the end of the frontier (1890, coincidentally, was the year of the census that Frederick Jackson Turner seized on to lament the passing of the frontier and to prophesy the coming of a new and uncertain age in American history), "ghost dancing" became a metaphor for the desperate and illusory attempt of a people to recover the unrecoverable. These notions are nowhere more evident than in the title of the most frequently cited historical account of the Lakota Ghost Dance, Robert M. Utley's *The Last Days of the Sioux Nation*. Of course, the Sioux Nation survives to this day, as does the symbolic power of Wounded Knee. By the 1970s the massacre had become a nationally recognized symbol of the brutality of American conquest. It formed the dramatic climax of Dee Brown's bestseller *Bury My Heart at Wounded Knee*, and in 1973 the radical American Indian Movement took over the tiny hamlet adjacent to the mass grave in a two-month siege that garnered international media attention. It is not surprising, therefore, that studies of the Ghost Dance religion have a hard time escaping the pull of Wounded Knee. As a consequence, the Ghost Dances are nearly always cast as expressions of endings, desperation, and death.

Yet viewing the Ghost Dances simply as a heartbreaking delusion ignores both the survival of the religion (it continued even among the Lakotas after Wounded Knee) and the far more complex issues of ethnic and racial identity raised by such movements. Among the Bannock- and Shoshone-speaking peoples of southern Idaho, the Ghost Dance religion—known in the Northern Shoshone dialect as *nazánga,* literally "to hold hands and walk"—was not a desperate religious fantasy that arose and was quickly abandoned after the prophesied golden age failed to return, but an old ceremony. Throughout the nineteenth century, native prophets and the Ghost Dance itself had been central to the religious lives of Shoshone and Bannock, or Newe (pronounced Ney-wa), peoples as they faced the growing domination of the Euro-American world. During the early years of reservation life, the Ghost Dance became part of a long-standing religious response to colonization, a response rooted in preexisting cultural practices and shaped by the emergence of ethnic and racial identity. The people who settled on the Fort Hall Reservation in southeastern Idaho—particularly those identified by white observers as Bannocks—were active participants in and missionaries of the religion. What was an old belief for Newe people became, in the 1870s and 1890s, a bridge to other American Indian peoples, the basis of two pan-Indian religious movements, and a powerful statement of a shared American Indian racial identity.

This evidence counters the standard view of the Ghost Dances and raises important questions. Why, for instance, did the religion survive at Fort Hall for decades when it was apparently short-lived elsewhere? And, if Bannocks were indeed the principal Ghost Dancers, why were they more active than the Shoshones, with whom they shared kinship bonds as well as the Fort Hall Reservation? In other words, what did it mean to be Shoshone or Bannock, or, for that matter, Indian? How did those identities emerge, and what are their connections to the Ghost Dance? The story that follows explores Shoshone and Bannock engagement with prophetic religion and their interactions with Euro-Americans in the nineteenth century as a means of answering these questions. The Ghost Dances were functional, not delusional. On one level they represented a culturally consistent appeal to a supernatural power aimed at restoring the flow of that power toward native people. But on another they were a vehicle for the expression of meaningful social identities. Moreover, the parallels between the Ghost Dances and the prophetic religion of Euro-Americans allowed native peoples to engage the dominant society in a conversation concerning American identities in an age of radical change.

Nearly four years after the massacre at Wounded Knee, the Lakota Ghost Dance apostle Kicking Bear received a letter from the Fort Hall Reservation.[2] The letter offers intriguing evidence of the role of the Ghost Dances in identity formation. On the surface it thanked the "Sioux Chiefs" for their recent visit to Fort Hall, but Captain Charles Penny, the acting agent at the Pine Ridge Reservation, suspected that the authors' true intent was to revive Ghost Dancing. The letter read:

"Kicking Bear" - LaKota's Ghost Dance Apostle

We the undersigned chiefs and headmen of the Shoshone and Bannock tribes of Indians, hereby write you our appreciation of the visit of your people to our reservation. Your people have seen with their own eyes what we are doing out here in the west. We still have all our old customs, providing such dances and sports do not in any way interfere with our work, etc.

We believe there is time for everything in this world—time for work, time for dancing and pleasure, and time for sleep.

We understand that in your country all the old Indian games and customs are abolished. We fail to see the humanity and justice in abolishing all our time immemorial pastimes and forms of worship. We see no harm in indulging in worshiping the Great Spirit in our old way, and also see no harm in our old games and sports, long as they do not interfere with our work.

We earnestly hope you shall explain to your agent and prove to him there is no evil in your customs of worship and dances, etc.

(signed)
James Ballard, Principal Chief
Joe Wheeler, Chief Justice, Court of Indian Offences [sic]

Whether Ballard and Wheeler were promoting the Ghost Dance religion in particular or were suggesting a more general resistance to the cultural oppression of the reservation system is not clear. But, considering the long history of the Ghost Dances among Shoshone and Bannock peoples, it is not unreasonable to suggest that both men viewed the religion as a "traditional" form of worship. Certainly they expressed their ideas in terms of a shared "Indian" identity that crossed ethnic, tribal, and historical boundaries.

Ballard and Wheeler illustrate the complex and contingent nature of social identity. Both men were leaders on the Fort Hall Reservation, but they had taken distinctly different paths to their positions and, seemingly, to their identity as Indians. Jim, or "Sheme," Ballard was often the agents' worst nightmare. He opposed every aspect of the federal government's assimilation program, from forced school attendance to the development of irrigated agriculture. He was, in the words of one Fort Hall agent, a leader of the "hunting, uncivilized, and nonprogressive element."[3] His following of about twenty Bannock and Shoshone families, like Ballard himself, was frequently identified as Bannock in official correspondence. In fact, Jim Ballard was a Shoshone. It was his rejection of assimilation programs rather than his linguistic affinity that led to this ethnic perception. Joe Wheeler seemed to be the direct opposite of Ballard: an English-speaking, "progressive" Shoshone who favored schools and "civilization."[4] Wheeler had indeed cut his hair, taken up farming, and served as a judge on the Court of Indian Offenses. But he also continued throughout the 1890s to live with two wives, a very non-progressive practice.[5] That these two men, so often at odds on a reservation marked by ethnic and political conflict, could find a common identity as Indians and extend their understanding of that identity to their Lakota friends is one of the crucial lessons that can be drawn from the Ghost Dance era at Fort Hall.

Human beings see themselves as individuals as well as members of one or more social groups. These conceptions, communicated inwardly to oneself or outwardly toward others, constitute identity. This study investigates the construction and expression of social identities, the concepts and images that lead some people to understand themselves as part of a group distinct from others. Every individual carries an array of social identities whose significance depends on the immediate social context. Thus, social identities—gender, class, ethnicity, and race, for example—are always intertwined and often contested. What's more, a person's conception of where he or she is situated in any one of these categories is always developed in conversation with the judgments of others.[6]

At its most basic level, an ethnic group is a named human population that shares a sense of solidarity. Ethnicity is a presumed identity, and unlike kinship, it is not based on blood ties or concrete social interaction. A number of features commonly mark ethnic groups: a proper name, a mythic common ancestry (including an origin story), shared memories of a past both mythical and historical, a link to a homeland, and common cultural elements, such as language, religion, and kinship systems.[7] Like all social identities, ethnicity is not primordial, innate, or unchanging. At various times, social, political, and economic factors have led to the emergence of new ethnic groups, a process known as *ethnogenesis*.[8] Yet even existing ethnic identities are historically contingent and socially negotiated through self-identification and assignment by others. "Ethnic identity," writes the sociologist Joane Nagel, "lies at the intersection of individual ethnic self-definition (who I am) and collective ethnic attribution (who they say I am)."[9]

In the past three decades, anthropologists, sociologists, and historians have increasingly explored the constructed nature of ethnicity and race. Since the pathbreaking work of Fredrik Barth, a number of scholars have come to consider the critical feature of ethnicity to be the ways in which groups maintain boundaries between themselves and others. As Barth argues (and as the case of Shoshones and Bannocks amply demonstrates), interethnic boundaries are not impermeable walls but rather "entail social processes of exclusion and incorporation whereby discrete categories are maintained *despite* changing participation and membership in the course of individual life histories."[10] The continuity of any ethnic group, then, depends on maintaining a boundary between it and other groups rather than on a discrete catalog of cultural elements or the individuals that the boundary encloses. Barth also demonstrated that ethnicboundary maintenance was not dependent on isolation but rather on social interaction and dialog between ethnic groups. The historian Alexandra Harmon has illustrated the ways in which native peoples around Puget Sound, mostly living outside reservations and often intermarried with non-Indians, redefined and asserted their Indianness. Kinship and trade relations, federal assimilation programs, and treaty fishing rights all became measures of Indian identity at different times. What it meant to be Indian might change, as might the set of individuals considered to be Indian, but, as Harmon demonstrates, "changes in culture and membership do not necessarily destroy ethnic categories themselves."[11] Like the work of Barth and Harmon, my study views ethnicity as a historical process of interaction and negotiation rather than as the innate essence of a people.

Race is an even thornier issue; it is perhaps the most divisive and misunderstood category in American society because it is a cultural construct that hides behind assertions of objective physical difference. There is no doubt that human populations of different geographic origins exhibit visible physical variations, but these differences alone do not constitute race. Human societies "make" races when they take perceived physical differences and combine them with historically and culturally derived perceptions of the Other. As European colonizers confronted new peoples, they made sense of difference in new ways. In time, ideas of difference based on climate, environment, and cultural practice gave way to the concept of race as inherent in the body and the blood. By the nineteenth century, European and Euro-American thinkers ascribed moral and intellectual characteristics to groups based on these perceived physical differences.[12] Racial categories are commonly understood as immutable and biological, but this is simply not the case. At times, ethnic and class divisions have overshadowed perceptions of biological difference in shaping racial divisions in the United States.[13]

The emergence and expression of social identities for American Indian peoples have been shaped by, and are made unique by, the development and coexistence of ethnic and tribal identities as well as a shared American

Indian racial identity. For the most part, minority peoples in American society are marked as either "ethnic" or "racial" groups: that is, they are understood as, or self-identify as, one or the other. American Indians, however, simultaneously hold strong ethnic identities—such as Shoshone, Bannock, Dine, and Lakota—and a racial identity as Indians. Anthropologists and other social scientists commonly distinguish between ethnic (social) and tribal (political) identity. My interest lies in the interplay of ethnic and tribal identity and race as separate but interrelated levels of social identity. The distinction between ethnic and tribal identity is important but secondary to the fact that each represents a less encompassing level of identity than race.[14]

The construction of ethnic and racial identity is a central theme of American Indian history. Before contact, American Indian peoples did not possess a shared identity, racial or otherwise. Identity could be expressed in ethnic or tribal terms, but even these concepts were amorphous; the essential basis for social organization was village or kinship ties. Native peoples sought to incorporate the European newcomers into these systems of understanding. They did not perceive a unity in Europeans that they did not see in themselves. Europeans and Euro-Americans, in contrast, treated native groups in a strangely dichotomous way. On the one hand, they recognized obvious ethnic and tribal distinctions; on the other, they ascribed a unity to these divergent peoples, lumping them together in terms of policy and attitude. Ethnic, and increasingly tribal, identities became more salient as relations with the colonizers came to dominate the economics and politics of native life. At the same time, American Indian peoples were exposed to Euro-American racial concepts through word and action, but it is unlikely that they accepted any suggestion of their own inferiority. Rather, they increasingly developed an Indian identity as a way of both incorporating the newcomers and positioning themselves in the new order.[15] None of this should suggest that native peoples simply discarded their cultural understandings. To the contrary, it was precisely their deep cultural practices, including kinship systems and religious beliefs, that provided the means for Indian peoples to make sense of the challenges they faced and reshape meaningful social identities that asserted their survival as a people.[16]

The Ghost Dances must be considered within these intertwined identities of ethnicity and race. Ghost Dances were certainly not the only way that Shoshones, Bannocks, or other native peoples expressed their ethnicity or an emerging sense of Indianness. At different places and in different times and contexts, American Indian peoples asserted, maintained,

Neolin
Delaware prophet
mid 18th Century

and reshaped social identities that reflected cultural meaning as well as the historical specifics of their relationship to other groups. Kinship, gender relations, legal rights, and political leadership have all been the basis for ethnic, tribal, and Indian identity.[17] And, from the time of the Delaware prophet Neolin in the mid–eighteenth century to the present day, religion has offered native peoples a powerful means to express identity. What follows is not *the* story of Indian identity, but one story of historic differentiation and identity formation, of religious persistence and innovation. Its premises are that beginnings are as important as endings and that the Shoshone-Bannock example provides a window onto the ways in which contingent events and deep cultural practices shaped the development and expression of social identities—ethnic, racial, and cultural—among American Indian peoples.

Writing the history of native peoples is fraught with political and cultural difficulties. The history that follows should not be misconstrued and misused by those bent on plundering native spirituality or sovereign rights. In this study I approach the Ghost Dance and other sacred beliefs as a scholar and an outsider. I treat religion as a social and cultural system, a set of sacred symbols that explain a people's creation, their relationship to the world and to others, and their destiny. This approach will undoubtedly seem alien to Indian people who view their spiritualism not as a cultural system but as an essence in their lives. From my perspective as an outsider, I cannot capture or explain the spiritual values that native peoples attach to these beliefs. Nor is it my intention, in describing American Indian religious beliefs, to provide a road map for non-Indian New Age "seekers" to appropriate these beliefs and warp them for their own purposes. For this reason such descriptions remain limited and focused upon illustrating the ways in which these beliefs could function as an expression of social identities.

Nor is it my intention in exploring the construction of social identities among native peoples to question the sovereign rights of American Indian nations. In the late eighteenth century, European colonists along the eastern seaboard of North America invented a nation and began to invent a national identity. The indigenous peoples that these new "Americans" encountered conceived of themselves and their relations to others in culturally and historically derived ways. The inability or unwillingness of Euro-Americans to understand and accept aboriginal conceptions of identity and social relations made identity formation a critical factor for the survival of native peoples. As the political, economic, and military power of the United States grew, older social identities and conceptions often gave way to newer and more salient expressions of identity. New social identities sometimes emerged from the shattering effects of epidemic disease, dislocation, and warfare. Others coalesced around the political demands of dealing with the United States. Whatever the reason, native groups made treaties and agreements in good faith with the United States and expected the same in return. To say that modern American Indian social identities are not the same as those held by indigenous peoples at contact in no way undercuts the legitimacy of modern Indian nations. Americans in 1776 did not understand or express their national identity in same ways as their descendants do today. To demand anything different of American Indian peoples represents an ethnocentric double standard and a profound misunderstanding of historical processes.

Throughout the text I make use of Shoshone and Bannock words. Representing these languages on paper is a complex and sometimes confusing task for a nonspeaker, given the number of living dialects and the variable writing systems that anthropologists have employed. Whenever possible I have adopted the spellings provided in Drusilla Gould and Christopher Loether's *An Introduction to the Shoshoni Language: Dammen Daigwape*, which focuses on dialects spoken on the Fort Hall Reservation. When I diverge from this system, I have identified the dialect and source.[18]

In what follows, part 1 examines the origins of Shoshone and Bannock ethnicity in a world that was, for the most part, of their own making. Until the beginning of the nineteenth century, no one of European descent had set foot in the Newe homeland. Still, the mediate, or indirect, effects of colonization had already begun to affect Newe life. Horses, European technology, and epidemic diseases initiated a process of historic differentiation felt to a differing extent by different groups, depending on their location and the choices they made. Eventually, Shoshone and Bannock groups coalesced into bands. With the growing immediate presence of Euro-Americans, new identities tied to band structure became increasingly important and ultimately formed the building blocks of Shoshone and Bannock ethnicity. Newe peoples made sense of the changes in their world in part through religious understandings rooted in shamanism and prophecy. But just as peoples do not live in isolation from others, beliefs do not exist in a vacuum. In the nineteenth century, Newe shamanism and prophecy entered into dialogue with the beliefs brought west by Indian peoples engaged in the fur trade and by

Christian missionaries. By the mid–nineteenth century, native prophets were preaching a syncretic religion that incorporated elements of Christianity with indigenous beliefs and asserted a native identity.

Part 2 follows the Shoshone and Bannock peoples through a period of declining autonomy as the United States exerted increasing control over their lives. Ethnic and tribal identities became more salient as individual groups sought to maintain their territorial and cultural integrity in the face of the expanding American empire. Yet, at the same time, the shared experiences of treaty making, reservation life, and aggressive assimilation programs helped confirm that in a racialized nation all American Indian peoples shared a larger identity that could encompass substantial ethnic differences. Shoshone and Bannock participation in the Ghost Dance movements of the 1870s and 1890s is inextricably linked to the construction of ethnic and racial social identities during these decades. The conclusion places the Shoshone-Bannock Ghost Dances within the larger context of identity formation and emerging nationalism that marked United States history in the nineteenth century. As Euro-Americans struggled to define the political and ideological boundaries of nationhood, prophetic religion often provided a common language for the dominant and the marginalized. For American Indian peoples, the nineteenth century saw warfare, dislocation, the destruction of native economies, and confinement on reservations, but it did not see their demise. To the contrary, it witnessed their emergence as a self-identified racial group. The shared discourse of prophecy was one means by which Indian peoples could mark off difference. Viewed in this way, the Ghost Dances were a prophetic expression of an American Indian identity that countered United States attempts to assert a particular national identity and to impose that vision on American Indians.

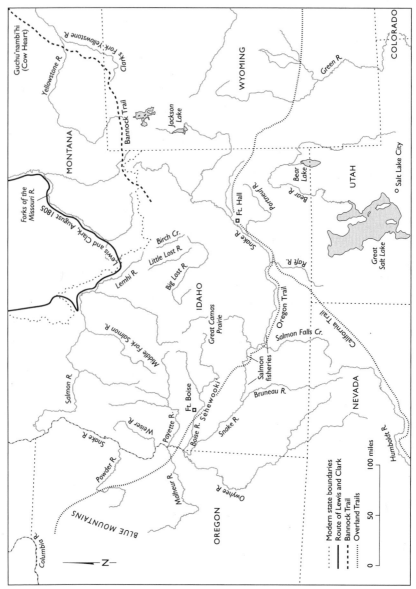

Map 1. Part of the Newe homeland, precontact to 1850s.

PART ONE

Identity and Prophecy in the Newe World

WHEN THE MEMBERS OF LEWIS and Clark's Corps of Discovery crossed the Continental Divide and descended into what is today Idaho's Lemhi Valley, they entered a complex and dynamic native world created by the ancestors of the modern Shoshone-Bannock people. The Newe world was not an untouched wilderness but a place with a long and rich social, religious, political, and economic history. It was also a world in the throes of great change. In the decades preceding and following that famous visit, the indirect and direct effects of colonization exerted a profound influence on Newe life. Horses, guns, disease, changing trade relations, and demographic migrations all affected older conceptions of social, political, and economic relations and identity. At the same time, native peoples west of the Rockies were enmeshed in a culturally rooted and ever-evolving set of religious beliefs, which provided a means for understanding the great changes in their lives and gave meaning to emerging identities.

CHAPTER 1

Snakes and Diggers

The Origins of Newe Ethnic Identities

During these years, the few whites then in that region called
the more miserable bands Diggers, or Shoshonees. . . . Their
condition is much poorer, having no horses. . . . Another
division of the Snakes . . . [the] Bonacks [are] better supplied
with all the means of Indian independence; horses, lodges,
guns, knives, and form bands annually to hunt in the buffalo
country.

Nathaniel J. Wyeth, 1848

By the time the Ghost Dance movements of the late nineteenth century
reached the Fort Hall Reservation in southeastern Idaho, government
officials and the local white population agreed that the reservation was
the home of two discrete peoples, whom they labeled Shoshones and
Bannocks. These same observers ascribed particular attitudes and behaviors to these ethnic identities, perhaps best illustrated by the "progressive" Joe Wheeler and the "nonprogressive" Jim Ballard. But these ethnic
identities were not age-old, fixed, or permanent. Rather, they were the
result of a historic process of social and economic differentiation beginning at the opening of the eighteenth century and stretching into the
reservation era and beyond. The first stages of this process took place at
time when the Newe peoples, who became the Shoshones and Bannocks,
enjoyed relative autonomy. In the 1600s, Newe peoples probably possessed a fairly uniform social structure and economy, tied together by an
intricate web of kinship. Into this world came horses, guns, and lethal
new diseases. Newe peoples incorporated or survived these Euro-
American agents of change, all the while modifying their culture to
exploit fresh opportunities and temper new restrictions.

Not all Newe groups responded in the same way. Horse ownership,
for instance, divided the Newes into mounted and foot-going groups,

drew Paiute-speaking people east, and led to the formation of bilingual "mixed bands." When the first white men set eyes on what is today Idaho, the process was already well under way. Early historic observers rarely recognized subtle cultural differences, but they did crudely note this most obvious feature of native life. In these early accounts the mounted groups were often called Snakes, whereas their foot-going counterparts were derisively known as Diggers.[1] It was the development of bands, which sprang from these socioeconomic distinctions, that by the reservation era provided the basis for Shoshone and Bannock ethnic identities.

Before there were Snakes, Diggers, Shoshones, or Bannocks, there were Newes. All of the Indian peoples who lived in southern Idaho at the time of white contact spoke a dialect of either or both Shoshone and Paiute, two closely related languages. Shoshone is a Central Numic tongue of the larger Uto-Aztecan linguistic stock. It is a widely dispersed language, its various dialects understood by Shoshonean peoples from Nevada to Wyoming and by the Comanches of the southern Plains. Paiute is a Western Numic language, and Bannock is a Northern Paiute dialect. It is intelligible by Paiute speakers from Fort Hall to the Mono Basin of California. Although mutually unintelligible, Paiute and Shoshone are very similar languages. A fluid social order and constant interaction between groups led to a great deal of lexical borrowing and bilingualism and prevented the emergence of deep dialectical differences. *Bannock* is an anglicization of *panákwate,* their name for themselves. *Shoshone* originates in the Shoshone word *sosoni',* a type of grass that was used to build conical dwellings. Some Plains groups referred to the Shoshones as "grass house people," and in 1805 William Clark reported, "This nation Call themselves *Cho-shon-nê.*" More accurately, they identified themselves that way to outsiders. Among themselves, the various Paiute, Bannock, and Shoshone speakers called themselves Numu, Neme, or Newe, meaning simply "the people."[2]

The starting point for any study of Newe social identities must be the protohistoric period, the era before direct Euro-American contact in which historical trends can be traced. There are, of course, models for understanding the earlier prehistory of the Great Basin, but all are subjects of intense debate. The most influential, and controversial, of these paradigms comes from linguistics. Proceeding from the theory that linguistic diversity is a function of time, the "Numic spread" theory posits that the area of the basin with the greatest dialectical diversity and the smallest language territories—the southwest corner of the Great Basin, near Death Valley—was the site from which a late and fairly rapid expansion of Numic-speaking peoples across the Great Basin and onto the Plains began. The large, fan-shaped area that Numic languages cover, with few dialectical differences, is used as evidence for this great population movement.[3] Before the Numic spread theory gained ascendancy, most archaeologists argued for a long period of cultural continuity, perhaps ten thousand years, in the Great Basin as a whole. More recent evidence from southern Idaho, however, has been interpreted to support the theory that Newe peoples did not occupy the area until the fifteenth century.[4] Regardless of archaeological or linguistic evidence, a clear understanding of prehistoric Newe social organization is essentially unrecoverable. The important, and established, fact is that the ancestors of the modern Shoshone-Bannock people lived in what is today southern Idaho at the opening of the protohistoric period.

There is no indication that the tribal or ethnic identities visible by the second half of the nineteenth century existed during the protohistoric era. The weight of ethnographic evidence suggests rather that the essential building block of pre-horse Newe society was the small "family cluster" or "kin clique"—several nuclear families that maintained close and consistent contact.[5] This view emerged most clearly from the work of Julian H. Steward and has often been overstated, misunderstood, and misused. Steward spent but six months doing his initial research among Basin peoples. Like many other ethnologists of his day, Steward viewed the Great Basin as a human laboratory in which to study the most "primitive" of peoples, hunter-gatherers. He asserted that the rigors of life in a harsh environment dictated a given people's social organization, and that Paiute and Shoshone speakers traveled in these small kin-based groups in order to exploit scarce resources. Band organization was nonexistent. Groups held a consensus right to the land, but because of the unpredictability of food resources and the fluid nature of the social order, these territories were not exclusive. Leadership was likewise rudimentary. The closest thing to chiefs or headmen were "talkers," men who kept track of the available foodstuffs and organized cooperative ventures. Families and individuals often switched groups in their never-ending search for sustenance. Steward characterized the hand-to-mouth life ways of basin peoples as a "gastric culture."[6]

Steward's analysis is fraught with problems and must be assessed with the utmost caution. Its most glaring flaw is his reliance on a crude environmental determinism that resulted in overstated generalizations and an underestimation of historical factors. For instance, Steward privileged the seed-gathering complex found in the more arid regions of the basin at the time of his research over all other subsistence strategies. Consequently, his simple "gastric culture" best describes some of the Shoshones and Paiutes of northern Nevada at only one moment in their history; it fails to capture the great diversity of subsistence practices and social organization evident among Newe groups at other places and times. The salmon-fishing populations along the Snake and Lemhi rivers, and especially the mounted buffalo hunters of the protohistoric and historic periods, do not fit neatly into Steward's model. Steward himself recognized this problem.[7] Moreover, there are questions concerning just how aboriginal a social order based on these small family groups actually was. Archaeological evidence suggests the presence of large, concentrated populations along the Humboldt River before the nineteenth century. Yet this is the very area where Steward developed his model and where it fits best. It is quite likely that historical factors, specifically the development of a trading and raiding route along the Humboldt after 1800, made that life-giving oasis a very dangerous place to live. Local groups probably withdrew from the river and traveled in small groups not only to exploit scattered resources but also to avoid roving "predatory bands" and stay alive.[8] Thus, if the family-cluster concept is to hold any analytical power, it is critically important to conceive of these groups not as ahistorical social isolates but rather as the building blocks of larger, nonpermanent social formations.

The key to understanding the development of Shoshone and Bannock ethnicity is kinship. Newe society was marked by intermarriage, bilingualism, and the easy transfer of families and individuals between groups. Descent was figured bilaterally: that is, just as in modern Euro-American culture, both sides of one's family are considered kin. Bilateral kinship allows individuals to activate a broad range of kinship ties at various times in their lives. Residence was initially matrilocal (with the wife's parents), but after the birth of the first child the couple felt free to live with other relatives. Fred Eggan has argued that marriage patterns elevated the "sibling group" to a central role in the social structure, a contention confirmed by Sven Liljeblad's research on family political leadership among the Bannocks.[9] Interaction between family clusters was extensive but informal, and there was no guarantee that the same people would travel, live together, or follow the same leader from year to year. The most stable units larger than the family cluster were winter camps. Established at attractive sites (sheltered, with wood, water, and forage), winter camps were used habitually, but it is impossible to determine from the historic or archaeological record whether the same families camped together each winter. Modern informants claim that families and individuals often wintered in different camps. Between the family cluster and the larger linguistic community, then, there were no *permanent* social institutions, and ethnic identities did not yet hold the saliency that they would gain by the reservation era.[10] Still, the groups with the strongest kinship ties gravitated toward each other as social and economic factors gave greater meaning to ethnic distinctions. Sibling bonds probably formed the basis for many family clusters and, by extension, the larger social groups that emerged later. In other words, the band and ethnic identities of the nineteenth century sprang from preexisting kin networks.

The social identities beyond family groups that existed among Newe peoples during the protohistoric era reflected the fluid nature of the precontact Newe world. Family clusters that habitually lived and traveled in close proximity and gathered together at various times for subsistence and ceremonial or defensive purposes often identified themselves and other Newe groups by the most important food source taken in an area. These "food names," however, did not represent discrete bands with a fixed membership or territorial range. Nor did they translate into fixed ethnic identities. For instance, *agai'-deka'*, or "salmon eaters," could refer to either Newes in the Lemhi Valley or those over two hundred miles away on the middle and lower Snake River. Moreover, many of the Lemhi Valley *agai'-deka'* also went "to buffalo," at which times they were *guchundeka'*, "buffalo eaters." (*Guchundeka'* also referred to the Eastern Shoshones of the Wyoming Plains.) Some group names referred to environmental adaptations. *Duku-deka'*, literally translated as "meat eaters," or more commonly "sheep eaters," was the name applied to the small Newe groups who lived and hunted at high elevations from the Wind River Range and Yellowstone Plateau of Wyoming all the way west to the Blue Mountains of Oregon. Many of the Lemhi Valley *agai'-deka'* were known as *duku-deka'* when they left the fisheries and returned to the mountains. Group names could also be geographic: the Newes who wintered on the upper Snake River in the vicinity of Fort Hall were known as *bohogoi'*, "people of the sagebrush butte," in reference to Ferry Butte, the prominent point visible in the northwest portion of the modern Fort Hall Reservation. A person's identity could remain fairly stable, but there was nothing to preclude the transfer of residence from one group to another.[11]

Nor did these social formations claim territorial rights exclusive of other Newe peoples. In the Western Shoshone dialect, the verb *nemi* means both "to live" and "to travel." Quite literally, to live was to travel across a large territory utilizing a wide range of resources. Yet, although a given group could range hundreds of miles each year, it also occupied a traditional "native land" (*tebíwa* in Bannock, *debia'* in the Northern Shoshone dialect). Here the group usually wintered and had uncontested access to resources. Rights to the *tebíwa* were not exclusive, but, out of respect, visitors from other Newe peoples always asked permission to join a people in the use of their native land.[12] Territorially as well as socially, then, the Newe world was a fluid and intricate network of kinship ties and extensive intergroup migration, and it cannot be assumed that the food-name groups constituted true bands, let alone tribal or ethnic identities.

Into this world of foot-going groups came the most important agent of social and economic differentiation in the protohistoric period: horses. Adopting an equestrian lifestyle, or dealing with peoples who had, revolutionized the lives of most of the tribes of the North American West. The Spanish settlements of New Mexico were the earliest source of horses for the intermountain and Plains peoples. By the 1640s Navajo, Apache, and Ute raiders regularly plundered the Spanish herds. The flow of horses out of New Mexico soared after the Pueblo revolt of 1680, and horses reached the Newe peoples of the Snake River region sometime around 1700, possibly as early as 1690.[13] There is a Newe tradition that their first horses came from their relatives, the Comanches, but it is just as likely that they obtained them from the Utes, who moved them north along the western slope of the Rockies. This western route was the most direct way to the Snake River Plain and the Columbia Plateau and avoided the hostile Apaches and Kiowas of the western plains.[14] The acquisition of horses revolutionized the social and economic lives of Newe peoples, increasing distinctions among them, drawing more Paiute speakers east, and intensifying conflict with the Blackfeet. All these factors in turn contributed to greater social cohesion among some Newe groups.

The first great consequence of horse ownership was the growth of significant social and economic distinctions between the mounted and the mostly foot-going groups. For the Comanches, the equestrian lifestyle became the basis for a new tribal identity. The Comanches split off from the main body of mounted Newes sometime in the late seventeenth century, and by the 1750s they had completed their migration south and southwest to supplant the Apaches as masters of the southern plains.[15]

The mounted Newes who remained on the upper Snake and Green rivers never developed so distinct a tribal identity, but they did increasingly incorporate elements of Plains equestrian culture into their established and varied economic culture. Mounted family groups could travel together for much longer periods, carrying far more equipment, food, and supplies. They could access a greater range of subsistence and trading sites—scattered over thousands of square miles—than their foot-going kin. Buffalo hunting, originally carried out on foot, gained increasing importance among the mounted groups. Still, they did not abandon established economic pursuits such as fishing, root and seed gathering, and small-game hunting.[16] The visible manifestation of this economic revolution was the influence of Plains material culture—parafleches, travois, Plains-style saddles and horse trappings, and skin-covered tipis—but just as their subsistence patterns retained important Basin orientations, so did their material culture. The mounted groups continued to use the ubiquitous conical baskets of Basin peoples as well as a complex fishing technology of the Plateau to exploit salmon runs on the Snake and Salmon rivers.[17] The mounted groups simply did not fit into neat culture areas, such as the "Great Basin," the "Plains," or "Plateau," and the economic distinctions that emerged between the mostly foot-going groups and the "wealthier" mounted groups was not a case of abandoning one way for another but of incorporating new opportunities.

The second great consequence of the acquisition of horses was the migration of Paiute speakers to the upper Snake River Plain, where they adopted the horse-bison economy then developing among the local Shoshone speakers and became an integrated minority within the larger group. It was this bilingual community that became the mixed bands of the treaty era and the Bannocks of the reservation period. The rich and varied economy that the equestrian life made possible attracted these migrants, but undoubtedly kinship ties were critical for determining exactly which families moved east. Mixed groups of Shoshone and Paiute speakers did not exist everywhere in the Great Basin. On the contrary, there was little intermixture of the two language groups. A possible explanation for this separation was that, in other places, both lived in similar landscapes and subsisted on essentially the same resources. In Nevada the line between the two language groups was fairly clear-cut. In Liljeblad's estimation there simply was no great incentive for one people to move into or share the other's territory. Only where more varied opportunities existed, to the north along the Snake and Salmon rivers, did substantial linguistic overlap occur. Yet even here bilingual alliance was not always the case. Most of the foot-going bands in the Snake River country between American Falls and the Boise River were exclusively Shoshone-speaking. During the historic period, the largest permanent Paiute-speaking presence was found on the upper Snake River Plain and in the Lemhi Valley, two centers of the equestrian economy and culture.[18]

The other important exception to this linguistic separation was found along the lower courses of the Boise, Payette and Weiser rivers, and it was there that Liljeblad surmised that the first mixed bands emerged. Known in Shoshone as *Sehewooki'* (*Séwoki'i* in Bannock), "willows standing in rows like running water," the area was a rich resource base.[19] The rivers abounded in salmon, and the nearby mountains offered root and hunting grounds. *Sehewooki'* was also one of the principal centers of the intertribal horse trade west of the Rockies during the protohistoric period and continued to host intertribal trade fairs until the late nineteenth century. Because of these advantages, the people who lived in these river valleys—oral traditions at Fort Hall hold that there was a mixed Shoshone-Paiute population at *Sehewooki'*—were the most sedentary of all Newe groups. For the same reasons, the area was also the westernmost stop in the regular rounds of the mounted Newe populations of the upper Snake River Plain. The kinship ties between the Boise-area people and those who wintered on the Fort Hall bottoms suggest that *Sehewooki'* was both the cradle of the mixed bands and the springboard for the Bannock migration to the east.[20]

How closely were Paiute speakers integrated into Shoshone society? Linguistic evidence can help answer this question as well as questions concerning the timing of the Bannock migration. According to Liljeblad, Paiute speakers within the mixed bands called their Shoshone companions *wihínakwate*, which is variously translated as "on the knife side" or "on the iron side." The Paiute speakers called themselves *panákwate*. (The equivalent Shoshone words are *wihiN-naite* and *bannaite'*.) Informants told Liljeblad, who studied Numic languages for over four decades, that *panákwate* meant "on the water side" or "on the west side." *Wihínakwate* and *panákwate* are essentially geographic referents to the original locations of the partners in the mixed bands. Primary evidence for this argument can be found in the account of the fur trader Alexander Ross, who reported that "Sho-sho-ne" meant "inland."[21] Liljeblad also emphasized that neither *wihínakwate* nor *panákwate* referred to a distinct "tribe" or people but rather to two "sides" of a bilingual "speech community." In accordance with bilateral kinship customs, people of mixed parentage could identify themselves either by the "side" whose language they preferred to speak or by the language spoken by the head-man they were then following. "In fact," wrote Liljeblad, "one cannot properly speak of a Bannock and Shoshoni tribal division."[22]

The third of the interrelated consequences of equestrian life for the Newes was an intensification of the conflict with their perennial foes, the Blackfeet. The same decades that saw the beginning of the Bannock migration also witnessed the ebbing of Newe residence on the northern Great Plains. As early as the 1720s, foot-going Newes ranged as far north as the Saskatchewan River, where they battled the Blackfeet. It is in regard to this struggle that the first references to the Newes appear in the historic record. In 1742 the de la Vérendrye brothers reported that the tribes of the northern plains were at war with the feared "Gens du Serpent" who lived to the west. Although it is not at all certain, it has long been assumed that these were the Snakes, or Newes.[23] There is more certainty that the Blackfoot war, coupled with a devastating smallpox epidemic, led to the Newe retreat from the plains of present-day Alberta and Montana in the mid– to late eighteenth century (the easternmost Newes continued to range east of the divide in central Wyoming).[24] War against the Blackfeet remained a constant in Newe life well into the historic period, and the consequent demands for defense influenced both the recruitment of Paiute-speaking allies and the emergence of band organi-zation, a crucial first step towards ethnic identity, among the upper Snake River Newes.

The best account of the Newe-Blackfoot conflict comes from the Northwest Company trader David Thompson, who spent the winter of 1787–88 in the lodge of Saukamappee, an elderly Piegan man who recounted his people's battles with the Snakes and the impact of horses, guns, and disease on the struggle. He was between seventy-five and eighty years of age at the time of Thompson's visit. His earliest recollec-tions dated to the 1720s, when Newe expansion onto the northern Plains had reached its zenith and the Piegans suffered the brunt of their attacks. Unlike the foot-going Piegans, the mounted Newes rode their horses swiftly among their enemies and "with their stone puk-a-mog-gan [and] knocked them on the head." The strange new animal alarmed the Blackfeet, "who had no idea of horses and could not make out what they were." The first horse Saukamappee ever saw was dead, having been shot out from under its Newe rider. He and many others flocked to the site to get a better look. The animal reminded them of a stag that had lost its horns, but as it was a "slave to man, like the dog" they named it the "Big Dog."[25]

The few horses the Newes possessed did not prove an overwhelming advantage in warfare. It was another European import, firearms, which the Blackfeet obtained from the French through intertribal trade, that turned the tide in the conflict. Until that time, large-scale battles were essentially shows of force, with each side taking refuge behind rows of shields and firing arrows with limited effect. The normally outnumbered Blackfeet appealed to Saukamappee's natal people, the Crees, for assistance. Sometime in the 1730s, the last "general battle" between the Newes and Blackfeet took place. Though again greatly outnumbered, the Blackfeet possessed a secret weapon: Saukamappee and nine other men carried guns. Lying beneath their shields, they crept to within sixty yards of the Newes, and when one of their enemy rose to shoot an arrow, the gunmen fired, with murderous effect. The disoriented and frightened Newes began to slip away, and when the Blackfeet charged, most fled the battlefield. The "terror" of the guns prevented future pitched battles. Ambushes and surprise attacks came to characterize the war. Here, the Blackfeet continued to enjoyed the advantage of guns and iron weapons as a result of their proximity to French, and later British, traders. The Newes, who had no traders among them, obtained only a few such items, either in battle or from their allies.[26] Moreover, by the mid-eighteenth century the Blackfeet had obtained horses. Facing a well-armed and now mounted foe, the Newes began their retreat from the northern Plains.

One final, devastating factor led to the Newe withdrawal to the southwest: disease. Saukamappee told Thompson how the Blackfeet came on an apparently abandoned Newe village along the Red Deer River in southern Alberta. Fearing a trap, the warriors cautiously watched the camp, but no one appeared. Horses, and even a herd of buffalo, grazed nearby. The Blackfeet attacked at dawn, cutting through the tents with their knives. What they found inside stopped them in their tracks: "There was no one to fight with but the dead and dying, each a mass of corruption." The Piegan warriors believed the "bad spirit had made himself master of the camp and destroyed them." They did not touch the victims but took the horses, the best tents, and any plunder that was "clean and good." But microbes are invisible, and diseases take no sides. Soon the pestilence struck the Blackfoot camp, killing more than half the population. For two or three years neither people felt much like fighting. When the conflict resumed, however, the Blackfeet advanced into present-day Montana, driving the Newes farther and farther south. As badly as the Blackfeet had suffered, the Newes suffered more: the catastrophic smallpox epidemic of 1781 made continued their residence on the northern

Plains untenable, except for a few small groups that took refuge among the Crows.[27]

By the time Lewis and Clark's Corps of Discovery made the first documented, direct contact with Newes in 1805, the process of social and economic differentiation was well under way. The expedition specifically sought out the Newes for assistance because they maintained large horse herds and because they were the natal people of the expedition's famed guide Sacajawea.[28] As chance would have it, Sacajawea's brother, Cameahwait, was a headman of the Newe group that the Corps of Discovery encountered in what is today Idaho's Lemhi Valley. Although the explorers' sojourn lasted less than three weeks among but a small portion of the larger "Snake Nation," and although the journals of Meriwether Lewis, William Clark, and others contain the ethnocentric judgments of their age, their detailed, vivid descriptions of subsistence strategies and social customs constitute the first Newe ethnography and provide a basic picture of Newe social identities at the beginning of the historic period.[29]

The journals reveal the effects of protohistoric trends such as the advent of the equestrian culture and the integrative effect of the Blackfoot war. "They have a great many fine horses, and nothing more," wrote expedition member Patrick Gass, "and on account of these they are much harassed by other nations."[30] Lewis reported that Newe warriors counted coup like their Plains enemies and added: "Each warrior keep[s] one or more horses tyed by a cord to a stake near his lodge both day and night and are always prepared for action at [a] moment[']s warning."[31] The source of such anxiety was the Blackfeet and their Gros Ventre confederates, who had forced the Newes from the Missouri headwaters and killed or captured twenty of Cameahwait's people in a recent attack. The explorers had expected to find the Newes around the forks of the Missouri and grew concerned as many miles, and precious summer days, passed without sight of their prospective allies. With fall fast approaching and the roughest segment of the journey at hand, it was imperative to make contact with the Newes and secure horses and information about routes through the mountains.

When Lewis finally crossed the divide and descended into the Lemhi Valley, he found a people who had suffered greatly at the hands of their enemies. They erected their only remaining tipi for the visitors' use; everyone else lived in conical brush lodges. The hostilities had forced the Newes into a defensive posture in which security was the first priority and food shortages were a constant threat. Out of custom and necessity, the Lemhi Valley Newes practiced a far more diverse subsistence cycle than their completely Plains-adapted enemies. This way of life was due in part to the presence of hostile tribes on the plains and in part to the varied opportunities available west of the divide. Fishing remained particularly important to all Newe peoples. The fisheries along the Lemhi River were some of the finest in the Newe country, and the people there exhibited a well-developed fishing culture and technology.[32] Hunting and gathering were also important aspects of their subsistence cycle. Serviceberry and chokecherry cakes were a staple in the lean times between the end of the salmon run and the Fall buffalo hunt. Antelope, taken after an arduous chase, and deer provided a more limited meat supply.[33] Many of the Newes, suspecting the strangers were in league with their enemies, were less than welcoming, and only through a long, pleading harangue was Cameahwait able to convince some of the people to help him assist the party.[34]

The Blackfoot war and the restrictions it imposed on Newe subsistence created a major impetus for the development of larger social formations among the buffalo hunters. Cameahwait's people remained in the Lemhi Valley for approximately half of each year, from May to September. Only in the fall, when the salmon runs had ended, did they venture back to the buffalo country of the Missouri drainage. That is why they were not where Lewis and Clark expected to find them. Lewis summed up their defensive subsistence tactics this way: "They never leave the interior of the mountains while they can obtain a scanty subsistence, and always return as soon as they have acquired a good stock of dried meat in the plains; thus alternately obtaining their food at the risk of their lives and retiring to the mountains, while they consume it."[35] When they did venture onto the plains for buffalo, the fear of their enemies was great, and consequently they banded together in the largest groups possible, usually joining forces with their allies, the Salish.

The Lemhi Valley Newes were preparing for the hunt just as Lewis and Clark arrived, and this timing partly explains their initial reluctance to help the explorers. To miss their meeting with the Salish would jeopardize the hunt and make starvation a looming possibility.[36] The anxious Newes nearly abandoned the explorers at one point, but, fearing the loss of valuable new trading partners, they continued to assist the expedition. After seeing Lewis and Clark safely into the Bitterroot Valley, the Newes hurried off to the forks of the Missouri.[37] Horses may have allowed larger groups of people to travel together for longer periods, but it was the demands of defense and hunting in hostile territory that were the real motivations for larger social amalgamations. By the turn of the nineteenth century, the elements were in place for the development of band organization among the buffalo-hunting groups, which in turn proved to be the first step toward more distinct ethnic identities.

The Lemhi Valley Newes were also embedded in a far-reaching trade network that illustrated both the mediate effects of European colonization and the importance of wide-ranging kin networks. Lewis saw horses with Spanish brands in their herds as well as "bridlebits and stirrips they obtained from the Spaniards, tho' these were but few."[38] It is unlikely that Cameahwait's people traded directly with the Spanish (which would have necessitated a long journey to California or New Mexico); rather, they most likely obtained these goods through a highly developed intertribal trade. By the early nineteenth century, an Indian trade route transporting horses stolen from the Spanish settlements of California had developed along the Humboldt River. At the same time, *Sehewooki'* emerged as a center of intertribal horse trading west of the Rockies.[39] Undoubtedly writing about the same area, Lewis wrote that the Lemhi Valley Newes obtained "perl oister they value very highly" from their "friends and relations who live beyond the barren plain" to the southwest. These people reportedly lived in a game-rich country and possessed more horses than the Lemhis, characteristics that suggest *Sehewooki'*. They also served as a conduit for Spanish and Indian goods, including horses, mules, metal, cloth, and beads.[40]

Regardless of these intricate trade relations, imperial decisions made on the other side of the globe limited Newe access to the most crucial trade items—guns. The French and English freely traded guns to the Blackfeet and other Plains people, whereas the Spanish prohibited trading guns to Indian nations. Consequently, the Newes possessed only the few firearms that they had taken in battle or could obtain from allied Indian groups. Lewis counted only three guns in a group of sixty Newe warriors and remarked that they were "reserved for war almost exclusively and the bow and arrows are used in hunting." Meanwhile, their well-armed enemies "hunt them up and murder them without rispect to sex or age and plunder them of their horses." Cameahwait attributed his people's precarious situation directly to their inferior position in the gun trade. He desperately wanted an adequate supply of guns so that his people "could then live in the country of the buffaloe and eat as our enemies do and not be compelled to hide ourselves in these mountains and live on roots and berries as the bear do."[41] Recognizing an advantage, Lewis threatened that no white traders would ever come among the Newes if they refused to aid his expedition. Hoping to open an unlimited trade, Cameahwait cajoled and pleaded with his people to continue to help the explorers.

Trade was important for survival, but it was also indicative of the intricate network of social and economic ties, based on kinship, that connected Newe peoples. Within this network there was a decided lack of ethnic consciousness. Social groupings larger than the family cluster were fluid, and individuals often spent time with different, widely scattered groups. Lewis unknowingly recorded evidence of this flexible social order when he sought information concerning routes through the mountains. Cameahwait suggested that an "old man of his nation," who lived a day's march away, could provide the necessary details concerning the country to the northwest. Presumably the man had spent time there, among the "pierced-nose Indians." He also introduced the explorer to another elder who knew the lands to the southwest. The "band of this nation" from which the man hailed lived some twenty days of difficult travel to the southwest across mountains, deserts, and a great plain divided by a large river. His people lived beyond this plain, in a fertile and partially wooded country, "not far from the white people with whom they traded for horses" and other goods. The old man was describing a trip across the Snake River Plain to the river valleys of southwestern Idaho and eastern Oregon, perhaps *Sehewooki'*. His home valley is impossible to determine, but his residence at Lemhi bears witness to the close and continuing associations that Newe peoples maintained across enormous distances, the fluid nature of residence and group membership, and corresponding lack of specific ethnic or tribal identities within the larger Newe world.[42] The distinctions among Newe peoples stemmed less from a well-defined concept of ethnicity than from the diversity of economic pursuits and the fact that certain groups, formulated through kinship ties, maintained closer relations than others. The old man who described the journey to the southwest also spoke of the "broken mockersons," a fierce, reclusive people who lived in the high country and "fed on roots or the flesh of such horses as they could take or steel [sic] from those who passed through their country." Judging by location and description, the "broken mockersons" were probably the *duku-deka'*, or Sheep-Eaters. Their separation from other Newe peoples was more a function of their location in the remote Salmon River country than of any nascent concept of ethnicity. Indeed, during the late nineteenth century, many *duku-deka'* came to live at the Lemhi Reservation and were never viewed as a distinct tribe. Ethnic, tribal, and band identities simply did not hold saliency among Newe peoples at the turn of the nineteenth century.

In the nearly six decades between the visit of Lewis and Clark and the advent of permanent white settlement, an ever-increasing stream of European Americans traversed the Newe homeland. These fur trappers, explorers, and overland emigrants traversed nearly every mile of the Newe country south of the Salmon River, and their journals and reports offer a more complete picture of the changes taking place during the first half of the nineteenth century. They witnessed not just the rounds of the buffalo hunters but also the lives of the foot-going hunting, gathering, and fishing groups. The first phase of white contact, the fur trade, was the least intrusive for the Newe peoples. Relations between the Newes and the trappers were generally good, buttressed by occasional intermarriage and, especially, a common enemy in the Blackfeet. Newe people never became specialized, full-time trappers and so offered little direct competition to Euro-American fur hunters. Nor were the trappers a threat to the Newes. They did not seek land cessions nor make permanent settlements outside a few small trading forts. Newe peoples looked on the trappers as allies in their war with the Blackfeet as well a much-needed conduit for manufactured goods.

Although they contain obvious cultural and gender biases, fur traders' accounts also contain the first evidence of emergent social, economic, and band divisions among the Newes. Some trappers and traders described fairly subtle differences. They recorded food names as well as free renderings of Newe words. Peter Skene Ogden even recognized that the "Upper Snakes" and the "Lower Snakes" spoke closely related yet distinct languages.[43] Most, however, were less observant and usually remarked only on the most obvious aspects of economic and social organization or, more likely, indiscriminately lumped all of their Newe allies together as Snakes. Typical was Alexander Ross, who described the Newe divisions as they appeared to Donald McKenzie during the latter's 1819 Snake River expedition: "The great Snake nation may be divided into three divisions, namely the Sherry-dikas, or Dog-eaters, the War-are-ree-kas, or fish-eaters, and the Ban-at-tees or Robbers. But as a nation they all go by the general appellation of Sho-sho-nes, or Snakes."[44] With their telltale suffixes, *Sherry-dika* and *War-are-ree-ka* are clearly versions of food names. Judging by their location and horse wealth, the *Sherry-dikas* were probably the mixed buffalo-hunting bands, while *War-are-*

a catchall term for the Newe groups living and fishing along
nd its tributaries. (It is impossible to determine with complete
which groups these labels actually referred.) Ross himself
at the trappers had but a "very confused idea of the Snakes,"
writing, "One would call them Bannacks, and another Warracks, while a
third would have named them dogs." Even after personally traveling
among the Newes, Ross cautioned that his observations could not "be
fully relied upon as correct."[45] No matter how confused, however, Ross's
account is still useful, for it identifies the essential divisions between
mounted and pedestrian Newe populations as well as the variations
found in the latter.

More troublesome is Ross's characterization of the Ban-at-tees, or
"robbers," which underscores the frequent confusion of Newe group
names in the historic record. Phonetically, *Ban-at-tee* is a close approximation of *bannaite'*, the Shoshone word for Bannock, yet Ross's description of these people bears little resemblance to the buffalo-hunting
Bannocks. They led, Ross reported, a "predatory and wandering life in
the recesses of the mountains, and are to be found in small bands, or single wigwams among the caverns and rocks." This description could con-
ceivably encompass the *duku-deka'*, or any number of small foot-going
bands found north or south of the Snake, all the way west into present-
day Oregon. Whoever they were, Ross's Ban-at-tees were clearly not the
mounted, Paiute-speaking migrants to the buffalo-hunting groups, who
were already becoming known as Bannocks in the literature. For
instance, the American trapper Warren Angus Ferris reported in 1832
that the people whom the trappers labeled "Ponacks" called themselves
"Po-nah-ke," a close approximation of the Bannocks' name for themselves, *panákwate*. Moreover, Ferris's Ponacks were mounted buffalo
hunters who often traveled in large mixed bands with the Snakes, indicating their continual presence among Shoshone speakers. The confusing, sometimes contradictory uses of *Bannock,* or variations thereof
(such as Pannack, Pawnack, and Bonack) are the most problematic
aspects of the early historical record concerning Newe social relations.[46]

Ross's crude ethnology also clearly illustrates the social, economic,
and gender biases of the fur hunters. Ross called the Sherry-dikas the
"real Sho-sho-nes, . . . [who] live in the plain hunting buffalo," but his
assessment of the War-are-ree-kas was far less charitable. He derided the
latter as "corpulent" and "slovenly" and claimed they were, although
numerous, "neither united nor formidable."[47] Taken with the Sherry-
dikas' wealth and prowess as warriors, Ross and countless other white

observers associated the equestrian lifestyle with a power and nobility they found lacking in the pedestrian groups. But, as Elizabeth Vibert has demonstrated, there were also gendered cultural assumptions at work among Ross and his fellow traders. The buffalo hunters, in European eyes, were more masculine, as was their principal food source. Red meat stood at the pinnacle of a European food hierarchy that saw fish and vegetable foods as feminized and far lower in status. So not only were the mounted bands critical as defensive allies against the Blackfeet and as suppliers of food, but their entire way of life appealed to the traders' gendered perceptions of worth.[48]

During his first trading expedition Nathaniel Wyeth, the founder of Fort Hall, drew conclusions similar to Ross's, suggesting three general life ways among the Newes. The "Pawnacks" often wintered near American Falls because of the abundance of buffalo. Farther downstream, Wyeth generally distinguished between peoples he called "Snakes" and those he called "Diggers" (although from time to time he encountered "Pawnacks" as well). Wyeth's Snakes owned horses, but they were not specialized buffalo hunters. Rather, they were a fishing people who kept Wyeth's party well-stocked with salmon during their march down the Snake River in August and September 1832. The Diggers, on the other hand, were "very poor and timid," living in smaller groups and fleeing at the approach of unknown parties.[49] It is unclear exactly what criteria Wyeth used to draw these distinctions, but he did not record subtle linguistic variations, as Ogden did, or any possible food names, as Ross did. Rather, it seems that his divisions depended as much on social integration as on economic orientation, and both were clearly more important than geographic location.

In Wyeth's scheme, Snakes, Diggers, and Pawnacks could at times be found in the same vicinity, often, indeed, visiting and traveling together. Moreover, both Snakes and Diggers were fishing people. The Diggers, however, were found in small, scattered encampments rather than at the major fisheries. Taken together, early accounts, such as Ross's and Wyeth's, and modern ethnographic resources suggest the general social and economic divisions apparent in the Newe world by the fur-trade era. To borrow Wyeth's nomenclature, the Snakes were the large Shoshonean populations along the middle and lower Snake. They owned horses and periodically joined in the buffalo hunt, but mostly they were fishing people who lived in relatively sedentary villages among the greatest fisheries in all the Newe country, *Sehewooki'* and Salmon Falls. The Diggers were the multitude of small, foot-going Newe groups and family clusters that continued to pursue a mixed subsistence strategy in more marginal environments north and south of the Snake River. Finally, the Pawnacks were most likely the mixed buffalo-hunting bands of the upper Snake River Plain, who in their annual cycle regularly visited and fished with their downstream friends and kin.

Despite such visible distinctions, these peoples were not separate tribes. They maintained close ties with one another, and indeed all were part of the greater "Snake Nation." That interrelationship was evident during McKenzie's winter encampment with the Newes near Bear Lake in 1819. People from all three Newe divisions were in a camp that reputedly stretched for seven miles. Taking advantage of the opportunity, McKenzie sought to negotiate peace between the Newes and the Nez Percés, his two principal trading partners, who were so often in conflict. The Sherry-dikas dominated both the camp and the council. Along with the War-are-ree-kas, they spoke in favor of peace and blamed the Ban-at-tees for attacks on both the Nez Percés and the whites. The latter people were eventually brought over to the council and told they must be good, and the "poor, trembling . . . Ban-at-tees" agreed.[50] None of these groups represented a separate tribe, but it is also evident that there was an unequal power relationship at work. This might have been due to the location of the Bear Lake encampment within the Sherry-dikas' *tebíwa*, or homeland. It is also possible that because the Sherry-dikas had developed a greater band organization and their leaders spoke for more people. Finally, because they often traveled with the mounted groups and relied upon them for protection, the trappers generally looked upon the equestrian people as dominant and ascribed greater power to them.[51]

The principal reason for the greater organization found among the mounted groups, and for their seemingly dominant status in the Newe world, was the continuing Blackfoot War. The demands of traveling and hunting in dangerous territory placed a premium on greater social integration among the mounted buffalo hunters of the upper Snake River Plain, who lived closest to the threat. By the 1820s, Blackfoot war parties regularly ventured deep into the heart of the Snake River country, as far west as the Great Camas Prairie; and the equestrian Newes, with long experience in warfare, most often battled the intruders. The men who led the fur brigades knew the danger well. In 1824, Ross feared the "Blackfeet and Piegan war roads [that] were everywhere in our way." But he was lucky and encountered only two sizable Blackfeet camps, both of which professed peaceful intentions.[52] Ross's successor, John Work, cautiously tried to keep the Newes between his party and the

Blackfeet. In September 1830, when he learned that the "great Snake camp" had already left for the buffalo hunt, Work wrote, "This is of advantage to us as they will be before us and amuse the Blackfeet." Work spent the harsh winter that followed near the future site of Fort Hall, constantly fretting over the Blackfeet and noting the passage of Newe bands downstream, which left his brigade exposed to attack.[53]

The Blackfeet may have been the terrors of the upper Snake River Plain, but they were not always successful in the brutal fighting. John Kirk Townsend, a naturalist who accompanied Wyeth's second expedition, recounted an intense battle on the upper reaches of the Big Lost River in August 1834. Caught on foot on the open plain, "the Blackfeet were run down with horses, and, without being able to load their guns, were trampled to death, or killed with salmon spears and axes." These unfortunate Blackfeet were probably a horse-raiding party intercepted short of their goal.[54] Still, the Blackfoot risk had grown so great that formerly safe havens, such as the Lemhi and Salmon valleys, had become dangerous "war roads."[55]

One of the consequences of the Blackfoot presence, then, was ever-larger social amalgamations. These were evident as early as 1805, when the Lemhi Valley Newe joined forces with the Salish to hunt in the Three Forks country. By the summer of 1819, when McKenzie's Northwest Company brigade fell in with a "friendly band of Snakes" as they traveled east along the Snake River, large defensive groups were necessary even in the heart of Newe country. The fur brigades that worked the northern Rockies commonly traveled with Nez Percé and Salish allies, but they also sometimes joined forces with the Newes. The group camping with McKenzie engaged the Blackfeet in a "severe battle" somewhere on the middle Snake Plain, and when the victorious Newes returned, Snakes appeared from every direction to join in a raucous celebration. Ross wrote: "They came in crowds from their hiding places and joining the victorious party in their scalp dancing and scalp singing, formed a host of at least five or six thousand. Their huts, their tents altogether resembled a city in an uproar, and their scattered fires exhibited rather an awful spectacle."[56] Although the Newe numbers were probably exaggerated, the reference to both huts and tents suggests the presence of both foot-going and mounted Newe, as does the suggestion of more timid Newes emerging from hiding places. It was late summer, and McKenzie's party was undoubtedly in the company of mounted Newes returning to the upper Snake River Plain after their annual trip to the fisheries of the middle and lower Snake. The foot-going people were at a decided disadvantage in warfare, and the mounted groups exhibited an increasing Plains influence, including the warrior complex. Indeed, Ross reported that the more sedentary fishing groups suffered most at the hands of the Blackfeet, while the mounted buffalo hunters held their own in combat.[57] Notwithstanding their differences, all of these groups were of the same "nation," and they came together in large groups first and foremost for defense.[58]

With larger social groups came important shifts in the power of Newe headmen. Bands formed around successful leaders of important cooperative endeavors. Liljeblad referred to these leaders as "bosses," although "talkers" is probably more accurate. For instance, the *baingwi-dai'-gwahni'* directed cooperative labor at the fisheries. The *dai'gwahni'* was literally "someone who coordinates or conducts a service for the people." He was an orator and mediator who smoothed over difficulties among his own people and with other bands. The *dai'gwahnee'* increased in importance as the mounted bands traveled ever farther to access the buffalo. The "band chiefs" whom European Americans encountered sprang from this political tradition. First and foremost, they had to be successful leaders of subsistence endeavors. Second, as the Blackfeet onslaught continued, larger groups coalesced around proven war leaders. Often these men possessed supernatural sanction for their abilities. Finally, by the mid–nineteenth century, the ability to act as effective intermediaries with European Americans became preeminent. Thus, the *dai'gwahnee'*, men already skilled as intermediaries, most often emerged as the "chiefs." Among the buffalo-hunting bands, the *dai'-gwahnee'* who spoke for the largest groups often fulfilled this role. The most successful band leaders balanced the needs and desires of their people against the demands of white society and, most important, negotiated their people's access to the land and its resources.[59]

Still, the power of these leaders should not be overstated. In such a fluid social world, political leadership developed on grounds that European Americans could hardly fathom. Newe headmen lacked the coercive power that white observers were accustomed to in leaders. Individual choice rather than stable allegiance marked Newe politics, and only the most capable leaders retained a following. In 1805 Meriwether Lewis wrote: "Each individual is his own sovereign master . . . the authority of the Cheif [sic] being nothing more than mere admonition supported by the influence which the propriety of his own exemplary conduct may have acquired him in the minds of the individuals who compose the band. . . . In fact every man is a chief, but all have not an equal influence on the minds of the other members of the community, and he who happens to enjoy the greatest share of confidence is the principal Chief."[60]

During McKenzie's peace council in the winter of 1819, the combined Snakes were led by two brothers, Pee-eye-em and Ama-qui-em, who, according to Alexander Ross, exercised remarkable control over their people. Perhaps their size had something to do with their power. Both men were of great stature, with Pee-eye-em reported to be much larger than the 312-pound McKenzie![61] But, clearly, their authority stemmed from their roles as successful *dai'gwahnee'*. Ross wrote: "Trade was no sooner over than Ama-qui-em mounted one of his horses, rode around and round the camp, and that itself was almost the work of a day, now and then making a halt to harangue the Indians, remind them of the peace, their behavior towards the whites, and to prepare them for raising the camp."[62]

In 1848 Nathaniel Wyeth remarked on the Newes' "almost entire absence of social organization," except at "salmon time" and during the buffalo hunt, when "some person called a chief usually opens a trade or talk, and occasionally gives directions."[63] Wyeth's original journal entries presented an image of greater respect and influence but still suggested that ability could only draw followers, not compel them. Writing of the great fishery at Salmon Falls and the Newe leader in charge, he recorded: "This chief is a good sized man and very intelligent and the President would do well if he could preserve the respect of his subjects as well or maintain as much dignity."[64]

The most famous Newe headman of the fur trade era, the Horn Chief, embodied all of the talents and characteristics necessary for effective leadership. The Horn Chief's role as *dai'gwahni'* was intertwined with his ability as a war leader. Living close to the buffalo herds on the upper Snake River Plain meant living in constant conflict with the Blackfeet. The Horn Chief, whom white fur hunters considered the "principal chief of the Snakes," was one of the most influential leaders because of his bold and successful tactics. Once, the story was told, while traveling alone across the open plain and armed only with a spear, he happened on a Blackfoot war party. Rather than flee, he charged into the enemy and killed six in hand-to-hand combat. "He always rushed headlong upon his enemies without fear of death," wrote the trapper Warren Angus Ferris, "and rendered himself so terrible . . . that his presence alone was often sufficient to put them to flight."[65] In addition to his prowess as a warrior, the Horn Chief also possessed a supernatural sanction for his leadership. He had survived countless battles, and it was well known among the

Newes that his tutelary spirit had rendered him invulnerable. Whites, of course, were usually incredulous, branding him superstitious, and lucky.[66] According to Ferris, the Horn Chief believed that "the moon was his guardian deity, this extraordinary Indian imagined that she instructed him in dreams during his sleep; and he taught his followers to believe that he never acted but in obedience to her directions, and that he could not be killed by metal."[67] Such beliefs were deeply rooted in the spiritualism of the Basin and Plateau. Newe peoples believed that tutelary spirits transmitted sacred knowledge and power, *bo'ha*, through dreams. These same spirits imposed dietary and behavioral taboos on their charges and protected them as long as they followed these proscriptions.[68] Although it may not have been necessary for leadership, the Horn Chief's formidable war *bo'ha* certainly buttressed his position among his people.

Just as important, the Horn Chief was a skilled intermediary. Captain Benjamin Bonneville remarked on the "great magnanimity" the chief had shown the whites. When some trappers had reportedly killed one of his relatives, the Horn Chief used his influence to halt his people's plans for revenge and declared himself a "friend of the white men."[69] In February 1831, Ferris experienced a similar situation firsthand. The Horn Chief forced some of his own people to return goods stolen from American caches. Then, when a few hatched a plan to kill the trappers and take all their goods, the Horn Chief again interceded. In full war regalia, he sat on his horse between his people and the Americans and "commenced a loud and threatening harangue." He bullied them and dared them to fire on him, until one by one they slipped off to their lodges. Considering his war record and his reputation for invulnerability, it is not hard to understand how his presence saved the trappers.[70] His motives for doing so might demand more explanation.

Although there were many important ramifications of white contact by the 1830s, the native world on the Snake River Plain was still one that operated essentially on Newe terms. Buffalo were still plentiful in eastern Idaho; white emigrants and their destructive livestock, miners, settlers, land claims, and reservation life still lay in the future. To protect and provide for his people, the Horn Chief dealt first with other Indian peoples and only secondarily with whites. His greatest adversaries were the Blackfeet; the trappers had become valuable allies and suppliers. Befriending the trappers offered more in the long term than did murdering them for their limited goods. Thus, the Horn Chief was a direct predecessor of Washakie, Taghee, Tyee, and Tendoy, the most influential

Newe leaders of the late nineteenth century. As a successful cultural intermediary, he remained on friendly terms with the whites while maintaining great influence over his people. In preserving this balance, he protected his people's interests and independence and brought access to the
white man's goods.

The Horn Chief's leadership during the fur-trade era illustrates the
growing importance of "bands" rather than "tribes." The latter was a
Euro-American concept that only gained importance with the treaty-
making and reservation eras later in the century. The Horn Chief was not
a dictator, nor was he ever the "principal chief of the Snakes." The periodic violence against trappers was mostly the work of opportunistic
young men seeking wealth and prestige through raiding. It was simply
impossible for the Horn Chief, or any other leader, to control all of the
Newes, especially when many did not even recognize his leadership. In
the winter of 1831, Work recognized the diversity of the Newe groups
camping together and the lack of a dominant chief: "The Indians assembled here are of different tribes of the Snakes and from different quarters
and many of them belong to no chief and are such wanderers that when
they commit a crime by stealing a horse there is no knowing where to
find them."[71] The Horn Chief may have been the most influential leader
the trapper knew, but he was not the "principal" chief because there was
no such position. The Horn was a *dai'gwahni'* who spoke first and foremost for his own people, a large, mounted mixed band of Shoshone and
Paiute speakers.

Nor could the Horn Chief's influence be easily transferred to other
leaders. He died in battle with the Blackfeet on the Big Lost River in the
fall of 1832. His village was large, two hundred lodges of "Snakes and
Ponnacks." It was attacked by 150 Blackfeet who disastrously underesti-
mated the Newe numbers. At battle's end some forty-five Blackfeet were
dead, as were nine Newe, the Horn among them. The story quickly cir-
culated that a Blackfoot warrior, aware of the chief's immunity to metal,
had loaded a piece of antler in his musket and thus killed the greatest
Newe leader of the day.[72] Not only the Newes mourned the Horn Chief's
passing. The trappers, too, had lost an important friend and protector
who held "sufficient influence over the tribe to restrain the wild and
predatory propensities of the young men."[73] During a visit to a large
mixed village of Bannocks and Snakes in the summer of 1835, Osborne
Russell concluded that fears of increased Newe raiding were warranted.
The Horn Chief's brother, Aiken-lo-ruckkup, or "Tongue Cut with a
Flint," was the group's nominal leader, but he lacked his sibling's domi-

nant influence. He told Russell that young men from the village had recently murdered two white trappers. The chief was angry that the whites had been killed simply for their possessions, which had already been gambled away. He guaranteed Russell's safety while in the village, but the trapper put little faith in the chief's ability to keep this promise.[74]

By the late 1830s, major changes in the Newe country were reinforcing the emergent band divisions. In 1837 another smallpox epidemic effectively ended the Blackfoot invasion of the upper Snake River Plain. Some bands were nearly wiped out; many of the survivors were elderly people who had weathered the 1781 epidemic.[75] In June 1838, Osborne Russell was working the Madison River with an outfit led by Jim Bridger. The trappers were following a Blackfoot band that was "to all appearances occasionally dying of the Small Pox." In an account reminiscent of Saukamappee's macabre tale of the 1781 epidemic, Russell wrote: "Today we passed an Indian lodge standing in the prairie near the river which contained 9 dead bodies." The trappers showed no mercy to their afflicted enemies, attacking and harrying them for several days before heading south for Henry's Lake. There they found more of their enemies and had "concluded . . . to smite [them] without leaving one to tell their fate." The approach of six suffering Blackfeet softened the trappers' hearts. "For we were ashamed to think of fighting a few poor Indians," Russell wrote, "nearly dwindled to skeletons by the small Pox and approaching us without arms."[76]

Such mercy was as rare for the trappers as it was for the Blackfeet; the enmity that had grown over the decades was hard for some outsiders to comprehend. Bridger's party traveled from Henry's Lake to the 1838 rendezvous on Green River. There they encountered a party of missionaries bound for Oregon. Among them was Sarah White Smith, one of the first white women to cross the continent, who condemned the fur hunters' actions: "It is dreadful to hear how the whites treat the Indians. Bridger's party have just been among the Black Foot tribe. This tribe have long been a terror to neighboring tribes & whites, but now their number is much reduced by the smallpox & it is still raging. The Indians made no attack on B's party but this party attacked them & shot 15 of them dead without excuse but to please their wicked passion."[77] Smith's sympathy was undoubtedly genuine, yet she also represented the first wave in a massive emigration that brought greater changes to the Newes, their allies, and their enemies than the trappers could ever imagine.

The Blackfoot withdrawal did not reverse the trend toward greater Newe band organization because the very same years saw the extinction of the buffalo herds in the Snake River country. The decline was evident by the late 1830s, and after 1840 buffalo could not be found in sufficient numbers to support the mounted bands. There were a number of reasons for the extinction. First, the Snake River Plain was a marginal environment for buffalo. The herds there, as elsewhere west of the Continental Divide, were never as large as the great biomass found on the Plains. As some Newe adopted Plains-style hunting on horseback, both their reliance on the herds and their hunting efficiency increased. Furthermore, large horse herds competed directly with the buffalo for grass and water. The Blackfeet, fur trappers, and early overland emigrants all increased the pressure on the buffalo herds. Ultimately the Snake River Plain could not sustain the number of animals necessary to support the mounted Newe bands.[78] In 1843 the famed explorer John C. Frémont called the recently extinct herds "pioneers" whose "experiment in colonizing the valley of the Columbia . . . had failed."[79] The extinction of the Snake River herds meant that although the Blackfoot threat had dissipated west of the mountains, the Newes still had to form into larger groups and travel long distances through hostile territory to find buffalo.[80]

Consequently, both band structure and individual political leadership became stronger among the mounted Newe. Julian Steward argued that the extinction of the Snake River herds was the catalyst for the emergence of "band chiefs" among the Idaho Newes and that before that point such leaders were relatively unimportant, with no real political power. While his theory minimized defensive needs and ignored earlier political developments due to the Blackfoot war, the major point was sound. Newe band organization came into its own after 1840, and it was the *dai'gwahnee'*, or hunt bosses, who most often emerged as leaders among the mounted bands. The intrusion of larger numbers of whites only increased political power. By the 1840s band councils existed, and, along with the chiefs, these bodies dealt with whites. Still, the power of the leaders and the Plains influence on the social order should not be overemphasized. *Dai'gwahnee'* could speak only for a specific group at specific times, and they could easily lose their following if they failed to maintain "unanimity by persuasion." The fluidity of Bannock and Shoshone society remained, and band chiefs and police societies never developed to the extent they did among Plains groups.[81]

During this period the ethnically mixed buffalo-hunting bands of the upper Snake River, most often identified as Bannocks, developed an even wider-ranging subsistence cycle that made them the "wealthiest" of the Newe groups. These bands already traversed great distances to access the best resources. Russell remarked in the summer of 1835 that the mixed band he visited had "just returned from salmon fishing to feast on fat buffaloe."[82] With the addition of the journey to Montana, the Bannocks' subsistence cycle reached its greatest extent. They usually wintered along the Snake River bottoms in the vicinity of Fort Hall. Early each spring they dispersed into smaller kin-based groups to hunt throughout eastern Idaho before journeying west, to the fisheries at Salmon Falls and Glenn's Ferry, to partake in the spring salmon run. Some groups continued farther west to *Sehewooki'* and beyond, where they fished and traded with local Newes and with the Umatilla, Nez Percé, and other Columbia Plateau peoples. During the summer, most drifted east and congregated on the Great Camas Prairie near modern Fairfield, Idaho. Here they dug roots, prepared for the fall buffalo hunt, and held a great trade fair attended by many Indian peoples. In late summer and early fall the Bannocks departed for the buffalo hunt. At first they hunted around the forks of the Missouri, but as the herds diminished they were forced to travel farther east. Beginning in the 1840s the mounted Newes utilized the Bannock Trail, which crossed modern Targhee Pass, traversed the northern reaches of the Yellowstone Plateau, and descended to hunting grounds near *Guchu'nambi'hi,* or "cow heart," northwest of modern Billings, Montana. The hunt lasted into the fall, and the people had to hurry back over the divide before the deep snows fell or else spend the winter east of the divide.[83]

With the completion of the Fort Hall subsistence cycle, the economic distinctions between Newe peoples reached their peak. These differences were critical to the emergence of band identity and, later, ethnic identity. Newes who possessed fewer horses sometimes spent a season or a year with their mounted kin, but generally they covered a much smaller area from year to year. Because they accessed fewer resources and trade, the pedestrian Newes were "poor." The division between wealthy mounted bands and poor foot-going groups was not simply a white imposition. The buffalo hunters of the Fort Hall region often referred to all downstream Newes, even the relatively well-off Boise River groups, as *detehaandee'* (*tedébiwa'a* in Bannock), literally "pitiful people." The term was not derogatory; it was used even by the "poor people" themselves. Rather, it was a recognition of the downstream Newes' relative lack of horse wealth and their consequent inability to completely access the bison economy.[84]

The band organization that emerged from economic developments ultimately became the source of ethnic identity for the equestrian Newes, but that is not the whole story. By the 1840s the mounted bands were increasingly known as Bannocks, even though Shoshone speakers were always the majority. It would be easy to attribute this usage to the ignorance of white observers, but the continued existence of the name and the language indicate something more. The continuing influx of Paiute speakers throughout the historic period is one explanation for the survival of the Bannock language and identity within the numerically superior Shoshone populations.[85] Just as important, Bannock speakers dominated leadership of both the buffalo hunts and most war parties. Sven Liljeblad believed that disproportionate Bannock leadership was due to an earlier unification of the Paiute speakers, who became Bannocks for defense and collective warfare. Even before they migrated east, he argued, they faced continual harassment and raids by the Nez Percé and other Plateau peoples around *Sehewooki'*, forcing a more organized response. Once integrated into the mounted Shoshone bands and facing the Blackfeet, the Bannock speakers continued this tradition. Kinship was another factor. Liljeblad also found that Bannock leadership was dominated by one family that had "risen to authority in the course of thirty years or less [and] discharged the duty of representing several mixed Bannock and Shoshone bands." Because so many Shoshones followed Bannock leaders, the misconception entered the historic record that the mounted mixed bands were actually Bannocks.[86]

By the late 1830s the fur trade was in decline, and both equestrian Bannocks and their pedestrian kin faced an invasion of unprecedented scale. Between 1840 and 1860, more than 250,000 emigrants crossed the continent to the Pacific coast, virtually all of them passing through Newe country. The emigration peaked in the years after the California gold rush, with some 60,000 making the trek in 1852.[87] Five years later B. F. Ficklin, an employee of the Pacific Wagon Road Office, kept an exact count of the wagons carried on the various Green River ferries. By August 15, some 850 wagons had crossed the Green, and the season was not over yet. Moreover, because most emigrants saved money by swimming their animals across the river, there were no comparable statistics for livestock. But by Ficklin's estimate, California-bound emigrants had driven some seventy thousand head of stock through the heart of Newe country. Frederick W. Lander, the superintendent of the wagon road, put these numbers in perspective when he wrote: "The above was a very small emigration, less than one-third of what it was in 1854."[88]

Aside from its scale, the concentrated impact of the emigration was unlike anything Newe peoples had seen before. The overland emigrants stuck to well-traveled riparian routes, which maximized their opportunities for living off the land but also intensified their environmental impact. They cut wood, hunted, fished, and grazed their stock within a very narrow corridor. As early as 1843, Charles Preuss, Frémont's cartographer, remarked, "The white people have ruined the country of the Snake Indians and should therefore treat them well."[89] Eight years later Richard Grant, the Hudson's Bay Company trader at Fort Hall, reported that the Newes around Fort Boise had been so terrorized by the Nez Percés and the emigrants that they would not remain at their fisheries and supply the fort's needs.[90] As Preuss's and Grant's comments suggest, the pedestrian Newes along the trails felt the greatest impact of the emigration. The emigrants consumed their resources first and most intensively, and, because they were less mobile than the mounted bands, these Newes had fewer options. They faced the choice of abandoning their most critical subsistence sites or possibly dying in the attempt to use them.

The equestrian groups also felt the effects of the emigration. Overgrazing was perhaps the most visible consequence. Grass was the fuel of the wagon trains, and the effect of tens of thousands of animals grazing within a narrow, semiarid corridor was profound. One historian has attempted to put a monetary value on the damage, but such numbers can never speak to the real impact of the emigration.[91] The mounted bands were usually far from the Snake River when the bulk of each year's emigration passed in late summer, yet when they returned to their choice winter camps along the Snake River bottoms, they found denuded pastures and little firewood. Overgrazing also hurt the emigrants. Indeed, horse theft increased west of Fort Laramie because the trail had been so stripped of grass that each night the animals had to be taken miles from camp to find sufficient forage.[92] Whether mounted or foot-going, Newe groups could not escape the effects of the emigration.

Violence was one of these effects, but it must be kept in perspective. The first overland emigrants had many fears about Indians on the trail—some warranted, some not. The Blackfeet caused the most trepidation during the earliest years of the emigration, but that threat faded with the smallpox epidemic.[93] Statistically, Indians of any kind posed relatively little danger compared with the other hazards of travel, and in fact emigrants killed many more Indians than vice versa. For example, the greatest number of emigrant deaths at the hands of Indians—sixty—came in 1851, a year when emigrants killed some seventy Indians. In only five years during the two decades of heaviest travel did white deaths exceed

Indian deaths. Overall, Indians killed fewer than four hundred emigrants between 1840 and 1860, accounting for only 4 percent of the estimated ten thousand emigrants who died along the trails. Disease was the greatest killer, causing nearly 90 percent of the casualties, and accidents too claimed more lives than violence.[94]

Indeed, it is striking how little contact many emigrants had with Indians. Clarence Bagley, who traveled to Oregon with his parents as a boy in 1852, remembered a rather gruesome game he played with a young girl from another emigrant family; they counted the fresh graves lining the Snake River portion of the trail. They saw 120 in a single day, and Bagley was sure there were many more that they had missed. But Indians were not to blame. "Most of these deaths were caused by cholera," he later recalled, "which by this time was making frightful inroads among the emigrants." He added, "On all our part of the trip we had no fear of the Indians except to protect ourselves from the pilfering of articles about camp and from stealing our horses at night." Horse theft was the emigrants' most common complaint, but only rarely did it involve a face-to-face encounter. The "one considerable excitement on account of Indians" that Bagley remembered came when an unidentified intruder attempted to steal a valuable mare while the train was camped on the Boise River.[95]

Newe people were more likely to trade with the white travelers than fight with them. Emigrants most commonly encountered Newes in the vicinity of Fort Hall, the great fisheries around Salmon Falls, and along the Boise River. Trade and peaceful relations usually prevailed, even in years of mounting violence. The sight of Salmon Falls, with hundreds of Newes engaged in fishing, particularly struck the emigrants. The Whitmans arrived there in August 1836, just a few days after a run had begun. Like the trappers who preceded them and the emigrants to follow, they traded with Newes for salmon. Two years later, at the same spot, Sarah White Smith wrote, "We have purchased salmon of these Indians, find it beautiful & are feasting on it." Salmon Falls was the source of extensive comment by members of Frémont's 1843 government expedition. Theodore Talbot described the colorful appearance of the large camp. "Round every hut are high platforms covered with drying salmon," he wrote. "They present quite a gay appearance for the meat of the salmon is a deep scarlet color." From Salmon Falls to the Boise, Frémont's party encountered Newes "strung out along the river at every little rapid where fish are to be caught, and the cry '*Haggai, haggai*' (fish) was constantly heard." (*Agai'* is more accurately translated as "salmon.") By the time the emigration peaked in the early 1850s, the Newes along the Snake River were still supplying the emigrants with fish. "All sorts of trades were made for fish," Bagley remembered, "The Indians had no use for money but were glad to exchange for clothing and particularly for ammunition." This last article of trade concerned Bagley, for by the 1850s tensions and violence between emigrants and Newes were on the rise.[96]

The social divisions between equestrian and pedestrian Newes became obvious by the time the emigrants reached Salmon Falls. Whereas the horse Indians, the Bannocks, often made them nervous, the travelers perceived little threat from the foot-going people; in fact, they usually looked down on them. Both Narcissa Whitman and Sarah Smith called the people there "diggers," even though they were well stocked with fish and roots. Smith was shocked by their poverty and lack of clothing and lamented, "It is out of my power to help them."[97] At Fort Hall, Grant drew similar distinctions between the "brave and numerous . . . Bonacks" and the "set called diggers or chochoukos [who] are miserable objects nearly altogether naked and starving the greater part of the year."[98] Talbot was one of the few white observers who spoke directly to the economic divisions in Newe life. Describing a visitor to Frémont's camp, he wrote: "There was one of these Indians who had belonged to the better class of Snakes, or to the rich Shoshonees, but he had been reduced by a succession of mishaps and was now abiding with his more abject brethren."[99] In essence, the effects of the large-scale emigration magnified the economic divisions in Newe life and soured relations between the travelers and the Newes.

Most often the immediate or remembered actions of the emigrants sparked the conflict. During the 1851 season one emigrant took revenge for the loss of a horse by shooting an unsuspecting Newe fisherman at Salmon Falls. It mattered not that the man was innocent; he was an Indian. That same summer, the Patterson train came across a Newe group camped at Rock Creek on the Snake River. Wanting the choice site for themselves, Patterson and several other men in the group fired shotguns over the Indians' heads and then chased them away on horseback. The Newes retaliated the next day, killing one emigrant and wounding two others. Later in the season, Newe warriors attacked a train near Fort Hall, killing eight and escaping with a good deal of property. Both government officials and members of the train blamed Patterson's arrogant and imprudent actions for the violence along the Snake River that summer (1851 was the bloodiest single year for the emigrants, and more than half of the killings took place along the Snake).[100] By the late 1850s the impact of the emigration was acutely apparent, and the pace of Newe raiding increased, although the emigrant death toll never again reached that of 1851.[101] Frederick Lander reported that "the Snakes or Shoshones have probably suffered more than any tribe from the passage of the emigration along the narrow vallies of their rivers." His sympathy rings hollow, however, for he had just surveyed a new road that offered "better grass and [a] more permanent supply of water" to the travelers. The route diverged from the Oregon Trail at South Pass and proceeded north and west to the Salt River and then to Fort Hall by way of the Blackfoot River and Ross Fork Creek. From there, it descended the Snake River to intersect the existing trails. Though more circuitous, "Lander's Cutoff" made up for the added miles by avoiding the alkaline deserts farther south and crossing the Green River so high that ferries or toll bridges were unnecessary; moreover, it provided "abundant" pasturage and water. It also directed the emigrants through the homeland of the mounted Newe bands. Lander estimated that 90 percent of the 13,000 overland emigrants of 1859 used his new road.[102]

Lander and other government officials recognized that resource damage seriously threatened peace along the trails. Emigrant deaths exceeded the Indian death toll in 1856, 1859, and 1860. Most of the killings came west of South Pass, in the Newe homeland. Lander knew his new road would cause problems as it encroached upon the "herding and camas grounds of the Shoshonee and Pannack tribes." One of his assistants, C. H. Miller, also singled out the new road for its impact on Newe life: "The animals of the emigrants will destroy the grass in the valleys where the Indians have kept the pine timber and willows burnt out for years as halting places in going and coming from their great annual buffalo hunts."[103] Miller felt that the mixed Newe bands of the upper Snake River Plain were the "most dangerous of all the Indians I have visited" and that the increased traffic would just make matters worse. Still, he blamed the emigrants for the tensions and denied that the Newe were "treacherous" simply because they killed intruders. On the contrary, he reported that they had "in the most manly and direct manner . . . said that if emigrants, as has usually been the case, shoot members of their tribes, they will kill them when they can." And yet another official of the Pacific Wagon Road office complained that the violence was a result of the "wanton annoyance of a class of emigrants, who never avoid an opportunity of attacking small bands of Indians whenever they are met with."[104]

In an effort to avert further violence, Lander toured the Newe country in the summer of 1859, and his report, filed in February of the following year, illustrates the effect of economic changes in Newe society
and the emergence of band organization. Lander first visited his closest
ally, the Eastern Shoshone headman Washakie, whose friendship had
been sorely tested. The previous summer Washakie had told Lander that
where he once saw a land filled with game, he now saw only "wagons
with white tops, and men riding upon their horses." When Lander
returned in 1859, he brought with him presents as a "reward for their
behavior in the past, and [as] payment for the destruction of their root
and herding grounds."[105] From the Green River, Lander moved west to
the valley of the Salt River and met with the Mopeah's band of three
hundred "Pannacks" who frequented the Blackfoot River. Midway
through the council, Tash-e-pah, or "French Louis," another Bannock
leader and "noted horse thief," arrived. It was mid-July, and Tash-e-pah
had left most of the "disaffected Pannacks at salmon falls." Lander
thought they were not "irreclaimably hostile" but feared that their
"horse stealing proclivities [would] prevent amicable arrangements with
them." He also questioned the two leaders' ability to control young warriors who were drawn to raiding by the promise of easy wealth and the
abusive actions of the emigrants. Also of concern were the "Western
Snakes" and the "Salt Lake Diggers," in particular Pocatello's band,
which had developed a reputation for raiding in the Raft River Valley
and Goose Creek Mountains.

Not dissuaded by wild rumors of hostility, Lander met with Pocatello,
who told the superintendent, "his tribe had received . . . 'assaults of
ignominy' from white emigrants on their way to California; that one of
his principal men had had his squaw and children killed by the emigrants quite recently; that the hearts of his people were very bad against
the whites; that there were some things he could not manage, and among
them were the bad thoughts of his young men towards the whites."[106]
Pocatello's people had adapted to violence and dislocation by becoming
raiders. In all Lander described seven major "bands" that lived along the
emigrant roads west of South Pass. All were Newe peoples, and Lander
wrote: "All the above Indians travel together and intermarry. They hold
the entire country." Yet he found enough social, economic, and political
difference to categorize them.[107] What separated the various Newe bands
and groups were economic conditions and the effects of the emigration.
The mounted bands and those foot-going bands, like Pocatello's, that
adapted to raiding along the trails had generally become more cohesive.

The opposite was true for many of the smaller pedestrian groups hardest hit by emigrant violence and resource appropriation. They were atomized and for safety probably withdrew from the trails and moved in even smaller groups.

From the beginning of the eighteenth century to 1860, Newe peoples experienced large-scale social and economic changes that for the first time established band organization and set the stage for ethnic identity. To a great extent, all of the bands shared territory and membership. On the upper Snake River Plain in the vicinity of Fort Hall were the mixed buffalo-hunting bands who exhibited the greatest social cohesion and band organization. Their annual range took them from the lower Snake River, where they fished, traded, and intermarried with the Newe people of the region, to the high plains of Montana and Wyoming, where they hunted and intermarried with their close relatives, the Eastern Shoshones. They were the Bannocks, although the majority were Shoshone speakers. In western Idaho, Shoshone populations along the Boise, Payette, and Weiser rivers owned horses and occasionally participated in buffalo hunts with the Fort Hall peoples. However, they never adopted an equestrian lifestyle to the extent of the latter group and were able to survive quite nicely as the most sedentary of Newe groups because of the rich resources of their homeland. With intensive white settlement, these people would develop a greater band identity as the Boise Shoshones, as would the Bruneau band that lived farther east.[108]

Scattered along the lower and middle Snake River were small, pedestrian Shoshone groups. They were far less mobile than the mounted people but lacked the resource base found farther west. Thus, they tended to exploit a wider range of resources in a more limited geographic area. They fished extensively, collected camas roots and piñon nuts at various times of the year, and hunted small game. Organized principally in small, kin-based groups, they wintered north and south of the Snake River from approximately Glenn's Ferry to American Falls. In the decades to come, white misconceptions and the effects of treaties and reservation would compress both lifestyles together, and these peoples, so often called Diggers, would become known simply as Shoshones.[109] The economic and social divisions evident by 1860 would later emerge as "ethnic" identities. Snakes and Diggers would become Bannocks and Shoshones.

CHAPTER 2

Shamans, Prophets, and Missionaries

Newe Religion in the Nineteenth Century

The Shoshone, or Snake Indians, and the Bannack Indians . . .
have united their forces for the purpose of making war upon,
and committing depredations on the property of, the white
people. . . . All these war movements are instigated and led
on by War-i-gika, the Great Bannack Prophet, in whom the
Bannacks and Shoshones have unbounded confidence and
faith.

James Duane Doty, 1862

Religion and identity are intertwined. Religions explain who a people
are, how they were created, and the nature of their relationship to the
world and to others.[1] Newe peoples made sense of the great changes in
their world in part through their religious beliefs. But, like people, belief
systems do not exist in a vacuum. Beliefs and events are inextricably
linked. Historical events are understood through the prism of culture:
that is, they acquire their significance through culture. At the same time,
cultures and their religions are products of history. As the meanings that
a culture applies to things, events, and people are put at risk in the material world, they are continually reevaluated and modified.[2] The material
changes in Newe life—the effects of Euro-American colonization chief
among them—had a transforming effect on native religion.

On the most direct level, Newe beliefs in shamanism and prophecy
entered into a kind of cultural conversation with ideas of Christianity
brought west by American Indians engaged in the fur trade and then by
Euro-Americans. In nineteenth-century America, prophetic religion
became a shared discourse of identity for Indians and non-Indians alike.[3]
To be sure, native and colonizer began from very different perspectives,

yet their concepts seemed similar enough to allow both peoples to express their identities in prophetic terms. By midcentury, Newe beliefs were part of a religious tradition among Indian peoples in the Great Basin and Colombia Plateau that integrated preexisting beliefs in shamanism and prophecy with the informal and direct introduction of Christian doctrine. The result was a powerful expression of Indian identity that provides the context for the later Ghost Dance movements within the cosmology, religious traditions, and religious innovations of Newe peoples.

Newe religion in the nineteenth century is treated here as a living product of culture and history. To construct a static picture of "traditional religion," and then compare and contrast it to the Ghost Dance doctrine in order to identify the Christian elements that Newe people integrated into their religious beliefs, would be simplistic, misleading, and indeed impossible. Religion, like any aspect of a culture, is never static. At some point every tradition began as innovation, and even the most conservative religions are not immune to change. It is impossible to establish a starting point that we can deem "tradition." Moreover, the fluidity and integrative nature of Newe religious beliefs make such static constructions untenable. This difficulty is compounded by the fact that native people seldom felt the need or the desire to explain their spiritual beliefs to Euro-Americans. When they did, most white observers took very little interest. Euro-American concerns were primarily economic and secondarily social (they had to live among the peoples they traded with), and their assessments of native religions were rudimentary and often derisive descriptions of Indian "superstitions." And by the time white observers arrived, Indian cultures and societies had already undergone considerable change. Thus the early historic source record must be weighed carefully in the context of later evidence and ethnographic sources and accepted as a temporally specific window on a process in motion, rather than as a baseline description of pristine culture.

Shamanism was at the core of Newe religious life in the nineteenth century. In many forms, shamanism remains strong among tribal peoples in North America and around the world. It exists in societies exhibiting various economic and social structures but has always been strongest among hunting and gathering peoples.[4] Shamanism is an animistic religion based on the belief that a spiritual power pervades the universe and that certain chosen and skilled practitioners—shamans—can access that power, bringing its benefits, or malevolence, to their people. In Polynesia this power is *mana,* among the Lakota it is *wakan,* and for the Iroquois it is *orenda.*[5] In the Northern Shoshone dialect of the Fort Hall Reservation, this power or "supernatural strength" is *bo'ha.*[6] *Bo'ha* is not a deity or a supreme being and is not worshipped as such. It is an essential life force, a sustaining healing energy, which can be tapped through ritual and sacrifice. *Bo'ha* is a mysterious and awesome presence found everywhere in nature. It is the source of healing and well-being, but in the hands of the incompetent or the malicious, it can bring disease, misery and death. It is a multifaceted entity, with seemingly discrete parts that are in fact a unified whole. All things—animals, plants, rocks, rivers—have their own distinct *bo'ha,* but in turn all share a connection with one another as parts of the larger spiritual force. The anthropologist Jay Miller suggests that *bo'ha* is best understood as a "pulsating web of power." He points out that American Indian grammars assume process and motion, that "people speak of living[,] not life[,] and moving[,] not staying, implying ongoing interactions and reciprocities."[7]

Bo'ha comes as a gift from spirit beings. These might be the spirits of fauna; certain rocks and mountains; natural phenomena such as thunder or lightning; mythical beings such as water babies, serpents, and mountain-dwelling dwarfs; and, more rarely, ghosts. Faunal spirits, the most common, were often associated with specific types of *bo'ha.* In Basin cultures, the "good" birds, most notably the eagle, were often the source of healing *bo'ha,* while the spirits of the wolf and bear exhibited strong war powers. Among some Basin peoples the rat dispensed incredible climbing powers, which were valuable for removing ceremonial feathers from an eagle's aerie. Some of the Shoshone-speaking peoples in the vicinity of Fort Hall felt that the strongest *bo'ha* came from ghosts and mountain dwarfs.[8] Usually, however, contact with ghosts was a horrifying experience that led to illness and required the intervention of a shaman. Likewise, some well-known spirits or mythical figures were never the source of *bo'ha.* One such was Coyote, the trickster of Basin mythology, whom many viewed as the cause of various maladies.[9]

The acquisition of *bo'ha* was not, and is not, limited to shamans. Many, if not most, people have contact with spirits or seek power at some time in their lives. Just as the demands of life are varied, there are many kinds of *bo'ha.* Among the Newes, people could solicit supernatural assistance in matters of war, love, hunting, and gambling. In these cases individuals sought power for personal reasons, and although such power certainly might affect others, it usually did not concern the community as a whole.[10] The trapper Osborne Russell, who spent nearly a decade among Newe peoples in the 1830s and left one of the few early descriptions of Newe religious beliefs, remarked on the importance of *bo'ha* in the life of every person. He wrote that every "warrior is protected by a pecular [sic] guardian Angel in all his actions so long as he obeys his rules [taboos] a violation of which subjects the offender to misfortunes and disasters during the displeasure of the offended Deity." As for shamans, the relationships of laypeople with their *bo'ha* were subject to taboos. However, Russell suggested that the relationship between shaman and spirit tutor was far more intense.[11]

Shamans differ from laypeople not in their acquisition of *bo'ha* but rather in the nature and extent of their power, the social recognition of that power, and their corresponding ability to exercise power for socially constructive purposes (such as curing illness and charming antelope) or destructive ones (such as witchcraft and sorcery).[12] Shamans can possess priestly powers—for example, they may serve as dance or ritual leaders—but their status is based on direct personal contact with *bo'ha* rather than on ritual knowledge. Both men and women can possess shamanic power. The focus of that power among Numic peoples is on healing and divination, and among the Newe the curing rite was the central performance of shamanism.[13] Some shamans possessed specialized and limited *bo'ha*, whereas others were more powerful "general practitioners." Specialists acquired their knowledge either through direct experience or through dreams of performing a cure. They were the first persons summoned in the case of routine illness or injury, and their power was an extension of well-known home remedies. In more severe cases, and when sorcery or soul loss was suspected, the family and community would call on the powerful "singing" doctors, who possessed the two most significant abilities of Basin shamans: they could suck disease-causing objects out of the victim and enter a trance state to recover lost souls. These powerful shamans were called *bo'hagande* among the Shoshones (*puhagem* by the Paiutes, and *puhá ga'yu* by the Bannocks)—literally, "powerful." This term could be applied to specialists, but it normally was reserved for the singing doctors.[14]

As a Northern Paiute told John Wesley Powell, "The doctor is made by dreams."[15] Contact with spirit tutors and the acquisition of *bo'ha* always occurred in the dream state. Power was never obtained in groups or at public performances. The dream experience could take two distinct forms: unsolicited visits by spirit tutors, and vision quests. Vision quests among Numic peoples in the nineteenth century were common but not as pervasive as among Plateau and Plains peoples.[16] Moreover, many Newes viewed *bo'ha* acquired in vision quests as inferior to that obtained through unsolicited dreams. At least one Fort Hall Bannock argued in the 1930s that men who sought their power were not true *bo'hagande* but only specialists. The curing ceremonies of these specialists were far simpler and lacked the singing and paraphernalia of a *bo'hagande*.[17] Spontaneous dreams were more prevalent among Basin peoples. Inheritance could prompt a dream experience, although it was not necessarily a separate method of obtaining *bo'ha*, because there was a cultural expectation that spirit helpers would attend the children of powerful shamans. Julian Steward recognized that the inheritance of shamanic power contradicted the overly simplistic view of Numic peoples he had presented, when he wrote: "It is of interest that in these societies which had few persons specializing in any kind of activity, shamanism or the predisposition to shamanism tended to be inherited."[18]

The tutor appeared to the future shaman repeatedly in dreams, prescribed in intricate detail the shaman's "medicine," and placed taboos on his or her behavior. Medicine bundles contained items symbolic of the curing *bo'ha* and of the spirit tutor. Some essential items appeared in all kits, such as a pipe, rattle, wild tobacco, special stones or beads, and feathers. In addition to these basic items, the spirit helper ordered the shaman to collect specialized paraphernalia. Bone whistles and tubes used to suck disease objects from patients were common. Every item in the kit held symbolic importance, and all had to be respectfully preserved in order for the shaman to maintain good health and *bo'ha*.[19] Most important, the spirit gave the shaman songs. In Northern Paiute dialects, the healing ceremony is called *tuníku'hu*—literally, "singing." It is through songs that the shaman contacts and communicates with the spirit tutor. Although a shaman may be taught certain songs at the outset of his or her training, the spirit tutor will reveal new songs throughout the shaman's life.[20]

Osborne Russell reported that Newe "Prophets Jugglers or Medicine Men" were instructed by "Deities," who "continually attended upon the devotee from birth gradually instilling into his mind the mysteries of his profession which cannot be transmitted from one mortal to another." Russell also alluded to the intricacy of spirit instructions when he wrote that these "supernatural directors" guided the potential shaman from early childhood, instructing him even in "his manner of eating drinking and smoking." Russell ascribed particular importance to smoking customs, as "every Prophet has a different mode of handling filling lighting and smoking the big pipe." The spirit tutor imposed numerous individual taboos on the shaman. "Some cannot smoke in the presence of a female or a dog," wrote the trapper, "and a hundred other movements equally vague and superstitious which would be too tedious to mention here."[21]

What was tedium for Russell was a matter of life or death for the Newe shamans. The spirit tutor's instructions were critical not only for successful shamanic practice but also for the shaman's physical health and well-being. Shamans who ignored repeated dreams, failed to follow the spirit helper's instructions in exact detail, or even modified their ritual paraphernalia without instruction could lose their power, become ill, or even die.[22] Shamanism was serious business, and constant contact with *bo'ha* was hazardous. Shamans were always at risk from people who unknowingly could cause them to violate their taboos. When shamans fell ill, the illness was often believed to be power-related. In these instances another shaman might attempt a cure, or, if the afflicted shaman could not understand his or her own dreams, a more experienced shaman might try to interpret them.[23]

Because of the highly personalized nature of *bo'ha*, every shaman dressed and painted in a unique manner. Painting was often more distinctive than dress. Dots and lines of red and white often adorned the doctor's face and body. Sometimes the shaman might wear feathers or dress in a certain manner, but it was just as customary for the shaman to dress exactly like the spectators. This increasingly meant wearing Euro-American clothing, especially by the twentieth century.[24] The Nevada Indian agent W. D. C. Gibson alluded to this trend during the Ghost Dance era, when he complained that, although most Northern Paiutes wore "citizen dress," he could not "prevent them from howling over their sick."[25] Clothes did not make the shaman. This was because *bo'ha* was never inherent in standardized ritual dress; it could be found only in items that the spirit tutors instructed the shaman to collect. Paints were usually part of this ritual paraphernalia, but clothing was not. The lack of any regular link between clothing and power raises important doubts as to whether the protective "ghost shirt" of the Lakotas could have originated within Basin aboriginal belief systems.

Power is essentially the opposite of sickness, and so the shaman's principal function was the healing rite. This ceremony was highly variable. The Newe healing rite was not a liturgy; there were no societies among Basin shamans, and, just as no two living shamans could share precisely the same *bo'ha*—with all its attendant taboos and instructions—no two shamans cured in exactly the same way.[26] The first step in the curing process was the decision that shamanic healing was indeed necessary.

This decision might occur after the failure of home remedies or when the patient's symptoms indicated a serious affliction. A trusted local doctor was usually called first. In more severe cases the family or the patient might seek out a shaman noted for strong power over the patient's particular condition. Shamans almost never refused a case, for to do so was viewed as a serious breach of taboo that could imperil the doctor.[27] The cost varied greatly, with more celebrated and powerful shamans charging higher fees. Remuneration was in the form of horses, trade goods, and, increasingly, cash. Like refusing a case, waiving a fee or overcharging was an act of disobedience toward one's bo'ha, and sickness or the loss of power could result.[28] Except in rare instances and emergencies, curing rites always occurred after dark. Until the ceremony the doctor remained isolated and might even retire to a special location to communicate with his or her bo'ha.[29] In most cases two performances, separated by one night, were necessary. Most took place outdoors, within the shelter of a semicircular brush enclosure. A fire burned at the center of the compound. In winter or in harsh weather, the patient's brush house was used instead of the simple sage and willow windbreak. (By the 1930s, nearly all curing ceremonies were held indoors, in the patient's home.)[30]

The curing rite itself was a combination of individual and communal contact with spiritual power. On arrival, the shaman discussed the patient's condition with relatives and smoked. Then, according to John Wesley Powell, who studied the Numic peoples in the early 1870s, the doctor "sits down and muses with his friend [spirit tutor] on top of the hut, or fire or sheet, until the hummingbird sings a song in his head. . . . When the hummingbird commences [the shaman] starts suddenly. . . . Then the doctor smokes and waits for another bird to teach him a song."[31] During a typical twentieth-century healing rite, shamans began with five short songs that honored the source of the curing bo'ha. The songs came directly from the spirit helper. Powell was probably referring to a related set of songs, for the hummingbird was one of the "good birds" known as a source of healing bo'ha. These initial songs were critical, for through them the shaman reenacted his or her original encounter with the spirit tutor and reestablished direct contact with the curing bo'ha.[32] The shaman's songs continued throughout the night, some for the purpose of diagnosis, some to effect a cure.[33]

The singing shaman was usually accompanied by at least two assistants. Most important was the poinabe or "talker."[34] Stephen Powers, who, like Powell, witnessed healing ceremonies in the 1870s, mistook the talker for "a male relative of the [patient], squatting by her side, [who] frequently ejaculated in a loud voice words intended to be encouraging to the woman and laudatory of the doctor's art." In fact the talker, who was not necessarily related to the patient, was repeating what the shaman had just said. Shamans preferred to use the same talker, who became familiar with the doctor's songs. It was the talker's job to prevent any mistakes in the ceremony by repeating the shaman's songs and words in a loud, clear voice so that the spectators could follow and sing along. Powers reported that the observers sometimes "joined in the chant in a low humming voice."[35] The talker, seated on the shaman's left, might also say prayers during the ceremony, some addressed to the sickness, which was warned of the presence of a great doctor and implored to leave, and others to the shaman, whom he praised and encouraged.[36] Throughout the long night the shaman also danced. "His dance was slow and consisted merely of a shuffle with both feet kept together;" wrote Powers, "and he kept time to it with a mournful wailing chant." Here, shamans often employed a second assistant, the *wütádu,* or dancer. Always a woman, the dancer mimicked the shaman's counterclockwise dance around the fire. She carried a bowl-shaped rattle and shook it in rhythm with the dance.[37]

Smoking was an important element of all healing ceremonies and illustrated the communal nature of the rite. After the talker filled the pipe, the shaman smoked first and then passed the pipe counterclockwise. Everyone in attendance was required to smoke the pipe. If anyone refused, the ceremony was stopped until that person cooperated. The entire ceremony was in jeopardy and the shaman suffered an insult to his spirit powers if these efforts failed. Usually, however, everyone cooperated, and the pipe made the rounds of the assembled crowd at regular intervals from the beginning of the ceremony to its end at daybreak.[38] Thus the curing ceremony was not only about healing an individual; it was also an important public performance that touched nearly everyone in the community. No announcement of the ceremony was made, yet word spread quickly, and normally everyone within easy traveling distance attended. Only menstruating and pregnant women were excluded from shamanic performances.[39]

Those present were not simply witnesses; they participated in the ceremony and communicated with the curing *bo'ha* as well. Their presence assisted in the shaman's struggle with the illness, and by singing and smoking they too established contact, through the shaman, with *bo'ha.* In this sense the whole community participated in the emotionally charged curing ceremony. On a more social note, rest breaks offered an opportunity to visit with friends and neighbors. The patient's family also provided a meal for the spectators (the doctor normally did not join in the feast). The cost of the ceremony could be substantial, and family members pooled resources, sold property, and sometimes slaughtered horses to provide for those in attendance.[40]

During the early hours of the ceremony, the shaman concentrated on determining the exact cause of the patient's illness. Generally, the shaman sang and danced around the fire until losing consciousness and entering a trance state, but, as with nearly everything surrounding shamanism, the precise way in which a doctor entered a trance was highly personalized and dictated by the doctor's spirit tutor. While in the trance, the shaman sought the cause of the illness and might also confer with his spirit helper regarding the cure.[41] When fully conscious, the shaman announced the cause of the illness, which could be one of three things: a breach of taboo, sorcery, or "ghosting." Taboo, or power-related, illnesses most often struck young people, especially those with powerful relatives and those who exhibited unusual talents or were themselves rumored to be powerful. In nearly all such cases an experienced shaman would try to determine which taboos had been broken and instruct the patient in avoiding future breaches. In effecting a cure, the shaman might remove the patient's power permanently or temporarily.

Sorcery was another very common diagnosis for Numic shamans, particularly in communities rent with conflict. Sorcery was also suspected if the illness came on quickly or if death was sudden. A sorcerer's malevolence usually manifested itself in the form of an object intruding into the body. In such cases, the shaman would find and remove the object, normally by sucking it out of the patient. Finally, "ghosting" occurred when spirits of the dead attempted to steal the breath of the living. This diagnosis was common among elderly patients, who had many friends and relatives among the dead who missed them and sought their company. Fainting spells, delirium, and unconsciousness were the usual symptoms. "Ghosting" also required the most highly specialized and risky curing method: soul recovery through trance. The ability to enter a trance and recover a lost soul was the hallmark of the most powerful shamans. These doctors could travel to another plane of existence to find the lost soul and guide it back to the world of the living.[42]

The dramatic conclusion of the ceremony often came when the shaman sucked the disease-causing object from the victim and displayed it for the assembled crowd. The moment the object entered the doctor, he was in a sense possessed and immediately fell into convulsions. Two or more men, designated earlier, quickly came forward and held the shaman down. The shaman struggled wildly against their grip for a time, then fell abruptly into a trance. On awakening the doctor coughed up the object: small snakes, toads and stones were common. It was then ritually disposed of by burning or burial.[43] The ceremony Stephen Powers watched closely followed this pattern. As the rite approached its climax, Powers observed "two large stalwart Indians" position themselves "as if they were about to pounce upon [the shaman]." He continued:

> Presently, as the doctor arose from one of his nasty vomits, he seemed suddenly to be seized with convulsions; he straightened up, his body grew rigid, he bent over backward as if about to fall, his eyes rolled, his arms were thrown wildly about. The two Indians now sprang forward and grappled with him, they seemed to struggle with him with herculean force, they swayed to and fro, they got the crick out of his back by doubling him forward. In a minute or two he was apparently restored, but he sank on the ground quivering and moaning as if with the exhaustion of the terrible struggle. The male relative [the *poínabe*] gave a loud shout of exaltation. . . . Now, what was the meaning of all this fanfaronade? Simply this—the old doctor had sucked the evil spirit out of the woman and received it into his own person, and it hurt him!

Powers deemed the shaman's performance "the most consummately acted humbug," yet he could not deny the effectiveness of the cure. The next morning the patient was "sitting up, eating a roast ground-squirrel and feeling much better." He attributed her rapid improvement to the "power of the imagination and of her belief in the efficacy of the old doctor's powwow."[44]

Indeed, Newe peoples believed in the efficacy of shamanism, and that belief provided the internal logic for the prophetic religions of the nineteenth century, including both Ghost Dances. Some aspects of the prophetic religions emerged directly from shamanism. The belief in the efficacy of dreams and the importance of following the prophecies revealed in them were fundamental parts of Newe cultures that allowed the incorporation of new ideas into an evolving religious understanding. Even though individual shamanic practice is based on a rigid set of taboos, shamanism itself survives precisely because of its ability to incorporate new beliefs and practices through a process of direct revelation. Other parallels between shamanism and prophecy are found in the ways prophets received their visions—essentially the same way that a shaman acquired power—and established their authority, through claims of weather control and invulnerability. Perhaps most important, in shamanic cultures, including that of Newe peoples, there is no clear distinction between physical and spiritual healing. All illness is in a sense spiritual, just as healing is spiritual.[45] The Ghost Dance prophets exhibited the one skill that set truly powerful shamans apart: they could enter a dream state in order to visit the land of the dead. Instead of returning with a lost soul, however, the prophets returned with a message of identity and community healing. Ghost Dances were a community curing rite that promised the restoration of a world free of disease, death, and spiritual disharmony.[46] The prophets proposed to heal the illness of the larger community rather than the individual, and, through group performance, to work a radical transformation of existence. Deeply ingrained shamanic beliefs made prophecy an understandable and consistently acceptable response to the demographic, social, and economic changes of the nineteenth century.

Prophecy was a second major aspect in the religious lives of Newe peoples and neighboring tribes of the Columbia Plateau and northern Rockies in the nineteenth century. Prophets could at times be shamans, but prophecy was in itself a specialization.[47] The first Columbia Plateau prophet was not a shaman, and neither Wodziwob nor Wovoka, the prophets of the 1870 and 1890 Ghost Dances respectively, were shamans when they began to preach. (Only later in their lives did the Ghost Dance prophets work as healers.) Prophecy must be understood as a separate but related aspect of Newe religion. As chance would have it, the agents of Euro-American colonization brought with them their own prophetic religion and often viewed their identity and destiny in prophetic terms. It was through the evolving prophetic tradition—both Indian and white—that elements of Christian doctrine became fused with native beliefs.

The prophetic tradition west of the Rockies was at the heart of a series of religious movements centered on the Columbia Plateau that preceded the Ghost Dances by decades and have been interpreted by some scholars as direct predecessors of the later religions. Leslie Spier's pioneering work on what he called the "Prophet Dance" challenged the common interpretation of native messianic movements as narrow responses to deprivation. Instead, he argued that the Prophet Dance was wholly aboriginal, precontact in origin, and rooted in a "common doctrinal background" found in Plateau cosmology: the "Earth-Woman" had a limited life span, and periodically the creator must return to renew the earth. According to the Nespelems, after he had made the world, the Old One, the creator, told the people:

I will send messages to earth by the souls of people that reach me, but whose time to die has not yet come. They will carry messages to you from time to time; and when their souls return to their bodies, they will revive, and tell you their experiences. Coyote and myself will not be seen again until the Earth-Woman is very old. Then we shall return to earth, for it will require a new change by that time. Coyote will precede me by some little time; and when you see him, you will know that the time is at hand. When I return all the spirits of the dead will accompany me, and after that there will be no spirit-land. All the people will live together. Then will the Earth-Woman revert to her natural shape, and live as a mother among her children. The things will be made right, and there will be much happiness.[48]

Spier argued that, long before white contact, strange natural phenomena set in motion religious movements based entirely on this aboriginal doctrine of world destruction and renewal. Prophets who, while in a dream state, had visited the creator or the land of the dead arose to preach a more righteous life. They also brought a ceremony, a "supposed imitation of the dances of the dead," and songs that would hasten the reunification of all people on a renewed earth. Spier believed that the Prophet Dances were the direct "source" of the Ghost Dances.[49] Although his premise is reasonable, the historical and ethnographic evidence suggests that the Prophet Dances should not be treated as a static tradition but rather as a dynamic, evolving element of American Indian spiritual life west of the Rockies during a century of tremendous demographic, social, and economic change.

The oldest recorded case of a Plateau prophet can be traced to the years after the "dry snow," a volcanic ashfall that took place sometime after 1790 and before the arrival of whites. (Volcanologists believe there was a major eruption of Mount St. Helens around 1800.)[50] In 1844 Cornelius, a Spokane chief, told Charles Wilkes how, after the ashfall some fifty years earlier, the "medicine-men arose," told the people to "stop their fear and crying," and then made a haunting prophecy: "Soon there will come from the rising sun a different kind of man from any you have yet seen, who will bring with them a book and will teach you everything, and after that the world will fall to pieces."[51] Oral traditions collected in the early twentieth century differ slightly in details but confirm that a prophet arose sometime around the beginning of the nineteenth century. Identified as "Michel," he may have been a Sanpoil who lived with the Okanogans. He was not a shaman and had "no curative or other magical powers." The story of his rise begins with the appearance of a two-headed, four-legged goose soon after the "dry snow." The people killed the bird and discovered wheat, which they had never seen before, in its two crops. They took this as a sign of the end of the world and immediately began to dance in a circle around the prophet. The dance "followed the pattern of one performed by the dead somewhere in the sky." Some of the dancers fell into trances and returned with their own prophecies, then joined the original dreamer at the center of the circle. Throughout the ceremony, the prophet exhorted the people not to "fight, steal, lie, commit rape, or sin in other ways." The religious excitement was so great that the people neglected their work, and some starved the following winter.[52]

It is reasonable to question the antiquity of prophecies that incorporated white contact. They might be interpreted as wholly postcontact explanations of epidemics, encroachment, and injustice, a spiritual explanation of the troubles that beset Indian America after contact. The oldest historically documented prophecies, however, came before the peoples in question were truly subjected to Euro-American domination. More convincingly, the prophecies may indicate mediate contact with the white world through wide-ranging "chains of communication." David Aberle and Deward Walker, among others, have argued that Spier's insistence that the Prophet Dances antedated all white contact is simply untenable. Epidemics spread in advance of white contact, and horses and competition for trade goods radically altered intergroup relations long before the first prophets arose. Plateau Indians knew of the whites, and their societies were experiencing major changes before the first explorers and traders entered their homelands.[53] The same was equally true for the Newes, who possessed items of Spanish manufacture when Lewis and Clark met them and regularly traded with Plateau peoples. Even more intriguing is Melburn Thurman's argument that the Prophet Dances were an extension of the Shawnee prophet Tenskwatawa's religion, suggesting a direct link between the Eastern Woodlands prophetic tradition, beginning with the Delaware Prophet in the 1760s, and the prophetic movements of the far West.[54]

Yet the motif of world destruction and renewal and indeed the prophetic tradition itself were not postcontact additions to Plateau cosmology. On the contrary, they were aboriginal ideas that provide a key for understanding Indian responses to the cataclysmic events that followed white contact. Elizabeth Vibert has argued that the important question here is not whether the Prophet Dances were inspired by aboriginal cosmology or by the effects of colonization but rather why the prophetic response seemed "natural and rational to . . . the prophets and their followers." She asserts that the devastating smallpox epidemics that struck the Columbia Plateau around 1780 and 1800 were largely responsible for initiating the dances. The Indians did not blame the whites for the diseases but rather interpreted them as an internal spiritual crisis for which the "Prophets held out the last and best hope for an end to the horror and a return to peace and prosperity." In this view the Prophet Dances are an example of how change, although it may be externally motivated, is internally ordered.[55]

The reception that native peoples gave Northwest Company's traders in the Columbia Plateau and the interior Northwest helps reveal how the former made sense of the vast changes that came with mediate white contact. In 1808, Simon Fraser, while descending the river that now bears his name, encountered hundreds of Thompson Indians, who welcomed him with elaborate greetings and prayers. The explorer made little of the ceremony in his memoirs, but over a century later James Teit collected stories from the Thompson Indians, who remembered this visit as the return of Coyote.[56] Three years later, in 1811, David Thompson descended the Columbia to its mouth and all along the way was greeted with similar ceremony. Near Kettle Falls, the trader remembered,

> the Chief made a short prayer, after which the dance commenced of the Men and Women, each separate, to the music of their singing, which was pleasantly plaintive. . . . Each line of Men and Women had a clear space of three or four feet within which they danced; at first the step was slow and the singing the same, but both gradually increased. . . . This lasted for about eight minutes, when a pause of two minutes took place; a prayer was made, and the dance and singing repeated twice: The whole was strictly a religious ceremony, every face was grave and serious, almost to sadness.[57]

A few days later, after witnessing more dancing, Thompson recorded in his journal, "I may remark that all their Dances are a kind of religious Prayer for some end—they in their Dances never assume a gay joyous countenance, but always a serious turn with often a trait of enthusiasm—the step is also most always the semblance of running, as if People pursuing & being pursued."[58] Because the Columbia River peoples had no tradition of a greeting dance, some scholars have asserted that Thompson had witnessed the Prophet Dance, and indeed his appearance might have even been interpreted by the Indian peoples he visited as the realization of prophecies that foretold of the arrival of the whites; hence the elaborate greetings at each village.[59] Or, it is possible that he, like Fraser, was welcomed as Coyote coming back to overturn and renew a world in disorder. This possibility is all the more likely considering that Thompson had been preceded downriver by the most famous and best-documented early prophet, Kauxuma-nupika, the Kutenai "manly woman."[60]

Arriving at Fort Astoria at the mouth of the Columbia during the summer of 1811, Kauxuma-nupika dressed as a man, carried weapons, and traveled with a wife. Thompson, coming in a few weeks later, recognized her as a woman once married to a Northwest Company employee. She had wintered at Kootenay House in 1808–09, and Thompson had expelled her because of "loose conduct." She returned to her people over a year later with a miraculous story: she claimed that the whites had changed her gender. She then changed her name to Kauxuma-nupika, "Gone to the Spirits," took on the roles and dress of a man—including marrying another woman—and claimed great spiritual power.[61] Kauxuma-nupika declared herself a prophet and traveled from "tribe to tribe," either in an attempt to proselytize followers or, as Thompson suggested, because her prophecies quickly made her unpopular. On her voyage down the Columbia in advance of Thompson's party, Kauxuma-nupika prophesied a coming epidemic and so alarmed the Chinooks that some of them threatened her life. At one village Thompson reassured the inhabitants and alluded to the danger facing the Kutenai prophet: "They as well as others enquired abt the Small Pox, of which a report had been raised that it was coming with the white Men & that 2 Men of enormous Size [were coming] to overturn the Ground [burying all the villages] &c. We assured them the whole was false, at which they were highly pleased, but had not the Kootanaes been under our immediate care she would have been killed for the lies she told on her way to the sea."[62] She approached Thompson for "protection" on the return trip upriver, and, according to Ross, the prophet delivered a very different message to the Indians she now encountered:

> The stories they gave out among the nonsuspecting and credulous natives
> as they passed, were well calculated to astonish as well as to attract
> attention. . . . They showed the Indians an old letter . . . and told them
> that they had been sent by the great white chief, with a message to apprize
> the natives in general that gifts, consisting of goods and implements of all
> kinds, were forthwith to be poured in upon them; that the great white chief
> knew their wants, and was just about to supply them with everything their
> hearts could desire; that the whites had hitherto cheated the Indians, by
> selling goods in place of making presents to them, as directed by the great
> white chief.[63]

It would be easy to argue, as Ross suggested and some scholars have accepted, that the prophet was a "cheat" who tailored her message to what Indian people wanted to hear, especially after her first prophecy nearly got her killed.[64] Regardless of the motives behind her shifting messages, however, Kauxuma-nupika and her prophecies cannot be understood outside the context of white contact, mediate or immediate. It was the whites who had "changed her sex," and their diseases and trade goods were integral to the world she foresaw. Yet native elements were also obvious in her prophecy: the two giants coming to overturn the earth were likely a reinterpretation of Coyote and Old Man on their way to renew the earth.[65] This interpretation may, in turn, explain the greetings Thompson received on his voyage downriver and illustrate the ways in which native peoples internally ordered and understood the effects of white contact.

In addition to disease and trade, a force with far greater psychic and emotional power reshaped the native prophetic tradition in the far West: evangelical Christianity. On a mystical plane where contact with supernatural power could impart the ability to foretell the future, native and Christian prophecy met, intermingled, and merged. At times, both native and colonizer expressed their identity through prophecy. For Indian peoples, the result of this religious "conversation" was a syncretic religion with the power to explain the impact of white colonization and inspire new identities.

The historical record suggests that Christian influences began well before the 1830s, the decade when, Spier asserted, a "Christianized" version of the Prophet Dance finally emerged. For instance, Alexander Ross, who lived among the Okanogans from 1811 to 1818, provided a different, far less positive, version of the world destruction and renewal motif in Plateau mythology from the one that Spier cited: "They [the Okanogans] believe that this world will have an end, as it had a beginning; and their reason is this, that the rivers and lakes must eventually undermine the earth, and set the land afloat again, like the island of their fore-fathers, and then all must perish. Frequently they have asked us when it would take place—the its-owl-eigh, or end of the world."[66] Ross also heard a version of the Okanogan origin story substantially different from the one Teit collected nearly a century later. The Okanogans told Ross that they were descendants of very white people who lived on an island called Samah-tuma-whoolah, "White Man's Island," which was ruled by a tall white woman named Scomalt. She expelled the wicked people by cutting off a portion of the island, drowning most of them in the process. One man and one woman survived, built a canoe, and made it to the mainland, "but they suffered so much while floating on the ocean that they became dark and dingy from the exposure, and their skins have retained that colour ever since. From this man and woman all the Indians of the continent have their origin; and as a punishment for their original wickedness, they were condemned by the great Scomalt to poverty, degradation, and nakedness, and to be called Skyloo, or Indians."[67] The parallels with the biblical tales of Adam and Eve and of the curse of Ham are obvious. They could be coincidence, they could arise from an Indian reinterpretation of biblical tales, they could represent Ross's spin on the matter, or they could be a combination of all three. There is simply no way at this date to draw a defensible line between a "pre-Christian" and "Christian" Prophet Dance or between pristine tradition and postcontact syncretism; but what can be surmised from the historic and ethnographic evidence is that Christian concepts entered Indian religious understandings through the shared discourse of prophecy.

Christianity likely transformed precontact belief with regard to the desirability of the end of the world and the return of the dead. The Modoc Dream Dance (which Spier interpreted as a southern extension of the Prophet Dance complex and a bridge to the later Ghost Dances) might provide one example of this process. The Dream Dance took place each fall when the aurora borealis became visible. "The boreal display proclaimed the sky on fire . . . with its light or smoke causing incurable sickness." The Modocs then took to the water, shouting and splashing to "ward off the sickness." After the ritual bathing, they held dances for two nights, "because they did not want the world to be destroyed." Yet the same elderly Modoc informant who witnessed the Dream Dance as a child in the 1840s and was a Ghost Dance activist in 1870 also said: "If the world should not burn, sickness would come and everyone die. . . . When the world is burned up, *Kumuk'a'mts* is going to make the world over again. . . . I do not know why he wants to make the world over. I never heard that the dead would be alive in the new world."[68] The end of the world was a frightening prospect for the Modocs in the 1840s; yet three decades later they participated actively in a religion intended to precipitate it. Could it have been that the "aboriginal" base of the Prophet Dances, as well as the Ghost Dances, was a prophetic and ceremonial tradition intended to prevent the end of the world, not hasten it? The key variable in this scenario would be the introduction of the Christian concept of the millennium, which transformed older beliefs in prophecy and world destruction, making the end of the world and the return of the dead acceptable, even welcome, prospects, while at the same time instilling the proselytizing zeal.

Christian influence on the prophetic tradition was obvious by the 1830s, and it was not Euro-Americans but Indians who transmitted and interpreted the doctrine. Iroquois and other Eastern Indians who worked as trappers for the Northwest Company were probably the earliest conduit for the informal introduction of Christian beliefs to the peoples of the northern Rockies, the Columbia Plateau, and the Snake River country. When Donald McKenzie led the first of his Snake River expeditions in 1818, his brigade was a cross-section of fur-trade society, including French Canadians, Métis, and Iroquois. Many Iroquois were devout Catholics and told the Western Indians of the "Blackrobes" and their power.[69] Alexander Ross described these "civilized Indians" as expert canoeists and woodsmen, but he had little faith in their religious understandings: "They are brought up to religion, it is true, and sing hymns oftener than paddling songs; but those who came here . . . retain none of its precepts."[70] Ross was correct insofar as their religious influence was neither uniform nor systematic: the Iroquois were trappers, not missionaries. Still, they lived among the region's Indian peoples and often took wives among these tribes. At the very least, they introduced Christian ideology for the first time and may have been the source of the manifestations of Catholic ceremony that later travelers witnessed among the Plateau tribes.

One particular group of Iroquois has been identified as prospective missionaries. Led by Old Ignace La Mousse, this group left the area around Montreal sometime after the War of 1812 and by 1820 had settled among the Salish. Old Ignace was a devout Catholic. He married a Pend d'Oreille woman and fathered three children, whom he brought up in the faith. In 1835 he took his two oldest sons with him to Saint Louis, Missouri (along with a number of other Indians), where they were baptized as Charles and Francis La Mousse. Two years later he again led an Indian mission bound for Saint Louis. Most of this ill-fated party, however, never made it. La Mousse, a Nez Percé, and the four Salish in the party were killed by Lakotas on the North Platte River. Only the missionary William H. Gray and two white companions escaped with their lives.[71] After La Mousse's death, Bishop Joseph Rosati of Saint Louis credited the Iroquois trappers with having "sown the first seeds of Catholicity in the midst of the infidel nations among whom they live."[72]

The religious influence of the Iroquois and the other Indian trappers must be assessed carefully. Some scholars, accepting Rosati's opinion, have placed Old Ignace La Mousse at the center of the evolving prophetic tradition.[73] But, the opinions of the Fathers in Saint Louis aside, there is no historical evidence that the Iroquois were active missionaries. The details of their daily lives in a nonliterate culture cannot be recovered. Alvin M. Josephy Jr., in his classic work on Northwest Indians, raises another important point from the historical record. Only in the early 1830s did the trappers routinely mention evidence of Christian influence. For instance, in 1824 Jedediah Strong Smith and his party of American trappers wintered among the Salish, but Smith's journals are silent on the matter of the Indians' religion. Smith was an atypical mountain man. Literate and well-read, he was a stern Methodist who studied the Bible constantly and often remarked on religious matters in his journal. Josephy infers from this absence of comment that the impact of the Iroquois Catholics had been minimal; something more must have happened to increase the Indians' interest in Christian concepts between the time of Smith's visit and the early 1830s, when nearly every Euro-American observer remarked on the startling elements of Christianity evident in the Indians' worship.[74]

That something was probably the return of two Indian youths to their homes after four years of schooling and religious instruction at the Hudson's Bay Company's Red River settlement. By the terms of its 1821 license, the company was required to provide religious instruction to the Indians. In 1824 company officials decided this meant educating and Christianizing a number of Indian children, and in April of the following year two boys, the sons of Spokane and Kutenai chiefs respectively, left for Red River. Both were given the names of company officials and thereafter were known as "Spokane Garry" and "Kutenai Pelly."[75] Garry and Pelly caused a great stir when they returned to their peoples in 1829. They dressed like whites, spoke English, and carried with them the King James Bible, the New Testament, and the Book of Common Prayer of the Church of England. Garry was the son of an influential headman who had died in his son's absence, and with the passage of time Garry became a headman in his own right. He was treated with great respect as he preached and sang hymns for his people. Indians from surrounding tribes, including the Nez Percés, took great interest in the young man's words, and his influence was probably the impetus for the famous Nez Percé mission to Saint Louis in 1831 to secure copies of the Bible for themselves. Less is known of Pelly, who died in 1831 after returning to the Red River school. But between them Garry and Pelly initiated a religious excitement with a doctrine that was not simply Christian but rather syncretic.[76] John

McLean, the company trader at Stuart Lake, British Columbia, wrote, "Two young men, natives of Oregon, who had received a little education at Red River, had on their return to their own country, introduced a sort of religion whose groundwork seemed to be Christianity, accompanied with some heathen ceremonies of the natives. This religion spread with amazing rapidity all over the country. It reached Fort Alexandria, the lower post of the district, in the autumn of 1834 or 1835."[77] Garry and Pelly's influence spread not only north but also east over the Continental Divide to the Salish, from whom it filtered south to the Newe peoples of the Salmon and Snake Rivers.

The fact that Indian peoples were reinterpreting Christianity was obvious to Nathaniel Wyeth during his first expedition in 1833. It is quite likely that the fur trader had at times witnessed a "Christianized" version of the Prophet Dance. For some time Wyeth's party traveled with a mixed Salish–Nez Percé village that treated each Sunday as a holy day. In the Flathead Valley, Wyeth described the Sabbath observance as a "parade of prayer," with trading, gambling, and even hunting and fishing put on hold until the prayers were over.[78] On two Sundays in May 1833, Wyeth also witnessed performances of what was probably the Prophet Dance. Disdainful of the Great Awakening ministers of his native New England and similarly suspicious of the Indian prophet's motives, he wrote:

> There is a new great man no[w] getting up in the Camp and like the rest of the w[o]rld [he] covers his designs under the great cloak of religion his followers are now dancing to their own vocal music in the plain perhaps ⅕ of the camp follow him when he gets enough followers he will branch off and be an independent chief he is getting up some new form of religion among the Indians more simple than himself like others of his class he works with the fools women and children first while he is doing this the men of sense thinking it is too foolish to do harm stand by and laugh but they soon will find that women fools and children form so large a majority that with a bad grace they will have to yield. These things make me think of the New Lights and the revivals of New England.[79]

Two weeks later the "medicine chief" of the same village performed a dance. He "formed them into a ring men women and children and after an address they danced to a tune in dancing they keep the feet in the same position the whole time mer[e]ly jumping up to the tune keeping the hands in front of them at intervals he addressed them."[80] By the end of his stay among the Indians, Wyeth paid little attention to their Sunday observances, recording only brief notations of their prayers in his diary. At the end of June, on the Camas Prairie north of modern Rexburg,

Idaho, he wrote, "Sunday Indians singing and dancing as usual. . . . These Inds. do nothing on sunday."[81]

Salish and Nez Percés actively transmitted these beliefs to Newe peoples. John Kirk Townsend, a member of Wyeth's second expedition, described a religious ceremony led by a group of Nez Percés and Salish visiting Fort Hall in July 1834. The Indians gathered in a lodge, and, after a "harangue" to remind the assembled of their purpose and to call for them to pray "with one tongue," the "chief" rose to his knees and began a series of short prayers, spoken "fervently" in short rapid sentences, meanwhile looking "beseechingly" to heaven. "At the conclusion of each sentence," wrote Townsend, "a choral response of a few words was made, accompanied by frequent low moaning." After about twenty minutes the "chief" bent his chin to his breast and began a song that all joined in. "It resembled the words, *Ho-hă-ho-hă-ho-hă-ha-a*, commencing in a low tone, and gradually swelling to a full, round, and beautifully modulated chorus." The chief ended the song with a "kind of swelling groan . . . [that] was then taken up by another, and the same routine was gone through." The whole ceremony had taken about an hour and a half.[82] Over the winter of 1834–35, according to Washington Irving, Capt. Benjamin Bonneville's party wintered on the Bear River in the vicinity of rival Newe and Ute villages. Irving suggested that the Newe headman's religious interest was simply another way of gaining the upper hand for his people over a traditional foe, in addition to their older forms of competition—shooting, horse racing, and the hand game. In describing the "senior chief of the Shoshonies," Irving wrote:

> He had been among the Nez Percés, listened to their new code of morality and religion received from the white men, and attended their devotional exercises. He had observed the effect of all this, in elevating the tribe in the estimation of the white men; and determined, by the same means, to gain for his own tribe a superiority over their ignorant rivals, the Eutaws. He accordingly assembled his people, and promulgated among them the mongrel doctrines and form of worship of the Nez Percés; recommending the same to their adoption. The Shoshonies were struck with the novelty, at least, of the measure, and entered into it with spirit. The began to observe Sundays and holidays, and to have devotional dances, and chants, and other ceremonials, about which the ignorant Eutaws knew nothing.[83]

While this assessment illustrates Bonneville's and Irving's inability to take Indian religions seriously, it also provides evidence of a direct link between Newe peoples and the religious excitement then existing to the northwest.

The old trade routes along the Snake River were doubtlessly a conduit for the spread of the religion. In 1835 a British physician visiting Fort Walla Walla described a religious ceremony strikingly similar to the one Townsend had witnessed at Fort Hall. Dr. Gairdner estimated that it had been "about five years since these things found their way among the Indians of the upper Columbia." He also noted the arrival of a Newe trading party. "In the evening the Indians say their prayers under one of the bastions," Gairdner wrote of the Newes, "and have the same religious ceremonies as the Walla-wallas."[84] There can be little doubt that long before the arrival of the first Euro-American Christian missionaries west of the Rockies, the region's native inhabitants, including Newe peoples, had already interpreted and incorporated Christian teachings into their own belief systems.

Moreover, it was an unlikely chain of events initiated by Indian peoples that brought the first white missionaries over the mountains. In 1831 the Nez Percés sent a delegation to Saint Louis in order to obtain "the book" and its knowledge for their people. The journey began with seven Nez Percés and a number of Salish, but in the end only four Nez Percés accompanied the returning supply caravan from the 1831 rendezvous all the way to Saint Louis. There they visited the Catholic Church and met with William Clark, then superintendent of Indian affairs. It was the first time he had seen Indians from west of the Rockies since his famous expedition a quarter of a century earlier. The Nez Percés fell ill. The two older delegates, Eagle and Man of the Dawn Light, died in Saint Louis and were buried in the Catholic cemetery. In March 1832 the two younger men began the voyage home. In the end only one, Rabbit Skin Leggings, saw his people again, and he died shortly after his return, in a battle with the Blackfeet. The sad end of the 1831 mission did not dissuade the Nez Percés, who joined in several more trips to Saint Louis, including the two led by Old Ignace. More important, the Nez Percé visit to Saint Louis became the catalyst for the evangelical Protestant missions that left for the far West in the coming years.[85]

While in Saint Louis, the Nez Percé delegation gained the attention of William Walker, who related their story to his friend G. P. Disoway, an influential layman in the Methodist church. Soon the story appeared in the church paper, the *Christian Advocate and Journal and Zion's Herald*, which editorialized, "Hear! Who will respond to the call from beyond the Rocky Mountains? . . . We are for having a mission established there at once. . . . All we want is men. Who will go? Who?"[86] The first to respond were Jason and Daniel Lee, who went west with Wyeth's supply train in 1834. But they continued on to the lower Columbia and soon settled among the burgeoning Euro-American population in the Willamette Valley, discarding their plans to minister to the Indians. The following year Marcus Whitman and Samuel Parker made the overland trek under the auspices of the American Board of Commissioners for Foreign Missions. The ABCFM represented the Presbyterian, Congregational, and Dutch Reformed churches, and its two agents were in search of prospective mission sites. At the 1835 rendezvous the two men met the Nez Percés and Salish and were so encouraged by their interest that Parker went on alone to the Columbia, while Whitman hurried back east to organize a missionary party for the next summer.

The evangelical missionaries who traveled west over the next several years stayed only briefly among the Newes, and their impact was transient. The party that Whitman and Henry Harmon Spalding led west in 1836 was one of the most famous in the annals of the overland emigration. Two members of the party aroused intense curiosity among the mountain men and the Indians: Narcissa Whitman and Eliza Spalding, missionaries' wives and the first Euro-American women to make the overland trek. Their mission field lay to the northwest of the Newe homeland, and by the end of the year the Whitmans were settled among the Cayuses along the Walla Walla River, while the Spaldings set up their mission at Lapwai among the Nez Percés.[87] More missionaries followed, but, as with the Whitmans and the Spaldings, their stay among the Newes was brief. In 1838, Sarah White Smith was among the missionaries who "reinforced" the Oregon mission. Unlike most of the others, she commented on the religious curiosity of the Newe people. On Sunday, 22 July, while encamped on tributary of the Bear River, she wrote, "The Bannock Indians have visited us. . . . Much interested in the singing & attentive to the other exercises. In prayer they fixed their eyes on the ground and looked devotional. When the sermon was about half done, some of them left & came again when the singing commenced."[88]

Smith's observations become understandable when considered in the context of Newe culture and religion. The sermon, delivered in a language few, if any, of the Newes could understand, held little interest. Singing, on the other hand, was a customary way of tapping bo'ha and an integral part of both shamanism and the prophetic religions. It is not surprising that it should have captured their attention. It is difficult to assess the effect, if any, of the pious evangelicals on Newe religion. They made no serious attempt to minister to the Newes, yet it seems likely that some of their beliefs filtered to the Snake River country through the same

Indian networks of trade and communication that brought word of earlier Christian doctrines. Within a decade of Smith's travels, however, another religious sect, itself imbued with a missionary impulse and a prophetic vision, came to settle permanently in the Newe homeland.

In July 1847, a little over four months before the Cayuses rose up and murdered the Whitmans, Brigham Young led the first contingent of Mormons into the valley of the Great Salt Lake. The prophet Joseph Smith had founded the Church of Jesus Christ of Latter-Day Saints nearly two decades earlier in New York. Smith's doctrines, particularly the institution of plural marriage, enraged many non-Mormons, who in turn persecuted the "Saints" and ran them out of Ohio, Missouri, and finally Illinois. Smith and his brother were assassinated by a mob while jailed in Carthage, Illinois, in 1844. By the spring of 1846, Brigham Young had assumed the church presidency and the title of prophet. He also formulated a plan for a great migration to the West, far beyond the reach of the "Gentiles," as non-Mormons were known by the faithful. The Mormons would began building their new Zion on the eastern edge of the Great Basin in the southeastern corner of the Newe homeland, just about where Shoshone speakers gave way to Utes.[89] Not only would the Mormons' location make them unique, but their doctrine and missionary practice exhibited an uncommon interest in American Indians that has forever linked them with the American Indian prophetic movements.

The core of Mormon doctrine is in essence an origin story that explains the existence of American Indians. The Book of Mormon, which Joseph Smith claimed to have translated from a set of golden plates, told the story of one of the "lost tribes" of Israel that fled to America around 600 B.C. to escape the Babylonian captivity of the Jews. Once in America, the family of the prophet Lehi split: the righteous followed his son Nephi, who led them deeper into the wilderness to escape the Lamanites, the evil followers of Lehi's other sons, Laman and Lemuel. Because of their wickedness, God cursed the Lamanites with a "skin of blackness." After his resurrection, the book continues, Jesus appeared in America and established a church that flourished for several centuries along with Nephite civilization, but as the Nephites' wealth increased, they strayed from the holy laws, and the struggle with their dark-skinned brethren began anew. Only a handful of Nephites survived the final battle, including the historian Mormon and his son Moroni. Mormon inscribed the history on the golden plates that his son then buried. It was the same Moroni who, as an angel, visited Smith in 1823 and told him of the plates.[90]

In the early nineteenth century, this story of American Indian origins was not far outside the mainstream of theological and scientific thought. Joseph Smith lived in an age when beliefs in folk magic and divination were strong.[91] Moreover, Mormon doctrine did not contradict the popular scientific or anthropological opinion of the age. The "lost tribe" theory was a widely held and popular belief, for it explained why there was no mention of American Indians in the Bible. Indeed, Smith was not the first to present a story purporting to explain this troubling omission.[92] And, more than any other creed, Mormonism based its claim of truth on "empirical" evidence. Eleven of the faithful swore that they had seen the golden plates before Moroni reclaimed them. In a time when the majority of Euro-Americans refused to believe that Indians could be responsible for such works, the massive earthen mounds constructed by Mississippians and the remains of Aztec and Inca cities were, to believers, evidence of the Nephite civilization destroyed centuries before.[93] One must also consider the curious parallels that native peoples, enmeshed in shamanism and prophecy, must certainly have seen in Mormon doctrine. Was not Moroni a spirit tutor who visited Smith in a dream and revealed sacred knowledge and a path to spiritual power?

On the secular plane, Mormon doctrine shaped the way in which the Saints approached the Lamanites. Mormon Indian policy was, on the surface, more sympathetic than federal or frontier policy in general, but this difference has also been overstated. Young's oft-quoted remark that it was cheaper to clothe and feed the Indians than to fight them obscured as much as it revealed about Mormon Indian policy.[94] Like most Euro-Americans, Young and his fellow Saints were convinced of the inferiority of Indian peoples; at the same time, conflicting land claims put them directly at odds with the people they aspired to save. Mormon settlements quickly sprang up in the most valuable sites at the base of the Wasatch range and in outlying areas such as the Cache and Tooele valleys. In every instance they evicted the native Shoshone and Ute speakers. Although the Saints recognized their trespass, they also excused themselves with the argument that their civilization was infinitely superior to native cultures. Peace and friendship with the Indians were Young's preference, but he was not above using force or even asking the federal government for aid in removing a people from the territory when friendly overtures failed.[95]

What truly made the Mormons' doctrine unique was how racial concepts were intertwined with their millennial vision and how they put these beliefs into action. Devout Mormons believed that the Lamanites could and indeed must be saved. Their salvation would be not just spiritual but physical as well. Mormons believed that when the Lamanites understood their true history and accepted the Book of Mormon, their skins would lighten and they would become a "white and delightsome" people.[96] These missions would happen in the "latter days," and according to the church doctrine they were a necessary precursor to the Second Coming. Thus, the Mormons, unlike any other millenarian sect, made American Indians integral to their prophetic vision.

Just as important, the Mormons carried with them a message of the inherent differences between the races. Mormonism was a product of the early nineteenth century and illustrated what Reginald Horsman has labeled "racialist" theories. The first half of the nineteenth century saw both the rise of scientific theories of racial difference and the "surging Romantic interest in uniqueness, in language, and in national and racial origins." By 1850, many Euro-Americans accepted as established fact the superiority of the "Anglo-Saxon race."[97] The Mormons reflected the racial hierarchies of Jacksonian America, yet they also "transcended conventional racial boundaries" in one radical dimension. In July 1831 Joseph Smith announced a revelation that "in time" Mormon men would take Indian wives so that their "posterity may become white, delightsome, and just."[98] Thus the redemption of the Lamanites would take place not only through conversion but also through the mixing of the more powerful white race with that of the Indians.

These beliefs translated into a strong and prolonged missionary effort among Indian peoples and led to a lengthy prophetic discourse between the Mormons and their prospective converts. On an objective level, missionary success was mixed. Baptism rates were high at times, but most of the conversions did not last. Still, the Mormon missionary effort was more systematic and long-lived than that of any other denomination except Catholicism. Young first concentrated missionary efforts to the south, among the Utes, but in the mid-1850s, after Newe leaders visited Salt Lake City, Young sent a mission among the "buffalo hunting Indians of Washington Territory." By mid-June 1855, the missionaries had arrived on a branch of the Salmon River, the same valley Lewis and Clark had visited a half century earlier. The Newe headman known as Le Grand Coquin invited them to stay. They named their settlement Fort Lemhi after a character in the Book of Mormon, and the name was subsequently attached to the valley and the river. The Lemhi Valley proved to be a prime mission site, for it was a crossroads of trade frequented by Nez Percés, Salish, and other Indian peoples, in addition to the Newes who called it home. In midsummer hundreds of Indians were present, and the Mormons found active interest in their services. The mission secretary, David Moore, recorded on 23 June, "When the Brethren met for prayers, the old chief [Nez Percé] and the Bannock chief [Le Grand Coquin] also met with them and united their voices in keeping time with the tune of the hymn sung, and during the time of prayer they observed the utmost attention and silence."[99]

Moore's comments are strikingly similar to those Sarah White Smith made seven years earlier. The Indians were clearly interested in whites' religion, but it was singing that provided a link to their own beliefs and attracted their greatest interest. When the majority of the Indians left for the buffalo country, the missionaries set out to learn the Shoshone language and instruct interested Indians in the Mormon faith. By October they had fifty-five converts, and the following month they baptized Snag, the local Newe headman. Their success brought a visit from Brigham Young in April 1857. He praised the missionaries' work and for the first time gave them permission to take Indian brides.[100]

The evidence from the Lemhi mission suggests that the Newe people saw the Mormon missionaries as sharing very similar beliefs. In one instance, the Mormon belief in faith healing proved instrumental in winning converts. George Washington Hill, one of the Lemhi missionaries, and later one of Brigham Young's closest advisers on Indian affairs, recalled how a young girl's illness led to a mass baptism. The girl's father had heard that the Mormons healed by the "ordinance of laying on hands" and asked Hill for help after she fell ill of "mountain fever." Hill told the man that the ordinance was reserved for church members, and if he cured the girl he expected the father to accept baptism. Then, along with Moore and B. F. Cummings, Hill "anointed the child and laid our hands upon her. When we took our hands off her head, her face was literally covered with large drops of sweat; the fever was gone, and the child got well immediately. On the Sunday following I baptized fifty-six, her father being the first in the water."[101] It is easy to see how the Newes could have interpreted the missionaries' successful actions within the context of shamanism. Their beliefs were not the same but appeared similar enough to allow for a temporary middle ground of religious understanding.[102] Indeed, Hill, like the Indians he ministered to, understood healing as a spiritual process. "The Lamanites are very much like other people;" he wrote, "some of them have great faith, and will be healed of any sickness, no matter how severe the attack, while others will not be benefitted in the least."[103] These parallels were at the heart of the prophetic discourse between Mormons and Newe peoples.

During the years that the Mormons operated their Lemhi mission, the number of emigrants and the level of violence along the overland trails increased, and it was here that the native prophetic tradition, the socioeconomic changes in Newe culture, and the hostility toward overland emigrants converged with the emergence of a Bannock prophet and a religion of resistance and nascent "Indianness." Stories of a prophet first reached the headquarters of the Mormon Church in Salt Lake City late in the summer of 1857. Dimick Baker Huntington, a Mormon adviser on Indian affairs, recorded the visit of two Bannock "chiefs" on September 16. "Piut" and "Korosokee" had come from Oregon City and told the Mormon Church president: "The Banack Prophet had sayed a great many things of late about Gods cutting off the Gentiles & that the tribes must be at peace with one another & that the Lariet of time was to be Broke that the sun was going to fall & the moon to be turnd into Blood that the Lord had cut off the Gentiles & throwed them all away."[104] The prophecy alluded to the destruction of the world and suggested the survival of Indian people on a renewed earth swept clear of the invaders.

   Whether the Bannock Prophet actually distinguished between Gentiles and other whites is impossible to determine from the diary. Other evidence suggests that he made no such distinction. Still, the Bannock leaders who visited Salt Lake City could have interpreted the prophet's message as including the Mormons among the saved. By the time of their visit, relations between the church and the federal government had reached their nadir. In early September, Young, aware of the approach of a U.S. Army column sent to enforce federal control, declared martial law, sealed the borders, recalled far-flung missionaries, and prepared to repel the army. Only four days after the Bannock visit, moreover, word arrived in the Mormon capital of the slaughter of an overland emigrant company at Mountain Meadows in southern Utah.[105] Although the "Utah War" of 1857–58 fizzled out, the hostility of the federal government and non-Mormon emigrants towards the church was well-known among the Indians and must certainly have suggested that the Mormons were a distinct "people."

   In any case, the Bannock Prophet's message was clearly intended for Indians and could damage the church's efforts as easily as it might enhance them. Ben Simons, a Delaware Indian who had married into Little Soldier's "Weber Ute" band[106] and sometimes served as an interpreter, visited Young on 1 November. Simons had heard of the Bannock Prophet's power and would use it to assess the truth of the Mormon religion:

> Ben sayed that the Banark prophet was his father & saw that there was or he had seen a great Light. or that thare was a deal of powder a going to burn in the west he sayed that thare was 3 Gentiles went from California to see the prophet and they Laught at him and made Derision of him when he asked them what he came for he was not their father but to the Indians when they commenced to cry & felt verry bad then they handed him a letter he took it and looked at it when a large portion of the letter dropped off like ashes & he said what thare remained was good & that which dropped off was good for nothing Ben says he has got the Book of Mormon & is going to take it to the prophet in the spring & if it drops to peaces then it is good for nothing but if it don't then he will be a Mormon.[107]

For Simons, a Delaware, the "Banark prophet was his father" and, indeed, a father "to the Indians." Clearly, the creation of an Indian identity is central to the prophet's message. He did not speak to a single ethnic group or tribe but to all Indians. His message included the concept of the unity of Indian people as well as their ability to control their own lives and resist white advances. The reference to a light in the west and the burning of powder suggests the coming of cataclysmic change. All of these ideas were recurring elements in the prophetic religions of Western Indians. It is uncertain whether Simons ever made his trip to see the prophet, but it is telling that he was drawn to the most millennial sect of white Americans to gauge their reaction to this prophetic statement of Indian identity.

Other Indians also communicated the prophecy to the Mormons, who must certainly have seemed to be speaking the same language. Some Mormons took a deep interest and saw the fulfillment of their own prophecies in the message of the Bannock prophet, just as the Ghost Dance excitement caused spiritual excitement among the Mormon faithful three decades later. George Washington Hill heard the message of the prophet firsthand and later retold it as a lesson for Mormon youth. In the church-published *Juvenile Instructor,* Hill recalled the visit by an Indian messenger to Lemhi in June 1857. The man wanted the prophet's message delivered to Brigham Young, but as it "contained prophecies so unlikely to come to pass," Hill discounted it and kept it to himself. Nearly fifteen years later, when his account appeared in print, however, the missionary had changed his mind.[108] The prophecy foretold the approach of Johnson's army during the "Utah War" in 1858 as well as the arrival of Connor's column and the construction of Fort Douglas four years later. In each case the Bannock prophesied that the Mormons would not have to fight. Even after another fort was built "up in the north" (perhaps a reference to Camp Connor near Soda Springs), the Mormons and soldiers would be at peace. But then, "the time would afterwards come when the mountains would be full of soldiers, and such fighting as there would be then had never been seen."

The prophet also foretold that if "his people" did as he said, they would never have to fight, for "he would do their fighting for them." He continued: "If their enemies came upon them he would meet them, and if they were determined to fight, he had the power to make the earth split and swallow them all up. He could then cause the earth to close up again, and they would all be gone. He had the power to create a whirl-wind of force sufficient to take the soldiers, cannon, wagons, mules, and everything else up and cast them upon the top of a mountain, and that would be the end of them."[109] When Hill asked the prophet's name, the messenger said that the prophet had anticipated this question. He said that at various times the soldiers had kept him captive or tried to bury him alive or burn him to death but had utterly failed each time, some-times paying with their lives. The prophet told the messenger that once Hill heard this, "he will know who I am." Although Hill left it to his readers to "draw their own conclusions," he believed that "all these things he certainly did tell, long enough before they came to pass, or before they were apparent to natural man, to entitle him to the name of prophet."[110]

Prophetic parallels notwithstanding, Newe peoples did not embrace Mormonism. On 5 February 1858, a force of about two hundred Newe warriors attacked Fort Lemhi, killing two of the missionaries and leading Young to withdraw the rest. An underlying cause of the attack was most certainly the ongoing intertribal conflict in the northern Rockies. The Newes, Nez Percés, and Pend d'Oreilles had become embroiled in a cycle of horse theft and retaliation that bordered on war. The missionaries, who did not understand these preexisting patterns, tried to stay aloof from the conflict and in the process alienated their Newe neighbors. The Mormons also charged that the army, and Gentiles employed by the army, had instigated the attack by arming the Indians and suggesting that if they plundered Mormon settlements, no one would punish them. There is corroborating evidence for this charge.[111] Finally, the attack might well have been inspired by the Bannock prophet. On 29 March 1858, just three days after Young had ordered the Lemhi mission aban-

doned, Little Soldier arrived with the ominous message that "Wahr-a-gi-
kah the great Banark Prophet had said to all the snakes & Banarks to be
ready when he should call for them."[112]

In the wake of the Lemhi attack, a growing number of government
officials reported the influence of the Bannock Prophet, who they feared
would use his message to disrupt white settlement and emigration. In
November 1858, C. H. Miller of the Pacific Wagon Road characterized
the "Pannacks" of Fort Hall as "a very dangerous, cruel, and vindictive
race," which ranged from Blackfoot Creek, north of Fort Hall, to the
Boise River valley. Although they respected Washakie and often hunted
with his people, he was not their chief.[113] Miller also charged that these
"Pannackes" had attacked and driven out the Mormons under the influence of the "celebrated prophet of the western Snake tribe, who reside[s]
in the vicinity of the old Hudson's Bay trading post of Fort Boisé, . . .
[and is] extremely hostile to the Mormons." Miller did not know the
prophet's name but wanted to visit this "man of great influence among
these dangerous tribes," for he felt the prophet's authority might "be
gained in behalf of the whites. . . . I consider him one of the most dangerous and desperate men now living west of the Rocky Mountains, for
the Indians have a superstitious reverence for him."[114]

The following year Frederick W. Lander, Miller's superior, reported
that the "Warraricas" or "Sun-Flower Seed Eaters," who ranged from
Fort Boise to the western slope of the Blue Mountains in Oregon, were
led by a chief and shaman named "Pash-e-co or Pa-chi-co." He was
reportedly the head of "all the Bannocks," and was "thought a wonder-
ful prophet by the Snakes."[115] Then, in 1862, the Utah Indian superintendent, James Doty, reported that this same leader, along with the afore-
mentioned War-i-gika, was planning a general war on the whites crossing
the Oregon and California trails. Once again, it was Little Soldier who
alerted the whites to the activities of the Bannock Prophet. He told Doty
that the Indians of northern Utah and southern Idaho had "united their
forces for the purpose of making war" on the settlers and emigrants. He
also alleged that the "Shoshone Indians have set aside Wash-i-kee, the
great chief of that nation, because he is a man of peace and a friend to the
whites, and have chosen in his place as their leader Pash-e-go, because he
is a man of blood." Finally, Little Soldier stated that "all these war movements [were] instigated and led by War-i-gika, the great Bannock
prophet, in whom the Bannacks and Shoshones have unbounded confidence and faith, who lives in the vicinity of Walla Walla, in Oregon and
Washington Territory."[116]

The confusion over the prophet's name suggests several explanations of his identity as well as the possible influence of yet another prophetic religion of the Columbia Plateau. One possibility is that this was in fact the Dreamer prophet Smohalla, whose religion was then gaining influence among the "renegades" who shunned the reservations and congregated along the Columbia River between the mouths of the Snake and the Umatilla rivers.[117] This theory could explain the reference to the Walla Walla country, but it is unlikely because of the hostility at that time between the Plateau peoples and the Snakes.[118] Moreover, this theory is inconsistent with the chronology of Smohalla's religion. The prophet was said to have begun preaching in his thirties, around 1850, and James Mooney believed that his theology had "materially facilitated" the Yakama confederation in the war of 1855–56. There is, however, no concrete evidence for Mooney's assertion. Several years after the end of the Yakama War, Smohalla was nearly killed in a fight with Moses, a powerful Sinkiuse headman, who believed that Smohalla was "making medicine" against him. Smohalla recovered, but, unwilling to return to his people in disgrace, he embarked on a long journey that at one point took him to Utah, "where he had seen Mormon priests in trances, getting commands direct from heaven."[119] After several years he returned home and declared that he had died and visited the Creator in heaven, who had commanded him to return to his people. The Indians' suffering and the presence of the invading white people, he told them, was due to "their having abandoned their own religion and violated the laws of nature and the precepts of their ancestors."[120] Smohalla's religion in its complete form apparently did not emerge until the early 1860s. It is far more likely that the Prophet Dance complex of the Columbia Plateau influenced both the Bannock Prophet and Smohalla.

Another possibility is that there was a single prophet and that both Huntington and Doty misunderstood Little Soldier. War-i-gika is a close approximation of Warrarica, the food name first used by Alexander Ross and attributed by Lander to the Newe peoples living around Boise. Perhaps Little Soldier had identified Pashego as the great prophet *of* the War-i-gika. Little Soldier's references to War-i-gika are the only ones in the historical record. Variations on the name Pashego (which is very similar to the Shoshone word for camas), continue to appear into the 1870s. In 1864, for instance, the agent John C. Burche met with leaders of the "Pannakés, the Pah-Utes, and Shoshonees" at two councils on the Humboldt River. Present was "Pas-se-quah, the chief of the Pannakés of Nevada and Idaho." Perhaps the "man of blood" had rethought the chances of a general war with the whites and promised Burche that no more attacks would occur between the Goose Creek Mountains and the bend of the Humboldt, presumably the area of his influence. Burche reported that, as of August 1864, Pashego had kept his word.[121] Less than a decade later, however, a prophet of the same name was preaching what was clearly the Ghost Dance doctrine of 1870 to the Newe peoples of southern Idaho.

By the late 1850s the prophetic tradition among the American Indian peoples of the far West had evolved into a discourse that interpreted the radical economic and social changes of the first half of the nineteenth century and expressed a shared Indian identity to rally resistance to colonization. Shamanism and prophecy were indigenous concepts that created a flexible religious milieu open to the incorporation of new elements and doctrines through the process of direct revelation. As chance would have it, the whites who settled among the Newe bands and their neighbors also carried prophetic conceptions of their own identities. Evangelical missionaries like the Whitmans and Spaldings expressed not only personal identity but also national identity in prophetic terms. More important, the Mormons who settled first among Newe people held an even more radical millennial vision of their identity and destiny that incorporated Indian peoples. Mormon and native prophecies emerged from different traditions yet were similar enough to enable the two peoples to speak to one another in prophetic terms. The Ghost Dances that spread across the West in the 1870s and 1890s were not a "new" religion for Shoshone and Bannock people. On the contrary, Ghost Dances were deeply rooted in the cultural and religious beliefs of Newe peoples. By the last decades of the nineteenth century, the dances were part of a prophetic tradition that explained the radical changes taking place in Newe people's lives, linked them with other native peoples, and gave hope that a distinctly "Indian" way of life would continue.

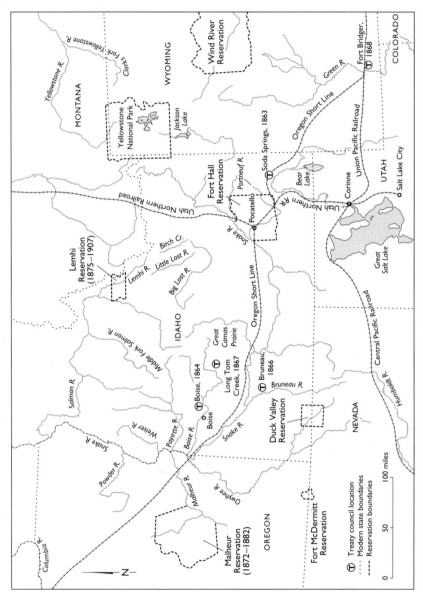

Map 2. Shoshone and Bannock treaties and reservations.

PART TWO

Identity, Prophecy, and Reservation Life

BY THE 1860s, Shoshone- and Bannock-speaking peoples lived in a world that was increasingly not of their making. On the heels of the massive overland emigration came the flood of permanent white settlement. The newcomers could not be overwhelmed or ignored. They demanded that native peoples give up most of their lands as well as their traditional life ways. Newe groups struggled to maintain their territorial and cultural integrity, in part by asserting more distinct social identities. Treaty making and reservation life gave ever-greater meaning to ethnic and tribal identities. Yet, at the same time, the broader message of the newcomers' aggressive assimilation programs was that in a racialized nation all American Indian peoples shared a larger identity as "Indians." The struggle to maintain some measure of cultural and political autonomy during these decades, as well as participation in the Ghost Dance movements of 1870 and 1890, helped to shape Shoshone and Bannock identity.

CHAPTER 3

Treaty Making and Consolidation

The Politics of Ethnogenesis

All the Bannock Indians will obey me and be good, but the
Sheep-eaters are not my people. They may steal and be bad,
but they are not my people and I cannot be responsible for
them. I will answer for the Bannocks. The Boises and Bruneaus
are poor; they cannot travel far; they have no horses to hunt
the buffalo, but they are good Indians, and are my friends.

Taghee, 1867

By the 1860s, the once-fluid social, political, and geographic boundaries
of the Newe world began to harden as the United States exerted ever
greater control over the lives and lands of Newe peoples. Social and economic differentiation had already resulted in a greater sense of social
identity among Newe peoples, best characterized by the existence of
bands. Bands, however, were not discrete, fixed, or formal polities.
Rather, they were loose-knit populations of family groups that formed
into larger bodies for ceremonial and subsistence purposes, for defense,
and, increasingly, for dealing with the demands of European Americans.
Cultural factors unified rather than divided bands. All shared a religious
heritage, and many of the bands contained both Shoshone and Bannock
speakers, with intermarriage so common that one early observer found it
"almost impossible to discriminate between them."[1] Still, some important differences existed between groups that evinced a localized ethnic
identity. Into this world came permanent, large-scale white settlement
and the treaty demands of the United States of America. The politics of
the treaty-making process and reservation life magnified band distinctions, making more sharply defined social identities increasingly salient.
During the treaty-making era, white officials began to treat the social distinctions evidenced by the various Newe bands as political or tribal divi-

sions, extending the power of the polities and leaders beyond family groups. Political loyalties became more relevant to identity as individual native leaders proved more or less successful in dealing with the United States. At the same time, white officials wanted to consolidate all of Idaho's Shoshone and Bannock peoples on a single reservation, in essence ignoring the very divisions they reified in treaty making. The contest over annuities and primacy on the reservation also magnified the importance of tribal identity. The treaty-making and early reservation years, then, marked a crucial phase in the move from the largely independent band organization that marked the autonomous Newe world of the mid–nineteenth century to the ethnic and tribal identities that formed in large part around political divisions and characterized reservation life.

The treaty-making process must be understood first and foremost as the meeting of two very different political systems. In a fluid social world, Newe political leadership was flexible, lacking the coercive power that whites expected. Bands formed around successful leaders of important cooperative endeavors, and the "chiefs" whom Euro-Americans encountered sprang from this political tradition. As the ability to act as an effective intermediary became preeminent, the _dai'gwahnee'_, the talkers who led cooperative endeavors, often emerged as the "chiefs." Successful leaders always walked a tightrope, balancing the needs and desires of their people against the demands of white society. Most important, they negotiated their own people's access to the land and its resources. As the United States became more powerful, outright hostility became impossible. There were simply too many white people, and they possessed attractive and increasingly necessary goods. As the power of the United States grew more obvious, the nature and exercise of native political power began to change. Capable leaders understood that they could use the whites and their wealth, no matter how unpredictable their presence, to buttress their own political leadership. But they had to do so within increasingly circumscribed bounds. The most adept _dai'gwahnee'_ understood this, retained more stable followings, and saw their influence grow. Other, less skilled leaders came and went.

If white Americans had a hard time grasping Newe politics, they were equally confounded by native conceptions of territory. A given band might range hundreds of miles each year, but it also occupied a traditional _tebíwa_, or native land, where the group usually wintered and had uncontested access to resources. Rights to the _tebíwa_ were not exclusive, but visitors always asked permission to join a people in the use of their native land. Here, the _dai'gwahni'_ spoke for his followers, negotiating access and dealing with visitors. His role was to maintain access to diverse areas and resources rather than to a fixed, exclusively owned territory. It was from this perspective that _dai'gwahnee'_ approached negotiations with white officials.[2] The attachment to a _tebíwa_ was also the principal reason that some bands chose to remain "poor." The Shoshones of the Bruneau Valley, for example, could not maintain large horse herds in such an arid setting. Consequently, they could not join the mounted bands on their annual rounds, and their "wealth" was limited. Yet they did everything possible to stay in the Bruneau Valley, including eschewing the equestrian lifestyle. Some white observers commented on the interrelationship between people, place, and leader, but none ever fully understood the indigenous concepts. "An Indian will never ask to what nation or tribe or body of people another Indian belongs," wrote John Wesley Powell of the Newe peoples, "but to 'what land do you belong and how are you land named?,' thus the very name of the Indian is the very title deed to his home."[3] In 1863 James Duane Doty commented on the seemingly communal use of the Newe world: "As none of the Indians of this country have permanent places of abode in their hunting excursions they wander over an immense region. . . . The Shoshones and Bannacks are to my knowledge the only nations which hunt together over the same ground."[4]

Doty saw that Newe peoples held a very different concept of land tenure, yet ultimately he, like every other white negotiator, failed to grasp fully the implications of these differences. Federal and territorial officials like Doty assumed that native leaders, like their white counterparts, represented fixed sociopolitical entities and exclusive property rights. In the name of economy and "civilization," they wanted to consolidate as many Indian peoples onto as few reservations as possible. To facilitate the process, white officials sought to work through influential yet tractable native leaders. They looked for a friendly "head chief." In the absence of such a person, they tried to create one. However, the concept of a head chief, as it was understood by Euro-Americans—a leader who could speak with authority for a discrete people and a territory—had no meaning for the Newes. When whites tried to consolidate numerous bands on a single reservation or impose the authority of one chief over these same groups, they again ran headlong into this problem. Essentially, they were dealing with _dai'gwahnee'_ who spoke only for their followers and sought to arrange access to their customary range, not transfer or reserve rights to exclusive property.

At the time of initial white settlement there were numerous Newe bands and _dai'gwahnee'_. The mounted buffalo hunters of Fort Hall looked to Taghee for leadership through most of the 1860s. Although they are usually called Bannocks in the historical literature, they were more accurately a mixed band that included a majority of Shoshone speakers. Farther east were Washakie's Eastern Shoshones, the largest of the mounted Newe bands. Their famed leader was, to white observers and officials, the most influential Shoshone leader of his day. In addition to these well-known headmen, whom whites assumed to speak for larger polities, there were other *dai'gwahnee'* who struggled to maintain their respective bands' autonomy through the treaty-making and reservation era. South and southeast of Fort Hall were the Northwestern Shoshone bands of Pocatello, Sagwitch, Bear Hunter, and others. To the north were mixed bands that wintered in the Lemhi and Salmon River country. This diverse group became known as the Lemhis, or, just as often, "Tendoy's band," after the skilled headman who remained the group's most influential leader for over four decades. Scattered throughout the mountains were small family groups of "Sheep-Eaters," many of whom would eventually join with the Lemhis. To the west were the Boise, Bruneau, Payette, and Weiser bands, the last led by Eagle Eye. Consisting mostly of Shoshones, these bands owned fewer horses and were less mobile than the mixed bands that hunted buffalo. They did, however, maintain a thriving trade with their mounted kinsmen, as did the Northern Paiutes and Shoshones who lived even farther to the west in Oregon. Of course, this is a very generalized description: band organization in Idaho was complex.[5] In the early 1860s, gold rushes wrought massive changes in the lives of all of Idaho's native peoples. The mines brought permanent white settlement, direct competition for land and resources, and territorial government for Idaho. By 1864 there was also a new territorial capital, Boise, in the very heart of the Newe homeland.[6]

With permanent white settlement came calls for treaties and the consolidation of Indian peoples on reservations. These demands did not lead to an organized, unified effort to negotiate with Indian peoples; confusion reigned. There were seemingly as many white polities as there were Indian ones. In addition to the Idaho territorial government, representatives of the federal government and the territories of Utah and Montana all dealt independently with Shoshones and Bannocks during the 1860s. Rarely, if ever, did the representatives of one territory know what the others were doing. Moreover, successive administrations in the same territory often followed very different courses. The ponderous bureaucratic and political process only made matters worse. Interminable delays and unratified treaties were rarely explained to native leaders, who were left to wonder why promises made face to face were never kept.

Amid the confusion, white negotiators did share one common goal: the consolidation of Indians onto as few reservations as possible. Consolidation, it was argued, would bring efficiency and economy to administration. It would make the jobs of the agents and farmers easier as well as speed assimilation. It would also open more land for white settlers. In the case of the Shoshones and Bannocks, moreover, it was assumed that consolidation would prove easy. People so closely associated, and who in many cases intermarried, should naturally accept a single reservation. Or so it was thought.

Typically, treaty making follows violence, and such was the case with the Newes. Beginning in the late 1850s and reaching a peak in the bloody summer of 1862, raids along the overland trails, coupled with growing Indian-white conflict in the Mormon settlements of northern Utah, drew the attention of the federal government. Along the western portions of the California Trail, from the Goose Creek Mountains to the Humboldt Sink, the principal motivation for the raids was hunger. In just over a decade, overland emigrants and their livestock had destroyed much of the game and grasses that the Northern Paiutes, Western Shoshones, and Gosiutes depended on. Some survived by begging food from local whites and emigrants; others turned to raiding. For the mounted Shoshones and Bannocks farther east, the attraction was plunder for its own sake. Washakie and other leaders struggled to keep the peace, but small emigrant parties were easy targets for young men seeking to gain wealth and prestige through raiding and horse stealing. Permanent white settlements also created anger, particularly among the Northwest Shoshones of the Cache Valley. After the Utah War of 1858 and the failure of an agricultural community in Tooele Valley, Mormon settlers moved into Cache Valley in force. They appropriated much of the best land and resented the "saucy" Indians who lingered around their settlements demanding food and presents.[7] In addition to hunger, encroachment, and the lure of plunder, there was also message of the Bannock Prophet. In August 1862 Little Soldier warned James Duane Doty that the Shoshones and Bannocks of northern Utah and southern Idaho, inspired by "War-I-gika, the great Bannock prophet," had decided to wage a general war on the settlers and emigrants.[8]

The message of an indigenous prophet meant little to Col. Patrick Edward Connor. A native of Ireland and a veteran of the Mexican War, Connor was living in Stockton, California, when the governor selected him to command a regiment of California volunteers in July 1861.[9] Like many of his soldiers, he would have preferred to fight rebels in Virginia; but Indians would have to do. Connor was ordered to march his troops to Utah, punish the Indian raiders, and secure the trails. His methods were brutal, though not uncommon: he ordered his principal subordinate, Maj. Edward McGarry, to "destroy every male Indian whom you may encounter in the vicinity of the late massacres."[10] The Californians arrived in Salt Lake City in October 1862, and soon the troubles in Cache Valley caught Connor's attention. In November McGarry marched north and, after a brief skirmish and the detention of the Northwestern Shoshone dai'gwahni' Bear Hunter, secured the release of a child believed to be the survivor of an earlier wagon-train attack. Then, in early January, Indians attacked two separate parties traveling to Salt Lake City from the Montana mines. These attacks led Utah Chief Justice John F. Kinney to issue an arrest warrant for the Northwestern Shoshone leaders Bear Hunter, Sagwitch, and Sanpitch. Connor had already made his own plans to punish the Shoshones, and, as he informed the territorial marshal, "it was not [his] intention to take any prisoners."[11] The troops traveled through bitterly cold nights and arrived at the Shoshone village on Bear River just before dawn 29 January 1863. The Shoshones were outgunned and surrounded, and the ensuing battle quickly turned into a slaughter. By most estimates at least 250 Shoshones, including Bear Hunter, died that day. Fourteen soldiers were also killed.[12]

The massacre gave Doty the chance he had been waiting for. "The fight on Bear river was the severest and most bloody of any which has ever occurred with Indians west of the Mississippi," he wrote. "It struck terror in the hearts of savages hundreds of miles away from the battlefield."[13] By the fall of 1863, often with the newly promoted Gen. Connor at his side, Doty negotiated five separate treaties with Newe peoples from Nevada to Wyoming. Doty's multitreaty approach seemed to reflect an awareness of the ethnic and social differentiation that had occurred among Newe peoples during the nineteenth century, but this was not truly the case. Although he recognized that a single treaty would be inadequate, Doty viewed the various Newe groups as far-flung arms of a single body and failed to understand the importance of the band divisions. He met first with Washakie's Eastern Shoshones and several allied bands of Northwestern Shoshones at Fort Bridger on 2 July 1863. Doty mistakenly assumed that Washakie's power extended far beyond his own band, and the subsequent treaties were based on the Fort Bridger agreement.[14] In mid-October, Doty and Connor negotiated the final treaty in the series with the "Mixed Bands of Shoshone and Bannack Indians" at Soda Springs.

Because of their strategic location at the intersections of the major trails, peace with the mixed bands was crucial.[15] One hundred and fifty men and their families attended the council, representing an estimated population of one thousand. Most of the "principal chiefs" of the "Bannocks" attended the council: Toso-Kwauberaht (Le Grand Coquin, also known as the Great Rogue), Mopeah, Matigund, and Taghee. Tendoy had already left for the buffalo hunt but sent word that he would accept the treaty's provisions. The treaty secured the peace and gave the government the right to establish forts, build telegraphs and stage stations, and grant railroad rights-of-way.[16] Though ostensibly an independent treaty, it included an article that bound the mixed bands to accept the provisions of the preceding Fort Bridger and Box Elder treaties. Moreover, Doty recognized no distinct territory as belonging to the Idaho Shoshones and Bannocks; he described their home range jointly with Washakie's. Nor were the mixed bands to receive their own annuity payments; rather they would share in those provided to the greater "Shoshonee Nation."[17] In a culture where leaders maintained authority in large measure through negotiating access to resources, the annuity provision of the Soda Springs treaty curbed the power of the Idaho headmen while increasing Washakie's influence.

The subsequent history of the Soda Springs and Fort Bridger treaties of 1863 underscored both the vast gulf between Indian and white political processes and the effects of these differences on native political systems. Because of a legal technicality, the Senate never ratified the Soda Springs treaty (all of the other Doty treaties became law).[18] The Bannock leaders who signed the treaty, however, believed it to be in effect. In particular, Taghee, who spoke as the principal *dai'gwahni'* of the buffalo-hunting bands, was dismayed at the government's inaction. He worked hard to fulfill his end of the bargain, but keeping the young men out of trouble was difficult when the promised annuities never arrived and no one came to explain the situation. At Fort Bridger, in contrast, Washakie and his people enjoyed the benefits of their treaty. Each year the wagons arrived with the Shoshones' goods, and each year Taghee saw his people drawn east toward Fort Bridger. Increasingly, white officials came to view Washakie as the "head chief" of both the Shoshones and Bannocks. His following was indeed growing. In September 1865, Luther Mann, the agent at Fort Bridger, attributed the growth to "those individuals who attracted by Washa-kee's rising home, have cast their lot with him."[19] Yet neither the Bannocks nor Washakie recognized his control over all of these peoples. The following summer Taghee led a band of four hundred Bannocks east to hunt with Washakie's people and visit the agent at Fort Bridger. Mann could offer the Bannock leader little in the way of either rations or answers.[20]

As long as Taghee and his people traveled with Washakie's band in the latter's *tebíwa*, the Bannock leader was subordinate to the Shoshone leader.

Bart Henderson, a prospector and adventurer, witnessed this relationship firsthand soon after the combined bands left Fort Bridger to hunt on the Wind River in September 1866. Henderson's crew quite literally ran into a Bannock hunting party, among them Taghee, while chasing buffalo. After sharing dinner with the "Chief of the Bannacks," Henderson accompanied the Indians back to their encampment. He estimated there were eleven hundred Shoshones, Bannocks, and Utes. His arrival caused a stir, and soon the "head chief" requested that the visitor come to his lodge. It was Washakie, resplendent in a long white duster and wearing a Colt dragoon revolver and cavalry saber, both gifts of Frederick W. Lander and symbols of his influence among the whites. The Shoshone chief entertained Henderson in high style. Dinner was served on a "very nice carpet, with teacups & saucers & very nice plates." In fact, Henderson recalled, "everything was very nice." The next morning Washakie and one hundred of his warriors accompanied Henderson back to his camp.[21] There is no further mention of the Bannock leader in Henderson's account. Once he had arrived at the Indian camp, Taghee faded into the background, and it was the place of the "head chief," Washakie, to demonstrate his wealth and generosity to the visiting stranger.

While Taghee struggled for recognition and the annuities due to his people, the Newe bands of western Idaho faced the onslaught of thousands of white miners and settlers who flooded into their lands, demanding large, permanent land cessions and the confinement of Indian peoples to reservations. The territorial governor Caleb Lyon, while pompous, self-serving, and arguably corrupt, was far more sympathetic to the Indians than was the typical white Idahoan.[22] He pursued a policy of establishing individual band treaties that recognized each group's autonomy and established reservations in their own *tebíwa*s. In October 1864 Lyon made a treaty with the Boise Shoshone headman San-to-me-co and his people. It stipulated a massive land cession but also guaranteed the Shoshones a reservation in their homeland as well as the "right of equally sharing the fisheries of said river [the Boise] with the citizens of the U.S."[23] Getting the Boises to accept the treaty was one thing; for a short time the governor even had the support of the notoriously anti-Indian *Idaho Statesman,* which celebrated the treaty as "all that could be desired by the settlers in the Territory." But getting Congress to ratify it was quite another. Like the Soda Springs treaty of the previous year, the Boise treaty languished in the nation's capital. After a year of Congressional inaction, Lyon was still trying to sell the treaty on the basis of its benefits for white settlers.[24]

Perhaps the greatest obstacle to Lyon's multiple-treaty, band-specific approach was that most white officials and settlers did not like its central implication: the creation of numerous reservations scattered across the southern portion of the territory. They wanted a comprehensive agreement that consolidated all of the "Indians of Southern Idaho" on one or two well-defined reservations. The secretary of the interior, James Harlan, recommended two reservations, one "at some point upon the Shoshone [Snake] River, embracing the fisheries on said streams, and a summer reservation in the vicinity of the Great Kammas Prairie."[25] He ordered Lyon to visit the Camas Prairie in the early fall of 1865 to investigate the viability of this plan. The governor assured the two thousand Indians there that if they maintained the peace the government would "guard their interests and protect their rights." Privately, however, he was less sanguine about the government's capability to keep such promises and protect the resources the Indians relied on. Nor did he conceal the fact that white interests always superseded those of the Indians. Reserving the Little Camas Prairie for the Indians opened the larger, more important Great Camas Prairie to white settlement, and, indeed, he stated that his actions were intended to secure the "better protection of the settlers on the Great Kammas Prairie and the travelers over the emigrant road along the Valley of the Shoshonee."[26]

By 1864, white encroachment and Indian retaliation had grown into the Snake War and made Lyon's work more urgent. The conflict flared up first in the Owyhee mining district south of Boise and by 1865 had engulfed the entire region. Sporadic raids led to a generally fruitless pursuit by volunteer and regular troops. The depredations engendered a seething hatred among local whites, who organized " Indian-hunting" expeditions and made little distinction between the guilty and innocent parties.[27] In February 1866, the *Owyhee Avalanche* proudly proclaimed that the citizens of Silver City and Ruby City resolved that "three men should be appointed to select twenty five men to go Indian hunting." Bounties were set at one hundred dollars for each male Indian, fifty for each Indian woman, and "twenty five dollars for everything in the shape of an Indian under ten years of age." To keep everyone honest, each scalp was required to "have the curl of the head, and each man shall make an oath that the said scalp was taken by the company."[28] Lyon tried to prevent the slaughter and collected 115 Shoshones near Fort Boise in February 1866. His actions, unfortunately, did not assure their safety. On 11 March 1866, a group of white vigilantes murdered sixteen Boise Shoshones near the near the mouth of Mores Creek. Two of the dead were men, the rest women and children. The *Idaho Statesman* celebrated the massacre and ridiculed the governor's "sickly sentiment" towards the Shoshones. "We long to see this vile race exterminated," wrote the editor. "Every man who kills an Indian is a public benefactor."[29]

In the face of vocal demands for extermination or removal, Lyon tried once again to solve the conflict with a band-specific treaty. This time he approached the Bruneau Shoshones, who, living in the midst of the conflict south of the capital, had borne the brunt of white hostility. The April 1866 treaty echoed the provisions of its failed predecessor. The Bruneaus ceded all of their land, including the Owyhee mining district, in exchange for a reservation south of the Snake River, the right to fish and hunt at their "accustomed grounds and stations," and the standard promises of agricultural and industrial assistance.[30] The fact that the government had finally recognized their plight pleased the Bruneaus, but most of all they welcomed a treaty that secured to them a reservation in their *tebíwa*. Far beyond sentiment, they felt a deep attachment to the land, from which sprang political authority. Their headman, Tcho-womba-ca or "Biting Bear," knew that the Bruneau Valley was where his people were supposed to be: "Father, I was born on this river. The bones of my fathers lie in the crevices of the rocks of these Cañons [sic] or in the springs of the valley. I want to stay here. Our wickiups are of straw, our arrowheads are stone. Skins are our clothes. Deer, elk, fish, antelope, roots and seeds are our food. This is given to us by the Great Spirit. We feel there is a better country when we die, but we do not know where it is. We desire to live here where we were born and to die here."[31]

It was a great day for the Bruneaus, full of hope and expectation. Lyon reinforced the solemnity of the day's proceedings by employing a ritual language of kinship relationships and by exchanging important ceremonial gifts: "I now hang upon the necks of your chiefs the silver medal of the Great Father at Washington, that you may have the memory of this treaty near your hearts, and may the Great Spirit of storm and sunshine help you to keep it."[32] But the medals and the memory of the treaty were all the Bruneaus would ever have. Like the Boise treaty of 1864, it disappeared into the abyss in Washington. Later, Lyon's successor, David W. Ballard, reported that he had heard of the treaty but could find no copy of it in Idaho.[33] Left to starve or be hunted by white vigilantes, over two hundred Bruneaus sought safety in the relative security of the Boise refugee camp.

After Lyon's failed Bruneau treaty, consolidation became the single-minded goal of territorial policy, and Fort Hall soon became the preferred site for the proposed reservation. In fact, the strategy had been suggested far earlier. In the fall of 1865, the special Indian agent George C. Hough had made an investigation of prospective reservation sites. "A reservation taking in Salmon Falls and extending up Wood River would be the most judicious selection that could be made," he believed. The proposal encompassed good fishing sites as well as access to the Camas Prairies. A second reservation might be established, perhaps along the Owyhee River, for the "southern Indians."[34] White settlement, however, precluded any chance of a reservation in southwestern Idaho. Fertile valleys, such as the Payette, provided a complex subsistence base for the Shoshones, Bannocks, and their neighbors, but they also attracted white farmers.[35]

Governor Ballard then began to consider Fort Hall as the place where he could consolidate the Indian peoples of southern Idaho. In the process he ignored a diversity of life ways and dismissed the distinctions existing between Newe peoples. Citing abundant fish and game, good pasturage, plentiful wood and water, access to supply lines, and few white settlers, he bragged that the area "presented by far the best facilities for the location of an Indian reservation."[36] In reality, the best camas grounds and fisheries were over one hundred miles away, as were the prime big-game hunting grounds of the Salmon River mountains and the Yellowstone country. The site was centrally located, and for the mounted, highly mobile bands that could access all of these resources, the Fort Hall area was a great place to winter. Indeed, it was their *tebíwa*. For the foot-going Shoshonean bands who had lived around the capital, however, the area was far less amenable. But these factors were unimportant compared to Fort Hall's relative isolation from white population centers. It was a place where Indian people could be consolidated and kept out of the way while assimilation and white settlement proceeded. Moreover, the governor either glossed over or completely misunderstood the nature of band divisions. "The various bands of Shoshone and Bannack Indians have constantly expressed a desire to be settled on a reservation and to be taught how to farm," he wrote, "and I anticipate little difficulty in inducing them to go to, and remain at this place."[37] His characterization of the "various bands" as a single people willing to accept a single reservation was common within the Indian department.[38] With preliminary boundaries drawn and signs posted to warn off any prospective white settlers, Ballard kept lobbying through the fall of 1866 and the spring of 1867. Success came on 14 June 1867, when President Andrew Johnson created the Fort Hall Reservation by executive order. Ballard now had a place to consolidate the "Indians in middle and southern Idaho"; the only task

that remained was getting them to go there.[39] Transferring the Boises and
Bruneaus to Fort Hall seemed simple, but the governor had yet to even
discuss the reservation with the more mobile, and often more disagree-
able, Bannocks.

The governor got his chance when the army detained two small
Bannock bands, numbering only seventy-five persons, found digging roots
on the Camas Prairie in June 1867. With the Snake War still smoldering
and rumors of white vigilantes organizing to annihilate them, the Indians
were brought to Boise for "safekeeping."[40] Ballard interviewed the headmen and brothers, Bannack John and Bannack Jim (also known by his
native name, Pagwite), and asked them about their people, their understanding of previous treaties, and their willingness to live on a reservation.
Both acknowledged Taghee as "head chief of all the Bannocks," and they
knew well of his frustration with white negotiators. They believed that the
Soda Springs treaty was in effect and that it guaranteed them access to a
wide resource area, including the right to "hunt buffalo and go into the
Boise country whenever they chose, so long as they remained friendly."
When the governor asked if they would "like to live on a reservation provided we build you houses, teach you how to farm, & [et]c?" the Bannock
headmen responded adamantly, "We want to hunt buffalo and to fish."
Ballard then asked whether, if they were allowed to do so at "proper
times," they would then go to the reservation. Both men agreed, but they
reminded the governor that they could not speak for all the Bannocks and
that "Tar-Gee would want to talk first." Ballard felt that the "general
Indian war" engulfing Idaho made it too dangerous for the Bannocks to
leave Boise, so they too found themselves at the refugee camp.[41]

The consolidation of Shoshone and Bannock bands at the Boise River
camp anticipated later conditions and attitudes at Fort Hall. For
instance, some of the "ethnic" characteristics that white agents perceived
at Fort Hall in the 1870s were first noted there. By the time the Bannocks
arrived, Capt. Charles F. Powell, who oversaw the camp, had moved the
Boise and Bruneaus to the confluence of the South and Main forks of the
Boise, some twenty-five miles from the capital city. He recognized that
the new location—attractively named Rattlesnake Camp—deprived the
Shoshones of any income from menial labor in the town, but he hoped it
would offer better opportunities for hunting and fishing. The loss of
domestic service probably shaped Powell's view of the Shoshones as
"very indolent indeed, not caring to exert themselves, except when
moved by hunger." He seemed more impressed with the new arrivals,
characterizing the Bannocks as "enterprising," "restless," and "athletic."

But they were also, in his opinion, harder to control, desiring the "wild freedom" they once enjoyed. He noted "many bad, vicious young men," but felt they would obey Bannock John.[42] Deep snows and lack of game forced Powell to move the camp to within six miles of Boise city that winter. The Shoshones returned to domestic service, and the captain's opinion of them improved. He now deemed them "remarkably industrious" and cited their "menial services" for local whites and their work as army scouts. He spoke little of the Bannocks, most of whom had been away during the fall and winter for their buffalo hunt.[43]

How real were such distinctions to the Indians themselves? Did the Bannocks view their Shoshone kin as docile domestic servants? Did the Shoshones share Powell's opinion that the Bannocks were excitable and prospective troublemakers whose habits would be "corrected" by reservation life? Obviously they saw themselves as distinctive peoples—some called themselves Bannocks and others Shoshones—but this did not mean their sense of themselves corresponded to Powell's opinions. Their self-identifications were likely based not on a defined sense of tribe or ethnic group but on which side of the bilingual Newe world they belonged to. The captain himself noted, "They are on the best of terms, all being more or less intermarried."[44] The difference between them was still essentially economic, and they had yet to fall into direct competition with one another for scarce resources. Both peoples continued to pursue an accustomed lifestyle in their respective *tebíwas* as best they could. Moreover, the Bannocks who returned to Boise represented only a small portion of that "tribe," probably those most intermarried and related to the Boise-area Shoshones. Still, the opinions of the captain and other white observers cannot be completely dismissed. If ethnicity is a process rather than an essence, such views are part of the historical process of interaction and negotiation that draws ethnic boundaries. The experience at the Boise camp suggests the ways in which self-identification intersects with ascription by outsiders to redefine ethnicity.

In late August 1867, Governor Ballard finally got his opportunity to convince Taghee to settle at Fort Hall. The governor began the council, held on Long Tom Creek (north of present-day Mountain Home) by stating the obvious: "As the whites approach your hunting grounds, the game recedes; as they cultivate the fields, wild roots, upon which you depend for subsistence, disappear." He told the Taghee that white people would only keep coming and that history demonstrated that where whites and Indians came in contact, the latter always suffered. Therefore, under the direction of the president, he had selected a reservation for the Bannocks and "other friendly Indians" at Fort Hall. "It is a good place for you," said Ballard, "with fish in the streams, game in the hills." In exchange for the reservation and government assistance and education, he asked the Bannocks to cede "all the country you have ever claimed."[45] Years of frustration boiled to the surface in Taghee's initial response. He lambasted the government for ignoring him and failing to fulfill the Soda Springs treaty of 1863:

> I thought when the white people came to Soda Springs and built houses and put soldiers in them, it was to protect my people, but now they are all gone, and I do not know where to go or what to do. The white people have come into my country, and have not asked my consent. Why is that? And why have no persons talked to me before? I have never known what the white people wanted me to do. I have never killed white people who were passing into my country. What you say to me I shall never forget.[46]

Taghee's frustration was understandable. He had performed his role as a Newe *dai'gwahni'* and made peaceful arrangements to protect his people and their life ways. The whites, however, had not fulfilled their promises. They had overrun his people's *tebíwa* but had sent no one to negotiate that access. They had promised annuity goods and then sent nothing. Now Governor Ballard stood before him and asked for even more concessions.

The prospect of living on a reservation with "other friendly Indians" also disturbed Taghee. Fort Hall was within the Bannocks' *tebíwa*, and sharing the reservation with others, over whom his authority was less than certain, presented problems. Taghee was confident that "all the Bannocks will obey me and be good," but he took no responsibility for other Newes. In particular, he singled out the Sheep-Eaters: "They may steal and be bad, but they are not my people, and I cannot be responsible for them." He assured the governor that the Boises and Bruneaus were "good Indians, and are my friends," but he also seemed hesitant to assume any obligation for them. He reminded Ballard that the Shoshones were "poor" in horses and could not follow the Bannocks on the buffalo hunt. His own people were suffering from want; some lacked horses, and those who could hunt buffalo had to travel farther and farther north each year to find the herds. In essence, Taghee told the governor he could only speak for his followers and could not be expected to provide for the "other Indians" who came to live on "his people's" reservation. Seemingly oblivious to the words Taghee had spoken, Ballard later reported that the Shoshones and Bannocks "are on terms of intimate friendship, and would harmonize on a reservation."[47]

Notwithstanding his frustration and anger, Taghee agreed to a reservation at Fort Hall. He set certain conditions, however, before he would take his people there:

> I want the Privilege of hunting the buffalo for a few years. When they are all gone away we hunt no more; perhaps one year, perhaps two or three years; then we stay on the reservation all the time. I want a reservation large enough for all *my people*, and no white man on it, except the agent and other officers and employees of the government. I want the right of way for *my people* to travel when going to or coming from the buffalo country, and when going to sell our furs and skins. I want the right to camp and dig roots on Cañon prairie when coming to Boise City to trade. Some of *my people* have no horses. They can remain at camas prairie and dig roots while the others go on. Our hunting is not so good as it used to be, nor *my people* so numerous. . . . I will go from here to the buffalo country, where I will meet all *my tribe,* and will tell them of this talk and the arrangements we may make [emphasis added].[48]

Again, Taghee was acting in the traditional role of a *da̲i'gwahni'*, protecting his people's *tebíwa* and negotiating access to a wide range of customary resources. Judging from his statements, he held a much more limited definition of "his people" than did the whites with whom he dealt.

The treaty that emerged from the Long Tom Creek council included none of Taghee's conditions. The brief document called for his people to take up permanent residence on the "Bannock and Shoshone Reservation" before 1 June 1868. The government promised necessary assistance and education, and in return the Bannocks relinquished their claim to all territory outside the reservation. Nowhere did the treaty even mention access to buffalo, camas, fish, or trade. Ballard claimed that the "articles were read, [and] explained" to the Bannocks before they signed the treaty.[49] Yet it seems unlikely that Taghee would discard demands he had made only moments earlier. Fortunately, the Long Tom Creek treaty suffered the same fate as all of its predecessors. Nearly a year would pass before Taghee and "his people" finally became a party to a ratified treaty.

The roots of the Fort Bridger treaty of 1868 lay in the events immediately following the Civil War, when the army and federal policy makers suffered embarrassing setbacks in their attempts to pacify the Plains tribes. On the northern plains, hordes of white gold-seekers traversed the heart of Lakota and Cheyenne hunting grounds on the Bozeman Trail. In 1865, this road and the army's attempt to keep it open touched off Red Cloud's War. At the same time, the southern plains were engulfed in a brutal war dating back to the Sand Creek Massacre of 1864. For many frontier residents, the answer was extermination, but other white Americans, most notably Senator James R. Doolittle of Wisconsin, sought a more humane resolution to the "Indian problem," one that would bring a final, all-encompassing peace to the Great Plains and beyond. Doolittle's committee investigation found that whites had provoked most of the hostilities and argued that reservations offered the only solution.[50] The senator's initial plan failed, but shortly thereafter Congress approved a very similar program of treaties and reservations, and the United States Indian Peace Commission was born.[51] The commission consisted of four civilians—Commissioner of Indian Affairs Nathaniel G. Taylor, Senator John B. Henderson, John B. Sanborn, and Samuel F. Tappan—and three generals—William T. Sherman, William S. Harney, and Alfred H. Terry. Gen. Christopher C. Augur often substituted for Sherman and eventually became a regular member of the commission. Characterized as "quietly competent" by two eminent historians of the frontier army, Augur did not share the opinion of many of his colleagues that the "Indian problem" demanded severe and brutal responses.[52] He was the lone commission member present at the Fort Bridger council with the Shoshones and Bannocks in 1868.

Augur viewed his mission at Fort Bridger as consolidating all of the bands on a single "Shoshone and Bannock reservation." The general asserted that the old ways of hunting must inevitably give way to the new path of agriculture. He warned that as soon as the transcontinental railroad was complete, whites would flood their country, so they must act now to select a reservation.[53] Not surprisingly, both the principal Indian leaders present—Taghee and Washakie—wanted their *tebíwa*s for their peoples' reservations. Washakie claimed "all the country lying between the meridian of Salt Lake City and the line of the North Platte rivers to the mouth of the Sweetwater" and wanted "the valley of the Wind River and lands on its tributaries as far east as the Popo-agi" for his reservation. Augur reported that "Taghee claims for the Bannocks in terms more general even, all the country about the Soda Springs, the Porte Neuf river, and the Big Kamas prairie to the northwest of it."[54] Augur then asked both men to settle their peoples on a single reservation. He told them that the "Great Father" wanted this because "more can be done for them in this way than if they are scattered over the country in small reservations." Washakie seemed amenable to the plan, especially because the proposed reservation in the Wind River Valley was within his *tebíwa*.[55] Taghee, however, adamantly refused to settle with the Wyoming Shoshones and thereby abandon his *tebíwa* and subordinate his authority to Washakie's. "As far away as Virginia City our tribe has roamed," he told Augur, "but I want the Porte-Neuf Country and the Kamas Plains." Taghee explained, "We are friends with the Shoshones and like to hunt with them, but we want a home for ourselves."

Augur then asked whether, if the Bannocks had a "separate home," they would agree to a single agency and "come to the Shoshone reservation for your annuities." Once again, the Bannock leader refused. He had spent the past five years waiting for the whites to fulfill their promises, all the while watching many of his people slip away toward Washakie. Taghee demanded that his people's annuities be sent directly to their reservation. Augur finally conceded to a separate Bannock reservation and agency and assured Taghee that until it was established their annuities would be delivered to Fort Bridger, "separate from those for the Shoshones." The treaty defined the boundaries of the Wind River Reservation, but because Augur was unfamiliar with Idaho, he postponed finalizing the borders of the Bannock reservation. Apparently he was unaware of the executive order that had established the Fort Hall Reservation over a year earlier, and the treaty promised the Bannocks a reservation encompassing "reasonable portions of the 'Port Neuf' and 'Kansas Prairie' countries."[56] The clause included the Bannocks' traditional winter camps on the Fort Hall bottoms as well as the critical root grounds Taghee demanded. The unfortunate misspelling of *camas* provided later white interlopers a specious claim to that area. Taghee knew nothing of the clerical error and must have ridden away from Fort Bridger hopeful but wary, believing that the treaty guaranteed his people a reservation in their *tebíwa*. Idaho territorial officials, on the other hand, had a very different vision for Fort Hall's future.

During the first decade of its existence, the Fort Hall Reservation was the scene of a struggle over primacy and survival among Idaho's Newe peoples that gave new significance to the ethnic identities of Shoshone and Bannock. Territorial and federal officials, unaware of or unsympathetic to the importance of band divisions, continued to promote consolidation. They believed that the distinctions between Newe peoples were inconsequential and that all southern Idaho's Indians could easily and happily live together on a single reservation. Ironically, their ignorance of band differences contributed to the emergence of sharper ethnic distinctions at Fort Hall, as social divisions became reified as political divisions. The practical effect of consolidation was to increase both the Shoshone population and the ethnic rivalry at Fort Hall. The Bannocks—meaning the mixed buffalo-hunting bands—viewed the reservation as theirs, a product of the Fort Bridger treaty. Throughout the 1870s, however, Fort Hall's Shoshone population increased rapidly, while Bannock numbers remained stable. Appropriations and rations were never sufficient, and, by the outbreak of the Bannock War in 1878, the Bannocks voiced a loud resentment of the interlopers who lived on their land and took their annuities. Thus ethnic identity at Fort Hall in the 1870s took shape in the conflict between the government's plans for consolidation and the native struggle for autonomy and survival on a poorly funded and undersupplied reservation.

The consolidation effort at Fort Hall was an extension of several long-standing and interrelated thrusts of federal Indian policy dating back to the removal era. Consolidation was first and foremost an issue of economy, and little, if any, thought was given to the social or ethnic ramifications of resettlement on Indian peoples. For many white officials, the Indian Territory still served as a model for efficiency in Indian policy. As late as 1878, for instance, Commissioner Hiram Price lobbied for the passage of a general consolidation bill, arguing that fewer, larger agencies would reduce the "expense attending the civilization of the Indians" while better protecting their personal and property rights. Proceeds from the sale of vacated lands would finance reservation operations and bring relief to taxpayers. Consolidation was, he wrote, "not only possible, but expedient and advisable."[57] Moreover, consolidation was often viewed as the first step on the government's grand scheme of assimilation by agriculture. Whenever the words *civilization* and *Indian* were spoken in the same breath in the late nineteenth century, *agriculture* was never far behind. For white policy makers, there were important cultural and economic assumptions behind this link. The dominant social theory of the age, which held that cultures passed through stages, with farming superior to and succeeding hunting, justified such self-serving goals. Combined with Jeffersonian notions of utopian agrarian capitalism, this theoretical construction led the well-meaning and the greedy alike to argue that the most promising way to turn native peoples into "Americans" was to make them farmers.[58] But the process would be neither quick nor cheap, and so it was also assumed that concentrating large numbers of Indians on fewer reservations, with supposedly greater supervision and instruction, would facilitate their transformation. As is so often the case, programs that seemed reasonable to their designers faltered when exposed to harsh realities. At Fort Hall, the government's inability or unwillingness to meet its treaty obligations created competition and resentments over scarce annuities and provisions and consequently sharpened the differences between Bannocks and Shoshones.

The Boise and Bruneau Shoshones were the first subjects of the government's consolidation policy. They had suffered through a miserable winter near the capital. White settlers had monopolized all of the timber lands and prevented the Indians from cutting firewood. The lack of warm clothing and a deadly measles epidemic increased the suffering. The bands started for Fort Hall in mid-March 1869, and by the end of April all but a few stragglers had arrived.[59] "They appear pleased with their new home," Capt. Powell wrote at the end of May, "and are traversing it in all directions fishing and hunting." Powell contracted for agency buildings, bought some stock cattle, and even recruited a number of Shoshones to plant crops. Within a month, though, his attitude had soured, and he blamed the Shoshones' "disposition to roam" for their initial failure as farmers. Strangely, he also reported that they "cannot be made to see the importance of drying fish for winter use."[60] It is hard to believe this indifference was due to laziness or ignorance, as Powell suggested. White observers, including the captain himself, had long reported Shoshones living on dried fish. More likely the Boises and Bruneaus planned to winter as they had customarily done, in small bands at opportune fishing sites, and by fall quite a few had left the reservation. The spring removal to Fort Hall was a welcome respite from the horrible conditions in the refugee camp, but the Boises and Bruneaus did not accept the move as permanent. Simply relocating them to the reservation could not make it their home. Nor was it certain to white officials that the bands could legally remain on the reservation and collect annuities.

The controversy over the status of the Boise and Bruneau bands at Fort Hall illustrated the new political realities that the United States was capable of imposing on native leaders and groups. Although Idaho territorial officials dearly wanted the Boises and Bruneaus to settle at Fort Hall, they questioned the bands' legal rights on the reservation. The Boises and Bruneaus been not been present at the Fort Bridger treaty council of 1868, and Col. DeLancey Floyd-Jones, Idaho's superintendent of Indian affairs, interpreted this to mean that no "definite treaty" existed with all of the Fort Hall Indians. The agent William H. Danilson also feared that many Shoshones would succumb to a severe winter if he lacked the authority to distribute clothing and blankets to them. The Shoshones told Danilson that they should be on the "same footing" as the Bannocks, and he supported their claim, citing their interest in agriculture and education and their acquaintance with "the customs and manners of the whites."[61] Some of the same officials, most notably Gov. Ballard, who had for years promoted consolidation, were now unsure how to proceed. Seeking official sanction to place all of Idaho's Newe peoples at Fort Hall, they awaited guidance from the Indian bureau in Washington. At first, Commissioner of Indian Affairs Ely S. Parker, the first American Indian to serve in that position, misunderstood the depth of the issue. Working from the premise that Fort Hall was first and foremost a reservation for all of southern Idaho's Indians and that the Bannocks merely wanted to be included there, Parker secured an executive order designating Fort Hall as the Bannocks' treaty reservation. The ethnic ramifications of the policy were never considered, and Parker ordered Floyd-Jones to "acquaint the Bannock Indians with the actions of this Department and the order of the President."[62] But the order did not resolve the real question: the exact nature of the rights the "other Indians" possessed. Floyd-Jones argued that the "fair interpretation" of the Fort Bridger treaty and, more important, the situation at Fort Hall was that the Shoshones "will enjoy all the privileges and benefits that are given . . . to their friends the Bannacks." The commissioner concurred and wired Boise, "Other Indians on the reserve will enjoy equal rights with the Bannocks."[63]

Thus, by the late summer of 1869, the Indian department had granted official sanction to the de facto policy of settling all of southern Idaho's Newe peoples at Fort Hall. There is ample evidence that this policy was never adequately explained to or understood by either the Shoshones or the Bannocks—or, for that matter, many white officials. For instance, Commissioner of Indian Affairs Francis A. Walker reported in 1872 that the Shoshones at Fort Hall had "no treaty with the government."[64] Consolidation represented a new political reality in a time marked by the loss of autonomy for native leaders and groups. In the years that followed, consolidation functioned to increase the saliency of ethnic and tribal identities at the expense of band identities and leaders.

The failure of the government to adequately fund and supply the reservation represented a second burden on native leaders. Taghee arrived at Fort Hall in June 1869 with five hundred followers after a troublesome winter on the plains. Buffalo had been scarce, and in April, while the group was encamped with Washakie's band near Wind River, a Lakota attack had claimed twenty-nine Shoshone and Bannock lives. The situation he found at Fort Hall, with no annuities and meager provisions, was hardly an improvement. Taghee demanded "to meet someone authorized by the United States to talk with them . . . that hereafter they can call this [Fort Hall] their country and permanent home." Most of all, he wanted their annuities sent directly to Fort Hall instead of Fort Bridger. Within days Pocatello came in with his band of two hundred. He too wanted a "talk" and to collect any annuities due to his people. Powell had little to offer either man but promised to explain their plight to Governor Ballard. Recalling their earlier meeting on Long Tom Creek and the promises made there, Taghee asked to speak with the governor personally.[65]

Taghee's reaction to consolidation and his demands for recognition must be understood within the context of the growing Shoshone population at Fort Hall. Approximately six hundred Bannocks "belonged" at Fort Hall, and by early counts the Shoshones at Fort Hall nearly equaled that number.[66] Yet the Fort Hall bottoms were the Bannocks' customary wintering grounds, and Taghee understood the Fort Bridger treaty as reserving the area for his people. Moreover, as the *dai'gwahni'* of the buffalo-hunting bands, he could speak only for his followers. He had previously warned Ballard that he could not be held responsible for all of the Indians the governor anticipated sending to "his people's" reservation. Taghee also feared that the government would try to force him to settle on the Wind River reservation and wanted "positive" assurance that he and his people "will not be removed" from Fort Hall. This concern makes Taghee's insistence that the Bannocks' annuities be sent directly to Fort Hall all the more understandable.[67] An official home and annuity distribution at Fort Hall were not matters of convenience but matters of physical survival for Taghee's people and of his own political survival as a *dai'-gwahni'*. And, as in the period preceding the Fort Bridger council, Taghee's frustration could in part be traced to Washakie's political influence.

In 1869 Washakie was enduring serious internal and external challenges to his leadership that had implications for Taghee's status at Fort Hall. The old chief still controlled the largest band of Eastern Shoshones, but an up-and-coming mixed-blood named Nar-kok was gaining influence. Nar-kok, who spoke fluent English, appealed to the younger, more militant Shoshones. When told he could no longer receive his annuities near Fort Bridger but must go to Wind River, Nar-kok loudly suggested to his followers that the only way to get their annuities might be to "steal a few horses and kill a few white men." Such talk shocked the agents, who lamented Washakie's apparent decline. The Wind River agent James Patterson had "no confidence" in Nar-kok, and Luther Mann at Fort Bridger characterized him as "crafty, and somewhat ambitious."[68] A second threat to Washakie's position came when several Northern Arapaho leaders expressed their wish to go onto the Wind River reservation. Washakie knew one of the Arapaho headmen, Friday, as a friend of his youth but was dismayed at the request. He told Mann that "he could not understand why the Arapahos, who had for years allied with the Sioux and Cheyenne

against him should now suddenly wish to join him."[69] Both these challenges led Washakie to seek more "reliable allies" to live at Wind River,
and Taghee's Bannocks, because of their long association and frequent
intermarriage with the Eastern Shoshones, were the most obvious recruits.

Washakie could not reject outright the government's desire to place
the Arapahos at Wind River, but he could use his control over annuities
to send a message that they were not welcome there. Moreover, by sharing his people's goods with desirable visitors, he could demonstrate his
power in the traditional role of _dai'gwahni'_. Since 1863 Washakie had
"utterly refused" to share his people's annuities with the Bannocks, yet in
1870 he took a very different stance. On annuity day Washakie had all
the Bannocks and Sheep-Eaters present share equally in the goods, while
he completely denied the Arapahos. His actions were a clear attempt to
draw more followers to Wind River and buttress his own political
power.[70] In 1869 and 1870, Washakie's influence drew Taghee's people
away to the east, just as they had been drawn in the years before the Fort
Bridger treaty. For Taghee to stop this movement and maintain his leadership, it was essential that the government recognize his primacy at Fort
Hall and deliver his people's annuities there.[71]

The government's inability to adequately supply the reservation, coupled with federal policy mandates, tied the success of consolidation to the
success of agricultural programs. Agent Danilson reported in August
1869: "The Indians, especially the Bannocks, are anxious to commence
farming in the Spring." The statement is curious, considering the
Bannocks' general resistance to farming. Forced to share Fort Hall with
growing numbers of Shoshones, the Bannocks may have tried to coun-
teract the Shoshones' growing influence by appropriating the most
potent symbol of Euro-American culture—farming.[72] Although the
Jeffersonian ideals behind this agrarian imperative meant nothing to
them, the Bannocks could not have missed the white men's obsession
with agriculture. In every council they had ever had, government officials
stressed that adopting "white ways" meant becoming farmers. By the
end of the summer, however, only thirty-five acres of the reservation
were under the plow, and the lack of supplies and facilities, combined
with the lure of the hunt, proved too great. Soon all the Bannocks
departed from the reservation, promising that "this winter's hunt in the
Wind River Mountains shall be their last" and proclaiming themselves
"anxious of settling down and living like white men."[73] The Boise and
Bruneau Shoshones who remained became the focus of the government's
plans. They cleared sagebrush, broke ground, dug irrigation ditches, and

planted potatoes. The Shoshones' efforts in the summer of 1870 so impressed Agent Danilson that he felt they would soon become independent farmers, "cultivating small patches for themselves." But that, of course, was what the Indian department wanted to hear. In truth, the farms were far from self-supporting, and by autumn Danilson was in a desperate race to obtain supplies before winter set in. By February the previous summer's crop had been consumed, and only a small amount of flour bought on the open market prevented starvation.[74] Danilson's experience was not the exception but the rule. Year after year, he and his successors struggled to provide the most basic subsistence for the Indians who took their chances with farming and remained on the reservation. The failure of early agricultural efforts helped to stall consolidation plans and would ultimately magnify ethnic differences between Bannocks, who generally rejected agricultural programs, and Shoshones, who participated in greater numbers.

The most common Bannock response to the agricultural assimilation program was to ignore it and treat Fort Hall as a single component in their subsistence cycle. For a people whose customary rounds covered thousands of square miles, it was an understandable choice. Other Newe peoples had followed similar strategies. The Cache Valley Shoshones exacted a regular tribute of food and presents from the Mormons who settled in their midst in the early 1860s.[75] A similar dynamic was at work at Fort Hall, with the added dimension that the Indians possessed a legally recognized right to the reservation. As long as their hunts were successful, the Bannocks saw no reason to starve at Fort Hall when periodic visits were enough to collect their annuities and provisions. This effectively meant that besides "old men and women, widows and their children, [and] men whose physical disabilities deter them from wandering about the country," the only Indians who stayed permanently on the reservation were the Shoshone farmhands. One agent lamented that "[Fort Hall] is a mere refuge for them; a place where they are to receive clothing and medicine, and, when desirable, or when other means fail, provisions."[76] Even with their greater mobility, the Bannocks faced a bleak future. Danilson noted their growing poverty when Taghee's band returned in June 1870, writing: "They had few robes, their horses were jaded, and the Indians themselves were badly off for clothing." More ominously, they were "loud in their demands" that the government fulfill its promises. Taghee told Danilson that he "had waited a long time . . . and unless something was done very soon he would not stand it." Superintendent Floyd-Jones hurriedly sent $3,000 from an "incidental fund," and Danilson issued blankets, calico, lead shot, percussion caps, and knives to the 520 Bannocks and 256 Shoshones present. The Bannocks still "felt they were not getting what they were promised." With the annuities distributed, there was literally nothing to keep them at Fort Hall, and, as Danilson expected, within a few days Taghee led his people off to "buffalo country" once again.[77] Although the Shoshones also came and went, the Bannocks' greater tendency to treat Fort Hall as a seasonal resort was a direct consequence of the social differentiation that had occurred during the eighteenth and nineteenth centuries. In this reservation context, social differences increasingly became political differences.

There was also the inherent difficulty, which the agents either failed to recognize or chose to ignore, of convincing any people to abandon familiar cultural patterns for an alien way of life. In the end, the agents' prescriptions for success always returned to the basic pleas for more money and more food. If only the reservation received proper funding, they argued, all the Shoshones and Bannocks would live happily at Fort Hall. Believing that regular rations and government promises would cause either group to discard its customs and become reservation farmers was ludicrous. The buffalo hunt for the Bannocks, like fishing for the Boise and Bruneau Shoshones, was more than a way to feed themselves and their children. It was also a source of identity: people did what they were supposed to in the places they were supposed to be. Many white Americans similarly attached substantial cultural meanings to farming. Some white officials recognized that the Indians' customary life ways would continue for some time, whether they liked it or not. Colonel Floyd-Jones thought it only natural that they would "visit when practicable, their hunting and fishing grounds," because it was simply "impracticable to insist upon their giving up these life-long pursuits, and adopting at once the domestic habits of the white man."[78] It was a legitimate explanation and one that future agents and superintendents continued to employ. Besides, the Bannocks had promised Floyd-Jones that the 1869–70 winter hunt would be their last. When they refused to stay on the reservation in 1870, however, the superintendent's attitude soured. "The Bannocks have not kept their promise," he reported. "They appear to make an annual visit of a month or two for the purpose of getting their clothing annuities . . . and then return to their hunting grounds on the Yellowstone and Wind River mountains." He also "regretted" that the annuity provisions of the Fort Bridger treaty had not been met, as "the Indians are fully aware" of the treaty provisions and were "very independent in their demands upon the agent."[79] Floyd-Jones's frustration was understandable, for as long as the Fort Hall Indians remained off the reservation—whether pulled by cultural patterns or pushed by lack of resources—consolidation was a failure. Even more disconcerting was the looming possibility that friction between whites and "roaming" Indians could lead to violence.

Such fears were magnified the following summer when the Bannocks returned to Fort Hall with news of Taghee's death near the Crow Agency during the fall of 1870. It was an important turning point for the Fort Hall Bannocks. Never again would they have a *dai'gwahni'* of such recognized stature and unifying influence. Years later, Stanton G. Fisher recalled: "Targie was a good friend of mine; a low-spoken, quiet, dignified, tall old man who, however, had perfect control over his people." But perhaps not enough control, for Fisher also had heard rumors that Pan-sook-amotse, or Otter Beard, Taghee's principal subchief and a cosigner of the Fort Bridger treaty, had killed him with "a dose of 'wolf medicine' (strychnine)."[80] True or not, such rumors spoke of great discord among the Bannocks, and it soon became apparent that no other Bannock headman could exercise similar "control" over his people.

The struggle to succeed Taghee as *dai'gwahni'* of the buffalo-hunting bands heightened internal divisions among the Bannocks. The agent Montgomery Berry believed that the question of succession was simple: Taghee's teenage son was the "hereditary chief" of the Bannocks. "His claims are fully recognized for the eventual chieftainship," wrote Berry, "but there is much anxiety among the ambitious men of the tribe as to who shall be *Regent.*" Berry imposed a more familiar, but utterly false, structure over the native political system. Among the Newes, leadership *could* be hereditary, but this was more expectation than requirement. One Bannock family had exercised great political influence during the nineteenth century, but there was no established hereditary claim to chieftainship. Wisdom, experience, and the ability to act as an effective intermediary with the whites were the true marks of leadership. Taghee's son, who was adopted by the Bannock headman Tyhee and later went by the name of Pat Tyhee, was simply too young and inexperienced to accept those burdens. By the 1870s, a leader could not be head chief without the recognition of both whites and his own people. Pan-sook-amotse assumed nominal leadership of the Bannocks, at least according to the agent. Yet neither he nor Pagwite, his major rival, was ever able to consolidate a standing as head chief.[81]

The political turmoil among the Bannocks caused concern to white observers. Agent Berry believed that, coupled with loud demands for annuities and presents, this unrest was evidence of either the interference

of troublesome whites or an "extensive conspiracy among them prepara-
tory to an outbreak." He held a long council with Pan-sook-amotse and
his councilors and impressed on them the government's "power, and
magnanimity, and resources." Just how he did this, considering the government's track record in supplying the agency, he did not explain. The
headmen reportedly set 1 September as the day for the "whole number of
Bannocks" to settle permanently at Fort Hall. But the summer of 1871
was to be no different from previous years: the Bannocks collected their
annuities and left for the buffalo country.[82]

Although the Shoshones appeared more willing to remain at Fort Hall,
the same problems that alienated the Bannocks drove many of them from
the reservation as well. At least thirty Boise Shoshones had traveled back
to the familiar lands around the capital by September 1869. The army collected them and sent them back to the reservation, and Superintendent
Floyd-Jones requested a permanent military force at Fort Hall to control
such "wandering."[83] The people who remained on the reservation faced a
winter of destitution. Danilson begged for winter clothing for the Indians
and argued that conditions at Fort Hall were much colder than around
Boise. When Congress had not appropriated money by December, he purchased the necessary clothing with $300 that the Wells Fargo Company
had paid to cut hay on the reservation. It was not the last time a Fort Hall
agent would be forced to use creative financing to meet treaty obligations.[84] With these conditions in mind, it is not surprising that many
Shoshones abandoned the reservation and struggled to continue their old
subsistence patterns. They remained in larger numbers than the Bannocks
because they lacked the mobility of the mounted people; and, more
important, whites had already appropriated the sites they depended on.

As a consequence, while the Bannocks were splitting into ever-smaller
factions in their efforts to maintain their customary life ways, the
Shoshones who remained on the reservation were moving toward greater
political and ethnic cohesion at Fort Hall. The Boise *dai'gwahni'* Captain
Jim (sometimes known as Boise Jim) emerged as the principal Shoshone
leader at Fort Hall during these early years. He had won over the agents
with his "laudable and politic administration," which essentially meant
he encouraged his adherents to farm. He personally "set an example by
planting potatoes for himself, and working with the volunteers in the
field." In a single year Captain Jim's following increased from sixty to
one hundred. Most of the additions were Utah Northwestern Shoshones,
along with a few Western Shoshones from Nevada.[85] Their older band
identity meant far less than Captain Jim's ties to the agents and their agri-

cultural programs. His growing influence illustrated the growing transition from a band *dai'gwahni'* to a Shoshone chief.

Captain Jim's rise was due to his skill as an intermediary, but his continued influence also depended on the success of the Indian farms and the fulfillment of the government's promises. Adopting agriculture made the Shoshones dependent on the reservation farms. A crop failure coupled with government neglect could mean starvation. Thus, Captain Jim's status and influence were constantly at risk. As hard as the Shoshones worked, the Indian farms never produced enough to sustain the growing population of the reservation. A grasshopper infestation nearly destroyed the entire 1871 crop, and by September Berry even asked the Shoshones to leave the reservation. Captain Jim led them off toward the Tetons in search of game. Berry now understood why previous agents had "pushed the Indians out on hunting and fishing excursions, for the purposes of economy." For as much as they lamented the Indians' "roaming," the agents knew there could be no other way for them to survive. Berry regretted sending them away but reasoned that it was better that they leave during late summer than have critical stores consumed before winter.[86] By late November the Shoshones were back, and Berry distributed annuity goods to 720 people. It appeared that more than five hundred Shoshones would remain on the reservation and require rations throughout the winter. Harsh weather and scarce game had already taxed the inadequate food supply. Berry put off addressing the issue for several days until he could "examine different Indians to guard against supplying wandering Indians who belong to other agencies." Nearly all were taken in and fed. Many were Northwestern Shoshones who "presented themselves for registry" at Fort Hall. Although Berry reported that the "Cache Valleys" had no agent, reservation, or "fixed place of habitation," he supplied them with annuities along with the other Shoshones whom he deemed to belong at Fort Hall.[87]

During the early reservation years, from 1869 to the outbreak of the Bannock War in 1878, the government's policy of consolidation, its neglect of the reservations and treaty obligations, and Newe responses to the realities of survival on an underfunded and undersupplied reservation were all factors in the creation of ethnic identities at Fort Hall. For the Newe peoples who came to live on the Fort Hall Reservation, consolidation was not a matter of embracing "civilization" but one of cultural survival. Life at Fort Hall entailed surrendering customary life ways, which no group was anxious to do. Both the Bannocks and Shoshones attempted to maintain their customary subsistence cycles for as long as possible. For the more mobile Bannocks, the reservation became a stop in their annual rounds. They saw no need to abandon their customary ways when they could simply incorporate the reservation into them. Moreover, considering the lack of proper facilities and appropriations, year-round residence on the reservation was an unattractive prospect. For the better part of the 1870s, the Bannocks came in briefly each summer to collect whatever annuities and supplies might be available. Scouring the plains for buffalo while fending off Lakota attacks might seem a hard way to live, but it was both culturally and physically preferable to starving at Fort Hall. It was a choice that irritated whites to no end.

The Shoshones seemed far more accommodating. Their compliance was due less to their allegedly docile nature than to their limited mobility. Even though foot-going Newe bands might cover an immense territory in a given year, they did not do so every year, and they used certain areas far more intensively than others. Unfortunately, these were often the same sites that white settlers coveted. By the time they had moved to Fort Hall, moreover, there was little incentive for them to adopt an equestrian lifestyle. Each year the buffalo became scarcer, and the Bannocks got poorer. Consequently, the Shoshones who fled Fort Hall in the early years sought not a new, "wealthier" lifestyle but a return to their traditional homes. Until the Bannock War of 1878, fairly large Newe bands lived throughout southern Idaho: in the Weiser and Payette basins, around Boise, and on the middle Snake River. Meanwhile, the Shoshones who remained at Fort Hall survived years of scarcity by accommodation and, in the process, won the agents' favor.

Treaty making and consolidation set the stage for the "ethnic" conflicts that marked the Ghost Dance era on the Fort Hall Reservation. Identities at the ethnic level that had emerged from social and economic distinctions hardened and became increasingly political. Native leaders approached negotiations with whites from the perspective of cooperative leaders who represented only those people who chose to follow them. Whites, on the other hand, expected leaders with coercive power and the ability to speak for a fixed polity and territory. In consequence, Newe peoples who understood their identity in terms of localized independent bands increasingly coalesced into two tribal entities: Shoshones and Bannocks. But just as these identities gained salience, the importance of another level of identity also grew. In the decades that followed, a shared racial identity as American Indians was negotiated between Shoshones and Bannocks at Fort Hall.

CHAPTER 4

Two Trails

Resistance, Accommodation, and the 1870 Ghost Dance

> There was a lot of confusion among our people at that time.
> Relatives and families were split. Some wanted to make a new
> life on the reservation while others wanted to stay out on the
> deserts and prairies where they would have to work a little
> harder but would still be their own bosses.
>
> Willie George, "Two Trails," 1963

The decade between the founding of the Fort Hall Reservation and the end of the Bannock War marked the last period of true off-reservation freedom for Newe peoples. It was also a decade for decisions as their options narrowed. As Willie George saw it, his people increasingly faced a choice between "two trails." White settlements expropriated or destroyed the very resources that made an autonomous life possible, while white settlers and politicians were increasingly calling for an end to the Indians' "roaming." Some groups, most notably the Fort Hall Bannocks, resisted the reservation system and maintained their customary life ways for as long as possible. Others chose a more accommodating path, either settling on the reservation and trying agriculture or casting their lot with the Mormons. Throughout this period of dislocation, adjustment, and warfare, the ethnic and tribal identities that gained such saliency in treaty making took on greater meaning. Yet as Shoshone and Bannock peoples made their varying choices, their shared experiences also suggested an identity that could encompass these ethnic and tribal differences. They often negotiated and expressed these competing identities through the discourse of prophetic religion. In this context, the waves of religious excitement that began with the first Ghost Dance prophecies of 1869 were not short-lived and desperate fantasies, as some observers have concluded, but part of an ongoing process of identity formation that would last for the rest of the century.

The Ghost Dance movement of 1870 was the first recorded pan-Indian religion to emerge from the Great Basin.[1] Unlike the more famous 1890 Ghost Dance, it remained obscure, mostly because non-Indian observers did not recognize the larger pattern from scattered reports of religious disturbances and rumors of Indian "outbreaks." James Mooney, who was among the first to recognize the existence of the religion some two decades later, believed that the 1870 prophet was Ta'vibo, or "White Man," whom he also believed to be the father of Wovoka, or Jack Wilson, the 1890 prophet. Ta'vibo reportedly began preaching around 1869 and died very soon thereafter. The finding gave a nice symmetry to the movements, but from the beginning there were uncertainties. Mooney also recorded the 1870 prophet's name as Waughzeewaughber but assumed that Ta'vibo, like his son, went by different names or that this man was simply a disciple of the Ghost Dance prophet.[2] It was not until 1939 that Cora Du Bois established that Wodziwob ("Gray Hair" or "Gray Head)" and Numataivo ("Indian White Man") were two different men. Numataivo was Jack Wilson's father, but he was not the "true originator of the 1870 Ghost Dance." According to Du Bois, Wodziwob died in 1872, whereas Numataivo lived until 1912.[3] More recently, Michael Hittman has confirmed Wodziwob's role as the principal prophet of the 1870 Ghost Dance, but he is far less certain that Jack Wilson's father played any important role in the religion. Hittman also asserts that both men lived past the turn of the century.[4]

Though the details of the prophet's life are in question, the outlines of his religion are fairly well established. Wodziwob's message was "transformative": by following the prescribed ceremonies, Indian people could radically transform the present through supernatural means. He prophesied a return of the old ways, with plentiful game and plant foods and all Indians, living and dead, reunited on a renewed earth.[5] The message was revolutionary, but the ritual was quite conservative. The ceremonial base of the both the 1870 and 1890 Ghost Dances was the traditional Paiute round dance. Round dances could be social occasions, but they often served important ritual purposes, like the increase rites performed at the beginning of a particular food-gathering season. It was in this context, during the annual piñon harvests, rabbit drives, and fish runs, that Wodziwob announced his prophecies.[6] Men, women, and children all participated. Forming a circle, they alternated sexes, interlocked fingers, and shuffled slowly to the left, all the while singing the numerous songs revealed to individual dancers in visions. The dances occurred five nights in succession, and the cycle could be repeated up to twenty times a year.[7] Theoretical approaches to the 1870 Ghost Dance mirror the debate on the earlier and later prophetic movements. James Mooney's emphasis on deprivation has by and large dominated both anthropological and historical treatments of the religion, whereas Leslie Spier and Cora Du Bois, coming from a diffusionist perspective, argued that "a recurring native pattern" was at the heart of the religion. Spier pointed to the Plateau prophet dances, whereas Du Bois situated these beliefs directly in Northern Paiute culture.[8] Hittman has sought to balance preexisting cultural elements with the effects of colonization. Although he accepts deprivation as the underlying cause of the movement, he also argues that historical and cultural factors help to explain its emergence and function.

Hittman thereby proposes an answer for one of the most persistent and troubling questions concerning the Ghost Dance doctrine among the Northern Paiutes: why would a people who practiced a ritual avoidance of the dead subscribe to a religion premised on their return? The key may lie with the prophet's birthplace. Wodziwob was a Paiute from the Fish Lake Valley of Nevada who had migrated to the Walker River Reservation, where he was also known as Hawthorne Wodziwob and Fish Lake Joe. The Fish Lake and neighboring Owens Valley Paiutes, unlike the Northern Paiutes of the Smith and Mason Valleys, where the Ghost Dances began, held an annual mourning ceremony, the cry dance. Hittman theorizes that Wodziwob introduced the cry dance to Walker River by grafting it onto the traditional round dance. This was a revolutionary step in a culture where ghosts were omens of disease and death, and where only the most powerful shamans were spiritually equipped to handle contact with them. In the process Wodziwob created what was both a community curing rite, seeking the return of the recently deceased epidemic victims, and an increase rite, which would return the environment to precontact conditions. Hittman thus refutes Spier's contention that there was no cultural basis for the Ghost Dances within Northern Paiute belief systems as well as Willard Park's insistence that shamanism had but a limited effect on the shape of the movements.[9]

The best-known manifestations of the 1870 Ghost Dance spread north and west into California and Oregon. The great proselytizer of the religion was a Paiute man named Frank Spencer. Also known as Weneyuga, Tsawenga, and Doctor Frank, he made converts among the Washoes, the Pyramid Lake Paiutes, the Surprise Valley Paiutes, and the

Paiutes and Modocs of the Klamath Reservation. The Modocs introduced the dance to the Klamaths, and a Modoc shaman, Doctor George,
carried the religion to the Modocs around Tule Lake, from where it
spread to the Shastas and Karoks. In contemporary but separate movements, the religion reached other California tribes, such as the Maidu
and Patwin.[10] The Ghost Dances proper lasted only a few years, and by
the fall of 1873 they had all but ceased. The reason most often cited for
the movement's decline is the failure of the prophecy. Yet among many of
the California peoples, the dances inspired revivals of preexisting religions (the Kuksu or "god-impersonating" cult) or were transformed into
new belief systems (the Bole-Maru and dream cults).[11]

It also appears that the 1870 movement lasted only briefly among the
people where it began. According to Du Bois, the last Ghost Dance at
Walker River took place in 1872, whereas Hittman argues that the
dances ended even earlier, in 1871. Du Bois suggested a series of causes
for the decline of the religion among the Northern Paiutes, including the
death of the prophet, the failure of the prophecy, the exposure of his leg-
erdemain, and a general Paiute skepticism of the doctrine. If Hittman's
identification of the prophet is correct, however, the first explanation can
be dismissed, as Fish Lake Joe lived well past the turn of the century.
Hittman's research also suggests that successful farming lessened feelings
of deprivation and that Wodziwob experienced a personal disillusionment with his own prophecy.[12] Even if the dancing ended quickly among
the Northern Paiutes of the Walker River Reservation, versions of the
Ghost Dance doctrine continued to circulate, if not from Walker River,
then from some other point in the Great Basin—perhaps from Frank
Spencer, who was said to have continued preaching for five years after
Wodziwob stopped. Moreover, Shoshone, Bannock, and Ute peoples
apparently did not become disillusioned.

The enduring practice of the 1870 Ghost Dance by Indian peoples in
the eastern Great Basin and Rockies counters the traditional historical
interpretation of the movement. Most historians have depicted the 1870
movement as a short-lived and inconsequential phenomenon that
affected only a few peoples north and west of its point of origin. Frank C.
Miller's comments in *The New Encyclopedia of the American West* are
typical: "As a movement the Ghost Dance of 1870 spread only to
California, Oregon, and other parts of Nevada; in some of these areas,
local prophets and cults arose. The movement subsided within a few
years when the prophecies did not come to pass."[13] But, in fact, there is
overwhelming primary evidence that the Ghost Dance of 1870 spread

Map 3. The Ghost Dance movements, 1870s and 1890s.

much farther east and was much longer-lived, particularly among Bannock and Shoshone speakers. How can one explain the longevity of the movement to the east when the Northern Paiutes dropped it so quickly? Some have suggested that the dances' staying power among certain peoples was a function of the structural complexity of the societies in question.[14] This interpretation, however, cannot explain the specific situation at Fort Hall. Bannocks reportedly took the lead in the religion, but the cultural differences between them and the Shoshones were simply not great enough to account for the different reactions. To understand the situation surrounding Fort Hall, it is far more profitable to examine specific historical processes, and in this regard David Aberle's theory of relative deprivation provides a useful analytical tool. In his study of Navajo peyotism, he argued that deprivation is always felt differently by different individuals or groups. What might strike one as deprivation could easily be interpreted by another as an improvement in life and status. Although relative deprivation is a general theory, its great strength lies in the recognition of the importance of specific historical situations.[15]

In this view, Bannocks at Fort Hall accepted, practiced, and proselytized the Ghost Dance more intensively than the Shoshones not because they were more "complex" but because they felt the specific deprivations of reservation life more keenly and in different ways. First, as mounted buffalo hunters (many Shoshone speakers were labeled Bannocks), they experienced worsening deprivation through the 1870s as white encroachment increased and the herds declined. In the aftermath of the Bannock War and the annihilation of the last buffalo herds, the old ways became impossible, and the Bannocks were increasingly restricted to life on an underfunded reservation. Second, they also felt deprivation because of the growing Shoshone population at Fort Hall and the corresponding erosion of their primacy on the reservation. The Shoshones, with less mobility, fewer options, and less hope that resistance could succeed, chafed less at the restrictions of reservation life. Their greater participation in the government's agricultural and assimilative programs meant that government agents visibly and vocally favored them, which in turn elevated their status and influence on the reservation. Many Shoshones, then, experienced these same events not as relative deprivation but as an improvement, albeit small, in their condition. Yet Shoshone speakers could still adopt, practice, and interpret the religion in their own way. And, indeed, they did so outside the reservation context, among the Mormon settlements of northern Utah. The Ghost Dances endured among Bannock and Shoshones speakers precisely because they could be interpreted variously as militant resistance and measured accommodation. Newe people who chose either "trail" looked to prophetic religion to make their choice understandable and proclaim their identity as Indians.

It was far from its origins in western Nevada that the Ghost Dance of 1870 received its first official notice. In May 1870, the interpreter at the Uintah agency, M. J. Shelton, traveled to Heber City, Utah, in an attempt to persuade two Ute bands camped nearby to return to their reservation.

One of the Ute leaders, Takona, introduced Shelton to "three strange Indians" from Fort Bridger, who had brought a message that all the Indians should "meet as soon as possible in the Bannock country . . . as they intend to reserect their forefathers and all Indians who wish to see them must be there."[16] The Utes had already sent runners to the southern bands and dismissed Shelton's pleas to return to Uintah, saying, "The White man has nothing to do with this, it is the command of the Indian God and if they do not go they will sicken and die." The appointed place for the resurrection was said to be in the vicinity of Wind River Reservation.[17] Both the *Deseret News* and the *Latter-Day Saints' Millennial Star* picked up on the story and indicated that the meeting place would be in the "Bannack country, about fifty miles east of Bear Lake." The papers also reported that the Indians intended to "engage in their traditionary religious rites," and that once finished they would peacefully disperse to their respective reservations.[18] The "traditionary" nature of the gathering is highly doubtful, as these peoples had never sponsored joint religious ceremonies before.[19]

Bannocks and Shoshones continued to cosponsor Ghost Dances in the Bear River area. In the spring of 1871, news of the Ghost Dances in western Nevada again spread rapidly among Numic-speaking peoples. Once again Shoshones and Bannocks appear to have been active missionaries. In May 1871, the Nevada agent C. A. Bateman ridiculed the "great fandango" that the Paiutes had "called to gratify the desires of some unknown prophet who, in some way, had succeeded in advertising the farce that God was coming in the mountains beyond with a large supply for all their wants, of what Indians most desire, game, and withal transform the sterility of Nevada to the fertility and beauty of Eden."[20] The advertising had spread much farther than Bateman knew. By May, Shoshones, Bannocks, and Utes had again converged on the Bear River to hold a Ghost Dance.[21] Then, in 1872, hundreds of Utes converged on Sanpete County, Utah, for what was probably a Ghost Dance. Joseph Jorgensen suggests that this was the last of the 1870 Ute Ghost Dances, although aspects of the religion were incorporated into the Ute Bear Dance, and individual Utes continued to join in Bannock and Shoshone Ghost Dances.[22] The eastward spread of the 1870 Ghost Dance suggests that Fort Hall Bannocks were active and important agents in transmitting the doctrine, just as they would be two decades later. Moreover, the doctrine as understood by the Bannocks, Shoshones, and Utes during the 1870s clearly carried a message of racial identity. Takona's statement to Shelton that the religion had nothing to do with the whites and that the

"Indian God" had called the gathering suggests that whites had no place in this vision of the renewed earth.

If the Ghost Dance of 1870 among the Bannocks, Shoshones, and Utes was indeed a religion of Indian identity and resistance to white encroachment and the reservation system, then the final disposition of whites in the prophecy is a crucial question. Mooney recorded two versions of the 1870 prophecy, both recounted by white observers nearly two decades after the fact. Capt. J. M. Lee of the Ninth Infantry visited the Walker River Reservation, where he heard tales of the Paiute prophet in the winter of 1869–70. According to Lee, the prophet had received three distinct revelations, each calculated to increase his standing among the Indians. In the first message, the "Great Spirit" had told him that there would be a great upheaval or earthquake that would swallow up the whites but leave their homes and property behind. The incredulous Paiutes asked how such an event could occur without destroying them as well. The prophet returned with a second message; the Indians would indeed be "swallowed up" along with the whites, but after a short period, perhaps three days, they would be "resurrected in the flesh, and would live forever to enjoy the earth, with plenty of game, fish, and pine nuts, while their enemies the white would be destroyed forever." As time passed and the prophecy went unfulfilled, many Paiutes lost interest, and it was then that the prophet returned with a third and final message: only the Indians who believed would be resurrected, and all the rest would "stay in the ground and be damned forever with the whites."[23]

Frank Campbell, the agency farmer at Walker River in the early 1870s, provided a very different and far more benign version of the prophecy in a letter to the commissioner of Indian affairs in 1890. He had lived among the Paiutes for over a decade and even claimed to have witnessed one of the prophecies. According to his recollection, "Waugh-zee-waugh-ber" began preaching the new religion in 1872. Campbell visited Wodziwob's camp while the prophet was in a trance state, and when it appeared to the Paiutes that the prophet's spirit was returning, "the Indians gathered around him and joined in a song that was to guide the spirit back to the body. Upon reanimation he gave a long account of his visit in the spirit to the Supreme Ruler, who was then on the way with all the spirits of the departed dead to again reside upon this earth and change it into a paradise. Life was to be eternal, and no distinction was to exist between races." After hearing the prophecy, Campbell told the Paiutes that "the preachings of Waugh-zee-waugh-ber were good and no harm could come from it."[24]

On the surface it might seem that Campbell's account was necessarily more accurate than Lee's. Lee, who had little respect for the "poor miserable Indians," presented the Ghost Dances as equal parts delusion and self-interest. Campbell, on the other hand, worked with and knew the Paiutes and spoke from firsthand experience. Yet it is quite possible that Wodziwob had altered his prophecy because of the farmer's presence. Campbell recalled that he had been "kept in ignorance" for several months after the preaching began, treatment that, in his opinion, was "remarkable considering the confidence they had always reposed in me."[25] In fact, the first dances at Walker River took place in 1869, and by the following spring the doctrine had reached Utah. So if Campbell's recollection of the date was correct, he had been kept in the dark for years rather than months. He believed that the Paiutes did not tell him of the religion because they feared ridicule, but it is just as likely they did not want Campbell to hear such militant prophecies. Regardless of Wodziwob's original prophecy, by the time the religion had reached the Bannocks and Shoshones of southern Idaho, the destruction of the whites was a clearly stated part of the doctrine.

When the message of the 1870 Ghost Dance reached the Fort Hall Bannocks, they were at an economic, social, and political crossroads. In the years since the reservation's founding, the government had never supplied adequate subsistence for the number of Indians it intended to concentrate at Fort Hall. Tension between Bannocks and Shoshones grew as the latter outnumbered the former. Moreover, there were obvious strains among the Bannocks as they sought to continue their customary life ways. In the wake of Taghee's death, the Bannocks split. In the fall of 1871, the buffalo hunters had again journeyed to the Montana plains as a single unit. After the hunt, however, one group followed Pan-sook-amotse to Fort Hall; another, Pagwite's, went directly to the Camas Prairie; and a third chose to remain at Wind River with the Eastern Shoshones. No Bannock leader could claim the status of "head chief." Pan-sook-amotse had not consolidated his standing during the winter's hunt, and Pagwite had always been marginal to Bannock leadership. There were also apparent generational divisions among the Bannocks. Pagwite appealed to the Bannocks, young men in particular, who had given up on the government's promises.[26] White encroachment only made matters worse, and the Great Camas Prairie became the focal point of Indian anger. The prairie was essential for all of Idaho's Newe peoples, who made annual visits to the high valley south of the Sawtooth Range to collect the edible bulbs. It was also a traditional "free trade zone," where Indian peoples from the Plains to the Plateau met for peaceful commerce each summer. Unfortunately, white herdsmen coveted the valley as a summer range for their livestock. The Indians rightly understood the prairie to be part of their reservation, regardless of the misspelling of Camas Prairie as "Kansas Prairie" in the Fort Bridger treaty. The agent Montgomery Berry knew the mistake was a "mere clerical error" but believed in 1871 that it was "of sufficient importance to give those who make it a business to encroach upon Indian lands a shadow of a claim." While no federal or territorial official ever cited the error as justification for white encroachment, neither did they move to protect the prairie for Indian use.[27] It was on the Great Camas Prairie in the summer of 1872 that social, political and economic tensions boiled over into violence and revealed the practice of the Ghost Dance among the Bannocks.

What white officials came to call the Wood River incident occurred on 23 June 1872. Pagwite's band had come to the prairie to dig roots and trade horses with the Umatillas and Nez Percés. They camped on the on the eastern margin of the Great Camas Prairie near the Big Wood River. A number of white stockmen were camped nearby, and days passed without trouble until some of Pagwite's young men asked the whites for assistance in rounding up their horses. Once they had lured the herdsmen out of camp, they attacked, killing one man and wounding two others.[28] After his initial investigation, the Fort Hall agent Johnson N. High concluded that Pagwite's young warriors had committed "premeditated murder . . . at the insistence of the medicine men." He described these shamans, or "Big Medicines," as "not necessarily doctors but necromancers, men endowed with supernatural power who are believed to be able to cause rain to fall[,] grass to grow. Who can cause the earth to burn up and cause sickness and death to fall upon whomsoever they wish, who cannot be penetrated by a bullet, and who have for these reasons more influence over the band than any one else and can command obedience to their will and excite all the malicious passions and frenzy in the savage nature of their followers."[29]

According to Stanton Fisher, the future agent and agency trader whom High had sent to the Camas Prairie, there were seven such shamans in Pagwite's band. They had incited the young men to "deeds of violence promising them plunder and at the same time no punishment," and claimed to "possess charms which render them invulnerable and that they can protect their followers from all harm." Fisher added, "The Indians as a class are strong believers in witchcraft and in the power of charms and incantations and look upon these 'Medicine Men' as beings of a superior order and do their bidding willingly." High recommended severe punishment for the killers and the removal of Pagwite from leadership. Perhaps being only partially facetious, he reasoned that the easiest way to curb the Big Medicines' power would be to publicly shoot several of them to death, disproving their claims of invulnerability and "prevent[ing] a new crop of truly dangerous individuals."[30]

Although neither High nor Fisher ascribed the troubles on Wood River to any specific prophecy, two facets of the shamanistic and prophetic traditions, and of the Ghost Dance movements, are unmistakable in their reports: claims of weather control and invulnerability. Weather control was a common method of legitimizing authority among shamans and prophets, including both the Ghost Dance prophets. Claims of invulnerability were even more widespread among spiritual and political leaders. Most telling is High's reference to the Big Medicines as necromancers, which suggests that they established their authority through communication with the dead. Ghosts were a frightening aspect of *bo'ha*, and this claim, which was far less common among Newe shamans, points to a direct relationship between the Big Medicines and Ghost Dance doctrine.

It was the report of a third white official that confirmed the link between the shamans in Pagwite's band and the 1870 Ghost Dance prophecy. Judge Clitus Barbour went to the Camas Prairie at Gov. Thomas W. Bennett's request. There he found some twelve hundred Shoshones and Bannocks equally divided between Tendoy's and Pagwite's camps. If his estimate was correct, Pagwite's following was far larger than it had ever been. For his own safety, Barbour camped with Tendoy on Soldier Creek. Like many in Idaho, the judge viewed the Lemhi headman as a stabilizing influence, and he suggested that all the Indians on the prairie should move to Tendoy's camp if they wanted peace.[31] Indeed, Barbour concluded that the Bannocks' failure to find a new head chief was the principal cause of the violence. But he also cited the influence of a new religious prophecy. When he sought a council with Pagwite, Barbour discovered that the Bannock leader had already left for Boise to return the stolen horses. In his stead came Pe-te-go, the "Big Medicine man and prophet." Judging by his name, prophecies and actions, Pe-te-go may have been Pashego, the Bannock Prophet and the "man of blood" blamed for unrest on the overland trails a decade earlier. Pe-te-go, who was said to have "immense influence" among the young men, freely admitted that the shamans had inspired the four warriors responsible for

the killing. At first Pagwite had tried to stop them, he said, but when they
started out a second time, "he crawled into his lodge and let them go."[32]
The prophet promised that Pagwite and his subchiefs would control the
young men in the future, but Barbour had his doubts. The major reason
for the judge's skepticism was a "pernicious" religious teaching that he
traced to the Northern Paiute leader Winnemucca. Barbour believed the
aging chief was trying to "rouse [the Shoshones and Bannocks] against
the whites through their superstitions." The specific prophecy stated that
"on a certain day, not far distant, all the dead Indians will rise from their
graves and collect in some plain, making a great and powerful army,
strong enough to overpower and wipe out all the white men." He argued
that the doctrine inspired other prophets or "imitators," presumably Pe-
te-go and the other "Big Medicines," and it was these "sour fanatics"
who turned religious passion into violence.[33] Winnemucca was not the
leader of a grand Indian conspiracy, but he was the subject of numerous
conspiracy theories in Nevada, Idaho, and Oregon in the 1860s and
1870s. Barbour was correct, however, in placing the prophecy's origin
with the Northern Paiutes. And although Barbour did not recognize it as
such, there can be little doubt that the prophecy originated in the Ghost
Dance. Militant resistance to the settlers' invasion, however, was not the
only way in which Indian peoples could interpret the Ghost Dance
doctrine.

To the south of the Snake River that summer, Ghost Dancing became
a religious conversation between native peoples and the most prophetic
of all Christian sects, the Mormons, concerning both peoples' identity
and destiny. By July rumors of Paiute "superstitions" regarding the
return of the dead had reached Utah, where the superintendent of Indian
affairs, George W. Dodge, fretted over the influx of Indians into the territory. The Uintah and White River Utes had once again left their agencies, and many Indians from Fort Hall as well as Washakie's band were
making their way into northern Utah. Dodge also claimed that thousands
of Indians, including many Lakotas and Cheyennes, were camped on the
Camas Prairie and would soon be heading south. (These were more
likely the same large Shoshone and Bannock encampments Barbour had
visited.)[34] Dodge mistrusted the Mormons and blamed them for these
unusual gatherings, but he also identified a native prophet. The Indians
gathering in Utah told Dodge that "the Great Spirit appeared to us and
revealed that we may remain [in their present camps] for two months
from the 4th of July, when the 'Voice from the West' will appear and
reveal more fully what we shall then do." Dodge even accurately deter-

mined the source of the prophecy as a Paiute "who made his appearance at Walker River reservation in Western Nevada last winter."[35] The use of Independence Day as a marker in the prophecy illustrates the truly syncretic nature of the Ghost Dances: a symbol revered by whites that would mark the beginning of a native renaissance. Ultimately the scope of the movement in Utah was never as large as Dodge had feared. By October, the Utes had returned to their reservations under threat of military action. In his final analysis, Dodge made no reference to Mormon interference or native prophecy but rather ascribed the whole episode to the miserable conditions on the reservations.[36]

Although the Mormon Church did not instigate the Ghost Dances, it was a beneficiary of the religious excitement engendered by the movement. As in the 1850s, the convergence of prophetic doctrines led some Indian peoples to seek out the Mormons and vice versa. Beginning in the spring of 1873, the church enjoyed some of its greatest missionary success among Shoshone- and Bannock-speaking groups. George Washington Hill, who as a missionary in the Lemhi Valley in 1855 had heard tales of the Bannock Prophet, led the northern Utah mission. In the process, he found confirmation of his own religious beliefs and identity. Beginning in 1871, he remembered, "the Indians from down the Humboldt, from Battle Mountain, Carlin, Winnemucca and all through that section of the country . . . had been begging me to come to their country and preach to them."[37] Finally, in May 1873, several Shoshone leaders visited him in Ogden and asked him to come and proselytize their people, who were camped along the Bear River near the town of Corinne, Utah. Hill, who had been instructed by Brigham Young to pursue such a mission, agreed but could not promise an exact date for his visit. On 5 May Hill took the train to Corinne and then set out on foot for the Shoshone village twelve miles distant. Along the way he met several Shoshones, who all told him the same miraculous story: that day their chief, Sagwitch, had arisen and told them to "clean up and stay home" as "Ink-a-pompy" ("Man with Red Hair") would arrive on foot that day. Hill was pondering how Sagwitch could have predicted his arrival when, "lo and behold, I met the chief [Sagwitch] coming to bring me a horse to ride to camp. That satisfied me that Father had something to do with it; so I resigned myself into His hands and said: 'Father thy will be done,' . . . the time had come for His work to commence among the Indians."[38] And commence it did. By the end of his one-day visit, Hill had baptized 102 Shoshones. Sagwitch, who had survived the Bear River Massacre a decade earlier and had resisted removal from his homeland ever since, had been moved to cast his lot with the Mormons. Although it was true that the church could offer some measure of subsistence and protection, there was more to Sagwitch's decision. Mormons, like Hill, viewed the world, and spoke, in prophetic terms that paralleled his own understandings. Indeed, it was the vision of an "old Bannock Indian" that Hill later credited with igniting the Indian fervor for the church.

In the summer of 1872, Hill recounted, Ech-up-way was camped with his people southwest of the Great Salt Lake when three strangers came into his lodge to discuss religious matters. In appearance they were Indians, but they counseled him to abandon Indian ways. They said, "The 'Mormons'' God was the true God, and that He and the Indians' Father were one; that he must go to the 'Mormons,' and they would tell him what to do, and that he must do it; that he must be baptized with all his Indians; that the time was at hand for the Indians to gather, and stop their Indian life, and learn to cultivate the earth and build houses, and live in them."[39] Then the strangers told him to look, and in place of the skin wall of his lodge was a vision of the Bear River country with prosperous Indian farms scattered across the land. The three men told him that once he settled there, they would visit again. He looked away and then back toward them, but they had disappeared. According to the missionary, it was not until four years later, after witnessing the scene the strange visitors had shown him, that Ech-up-way told Hill of the vision and his reason for seeking baptism.[40] Thus, while some Indian peoples interpreted the Ghost Dance prophecy as a message of militant resistance, others interpreted it as a sign to seek power through people who seemed to understand the world in the same way. In essence, Indians like Sagwitch and Ech-up-way and white Mormons like Hill created a religious middle ground, a set of creative misunderstandings that, at least for the moment, brought them together.[41]

Most white officials and observers dismissed or ignored the spiritual dimension of the unrest of 1872 and instead looked for more material ways to control the Indians' "wild freedom." In Idaho this meant renewed demands to consolidate and keep all Newe peoples, especially the Bannocks, at Fort Hall. Agent Johnson High placed the blame on the government rather than the Bannocks and suggested a simple solution: the government must fulfill the promises it had made at Fort Bridger. "There should be provisions made for subsisting them at home [Fort Hall]," he argued, "at least until they find among their number a chief with influence enough to control them." Then, as long as the government kept faith, the transforming effect of agriculture would do the rest, and even the "wild blanket Indians" would become upstanding farmers.[42] The *Idaho Statesman* was far less optimistic and suggested an equally simple, if less humane answer: kill any Indian who left the reservation. Charging that "there really are no limits to the reservation," the paper attacked the "pretended treaty" and identified independent Newe bands living on the Weiser, Owyhee, Malheur, Bruneau, Bitterroot, Salmon, and Lemhi rivers, and even one small group on the Boise River three miles from town.[43] Although the perception of great numbers of Indians roving the countryside was common among Idaho settlers, many Indians sought to avoid the conflicts by staying on the reservation. By January 1873, there were between 1,200 and 1,500 people scraping by on meager rations at Fort Hall.[44]

Gov. Bennett, who did not relish the prospect of a general Indian war, promoted what became the most acceptable solution to white officials: a new, more restrictive agreement with the Bannocks and Shoshones. The governor believed that troubles would persist until the "liberal and loose provisions" of the Fort Bridger treaty had been "reformed." Specifically he meant article 4 of the treaty, which guaranteed the Indians a broad right to hunt on the "unoccupied lands" of the United States. Legal or not, Bennett argued, well-armed "painted savages" roaming around isolated settlements created "intense excitement and fear."[45] He felt war was imminent unless settlers believed the "government was taking steps to protect them," yet also argued that "good faith with the Indians should be fully observed." Bennett proposed a new agreement that "*definitely* and *particularly*" described the root grounds, hunting areas, and fishing sites outside the reservation protected for Indian use. Once these areas had been defined, the Shoshones and Bannocks would be "resolutely kept in these lands, and their rights vigorously guarded."[46] The secretary of the interior agreed and appointed Bennett, the Fort Hall agent Henry W. Reed, and Rep. John P. C. Shanks of Indiana to negotiate a "reformation" of the Fort Bridger treaty.[47]

When the commission met with the combined Shoshones and Bannocks at Fort Hall in early November, Reed reported that the results were "apparently satisfactory to all concerned." That satisfaction may have had more to do with the distribution of annuities than with the agreement itself. Without precise council minutes, there is no way to gauge the understandings of the native leaders involved. What is clear is that the agreement achieved the commission's principal goal. The Fort Hall tribes would relinquish their right to hunt outside the reservation without the agent's written permission. For its part, the government would strictly forbid white trespass on the reservation. Finally, any Indian who decided to settle down and become a farmer would receive a house and a milk cow provided by the government. But despite Agent Reed's assertion that native rights to the Camas Prairie must be protected if there was to be a lasting peace, the agreement did not reaffirm Indian rights to the area or call for any concrete steps to protect those rights.[48]

The 1873 agreement proved to be no solution at all. Congress never ratified it and even made matters worse the following year: a provision of the 1874 Indian appropriations bill required all able-bodied men to work for their rations. Reed immediately requested an exemption for Fort Hall. Enforcing such a policy, he argued, would simply drive Indians, especially the Bannocks, off the reservation: "Our Indians *know* that they can get something of a living by hunting, digging camas & roaming generally, especially with their annuity goods, the matter of getting a living from agriculture is an experiment, especially when the crops are liable to be destroyed by crickets and grasshoppers." He estimated that it would take years to convince the Bannocks to live by agriculture and stock raising alone.[49] The now-old story of inadequate funding and rations continued for the remainder of the decade as conditions spiraled downward at Fort Hall. As the reservation struggled through the 1870s, the government was unwilling to commit even the barest of resources to facilitate its stated goal of consolidation. Ultimately, no government plan or program did as much to encourage consolidation as did white encroachment and destruction of the native subsistence base. Life away from Fort Hall became increasingly difficult during the 1870s, until the Bannock and Sheep-Eater wars at the end of the decade made it next to impossible for large bands to live safely off the reservation.

Tyhee's emergence as the principal Bannock chief at Fort Hall in 1874 marked a move toward accommodation among the Bannocks and illustrated the complexities facing native leaders during the early reservation era. Pan-sook-amotse had died over the winter of a "lingering illness," and Pagwite spent most of the next several years off the reservation. Unlike these men or Taghee, who preceded them, Tyhee's status was clearly that of a "reservation" chief. His core following consisted of the small but growing number of Bannocks who remained on the reservation. He had little influence over the majority of the Bannocks during their time off the reservation. Like the Shoshone leader Captain Jim, he appropriated the crucial symbol of agriculture, which improved Agent

Reed's view of the Bannocks. The Shoshones' "reputation, at least, is the best by far," but the Bannocks, he argued, were not that bad. With the exception of a few wild young men, Reed felt "they can be managed as easily as other Indians." The Bannocks were also particularly fond of herding, and the agent believed that stock-raising, rather than agriculture, held the greatest promise for their future. In December 1874 Tyhee and the other "chiefs and headmen" asked the agent for the necessary plows, wagons, and harnesses to begin farming. That spring five families, including Tyhee's, planted some forty-two acres. William Danilson, who had returned for a second stint as agent by the summer of 1875, was optimistic that another twenty families would take up the plow within a year. The Bannock chief again set the example: "Tyee has a very comfortable house on his farm in which he lives, and the other families desire houses on their farms."[50] Tyhee perhaps understood better than the rest of his kinsmen the restrictions that they faced. His actions that summer reveal an adept political leader whose influence grew as options outside the reservation vanished.

In 1875, however, many Bannocks could still envision a more autonomous life and completely rejected the government's attempts to turn them into white men. While Tyhee took up farming, the "nonprogressive" Bannock faction, led by Pagwite, brought the downfall of the first great symbol of the assimilation program, the Fort Hall school. Agent Reed had hired Peter O. Matthews, "an educated Indian," from Tulare Lake, California, as teacher the previous year. Pagwite charged that Matthews had traded annuity goods for sex with some of the schoolgirls. Reed and his successor Danilson supported the teacher, even when allegations arose that Matthews had threatened to "measure arms" with Pagwite unless the latter kept his mouth shut.[51] The agents lumped all of Matthew's accusers together as an undesirable element and argued that the charges were but a thinly veiled attack on the school and "progress." Reed also believed that the Catholic Church and its missionary, Father Touissant Mesplie, were working against the school.[52] Danilson made no mention of the religious angle but rather blamed a coalition of disgruntled Indians and meddling white men. "The Indian Pagwite is not a chief," he wrote, "and is one of the most miserable and worthless Indians in the Bannock tribe." As for J. M. Fisher, who detailed Pagwite's charges in a letter to the commissioner, Danilson reported that he had fired the man as an "unfit person to be on the reservation" only one day before he wrote to Washington. Finally, Danilson characterized James Dempsey, who had also made allegations against

Matthews, as a "Squaw man [who] because of his meddlesome, lying, mischief making proclivities was forcibly ejected from the reservation in October 1875." Matthews himself soon left Fort Hall, and two years later, while serving as teacher at Fort Peck, he was still trying to clear his name.[53] The Matthews affair may well have indicated another bid by Pagwite to assume leadership of the Fort Hall Bannocks. It certainly foreshadowed the long struggle over the Fort Hall school that epitomized the cultural wars of assimilation in the 1880s and 1890s.

The majority of the Bannocks, however, continued to spend the greater part of the year away from Fort Hall, while the Shoshone population on the reservation increased. "Quite a number of the Bannacks" had decided to settle down and remain at Fort Hall over the winter of 1874–75, but with such a large combined population the beef supply ran out by January. "They became thoroughly disgusted with the reservation," wrote Danilson, "and early this summer struck out for their old hunting grounds." Danilson estimated that 1,500 Indians—600 Bannocks and 900 Shoshones—"belonged" at Fort Hall. Yet only five hundred were present when he took a count in July 1875. He carried out a more exact census in November, when most of the Indians had returned, and found 964 Shoshone and 398 Bannocks. He estimated that another 250 Bannocks were off on the hunt. In the autumn of 1876, only 212 Bannocks were present on annuity day, compared to 845 Shoshones.[54] Quite clearly the Bannocks had no faith in the government's promises if not even the lure of annuity goods could draw them from the ever more precarious buffalo hunt. Meanwhile, the Shoshones came to demographically dominate the reservation, and Bannock resentment grew.

In 1875, as conditions on the Fort Hall reservation reached their nadir, another wave of Ghost Dance excitement washed over Indian peoples as well as their white Mormon neighbors. Among the first to hear of the doctrine were the Southern Paiutes in the southwestern Utah. A. H. Thompson, who led a party from the United States Geological Survey into the area in the spring of 1875, recalled that "a great excitement was caused among the Indians by the report that two mysterious beings with white skins . . . had appeared among the Paiute far to the west and announced a speedy resurrection of all the dead Indians, the restoration of the game, and the return of the old-time primitive life. Under the new order of things, moreover, both races alike were to be white."[55] The two prophets may have been Wodziwob and Frank Spencer, who by 1875 was probably the principal proselytizer of the religion.

There is also the possibility, as James Mooney hinted, that Mormon influence was in some way related to the excitement.[56] The parallels between Mormon and Ghost Dance doctrine reported by Thompson are striking, and it appears that once again Mormon leaders sought to engage their followers as well as Indian peoples in a prophetic discourse. The white-skinned prophets bring to mind stories of Mormon theology's Three Nephites, celestial beings who were expected to appear on earth in the last days. Although Mooney was apparently unaware of this aspect of Mormon doctrine, he did report that the "Mormon priests accepted it [the Ghost Dance doctrine] as a prophecy of speedy fulfillment of their own traditions." Orson Pratt, a prominent Mormon leader, was said to have preached a sermon "urging the faithful to arrange their affairs and put their houses in order to receive the long-awaited wanderers."[57]

The intersection of Mormon and Ghost Dance doctrine, combined with the general mistrust of the church's activities among American Indians, led many nineteenth-century observers to conclude that the Mormons had instigated the Ghost Dances as part of a wider plan to disrupt federal authority in the West.[58] The church's successful missions among the Shoshones, Bannocks, and Paiutes led to a flood of accusations. One Idaho official charged that the missions had made the Indians "entirely subservient to the authorities of the Mormon Church." The Wind River agent reported that a number of Shoshones had been baptized and exhorted to "drive the gentiles out of Utah, and take possession of their ranches and property." And the Nevada agent C. A. Bateman feared that the baptisms would recall the "spirit actuating the famed Mountain Meadows massacre."[59] Although it is certain that the Mormons did not invent the Ghost Dances, considering their residence among the Bannocks, Shoshones, and Paiutes, their millenarian doctrine, and their prolonged missionary activities among Indian peoples, it is quite possible that parts of their doctrine had merged with the Ghost Dance doctrine. Whether the events of 1875 were evidence of a Mormon conspiracy, as Danilson believed, is debatable. Later observers made much of the promise of invulnerability and suggested that Mormons inspired the idea of the bulletproof "Ghost Shirts" worn by Lakota dancers in 1890. It is far more probable that Mormon missions among the Indians in the 1870s owed their success in part to the convergence of prophetic doctrines in the Great Basin. And, as with the Mormon fascination with the Bannock prophet nearly two decades earlier, the events prompted Mormons themselves to reexamine their own beliefs.

The charges of Mormon interference and Ghost Dances at Fort Hall must also be understood in the immediate context of the Mormon mission among the Shoshones of northern Utah and the "Corinne Indian scare" that it engendered. Hill had established a new settlement on the Bear River near the Gentile town of Corinne in April 1875. The Indians, mostly members of Sagwitch's Northwestern Shoshone band, went to work planting, and by late summer the mission had counted nearly six hundred baptisms. It also created near hysteria among the notoriously anti-Mormon residents of Corinne. The fact that all of this took place against the backdrop of the trial of John D. Lee, the only man ever charged in connection with the Mountain Meadows Massacre of 1857, only increased tensions.[60] Many of the Indian converts drawn to Bear River were from Fort Hall, and Agent James Wright also complained bitterly about the Mormons: "These Indians are being operated upon by the Mormons, many of them Baptized, others taken through the 'Endowment House' (whatever that is or means) and then called 'The Lords Battle Axes.' The Mormons say that they have appointed missionaries to labor among the Indians. All this means mischief. The Indians are not made better, but much worse."[61]

Wright argued that the civil authorities in Utah had been "sold to the church" and suggested that a special federal agent, supported by the military, was needed to force the Indians back to Fort Hall.[62] Three weeks later Wright reiterated his charges of Mormon interference: "The Mormons have sent Indians to this Agency and Wind River, to inlist the Indians in their favor. Unless the Indians are very soon taken out of Utah there will be trouble."[63] In his annual report, Agent Danilson recounted a version of the doctrine—an intriguing mix of the Ghost Dance beliefs, Mormon theology, and shamanism—which the Mormons were allegedly teaching to the Bear River converts, who in turn brought the message to Fort Hall. The Indians "were told that by being baptized and joining the church, the old men would become young, the young men would never be sick, that the Lord had a work for them to do, and that they were the chosen people of God to establish his kingdom upon the earth, &c.; also that Bear River Valley belonged to them, and if soldiers attempted to drive them away not to go as their guns would have no effect upon them."[64] An earthly paradise was the ultimate promise of the Ghost Dance, and claims of invulnerability were standard within the shamanic and prophetic traditions. Telling the Indians that they were an instrument of God was not unusual for Mormon missionaries, but telling them that they owned the Bear River Valley seems far more risky: why would the

Indians stop with the destruction of the Gentile town of Corinne? Why would they not then question Mormon rights in Utah?

Ultimately it was Sagwitch's and Hill's mission community that became the casualty of the fear and suspicion. On August 9 the *Corinne Mail* screamed: "Mormons Meddling with the Indians! Mountain Meadows to be Repeated!!" The paper charged that Brigham Young himself had visited the mission and "pronounced a curse on the town," intending to destroy it with his Indian army. But after one alleged attack on the town, it was U.S. troops who arrived and ordered the Indians to disperse. They did so, abandoning most of their crops in the field.[65] According to Danilson, at least, the scare had destroyed the Mormons' credibility. "[The Indians] seem very much disgusted with the whole proceeding," he wrote, "[and] have lost faith in the Mormons." The agent also drafted a letter for the "Bannock and Shoshone Chief and Headmen" to the commissioner of Indian affairs, assuring him of their loyalty. "The Mormons are all the time making bad talk," read the letter; "they have deceived us in many ways and we will not believe them any more." The leaders had called for their people to come home to the reservation from the "Cammas and Yellowstone countries." Many others, of course, had abandoned their fields and crops on Bear River, and they too moved to the relative protection of the Fort Hall reservation. Once again, an increasing population might cause disaster. "Our beef and flour will not last all winter," said Bannock and Shoshone leaders. "What are you going to do?"[66]

The hardships that the Shoshones and Bannocks faced during the winter of 1875–76 were the worst in the reservation's brief history. Congress had again required that all Indians work for their rations. Danilson followed the policy during the summer, when most of the Bannocks and many of the Shoshones were gone, but it became impossible in the fall, when all returned. He acquired an exemption from the secretary of the interior, but that only relieved a legal concern. There was still the problem of actually feeding the people. The weekly beef issue was enough for one square meal; the flour and potatoes might last five days. By 1 March, the supplies were nearly exhausted, and Danilson returned to the policy of feeding only the farmhands. By 1 April, he could not even do that, and instead he issued rations only to the "old and infirm." The rest would have to fend for themselves—with snow still on the ground and little game. "It is not an easy matter to describe how an agent with any feeling of humanity is affected under these circumstances," he wrote, "or to convince the Indians it is not his fault that more food is not furnished."[67] That same year, an army officer who visited Fort Hall reported the miserable conditions and "dissatisfaction" he found. Capt. J. L. Viven reported that the Indians were upset that they could get no word on the 1873 agreement; they could not understand why the government did not live up to its promises when they had fulfilled their own. There was little choice but to allow them to go to the Camas Prairie and hunt for a living. He also ominously noted, "All of them have horses and can mount the various members of their families and be off in an hour's time, besides, many have very fine and good fire-arms."[68] Within two years, Capt. Viven's ominous words came true.

Each summer from 1877 to 1879, warfare visited the Idaho Territory. The first and most famous of these conflicts was the Nez Percé War. The story of Joseph's people and their flight toward Canada became the stuff of legends. At the other end of the spectrum was the Sheep-Eater War of 1879. This little-known series of skirmishes in the remote Salmon River country was less a war than a manufactured conflict. Between the celebrated and the forgotten came the Bannock War of 1878, which was a little of both. Prominently remembered by Idaho's pioneer generation, it merits barely a footnote in most modern histories of the West and of American Indians. In fact, it was a turning point in the history of the Newe peoples. It marked the end of militant resistance to the reservation system and crystallized the Bannocks' reputation as hostile, intractable opponents of the white men and their programs. More important, the disaffection between Shoshones and Bannocks that had grown during the early reservation years became evident in the months preceding the war. The social differentiation and conflict over scarce resources that had given rise to distinct reservation "peoples" helped determine who participated in the hostilities. The war sharpened those distinctions at the same time that it demonstrated the growing expression of an Indian identity.

The reasons for the Bannock War are complex. On one level, the war was clearly a response to relentless white intrusion. The Wood River incident six years earlier had not prevented a steadily increasing number of white stockmen from driving thousands of cattle and hogs onto the Great Camas Prairie. But the growing ethnic distinctions between Bannocks and Shoshones also shaped the conflict. Like nearly ever other "Indian war" in American history, this was not a racial war. Only a minority of the Newes chose to fight, and ethnic animosity was an important factor in an individual's decision to go to war or stay out of the fray. Both the growing Shoshone population at Fort Hall and the constant struggle over annuities raised and focused Bannock dissatisfaction and anger. The hostile force consisted principally of the young men of the buffalo-hunting bands, the Bannocks. Their sense of ethnicity was a product of the social and economic change magnified by the political demands of the treaty and reservation eras. Yet on several occasions the militants attempted to overcome ethnic divisions and recruit allies by appealing to a new racial identity: a sense of Indianness. In 1878 the appeal failed, and thus the Bannock War testifies to the social identities that separated Indian peoples more than to those that united them. The Bannock War must also be understood within the tradition of religious militancy that marked resistance to white expansion and the reservation system in the 1870s. Once again, the messages of native prophets instilled a sense of Indianness and rallied opposition.

In the summer of 1877, anxiety over the Nez Percé War gripped all of Idaho Territory. Fearing that the disputed root grounds on the Great Camas prairie would be the wellspring of a second Indian war, Governor Mason Brayman met with fourteen Newe leaders, including Captain Jim, the Shoshone chief at Fort Hall who had left the reservation; his brother, Major George, a Bannock headman from Fort Hall; Bannock John, who spent his winters at Salmon Falls on the Snake River; and Major Jim, a subchief of the Lemhi band.[69] Major Jim got to the heart of the problem when, after forcing the governor to admit that the Indians had owned the Great Camas Prairie first, he said:

> Your people make farms and fence up all the country, the Indians make their farm too, which is the Great Camas Prairie, where our women dig roots to feed them and the children. The white men drive too many hogs and cattle upon the prairie, which eat up the roots of the camas and destroy the plant. We cannot eat without food, and the camas root has always been our food. When the camas is destroyed our children will suffer from hunger. . . . We never sold or gave away the Camas Prairie. We had nothing to do with any treaty which would take it away from us.[70]

Also present at the council was a young Bannock warrior named Buffalo Horn, who had made a name for himself during the Lakota campaign of 1876–77. As the lone Bannock among the Crow scouts, he gained renown for his bold and fearless style. In his most famous exploit, he took a dispatch from Crook's camp on the Powder River to Nelson A. Miles's column on the Yellowstone. Riding in the company of Thomas Leforge, the "White Crow Indian" who commanded the scouts, and William F. "Buffalo Bill" Cody, he passed through miles of dangerous territory with the message.[71] The *Idaho Statesman* trumpeted his "distinguished service" and reported that he had personally killed a Lakota chief at the Battle of Wolf Mountain.[72] When the army wanted scouts for the Nez Percé campaign, it needed to look no farther than the Newe encampments on the Camas Prairie. Buffalo Horn was among the first group of twenty scouts to join General Oliver O. Howard's pursuit of the Nez Percés in late July.

As the war scare spread, most of the Shoshones and Bannocks returned to the relative safety of the reservations, aggravating the shortages of food and supplies. The annual appropriation for Fort Hall was adequate only if most of the Indians abandoned the reservation during the summer. On the eve of the Nez Percé war, slightly more than 500 Indians were living full-time at Fort Hall, with approximately 100 more "coming and going." Danilson estimated that 700 were camped on the Great Camas Prairie, with 50 more in the Cache Valley of northern Utah and a band of 150 hunting in western Montana. All were absent with his permission, and the agent felt that white settlers, "feeling revengeful towards all Indians," posed the greater risk to the peace.[73] Agent Fuller reported similar conditions at Lemhi, with two large groups under Tendoy and Pegge absent with his permission.[74] With the outbreak of war, hundreds who normally would have been hunting, fishing, and digging roots over thousands of square miles returned to the reservation. Danilson feared that if they were not fed, they might join the hostile Nez Percés. By July there were seven hundred Indians at Fort Hall and no flour left. The following month the population had reached nine hundred, nearly twice as many as any previous August. Eventually the Indian Department allowed Danilson to purchase three months' worth of emergency rations.[75]

The additional food averted starvation, but Fort Hall did not emerge unscathed from the Nez Percé conflict. As Joseph's people fled east, wild rumors swept the agency. The unrest peaked on the morning of 8 August 1877, when a white "tramp" who lived on the reservation claimed he had been accosted by hostile Indians. Word spread that the Nez Percés were close at hand, and soon the Bannocks were "riding back and forth hurriedly, driving in their horses." "The excitement increased as the day advanced," wrote Danilson, "and about 10:00 o'clock A.M. a young Bannock warrior started on the war path alone."[76] His name was Pe-tope, and, wearing his finest "war habiliments" and armed with a Winchester rifle and a revolver, he rode toward the agency. He soon encountered two teamsters and shot one in the neck. Several Indians saw the attack and gave chase, but before they could overtake Pe-tope, he fired on another freighter, wounding him in the leg. Both men survived.

Danilson reported that "the headmen of both tribes denounced the shooting, and promised that the murderer should be arrested and severely punished."[77] Pe-tope, however, had escaped from the reservation, and arresting him would be no simple matter. Danilson therefore jumped at the army's request to recruit more Indian auxiliaries at Fort Hall. He hoped that the additional enlistments would, in a single stroke, reduce the reservation's population, relieve the food shortages, and quiet the most troublesome element at Fort Hall.[78]

Although they are known in the historical record as the Bannock scouts, many Shoshones also joined the unit. Stanton G. Fisher, the autocratic, fearless Fort Hall trader and future agent, served as chief scout. Madison John, Pagwite, Jerry Ballard, Good Year, and Bronco Jim were his sergeants. Four mixed-bloods, who acted as Fisher's aides and intermediaries throughout the campaign, rounded out the company. The half-Shoshone Rainey brothers, Charley and Joe, worked as Fisher's interpreters and remained close associates during the agent's long career at Fort Hall. Jules Chimeneau was a mixed-blood Cheyenne, and Baptiste "Bat" Avery was "a little French-man [and Flathead] one shade darker than Rainey." Avery also became a fixture at Fort Hall. After his term with the scouts he married a Shoshone woman, settled on the reservation, and was eventually put on the tribal rolls as a Shoshone.[79]

The scouts' experience during the war was less than satisfying. They possessed very different motivations and expectations from those of their white commanders. In a world where white settlers destroyed the root grounds and game was disappearing, reservation life promised only monotony and starvation. The Nez Percé War was a welcome outlet, one that was particularly appealing to young men who had seen few chances to prove themselves in battle. The scouts who left Fort Hall on 19 August sought prestige and honor in warfare. Two days later messengers arrived with word of the battle at Camas Meadows, only a day's ride from their camp. The scouts threw away their breakfast and "struck out pellmell" for the action.[80] Such opportunities could not be wasted. Arriving at Camas Meadows too late for the fight, the Fort Hall scouts enjoyed a boisterous reunion with their kinsmen. But soon relations between the scouts and the high command soured, culminating in the arrest and detention of Joe Rainey and nine others after a good portion of the teamsters' horse herd went missing. Rainey was eventually sent on to Fort Ellis as a prisoner because of his "cross and mutinous" demeanor.[81]

One humorous yet telling incident during the Nez Percé campaign illustrated the amorphous nature of ethnic and racial identity. It occurred during the scouts' last major engagement. By Fisher's estimation, Charley Rainey's "Injin ambition" had gotten the better of him. Dressed in a "scarlet war rig top[p]ed out with an eagle feathered war bonnet," Rainey and Bat Avery rode off to attack the Nez Percés in a running gun battle. Rainey believed that the nearby soldiers would recognize his distinctive "rig" and hold their fire. When the two scouts stopped in a clump of sagebrush to clean their guns, however, a second group of troopers happened by, mistook them for the enemy, and opened fire. Bullets knocked the feathers from Rainey's bonnet and reportedly ripped through the men's clothing, but neither was injured. At that instant Avery burst from the brush and screamed, "You dam fools you cant tell Injin from white man yet!"[82] The nature of racial and ethnic identity was indeed slippery, and, as demonstrated by Avery, the mixed-blood Salish Frenchman who was soon to become a Shoshone, self-identification was often a determining factor.

Ultimately the scouts' enlistment had no effect on the dire situation at Fort Hall. After a brief visit to the Crows, they returned to a reservation in disarray, with too many people and too little food. Moreover, the Indian bureau was pursuing a course that seemed calculated to ensure unrest. On 17 October, the commissioner of Indian affairs ordered Danilson to cease issuing hunting passes except in an emergency. It was an unreasonable request, and the agent argued that the bureau had for years tacitly accepted hunting as a substitute for proper appropriations.[83] Plans to consolidate even more Shoshones at Fort Hall made the situation worse and threatened to intensify the nascent ethnic animosities. In November the Indian Bureau notified Danilson of plans to move 240 Northwestern Shoshones, then living along the Bear River, to Fort Hall. He accepted that this group "belonged" on the reservation—they were Shoshones and had "friends and relatives" there—but he cautioned that current supplies were inadequate. Danilson also cited open Bannock anger over the growing Shoshone population at Fort Hall. In 1869, he had counted six hundred Bannocks and five hundred Shoshones. Eight years later there were approximately one thousand Shoshones, but the annual appropriation had not increased.[84] A year later (in the aftermath of the Bannock War) Danilson was much more explicit. He argued that the government had "to a certain extent" broken the Fort Bridger treaty of 1868 by concentrating all the "roaming Indians in southeastern Idaho" at Fort Hall. At first the Bannocks appeared unconcerned; they outnumbered the Shoshones, and their subsistence cycle took them away from the reservation for much of the year. As buffalo became scarce, the "Shoshones kept coming," and the government furnished no additional supplies, the Bannocks began to resent consolidation. In the months before the Bannock War, "the Bannocks complained about the Shoshones having their supplies, and looked upon them as intruders on their lands. There was a bad feeling existing between the two tribes; the Bannocks were restless, were inclined to be quarrelsome, and were constantly committing petty thefts against the Shoshones."[85] The events of the fall of 1877 and the winter and spring of 1878 demonstrated that conditions on the Fort Hall reservation were just as important as the invasion of the Camas Prairie in fostering the outbreak of the Bannock War.

The arrest of the Bannock fugitive Pe-tope was the first in a series of incidents that magnified the growing rift between the Bannocks and Shoshones. By November Pe-tope had returned to the main Bannock encampment. Danilson told the Bannock headmen that they must bring him in, and, to his surprise, they complied. The ease of the transfer amazed Danilson, but just one hour later a young Bannock, a friend of Pe-tope, murdered an employee of the agency beef contractor.[86] The spiral of events leading to the Bannock War had begun.

The hunt for the new fugitive proved even more disruptive and enraged the Bannocks. The morning after the shooting, Agent Danilson and Capt. Augustus Bainbridge, the commander of the Fort Hall military post, told a large assembly of Shoshones and Bannocks that the murderer, Tambiago, must be arrested and tried for his crime. But at this point the search for the killer ran head-on into ethnicity at Fort Hall. The Shoshones refused to help, saying "had he been one of their tribe they would have arrested him at once, but as he was a Bannock he should be arrested by his own people." The Bannocks then agreed to arrest the wanted man but returned empty-handed. After several more attempts to arrest Tambiago, Danilson "became convinced that they did not want to or else were afraid to make the arrest." The agent also feared "that the majority of the Bannocks were hostile" and was "satisfied they [were] purchasing ammunition . . . and otherwise preparing for war." He saw no option but to call for troops, as "there were more Bannocks here than there had ever been at one time and they were as wild and untamable as could be."[87]

The troops arrived a few days before Christmas, under the command of the arrogant and imprudent Col. John E. Smith. While lamenting the lack of a "head chief" at Fort Hall, Smith believed he could bully the Bannocks and demanded the immediate surrender of Tambiago. The

Shoshones said he was in the Bannock camp but reiterated that it was not their place to arrest him. The Bannocks denied that Tambiago was still on the reservation and claimed they had been prepared to turn him over until they heard that the soldiers were coming. Smith dismissed the Bannock version of events and issued an ultimatum sure to enrage the Bannocks and drive a wedge between the two peoples at Fort Hall. Most of the Fort Hall scouts were in attendance, expecting their pay from the previous summer's campaign. Smith announced that he would withhold the Bannocks' earnings and that if they did not surrender the murderer, "they would not get it at all." "The Shoshone scouts were paid," the colonel reported, "as I wished to show them that a discrimination would be made in favor of those we considered friendly." Smith was not finished. He threatened to cut off rations to the Bannocks and told them that if they did not turn over the accused, he would be "ordered to attack them."[88] It is hard to imagine how Smith could have mishandled the crisis more thoroughly. He knew of the tensions between the Shoshones and Bannocks and of the latter's threat to "kill all the whites in the vicinity, also friendly Indians," yet he chose to aggravate the situation. After all his threats, he did conclude that it would be unwise to "stir [the Bannocks] up" until mounted reinforcements arrived.[89]

In the meantime, it still seemed possible to defuse the crisis. The Bannocks had returned to their camps at the cedars, a heavily wooded area two and a half miles from the river. On 9 January 1878, Tambiago was arrested north of the reservation. With the killer in custody, Danilson asked that the military "let matters drop" until the Bannocks could be permanently removed from Fort Hall.[90] But the army could not be dissuaded. At 2:00 A.M. on 16 January the cavalry rode into the two Bannock camps. The fifty-three warriors present put up no physical resistance but hurled "threats and insults toward the soldiers." The troops tore down the lodges, seized thirty-two old rifles and approximately three hundred ponies, and marched the Bannocks, Tambiago's father and brothers among them, to the agency. Danilson was aghast. The horses were not the best of the Bannock herds, and the haul of only a handful of aging weapons (Danilson stressed that "*no* pistols" were found) meant the Bannocks had hidden their best firearms. With Col. Smith's threats hanging in the air, the army's action had come as no surprise to them. The cavalry was scheduled to leave in two days, and Danilson begged that they take all the Bannocks with them.[91] In his view, in exchange for a few worthless old weapons, the army had guaranteed a war come spring.

Soon reports began to suggest that war was indeed imminent. One local observer, Frank J. Parker, predicted that the settlers had little to fear from the Shoshones. "The Shoshones fear the Bannocks," he wrote, "and therefore they naturally hate them and will assist the whites in case of an uproar." He warned, however, that if the Bannocks chose war, nothing stood in their way. The early months of 1878 saw little snow and consequently few obstacles to travel.[92] Indeed, the most militant Bannocks had already decided on war, and Parker had a good idea of who would lead them: "Buffalo Horn and the remaining young are off and away, no one knows wither. . . . Some say that Buffalo Horn is now a Chief, in which case mischief is certainly brewing."[93] Though his analysis greatly overstated the hatred between Shoshones and Bannocks, Parker's other predictions proved accurate in the spring of 1878. Other observers also saw ethnic dissension between the Bannocks and Shoshones. George Chapin of Goose Creek reported: "There are about 50 Shoshones in Marsh Basin who say they have left the reservation in consequence of threats against them made by the Bannocks."[94] Just who these Shoshones were is not known, but it is clear that, by early 1878, the ethnic struggle at Fort Hall and the crises beginning the previous summer had led them to fear for their lives.

In fact, "friendly" Indians throughout southern Idaho seemed to be preparing for war. At the end of January Captain Jim called on Governor Brayman. He asked the governor to write his brother, Major George, a Bannock leader at Fort Hall, to tell him to remain on the reservation, be friendly to the whites, and side with the soldiers in case of trouble. The governor happily obliged, but less than a month later Captain Jim was back, this time seeking permission for his brother's band to visit his camp on Indian Creek, south of the capital. The sudden change in plans aroused Brayman's suspicions, but neither Captain Jim nor his English-speaking son-in-law, Sandy, would directly answer the governor's questions about Major George's motives and the "disposition of the Bannocks." They did tell him, however, "the old men—the good Indians—want peace, the young men were very bad." From this the governor inferred that "Major George sees trouble ahead and wishes to be out of the way."[95]

By early spring, Buffalo Horn and the militants had begun recruiting allies. They did so in part by appealing to a shared identity. They began their efforts among the Western Shoshones of the Duck Valley Reservation. In early April, the agency farmer Levi A. Gheen heard reports that the Bannocks were seeking allies and had threatened to kill him and

Captain Sam, the "main Captain" or dai'gwahni' at Duck Valley, if they stood in the way. When the agent arrived at Duck Valley, he found Captain Sam's band, as well as some Bannocks "from the Camas Prairie" and Shoshones from Fort Hall. The latter told Gheen that only a few Bannocks wanted war, but that these "unruly ones" held great influence. They asked the agent to intercede in the conflict by doing whatever he could to get the troops withdrawn from Fort Hall and the captured ponies returned. They promised that if the farmer did this, they would peacefully return to Fort Hall.[96] They may have been trying to scare Gheen, but it is just as likely that the Fort Hall Indians were measuring his willingness to help them. Gheen was well-liked by the Western Shoshones. He spoke their language and had served as an agent and farmer for nearly a decade. His close alliance with Captain Sam was instrumental in the selection of Duck Valley as a reservation.[97] The visitors certainly knew of Gheen's reputation and may therefore have sought his intervention to stop the war. The agent, however, told them that the Western Shoshones would never join in a war against the whites, that he had no influence at Fort Hall, and that they should return to their home reservation. Stinging from Gheen's rebuke, the Bannocks and Shoshones rode off, repeating their threats against him.[98]

In a later statement, Captain Sam suggested that the Bannocks had used a racial sense of Indianness in their appeal for allies. They designated the whites as a "common enemy" of the "Indians." After Captain Sam refused their demands for alliance, they had grown angry and promised that "when they had destroyed the railways and killed the whites, they would divide both sides of the world among their friends and kill all the Indians who had not united with them."[99] This "promise" was reminiscent of Pashego's prophecy five years earlier, after the Wood River murder, and calls to mind the more militant versions of the Ghost Dance doctrine. In essence they were saying: If you are not with us, you are not an "Indian." Captain Sam declined to join the hostile alliance, but he understood its motivations and played on his loyalty to the whites to help his people. Such loyalty could be dangerous, and during the conflict Captain Sam's control over his people was sorely tested. In one incident a group of whites opened fire on two of his young men. They escaped unharmed, with a wounded horse and a lesson in racial attitudes. Captain Sam told the Nevada superintendent, A. J. Barnes, that the government would be well-advised to intervene and prevent "bad white men from imposing on Indians and forcing them into retaliation." Another Western Shoshone told Gheen, "There was no dependence to be put in the white people, that while the Shoshones were doing all in their power to protect them, the whites were trying to kill them."[100] It was a simple fact that, more often than not, white settlers did not see a Shoshone or a Bannock; they saw only an Indian. Such shared experience could help forge a new shared identity.

The Bannocks' entreaties failed at Duck Valley, but they succeeded among the Northern Paiutes at the troubled Malheur Reservation. Created by executive order in 1872 for "all the roving and straggling bands in Eastern and Southern Oregon," Malheur's history was similar to Fort Hall's in that government appropriations never met the needs of the population.[101] Yet during the reservation's first years, the situation seemed manageable. The energetic and sympathetic agent Samuel B. Parrish formed a strong alliance with the Paiute leader Egan. A Cayuse by birth, Egan was captured as a small boy and rose to prominence as a war leader during the Snake War of the 1860s. Afterward he settled at Malheur, where his friendship with Parrish paralleled the Gheen–Captain Sam alliance at Duck Valley. Both men benefited; Parrish saw agricultural "progress," and Egan enjoyed the respect and influence due to a successful leader. According to O. O. Howard, "Through Egan the Indians came to love Major Parrish."[102] All that changed in 1876, when a new, far less sympathetic agent came to Malheur. W. V. Rinehart was allegedly corrupt, arguably incompetent, and clearly hostile. He treated the Paiutes like obstreperous children and in the process undercut Egan's influence. He told them that the government owned the reservation, and if they wanted food and clothing, they must labor for a dollar a day. Rinehart also fired Sarah Winnemucca, daughter of the famous Northern Paiute leader, from her position as agency interpreter after she had made charges against him. On the eve of the war, it was to Sarah that Egan turned, asking her to plead their people's case to Washington.[103]

Corruption and deprivation alone cannot explain Malheur involvement in the Bannock War; there was also a religious dimension. Although Egan was the acknowledged civil leader of the Malheur bands, Oytes was an influential headman, a spiritual leader, and a disciple of the Dreamer prophet Smohalla.[104] He was also a shaman and was feared as a witch. Rinehart reported that it was Oytes who kept Winnemucca's band from settling at Malheur. He wrote that it was the old chief's "unshaken belief" that "Oits . . . has the power of witchcraft, and he will practice his evil enchantments until every Piute except his own little band is driven through fear from the agency."[105] It is also clear that Oytes used the prophetic complex, if not the Ghost Dance doctrine itself, to garner support during the Bannock War. In his official report of the campaign, Gen. Howard reported that Oytes had "prophesied that the time had come when the Indians were to destroy the whites and recover their country."[106] The shaman himself reportedly exclaimed, "I can defeat all my enemies! No bullet can hurt me. I have the power to kill any of you! It is wrong to dig up the face of the earth—the earth is our mother; we must live upon what grows of itself."[107] Oytes's statement is a revealing combination of Smohalla's doctrine—the proscription against plowing Mother Earth—and traditional aspects of Great Basin shamanism, such as the claims of invulnerability and threats of sorcery. Parrish had been able to keep Oytes in check, sometimes in novel ways. He reportedly once offered the prophet $350 if he would allow the agent to fire a bullet at his chest. Oytes declined the challenge. General Howard believed that only after Rinehart replaced Parrish did Oytes' power and influence increase.[108] Likewise, in her account of the Bannock War, Sarah Winnemucca depicted Oytes as an evil, power-hungry man who led the Northern Paiutes into the conflict and the good chief Egan to his death. Her opinions were no doubt biased by her father's experience and her sympathy for Egan, whom she viewed as the legitimate leader at Malheur.[109]

The first Bannock runners had arrived at Malheur at the end of March, and others followed throughout the spring of 1878. They carried word of the trouble at Fort Hall, suggested that the army had similar plans for the Northern Paiutes, and revealed that "when the grass came, the women and children would leave Fort Hall and go to Camas Prairie; that the men would go to the buffalo country to fight the soldiers."[110] Within three weeks, more Bannock emissaries had arrived, and in an angry meeting on 14 April the Northern Paiutes accused their agent, W. V. Rinehart, "of concealing the true state of affairs in order to deliver them over to the military." Rinehart became more concerned over the next several weeks, as Paiutes and Shoshones streamed onto the reservation at the very time they would normally have left for the root grounds and fisheries.[111] On 13 May the Owyhee County sheriff telegraphed Fort Boise complaining that a band of nearly one hundred Bannocks camped near Silver City were "endeavoring to induce the Piutes to join them to go on the war path."[112] When troops arrived they found only an abandoned campsite. Shortly thereafter, Thomas Silvey, who kept substantial herds on the Great Camas Prairie, sent word to Boise that large numbers of Indians were heading there.[113] In all probability, the combined Bannock–Northern Paiute camp near Silver City had dispersed along with the core group of "hostile" Bannocks following Buffalo Horn toward the Camas Prairie and the Malheur people returning to the reservation in Oregon.

Rumors of the impending war swirled as the annual gathering of Shoshone and Bannock bands began on the Great Camas Prairie. Some of the "hostile" Bannocks were already there, as were larger numbers of "friendly" Indians. There were also a number of white herdsmen and an estimated 2,500 head of cattle on the prairie.[114] Buffalo Horn had not gone straight to the Camas Prairie but stopped in Boise, most probably fresh from the council with the Malheurs, looking for ammunition. After the officers at Fort Boise and several merchants denied his requests, the Bannock leader appealed to Governor Brayman. He assured the governor that after his people had dug the camas, they would return to Fort Hall. In light of Buffalo Horn's previous service, and hoping to ease tensions, Brayman scribbled a short note to a local storekeeper: "Buffalo Horn wants say $2 worth Winchester cartridges for deer hunting. He is loyal." The Bannocks then purchased one hundred cartridges and a pound of powder, and several days later they left for the Camas Prairie.[115] Although the governor may have believed, or more likely hoped, that Buffalo Horn would keep the peace, he also feared that conflict was becoming unavoidable. Two weeks after Buffalo Horn visited Boise, Brayman wrote prophetically to Gen. Oliver O. Howard, "I do not think the Bannocks intend war, but do fear personal collision and bloodshed, with their wide-spread consequences." He suggested that the cavalry commander at Fort Boise make a "pleasant summer march to Camas Prairie, and *show* his force."[116]

Before Brayman's recommendation could reach Howard, the "personal collision" he so feared occurred. Just after dawn on 30 May 1878, two Bannocks rode into the Silvey cattle camp on the Camas Prairie. One was Bannock John's son Joe, reportedly a "wild, young, and quarrelsome" man who had spent the previous evening gambling and drinking. He offered to trade a buffalo robe to the three white men present. When they examined the robe, Joe opened fire, severely wounding two of the men. While the herdsmen made a desperate escape, their assailants returned to the Bannock camp, where Joe's rash action forced a moment of decision. Remembering the army's threats that all would suffer for any depredations by any one of their kinsmen, Buffalo Horn reasoned that since they would all be punished, they "might as well start in, go on the war path and get some horses and property."[117]

The decision to go to war shattered the Indian encampments on the prairie. Major Jim and Joe Rainey, who were traveling from Lemhi toward Camas Prairie when they met the retreating bands, claimed that the Bannocks had nearly begun fighting among themselves. Ultimately the peaceful faction headed for Fort Hall or Lemhi; those for war—totaling no more than two hundred, mostly young men—followed Buffalo Horn south toward the Snake River. The typical militant was young and a member of one of the "wealthier" buffalo-hunting bands. Many were Shoshone speakers. These men felt the pressures of reservation life most acutely. Although women, children, and older men went just as hungry when the supplies ran out, they were not subject to the same cultural pressures as the young warriors. Their frustration and hostility increased as opportunities to prove themselves in battle and provide for their people diminished. They envied Buffalo Horn, one of a handful of young men who had gone to war in the 1870s and emerged a famed and feared warrior. For some, these concerns overrode ethnic, band and generational factors. In the mid–twentieth century Willie George, a Boise Shoshone, recalled his father's and grandfather's reasons for following Buffalo Horn: "I guess father forgot about the good things he learned at Fort Hall and began to think he might get his chance to live like an old-time Shoshone after all. And apparently my grandfather decided he would rather die as a free Shoshone than a reservation farmer."[118] The abandoned lodge poles standing like skeletons in the Bannock camp testified to the haste of the decision. As word spread to the other Indian camps, a general exodus from the Camas Prairie began. A few more Shoshones and Bannocks undoubtedly rode off to join Buffalo Horn, but once again the vast majority chose peace. Tendoy started his people for Lemhi the next morning, while Captain Jim left for Fort Hall with a mixed group of Shoshones and Bannocks.[119]

The shattering effect of the outbreak was not restricted to the Idaho bands. At Malheur, Egan made one last effort to hold his people together and prevent them from joining the Bannocks. On ration day (1 June) forty-six Bannocks were among the Northern Paiutes. "Chief Egan begged me to give them rations as visitors," Rinehart reported, "and upon my refusal he divided his own with them and both parties left at once."[120] Egan's request was a symbolic test and a final attempt to convince his people that his influence with the government was still strong and that war was not necessary. Rinehart missed the message entirely. He saw "no evidence of hostile intent" in Egan's actions. But he could not ignore what happened next. At noon on 5 June "all the working Indians quit and left the agency without giving notice or assigning cause." The next day, the few remaining Paiutes slipped off the reservation; then, fearing for his life, Rinehart also fled.[121] Although neither the Paiutes nor the agent could know it, that day effectively marked the death of the Malheur Reservation.

As the war began, Buffalo Horn and his followers tried to overcome the divisions that consistently hindered their search for allies by asserting a racial sense of "Indianness." If reservation life at Fort Hall had helped reify social divisions as ethnic identity, federal policy also exerted a simultaneous and seemingly contrary effect: the creation of a racial identity out of shared experience. Similar processes, though not always involving the creation of racial identity, have taken place throughout American history. The literature on African Americans and the southern and eastern European immigrants of the nineteenth and twentieth centuries demonstrates how individuals with widely divergent cultural backgrounds can find a common identity through shared experience.[122] Likewise, one of the metahistories of Indian America is the creation of one out of many. Although Bannocks and Shoshones responded differently to reservation life, both groups were subject to the dispossession of their lands and near starvation rations on the reservation. The growing saliency of ethnic identity was part of the reservation experience, but so was the inescapable fact that ultimately Shoshones and Bannocks were more alike than different.

Buffalo Horn was voicing these developments when he demanded that all "Indians" join him. For the most part his appeal failed, but it illustrated the both the nascent quality of racial identity and the complexities of survival. Moving south and west from the Camas Prairie, the hostile group raided along the Snake River toward the Bruneau Valley. Near Glenn's Ferry, Bruneau John and his family encountered Buffalo Horn, who demanded that they join his band. Bruneau John refused, arguing that it was impossible to kill all the white people because "they keep coming just like the grass." Besides, he added, he did not own a gun. To this, the enraged Bannock responded: "You have the same kind of skin as I have, and if you don't join me I will kill you too. . . . I am going through Bruneau and Duck Valley and I will eat you and the whites too."[123] Bruneau John and his family slipped out of the Bannock camp that night. He decided to cast his lot with the whites and hurried downstream to Dorsey's ferry at the mouth of the Bruneau River. With the boat on the far shore and no ferryman in sight, Bruneau John made a desperate swim across the Snake River and returned with the boat. He and his family rode on to Abraham Robinson's ranch, and from there Robinson and Bruneau John raised the alarm down both banks of the Bruneau River. By the time the Bannocks arrived in the valley, nearly all of the settlers had safely "forted up" at Robinson's Ranch. Bruneau John served as an army scout for the duration of the war, and on his death in 1898 he was heralded as the Paul Revere of Idaho.[124] Rarely were Indian wars clear-cut racial conflicts. Bruneau John's decision to help the settlers reflected the complex reality in which he found himself. Weighing his life and the safety of his family against an amorphous sense of racial loyalty, Bruneau John chose to protect those closest to him. In every conflict, Indian people fought for as well as against the whites. The Bannock War was no different.

Indeed, many of the Indian casualties of the Bannock War came at the hands of other Indians, including Buffalo Horn, who died in the first major clash of the war, near South Mountain, Idaho, on 8 June. Four white volunteers and two of their Paiute scouts also died in the battle. Piute Joe, the lone surviving scout, took credit for killing the Bannock leader. He told Sarah Winnemucca that the Bannocks were "killing everything and everybody, Indians and whites," so he and the other two Paiutes decided to join the volunteers from Silver City. In the heat of battle the company scattered, leaving Joe, according to his own account, to face his death. With no chance of escape he stopped and, using his horse as a shield, fired on the charging warriors. When Buffalo Horn fell from his horse mortally wounded, his shocked and disoriented followers broke off the attack.[125] A tradition among the Paiutes of Fort McDermitt, Nevada, holds that just before the battle, Buffalo Horn had argued with a Paiute leader, who then slipped soap into Bannock warrior's tobacco bag, thus violating a taboo and making him "soft." It is also said, in a story reminiscent of the Horn Chief's demise, that the Paiute scout did not fire a bullet but rather the brass button from a soldier's uniform, which killed the Bannock leader.[126]

After South Mountain, the leaderless Bannocks moved west to meet the Malheur Paiutes at Juniper Lake near Steen's Mountain, Oregon. The scene played out at that encampment mirrored the occasion of the Bannocks' decision to go to war. Winnemucca had left Fort McDermitt on learning of the outbreak, with the intention of keeping the Paiutes out of the fray.[127] But the old chief's declining power over the previous became evident; he had little influence over the Malheur people. Egan was in a better position to argue for peace, but that hope was fading as well. Even before the council at Juniper Lake, Egan reportedly told a white man at Camp Harney that he knew "that there were not enough Indians to whip all the whites, but he would fight as long as he could, and then he thought the Great Father at Washington would give him more supplies, like he did when they quit fighting before."[128] At Juniper Lake, Oytes held sway and for a time, according to Sarah Winnemucca and Gen. Howard, even replaced Egan as chief.[129] But when it became clear that the majority of the Malheurs were for war, and "after long reflection and saving the lives of several friends, whites and red men," as Howard wrote, "Egan at last consented to be their war-chief."[130] Still, many Paiutes rejected war. The militants resorted to promises of "arms and plunder" and then "threats and coercion" to convince some to join them. Sarah Winnemucca, who was working for Howard, secretly arrived in the camp around 14 June. By this time her father was a virtual prisoner of the war faction. She was able to escape with him, most of her family, and a substantial group of antiwar Paiutes. When the hostile faction discovered the escape, they rode out in pursuit and overtook some of the fleeing Indians, whom they forced back to the encampment. Sarah made it safely to Gen. Howard's camp the next day.[131]

The war that followed was devastating for the Bannocks and Malheur Paiutes, and throughout the conflict the militants sought spiritual power. According to Willie George, while encamped at Pa-sego, near present-day Baker, Oregon, the Bannocks held a Ghost Dance. Other warriors "went into the hills to sleep in hope that a spirit would come to them and give them some extra war power. Men who already had what they thought was good power went alone into the hills to pray and meditate so that their power would be strong when they needed it."[132] But the Bannocks' war power could not overcome the soldiers. Egan was severely wounded at Curry Creek on 23 June, and the hostile band then moved north, Howard believed, in an attempt to enlist the Cayuses and Umatillas.[133] On 8 July, Howard's troops defeated the Paiute-Bannock coalition at Pilot Rock, and the collapse began. Small groups scattered in all directions. Some tried to cross the Columbia River, only to be shot out of the water by army gunboats.[134] At least a portion of the hostile coalition made it to the Umatilla Reservation, forcing the Umatillas to finally take sides.[135] On the afternoon of 15 July, under a flag of truce, a Umatilla party killed Egan and brought in his scalp. Apparently that was not enough for Col. "Rube" Robbins, the chief of scouts, who returned to the scene and "took Chief Egan's head and wounded arm from his body."[136] The grisly evidence was meant to confirm Robbins's claim to have mortally wounded Egan at Curry Creek. Gen. Howard remembered that Egan's severed head was sent "as a fine specimen of an Indian head of large brain to the Medical Museum in Washington. . . . The Piutes felt keenly this last and greatest humiliation, . . . that their much loved chieftain's head should have such a dreadful and ignoble resting place."[137] With Egan's death, the war turned into a pursuit. Oytes and many others surrendered, while small groups of Bannocks and Shoshones headed east toward the reservations or perhaps in the hope of reaching Canada.[138] The soldiers harried the retreating groups until the very last surrendered in Yellowstone National Park in early September.[139]

The Bannock War effectively marked the end of militant resistance to the reservation system, but it did not mark the end of the Ghost Dance religion as a powerful expression of identity. In the 1879 report of the Smithsonian Institution, Col. Albert Brackett wrote of the "Religion, Superstitions, and Manners" of the "Snake Indians." He described them as "marvelous storytellers" and "willing listeners." Apparently tales of the millennium were among their favorites, for Brackett wrote: "Almost every summer they get thoroughly frightened by some prophet predicting the speedy end of the world." In response to these prophecies, "old and young mount their ponies, and, crossing the mountains, assemble near Bear River, where they go through a series of dances, incantations, and rites until they are almost beside themselves with excitement. This excitement disappears as quickly as it makes its appearance, and then all hands pack up again and bundle themselves off home as contented as can be."[140] The colonel felt the gatherings were beneficial, as they diffused pent-up anger and excitement and kept the Indians from raiding white men's herds. The patronizing and arrogant tone aside, Brackett's article suggests that Shoshones and Bannocks still commonly practiced the Ghost Dance in the late 1870s.

By the end of the Bannock War, the trails open to Bannock and Shoshone people were few, and they increasingly converged on Fort Hall. Some groups struggled as best they could to maintain a semblance of their customary ways in their own homelands, and a few succeeded well into the twentieth century. Sagwitch and a good number of his followers remained among the Mormons, as do many of their descendants to this day. But for most, life on the reservation was the only real choice. There, Shoshones and Bannocks seemingly confronted two opposite trails. One led to a supposed agricultural paradise and was imbued with the prophetic spirit of the evangelical Protestant "Friends of the Indian." The other trail led in the opposite direction, and those who followed it increasingly defined their identity and that of "Indians" in opposition to white America and its assimilationist policies. In reality, of course, the choices and decisions were never clear-cut, and individuals and families could and often did cross back and forth. In the 1880s and 1890s the contest over Indianness continued on the reservations, and the Ghost Dances remained an important means of expressing that identity.

CHAPTER 5

Culture Wars, Indianness, and the 1890 Ghost Dance

This extermination and resurrection business is not a new
thing here by any means as it has been quite a craze with them
every few years for the last twenty odd years to my certain
knowledge.

Stanton G. Fisher, Fort Hall agent, 1890

In the years after the Bannock War, another conflict raged on the Fort Hall Reservation. In a few rare instances it became violent, but for the most part it was a political, social, and cultural fight. In essence it was a conflict between two competing visions of the future of Indian America. One vision prophesied the end of American Indians. Taken by the hand and led to civilization by well-meaning Christian reformers, the Bannocks, Shoshones, and all other Indian peoples would adopt the ways of white America and become indistinguishable from all other citizens. The second vision, asserted by Indian peoples themselves, expressed resilient and sometimes new identities both as ethnic peoples and as one people who shared a racial identity and a future. At Fort Hall, the cultural war of assimilation sharpened and in some ways redefined the ethnic and tribal identities that had emerged early in the century. Ethnicity after the Bannock War was often determined by the stance that Indian people took with regard to assimilation. Yet while the conflict over assimilation defined ethnic difference, it also provided the means to overcome this division. For Bannocks and Shoshones the experience of reservation life was instrumental in the development of a new shared identity as American Indians, and the Ghost Dance religion was an important factor in the formation of an Indian community and identity as well as a potent means to resist the prophetic vision of Americanness that reformers sought to impose.

The assimilation program that Shoshones and Bannocks faced during the last decades of the nineteenth century was nothing less than a cultural war driven by a prophetic vision of American society. The "Friends of the Indian" who led the campaign were heirs to the reform zeal of the Second Great Awakening. This movement taught that salvation was a rational choice and that American society was perfectible, if only all Americans made that choice. Much had changed in the United States between the 1830s and the 1880s, yet the reformers' vision of American greatness was still based on conformity with their own narrow definition of what it meant to be an American. Individualism, capitalism, and, most important, Protestant Christianity were the hallmarks of that vision; diversity was the enemy.[1] Groups that did not share their vision and appeared cliquish were targeted for assimilation. So it was that eastern and southern European immigrants, like American Indians (and Mormons, for that matter), became the subjects of "Americanization" programs. In each case it was a perceived communalism, which supposedly blocked individual freedom and choice, that had to be eliminated. The violent metaphors that these "humanitarian" reformers employed to describe their goals revealed the depths of the supposed threat. In 1900, the prominent reformer Merrill E. Gates called the Dawes Severalty Act a "mighty pulverizing engine for breaking up the tribal mass." And, perhaps most famous of all, Richard Henry Pratt, the founder of the Carlisle boarding school, proposed "killing" the Indian in order to save the "man."[2]

The Friends of the Indian employed a number of weapons in their campaign. Land ownership in severalty and agricultural labor were to transform the adults, while schools, preferably boarding schools, would culturally reeducate the youth. White understandings of justice were to be imposed through reservation police forces and Courts of Indian Offenses. Finally, the activities of Christian missionaries and white medical doctors would convince the Indians that their spiritual beliefs were mere superstitions. For indigenous peoples, the reformers' vision meant the end of tribal identities and the acceptance of a new life as individual Christian Americans.

But American Indians did not disappear. To the contrary, during this period an identity that united all American Indian peoples became increasingly possible and salient. Expression of and control over one's identity has been a key form of resistance among subject peoples, and the great unintended consequence of the assimilation program was a stronger American Indian identity. Wearing "white man's" clothing, cutting one's hair, and learning how to farm did not kill the Indian. Rather, the attempted imposition of white culture often functioned as a shared experience that reinforced similarities among Indian peoples as well as magnifying their differences with the whites. For example, many of the students sent away to boarding schools returned with a new sense of Indianness as well as established ties to fellow students—Indians—on reservations across the nation. This shared identity was not a product of the assimilation program alone. The Ghost Dance religion was one of the most important indigenous expressions of that identity. For Shoshones and Bannocks the Ghost Dance was not new, but the waves of excitement it generated provided a bridge to other Indian peoples and allowed the incorporation of new and powerful Christian doctrines. The Ghost Dance taught Indian peoples that they were a distinct group with a distinct origin and way of life and a destiny separate from white America.

The social and political divisions visible at Fort Hall in the 1880s seemed to belie any possibility of a shared identity. For many white observers during the last three decades of the nineteenth century, Shoshone and Bannock ethnicities were well-established and evident in the respective peoples' reactions to assimilation. The Shoshones were "docile" and "tractable," hard workers and eager participants in the government's agricultural plans. In 1872, Johnson N. High praised the Shoshones' work habits. "They are excellent farm hands," he declared, "and I have no difficulty in getting as many as a hundred volunteers in the field at a time." Fifteen years later Peter Gallagher echoed these sentiments, writing, "The Shoshones take more kindly to labor and are more disposed to settle down."[3]

Reactions to the Bannocks were more ambivalent. At times the agents expressed an almost romantic appreciation for their "athletic" and "energetic" traits, but frustration with the Bannocks' "turbulent and rebellious" nature always tempered such praise. Some agents saw a "extensive conspiracy existing among [the Bannocks]"; others were less fearful but still chafed at the Bannocks' refusal to remain at Fort Hall and become farmers.[4] Memories of the Bannock War also shaped exaggerated images. Until after the turn of the century, Indian scares were common in Idaho, and invariably it was the Bannocks who struck fear in white settlers.[5] William Parsons, a Bureau of Indian Affairs (BIA) special agent sent to Fort Hall in 1885, even declared:

> You cannot reason about the Bannock Indians as you can about the
> Shoshones and other less savage tribes. The Bannocks have been warriors
> and hunters since time immemorial, the smell of blood converts them into
> tigers; they care not for the justice of the quarrel, blood must be expiated

with blood, and they are by no means particular from whose veins the expi-
atory blood is drawn; and it therefore is necessary in order to quell them
when excited, to confront them with the absolute certainty of death. . . .
The Bannocks are, in my judgement, the most savage, cruel, treacherous
and dangerous Indians in the West.[6]

Although Parson's words are the stuff of a dime-store novel, they illustrate how easily and completely Euro-Americans associated militant
resistance to "progress" with the Bannocks. These views had a great
influence on the Indian bureau's actions toward Fort Hall Indians. The
anger and frustration with the "nonprogressive" Bannocks led the
agents to favor the "progressive" Shoshones and undercut the former
people's claim to primacy at Fort Hall. In fact, on a number of occasions
agents actually proposed the complete removal of the Bannocks from
Fort Hall.

Yet how real were these divisions to the Shoshones and Bannocks
themselves? Their responses to reservation life suggest that although they
did not share the views of whites, they drew their own important distinctions. Moreover, their reactions illustrate the ways in which ethnic
boundaries are drawn and maintained through a combination of self-
identification and ascription by outsiders. The use of white-imposed
labels as well as the concrete physical responses to assimilation were
ways of expressing their differences. For instance, the power of these
Euro-American perceptions was not lost on the Shoshones, who at times
used the Bannocks' savage reputation against them. In April 1891, for
example, after a young Fort Hall Bannock murdered two white ranchers,
the *Idaho News* from Blackfoot reported: "The Shoshones congratulate
themselves that the murderer was not of their tribe. . . . Captain Jim,
Chief of the Shoshones, says his heart is deeply troubled over the murder
and he wants the white men to know that his people are friendly and will
not fight."[7] Over half a century later, Willie George told Jack Contor that
Shoshones at that time often understood their word for the Bannocks—
pánaite—as " 'someone who doesn't care about anything'—they're just
wild."[8] Thus, Shoshones could and did use their reputation to their benefit. And although they certainly did not see their words and actions as
making them less Indian, these characteristics did represent very real differences in the political stance people took towards assimilation, and by
extension a new way of defining Shoshone and Bannock ethnicity. One
tragic event illustrated the depth of these divisions.

On the afternoon of 5 December 1882, a young Bannock boy ran into
the flour mill at the Fort Hall agency. As ten-year-olds are wont to do, the

boy had chosen a dangerous place to play, and when his blanket got caught in the cogs there was no one to help him. Unable to free himself, the boy was dragged into the machinery and crushed. He lived only a short time after being rescued, and died in his father's lodge.[9] As news of the boy's death spread, the reservation braced for trouble. Pokibero, the boy's father, had fought alongside Buffalo Horn four years earlier, and Agent A. L. Cook remarked that "he belongs to the worst element of the Bannock tribe."[10] That night, one of his wives fled to the agency, fearing that Pokibero would blame her and take his vengeance. Several mixed-bloods warned the miller to watch his back, and Cook made it a point to visit the father as soon as he returned home and learned of his son's death. But the agent found a remarkably calm man, who simply asked for a coffin to bury his son. "He said his heart was bad when he found the boy dead, but he knew that no one was to blame and his heart was not bad now." Cook was relieved. Perhaps things would not go bad. The mixed-bloods no longer feared trouble, and only one Indian policeman was left at the mourning lodge to watch the father. The next morning the mill burned to the ground, taking with it 1,500 bushels of wheat and 12,000 pounds of flour, nearly all of which belonged to Shoshone farmers. News of the fire consumed the agency and spread to the outlying camps. Some of the Bannocks rode in armed and "caused considerable excitement." "The Shoshones looked at the ruins and quietly returned [to their homes]," wrote Cook, "thinking that the Bannacks had burned the mill to injure them." The agent would never be able to prove that the fire was arson, but, like the Shoshones, he suspected Pokibero, who was the first to report the fire.[11]

The weeks that followed revealed the depths of the divisions between Shoshones and Bannocks at Fort Hall. Many of Pokibero's former companions, warriors who had ridden with him during the Bannock War and who were rarely seen around the agency, came in from their camps along the Snake River. They were all heavily armed, and Cook suspected that they meant to prevent Pokibero's arrest. The BIA special agent Arden Smith, who was at Fort Hall on an inspection tour, also felt that the fear of revenge motivated their actions. He wrote, "They believed that the Shoshones, whose wheat and flour had been destroyed, would come in force [and] would kill [Pokibero] on the Indian traditional principle of an eye for an eye."[12] Although Smith ascribed a Biblical law to the wronged Shoshones that they did not in fact hold, he did recognize the growing rift between the two ethnic groups on the reservation, and he feared it would lead to civil war. Throughout the day more Bannocks rode into the agency, "some riding in circles and gesticulating furiously, seemingly working themselves into a white heat of passion, as they did in '78 [during the Bannock War]."[13] Agent Cook, Smith, and the Rev. M. B. Bristol, superintendent of the Fort Hall school, attended the boy's funeral on 7 December. Pokibero buried his son in the nearby foothills. The boy was dressed in a "costly Indian war suit," complete with feathered bonnet. The father removed the corpse from the coffin and held it up as the finest horse in his herd was led past. The boy was then buried, and the horse, along with two others, was killed at the gravesite.[14] While this "grim spectacle" shocked the white agents (and reinforced their view of the Bannocks as nonprogressive), the funeral had a cathartic effect on the Bannocks. Afterwards, the head man Race Horse told Cook, "No more bad Indians, all have good hearts now."[15] Still, the question of responsibility remained.

The commissioner of Indian affairs ordered Pokibero's arrest, but Cook and Smith knew they could not move quickly without risking further unrest. They lacked sufficient evidence to prove the father's guilt, and, more important, they were aware of the sensitive ethnic issues the death and fire had raised. A Bannock had been killed by Shoshone property (in fact, the mill belonged to the agency, but it primarily served Shoshone farmers), which in turn, allegedly, had been destroyed by a Bannock. But there the violence had ended. The Shoshones did not retaliate, even though they outnumbered the Bannocks at Fort Hall by three to one. The Bannock warriors riding wildly about the agency were unnerving but harmless, as long as another event did not unleash their anger. Both men feared that arresting Pokibero would provide that spark. Yet Smith also feared that if the arsonist went unpunished, the seriousness of the act would escape being "firmly impressed on the Indian mind." His suspicions were inflamed when, following the funeral, Tyhee remarked to Cook that the Bannocks would do nothing more with regard to the boy's death. The inspector took this to mean that the Bannocks were guilty and "the destruction of the mill was sufficient appeasement and reparation for the death of the boy." He concluded, "The Bannocks will not punish the Incendiary and if left to the Shoshones, as the only judges and jurors, the probability is that they will be afraid to do so."[16]

Smith and Cook then hatched an ill-fated plan to expose the guilty party. On annuity day, 18 December, Cook confronted the Bannocks in council and openly blamed them for the fire. Presumably the timing implied that their annuities could be withheld if they continued to protect the arsonist. The plan backfired. The Bannocks, led by Tyhee, Race Horse, Pagwite, and several other headmen, refused to be blamed for the fire. Tyhee in particular was incensed and told the agent that if the Bannocks knew who set the fire, they would have turned him in. He then suggested that the miller, who had acted like a "frightened child" after the boy's death, had been careless and left the fires burning. Pokibero then told his side of the story. He said that when he discovered his son's death, "I got right down on my hands and knees over my boy and staid there till I heard a train coming in the morning." It was at this point that his sister told him of a strange light coming from the mill. When Pokibero had finished, Tyhee asked Cook if the man looked ashamed or guilty. The agent did not answer but told the Bannocks that Washington must know that they had not intended the mill to be destroyed and would turn over the arsonist. Tyhee said the Bannocks would continue to talk over the matter, but suggested, "The Shoshone Indians are talking a good deal and may be one of them did it."[17] Not only had the agent's attempt to affix blame failed, it had also brought Fort Hall's ethnic animosities to the surface once again.

The same night that Cook met with the Bannocks, Poor Buck, a son of the Shoshone chief Gibson Jack, rode into a Bannock camp on the Snake River and shot his estranged wife. The girl's mother managed to stab Poor Buck in the face, but he escaped and rode to within a short distance of his father's lodge, where he shot himself. Because the victim was a Bannock and the attacker a Shoshone, the agents worried that ethnic resentments stirred by the mill incident would explode into violence. In a morbid way, Smith felt that Poor Buck's attempted suicide might defuse the situation. "If he dies and the girl lives," he wrote, "which is most improbable, there will be the end of it."[18] Things did not work out as Smith had hoped. Poor Buck died on 23 December, and his wife died on New Year's Day 1883.[19]

The feared interethnic violence never occurred. Bannocks and Shoshones alike viewed the murder-suicide as a crime of passion. Incidents of personal violence and revenge were familiar in Newe cultures. Poor Buck had not attacked a Bannock because of ethnic resentments, but rather, in a fit of rage and jealousy, he had attacked the woman who had left him for another man. The responses to such an act could include violence, either blood revenge or the destruction of the offender's property, but they were the responsibility of the victim's family and friends, not of the tribe.[20] In a situation such as that at Fort Hall, with two groups so closely related and intermarried, there could be no other way, unless constant interethnic violence was acceptable; and, of course, it was not. Only a few years before the mill fire, the prospect of a war between Shoshones and Bannocks would have been inconceivable. Bannocks had always killed Shoshones, of course, and vice versa. But the motivations were always personal or kin-based, as in the Poor Buck incident. One group did not kill the members of the other simply because they were the *Other*. Poor Buck's case was, therefore, qualitatively different from the death of Pokibero's son. The latter represented a new category. The murderer was not even a human being, but a Shoshone mill, a symbol of ethnic boundaries during the assimilation era.

Living together on a single reservation, however, demanded more peaceful means of mediating disputes. Both Shoshone and Bannock leaders understood this, as well as the restrictions they worked under. Neither group could pursue a life completely independent of the Indian department and the reservation. The agents' charges might anger Tyhee, but he also knew that he could not ignore them. In the first weeks of the new year, all sides worked to diffuse the tensions that resulted from the mill incident. Agent Cook took the first step when he decided that he could not punish the Bannocks without absolute proof. He even accepted the possibility that the fire was an accident and suggested that the new mill be constructed on the Portneuf River in order to employ water power. The Bannocks also moved to ease the tensions and seemingly took some responsibility for the fire. Tyhee told Cook, "If Washington will build another mill we will sell hay and ponies and pay for it . . . and maybe some of the Shoshones will help some."[21] Tyhee and the other Bannock leaders knew they must try to heal the rift with the Shoshones. It is also possible that Pokibero was indeed the arsonist, but, because the Bannock leaders felt he was justified in setting the fire, they refused to turn him in, preferring that the entire group take responsibility. Whatever the motive, the crisis had passed. The ethnic tensions that the mill incident had revealed continued to smolder under the surface, but, just as the crisis revealed deep divisions, its outcome illustrated how reservation life demanded a consensus that could lay the groundwork for the creation of a reservation community and new understandings of identity.

In very similar ways, dealing with outsiders demanded that Shoshones and Bannocks work together. In the process, both groups called upon older ideals of territory and political leadership in order to create a working political community at Fort Hall.[22] The pressures of consolidation continued in the aftermath of the Bannock War, and thus the essential cause of earlier ethnic animosities continued to divide Fort Hall Bannocks and Shoshones. The realities of consolidation, however, were far more complex and also worked to draw the two peoples together. Negotiating with government officials demanded that Shoshone and Bannock leaders find agreement. The Bannocks might claim a greater right to Fort Hall and resent the Shoshone presence, but the latter people, who were by far the majority and whom the government considered the more "worthy" people, could not be ignored—especially when the government wanted to send even more people to Fort Hall, and local white settlers cast greedy eyes on reservation lands.

White encroachment became a serious threat at Fort Hall by the late 1870s. Some fifty white families lived at the southern end of the Marsh Valley, within the reservation's boundaries. The relentless advance of the railroads posed an even greater threat, as they invariably brought more settlers hungry for land.[23] Meanwhile, the bureau sought to close the Lemhi Reservation and move Tendoy's people south. It was an effort to settle these issues that led the commissioner of Indian affairs in March 1880 to direct Agent John A. Wright to bring Tendoy and other prominent leaders from Lemhi and Fort Hall to Washington, D.C. Tissidimit and Grouse Pete also came from Lemhi, and Gibson Jack, Captain Jim, and Tyhee represented Fort Hall. Tendoy's son Jack and Charley Rainey, acting as interpreter, rounded out the delegation.[24] The agent viewed the trip as a means to impress the Indians with the "population, industrial pursuits, education, and other advantages enjoyed by the whites."[25] But the real purpose was land cession and consolidation. On 14 May 1880, the delegation signed an agreement that provided for the closure of the Lemhi reservation, the removal of the Lemhi Indians to Fort Hall, the cession of the disputed lands in Marsh Valley, and the survey and allotment of the entire Fort Hall reservation.[26] Within two months of the visit, however, the agreement started to unravel. Tendoy rejected the move, saying there was misunderstanding "as to the particular part of the [Fort Hall] reservation to be occupied by his tribe." The powerful merchant and politician George Shoup suggested a second meeting to iron out the difficulties, but by late summer the commissioner had given up on Lemhi removal for the time being. "So far as the Lemhi Indians are concerned," wrote the commissioner, "that part of the agreement which relates to them becomes inoperative, the tribe having since declined to remove to Fort Hall." He recommended that Congress ratify the portion of the agreement concerning Fort Hall.[27] It would be nine long years, however, before Congress acted.

The 1880 Washington delegation and agreement illustrated the internal factionalism within the various Shoshone and Bannock bands. The politics within each group always made the situation more complex than a simple ethnic split. Tendoy's leadership of the Lemhi contingent came as no surprise. Although not unchallenged, he had been the most influential and vocal Lemhi leader for nearly two decades.[28] At Fort Hall the situation was far more complicated. Captain Jim and Gibson Jack were both progressive Shoshone leaders and proponents of agriculture. It is easy to understand Wright's motives in selecting them for the delegation. But he could not ignore the Bannocks. Tyhee, the single Bannock representative, though at times a thorn in the agent's side, more often assumed a "progressive" stance on indicator issues such as agriculture and land cessions. Throughout the 1880s, Tyhee remained among the reservation's leading farmers. Tyhee's principal challenger for influence among the Bannocks was Pagwite, who by 1880 had developed a reputation as an intractable foe of "progress." His exclusion, like Tyhee's inclusion, makes perfect sense in the context of the agents' attempt to engineer a land cession. The experience of the delegation and those who were excluded from it reveals that the Bannocks had neither a unified leadership nor an agreed-on response to the demands of consolidation and assimilation. Tyhee and Pagwite represent points on a continuum of opposition. Tyhee, the well-established reservation leader, more often assumed the role of mediator and conciliator, while Pagwite, who was never able to secure a consensus among the Bannocks (let alone the Shoshones), spoke directly against Euro-Americans and their programs. Ultimately Tyhee, who employed older ideals of the _dai'gwahni'_, would prove the more influential.

At times the ethnic divisions at Fort Hall seemed to shatter any hope of consensus and unified action. In the summer of 1881, with the original Utah and Northern Railroad right-of-way still unresolved, the government sought yet another right-of-way for a Union Pacific subsidiary, the Oregon Short Line. In a preliminary council both Shoshone and Bannock leaders agreed to a survey of the right-of-way, but during the main council, more than two weeks later, the Bannocks balked. The interpreter informed Assistant Attorney General Joseph K. McCammon, who represented the government, that "The Bannocks don't agree. They say the Shoshones have done all the talking, and they have not had a chance to say anything." Pagwite was the most vocal of the Bannock critics. He recalled earlier promises that no whites would be allowed to trespass on the reservation and was angry that these promises had not been kept.

McCammon promised that soldiers would evict the trespassers and then asked Pagwite if he thought the settlement of six thousand dollars was unfair. Pagwite responded that he thought the amount was fair but that he would "be better satisfied when he gets the money in his own hands."[29] He accepted McCammon's promise, which of course the assistant attorney general had no power to make, and the Indian leaders signed the agreement. Backed by the powerful Union Pacific lobby, the agreement quickly made its way through Congress. The payment to the Indians, however, took some time to reach Fort Hall.[30]

The continuing growth of the Shoshone population and influence at Fort Hall remained a source of friction. The increase, though not large, was steady.[31] If the Indian bureau were to have its way, the trickle would turn into a flood. In January 1884 the special agent Cyrus Beede arrived at Fort Hall to convince the people there to accept more immigrants, as the bureau sought to close both Duck Valley and Lemhi. The Bannocks, led by Tyhee and Pagwite, and the Shoshones, represented by Gibson Jack and Captain Jim, agreed to accept the new people if the government built them a new flour mill. Even so, they feared that the increased population would mean greater hardship. Beede agreed that rations would not be reduced but made no promises about the mill.[32] When Beede visited Duck Valley, however, the Shoshones there steadfastly refused to go to Fort Hall. The government had not offered any compensation for their reservation or promised them a permanent place at Fort Hall. The Shoshones also told Beede they did not want to go onto "the same reservation with the Bannock Indians."[33] Captain Sam complained there were too many railroads and whites surrounding Fort Hall, but Beede sensed he was "afraid of the Bannock Indians, he having some misunderstanding with them not long ago." Most likely, it was resentments left over from Captain Sam's refusal to join the hostilities during the Bannock War that underlay his concerns.[34]

Beede was no more successful at Lemhi, where Tendoy's people were reluctant to leave their homes and the "graves of their departed friends and relatives" and knew full well of the miserable conditions at Fort Hall.[35] Some feared a cut in rations; others wanted to talk to George Shoup before they made a decision; but there also appeared to be an ethnic barrier to consolidation. In frustration Beede wrote, "Again, the 'Shoshones' wherever I meet them, seem to have a dread of the 'Bannocks' and fear their confederation with them."[36] Seemingly recognizing the confusing nature of ethnic identity among people so closely allied and intermarried, it was the special agent who put "Shoshone" and

"Bannock" in quotation marks. The important division was as much political as ethnic. Like Captain Sam at Duck Valley, Tendoy had long-standing disputes with the Fort Hall Bannocks and would lose much of his legitimacy as a _dai'gwahni'_ by leaving his homeland. By May the Lemhi removal was again on hold, and Agent Harries wrote: "Nothing short of actual force will accomplish their removal."[37] In the end, force was unnecessary, but the Lemhis staved off removal until 1907.

The government proved far more successful in pursuing land cessions at Fort Hall, and it was this relentless pressure that led Shoshone and Bannock leaders to find consensus by applying older political ideals in a new reservation context. In May 1887, the Indian bureau dispatched inspector Robert S. Gardiner to negotiate the sale of the Pocatello town site (where most of the residents, numbering more than one thousand, squatted on reservation lands) and settle the still-unpaid-for Utah and Northern right-of-way.[38] Although both Shoshones and Bannocks eventually agreed to the sale, the ethnic divisions at Fort Hall were again evident. On several occasions the Shoshone leaders deferred to the Bannocks, seemingly accepting the latter people's primacy on the reservation and the leadership of Tyhee, the Bannock headman. Gibson Jack alluded to the Bannock resentment of the Shoshones: "The Bannocks claim they have more right to this reservation than the Shoshones, and that they have the best right to talk first."[39] Then, after several Bannocks vocally opposed the sale, he said that he had changed his mind about supporting the agreement "because there is so much talk among the Bannocks, and I feel awfully bad about it." Padzee, who claimed to be "head of the Shoshones in this talk," also deferred to the Bannocks, saying: "I always say what Ty-Hee told me." Captain Jim also accepted the Bannock leader's prominence, saying: "I believe you are aware I was brought here from Boise. Ty-Hee told me to come here and to go to work farming and make a living for myself and my children." And finally, Captain Joe, apparently in reference to a marker that the Bannock chief had placed on the reservation, remarked: "When Tyhee put up that post, they told us no white man would come here." He concluded: "We need the land to plow and do not want white man on it to bother us." The Bannock leaders opposed the sale, but for different reasons. Ke-O was not interested in farming and opposed the sale because he wanted to live as he always had. "This is a small mountain and there is not much land or ground to hunt upon," he said, "I like this land because I have lots of children to run over it, and the land is too small for me." Race Horse then expressed dismay that "Washington" was again asking for more land. He concluded, "God gives us this land and that is the reason I want my land yet, and it makes us feel bad when you ask us about it."[40]

The Fort Hall agent Peter Gallagher cajoled and ridiculed the Bannocks and Shoshones, but he ultimately had to turn to Tyhee to convince the leaders to sell. Gallagher reinforced Tyhee's status, leaving no doubt about who "Washington" considered to be the head chief at Fort Hall. "He wants to resign his chief-ship," the agent remarked, "but so long as I am here I will keep Ty-Hee in the first rank."[41] Tyhee then spoke for consensus among all the Indian leaders: "I do not like the way they have been talking here, one, one way, one another, they do not agree and it does not suit me. . . . Now I want you all to come to one understanding and agree to sell Pocatello." He then asked what Gardiner and Gallagher thought of his view. They both agreed that it was "precisely right." One by one the other headmen, including Pagwite, fell in behind Tyhee and agreed to sell the Pocatello townsite.[42]

The Pocatello cession of 1887, like the mill incident four and a half years earlier, provided a window on the nature of ethnicity and the operation of native politics at Fort Hall as well as on the effects of shared experience. New situations demanded new responses, but those responses did not emerge from whole cloth. Older ideals and systems provided the fabric for new understandings. The Bannock claim of primacy was based on the fact that Fort Hall lay within their *tebíwa* and was buttressed by their understanding of the Fort Bridger treaty as the document that created the reservation. The Shoshones were clearly conscious of this claim. They deferred to Tyhee because he was the recognized chief of the Bannocks and, no doubt, because of his success as a mediator as well. Tyhee's authority among the Bannocks was based on this same ability, which in turn depended on his influence with the whites. Thus Tyhee acted in many ways as a traditional *daí'gwahni'*, negotiating his people's access to resources. Unlike earlier leaders, such as Taghee, he also assumed some leadership over the Shoshones. He could not ignore the Shoshones, who were the majority on the reservation and who enjoyed the agents' favor. In situations such as land cessions which demanded consensus, Tyhee was the only leader with substantial influence among the Bannocks, Shoshones, and Euro-Americans and thus the only one who could create consensus on a divided reservation. He continued to fulfill this role as part of a delegation to Washington in 1889 seeking Congressional passage of the Pocatello cession as well as the long-delayed Marsh Valley cession agreement.[43] These same dynamics were evident in the way Bannocks and Shoshones responded to the government's assimilation programs. On the surface, the two peoples responded differently, but ultimately the shared experience of reservation life outweighed ethnic differences. And on this cultural level, the Ghost Dance religion was both a symbol of different reactions and the means to overcome them.

The Numu (Northern Paiute) prophet Wovoka experienced his first vision on New Year's Day 1889, when a solar eclipse darkened the skies throughout the West. After traveling to heaven and seeing all the dead people living there "happy and forever young," Wovoka reported, God told him to go back to earth and tell all the people to be good and love one another, and promised that if they "faithfully obeyed his instructions they would at last be reunited with their friends in this other world, where there would be no more death or sickness or old age." Wovoka then began to preach to the Numu of the Smith and Mason valleys in western Nevada. Although at the time he claimed no healing *bo'ha,* he demonstrated the power of his prophecy in ways common to Numu shamans: weather control and invulnerability. He predicted and took credit for rains that ended a prolonged drought, and this success won him an instant following on the nearby Walker River Reservation. The first dances probably took place in the spring of 1889, with only local Numus attending. News of the religion spread quickly, and when the second dance was held, many visiting Indians were there, including some from Fort Hall.[44]

Ceremonially, Wovoka's Ghost Dance was very similar to the 1870 religion, but there were important differences in intent and effect between Wovoka's doctrine and that of Wodziwob. David Aberle has argued that the 1890 doctrine was as much "redemptive" as "transformative." A redemptive movement seeks to find "a state of grace in a human soul, psyche, or person" and is defined by a search for a "new inner state." While on one level the intent of the 1890 Ghost Dance was clearly transformative—it purported to bring a renewal of the earth and reunification of all people—its impact on Indian communities and individuals was often redemptive.[45] Wovoka preached a gospel of peace, love, and accommodation that, by eliminating many of the causes of internal discord, served to strengthen Indian communities. And as such his religion survived in modified forms well into the twentieth century. The revival of the Pawnee Hand Game and the New Tidings religion among the Sioux of Saskatchewan are but two examples.[46] In his own homeland, Michael Hittman has argued, Wovoka's vision of "racial harmony on earth, pending everlasting life in Heaven" was entirely consistent with the "biculturalism and aspirations" of the Numu during the final years of the nineteenth century.[47]

Wovoka's prophecies also exhibited a much greater Christian influence than the earlier religion. A number of observers, Indian and white alike, reported that Wovoka claimed to be Jesus, going so far as to show visiting Indians the stigmata of his crucifixion.[48] Wovoka never made this particular claim to James Mooney or any other official investigator, but he left no doubt that he was a messenger sent by God. At about the age of eight the future prophet began working on the Mason Valley ranch of David and Abigail Wilson. He became the constant playmate of the couple's three sons and was accepted into their home, where he was known as Jack. (Indeed, he was commonly known by Indians and whites alike as Jack Wilson.) The Wilsons, devout United Presbyterians, exposed Jack to Bible readings and prayers. Although it is impossible to recover what he heard or how he interpreted it, it is reasonable to suspect that this early exposure to Christianity influenced the development of the Ghost Dance doctrine. According to Edward A. Dyer, a local merchant and long-time friend of Wovoka who spoke fluent Paiute, it was these youthful experiences that led Wovoka to a life of prophecy.[49] Michael Hittman has even suggested specific biblical passages that might have inspired Wovoka's prophecies and has argued that his career demonstrated a desire to emulate the "saddle-bag preachers, or traveling evangelists who conducted revival meetings in the Walker River area."[50]

Others have suggested a strong Mormon influence on the religion. At one level these assertions revolved around conspiracy theories. Even before the "Sioux Outbreak," Gen. Nelson A. Miles had blamed the Mormons for the Ghost Dance religion and the associated unrest on the reservations.[51] A number of other official reports also seemed to suggest Mormon involvement. The Northern Cheyenne holy man Porcupine, for instance, told an army investigator that many of the whites he met between Fort Hall and Walker River participated in the dance.[52] In October 1890, the commander of Fort Washakie, Wyoming, identified Pagwite as the "Indian Christ" and claimed that the Bannock headman was a Mormon and that by extension the church had instigated the entire affair. Pagwite was certainly a Ghost Dance activist, but he never became a Mormon.[53] None of these observers were concerned with the doctrinal similarities between the Mormon and Indian prophecies or the incorporation of Christian concepts into the religion. Rather, they wanted to assign blame in the aftermath of Wounded Knee. For those who could not accept the Ghost Dance as an native-inspired and native-led movement, and who believed that "designing" white men must somehow be responsible, the Mormons became popular scapegoats because of their history of involvement with Indian peoples and their sour relationship with the federal government.[54]

Mooney also tried to assess the Mormon influence on the Ghost Dance, but from the perspective of a social scientist. He was fascinated by the intersection of Mormon and Indian prophecies and believed that each informed the other. As in 1875, it appears that the Ghost Dance prophecy aroused interest among some Mormons who found validation of their beliefs in the arrival of the Indian Messiah. Mooney reprinted portions of a pamphlet that appeared in Salt Lake City in 1892. Written by Mormon dissidents angry with the 1890 manifesto renouncing polygamy, the tract claimed: "The Mormons have stepped down and out of Celestial Government—The Indians have stepped up and into Celestial Government." The authors argued that the Ghost Dance prophecy was a sign of the impending millennium as well as an indication that God had forsaken the Mormons because of their official rejection of plural marriage.[55]

Mooney also theorized that a Mormon belief in protective garments had inspired the supposedly bulletproof "ghost shirts" among the Lakotas. Noting that protective medicine had not previously taken the form of clothing among the Lakota, he suggested that Ghost Dance pilgrims formulated the concept of the ghost shirt after encountering Indian converts who connected the aboriginal concept of protective medicine to clothing. Believing that the Wind River reservation was the likely source of the concept, he wrote: "It is easy to see how an idea borrowed by the Shoshoni from the Mormons could find its way through the Arapaho first to the Sioux and Cheyenne and afterward to more remote tribes."[56] Although he greatly overestimated the success of the church's missions,[57] Mooney's suggestion that Mormon doctrine, like other Christian elements, could have been incorporated into Ghost Dance doctrine is completely plausible.

Wovoka's doctrine was distinct but had a very important similarity with the earlier movement: both left plenty of room for interpretations as diverse as the religious traditions and historical experiences of the peoples who accepted them. Mooney pointed out that on the basic foundation of Wovoka's vision, "each tribe has built a structure from its own mythology, and each apostle and believer has filled in the details according to his own mental capacity or ideas of happiness, with such additions as come to him from the trance."[58] The variability was even obvious to observers who were not ethnologists. Agent Fisher observed that the dance as practiced at Fort Hall was "not the same as the 'ghost dance' now being carried on by the Sioux and other eastern tribes." He added: "Scarcely any two tribes have the same ideas as to what they must do to bring about the desired result." (Fisher, unfortunately, did not provide a detailed description of the ceremony at Fort Hall.)[59] Such doctrinal flexibility meant that the religion could be interpreted both as a message of universal peace and brotherhood and as an inspiration for militant resistance. Moreover, as the experience at Fort Hall demonstrates, individuals of the same group could hold substantially different understandings of the meaning and use of the doctrine.

Likewise, there is conflicting evidence concerning the ultimate fate of the whites in the prophecy: Would they be destroyed? Would they survive along with Indians in the new paradise? Would Indians and whites become one people? Unlike the 1870 movement, the 1890 Ghost Dance supported numerous versions of the prophecy, several of which included the violent destruction of the whites. In the fall of 1890, Captain Dick, a Paiute at Fort Bidwell, California, told an investigator that when "Old Man [God]" returned, all the Indians would climb up into the mountains to escape the flood that killed all the white people.[60] Another militant version of the doctrine was recorded among the Lakotas. Short Bull, one of two principal Lakota Ghost Dance leaders, reported that, during his visit to Nevada, the Indian "Messiah" told him that he had returned to the earth once before, but the white people had murdered him. He then showed the pilgrims the wounds on his hands and feet.[61] On October 31, 1890, Short Bull reportedly spoke to his people at the Pine Ridge reservation:

> My father has shown me these things, therefore we must continue this dance. If the soldiers surround you four deep, three of you on whom I have put holy shirts, will sing a song, which I have taught you, around them, when some of them will drop dead. The rest will start to run, but their horses will sink into the earth. The riders will jump from their horses, but they will sink into the earth also. Then you can do as you desire with them. Now, you must know this, that all the soldiers and that race will be dead. There will be only five thousand of them left living on earth. My friends and relations, this is straight and true.[62]

But not all Indian versions of the doctrine prophesied the destruction of the whites. Porcupine, who like the Lakotas had seen the stigmata, did not suggest that the "Messiah" had abandoned his white children or planned their elimination. On the contrary, "He spoke to us about fighting and said that was bad. . . . He told us not to quarrel, or fight, nor strike each other, nor shoot one another; that the whites and Indians were all to be one people."[63]

The earliest direct account of Wovoka's doctrine came from Arthur I. Chapman, an officer sent to investigate the reports of an "Indian Messiah." Chapman arrived at Walker River on the last day of November 1890. He first interviewed Josephus, the captain of the Indian police and a Ghost Dance believer, who attested that Wovoka's religion was one of universal peace and brotherhood. In heaven Wovoka had seen both Indians and whites "dancing, gambling, playing ball and having all kinds of sports." God told the prophet "to tell all the [living] people that they must not fight, there must be peace all over the world; that the people must not steal from one another, but be good to each other, for they were all brothers."[64] On 4 December 1890, at Wellington, Nevada, Chapman conducted the first known interview with Wovoka himself. The prophet said that God had told him that the Indians must not "fight the white people or one another; that we are all brothers and must remain in peace; . . . that God told him or gave him the power to destroy this world and all the people in it and to have it made over again; and the people who had been good heretofore were to be made over again and all remain young."[65] The implication is that race did not matter: "bad" people would be destroyed and "good" people would be reborn. It is difficult to gauge whether or how much Wovoka tailored his statements for Chapman. He exhibited some mistrust of the whites, telling Chapman that they often mistreated his people. Tensions were already running high on the Lakota reservations; this unrest was the reason for Chapman's visit. Wovoka was well aware of the excitement and told Chapman, "I heard that soldiers were coming after me."[66] Even before Wounded Knee, it is reasonable to assume that Wovoka might be reluctant to tell a white investigator everything.

The only written version of Wovoka's doctrine recorded by an Indian is the famous "Messiah Letter" of 1891, which exhibits a certain ambivalence about the fate of the white race. The Messiah Letter exists in three versions. Casper Edson, a young Arapaho who had attended Carlisle Indian school, wrote down the first in broken English at the very moment Wovoka addressed the Arapaho and Cheyenne delegation. On his return to Oklahoma, the Cheyenne delegate Black Sharp Nose dictated the second, or "Cheyenne," version to his daughter, who wrote it "somewhat better English" on the back of the sheet of paper that held

Edson's version.[67] Finally, James Mooney provided his own free rendering of the letter. In all three versions it is clear that Wovoka was not preaching violent resistance to the whites, yet it is not at all clear that whites would survive to share the renewed earth. One of the critical passages in Edson's version reads: "No hurt anybody. no fight, good behave always, it will give you satisfaction." Mooney's rendering of this passage has become perhaps the most-quoted portion of Wovoka's doctrine: "You must not fight. Do always right. It will give you satisfaction in life." This passage suggests that the religion was indeed one of universal peace. Yet only a few moments later the prophet told the assembly "Dont tell no white man" that Jesus had returned to earth and that the dead were alive again. Edson then recorded this advice: "Work for white men never trouble with him until you leave, when it shake the earth dont be afraid no harm anybody." The Cheyenne version of this passage reads: "Do not refuse to work for white man or do not make any trouble with them until you leave them. When the earth shakes do not be afraid it will not hurt you."[68] While the statement expresses no clear indication that whites would be destroyed, the phrase "do not trouble with him until you leave" suggests that they would be left behind. Thus, although Wovoka told the pilgrims to lead honest, peaceful, and "redemptive" lives, they could still have left the meeting believing that whites had no place on the renewed earth.

When Mooney himself visited Wovoka in 1892, the prophet "repudiated any idea of hostility toward the whites, asserting that his religions was one of universal peace." He also "disclaimed all responsibility" for the Lakota ghost shirts. Still, Mooney suspected Wovoka had not told him everything, "as no Indian would unbosom himself on religious matters to a white man whom he had not had a long and intimate acquaintance." Mooney also suggested that the "warlike turn of affairs . . . across the mountains" might have effected a change in the nature of Wovoka's prophecy. He found that Wovoka, while not exactly in hiding, was making himself scarce. Edward Dyer, who acted as an interpreter during the meeting, concurred.[69] Mooney concluded "though certain medicine men . . . [anticipated] the Indian millennium by preaching resistance to the further encroachments of whites, such teachings form no part of the true doctrine."[70] Perhaps, if one defines the "true doctrine" as that espoused by Wovoka. But, as Mooney was fully aware, no two Indian peoples' understood the doctrine in precisely the same manner. At Fort Hall the Ghost Dances functioned as a religion of resistance, if not against physical encroachments, then certainly against the cultural

inroads of assimilation. In the process the religion contributed greatly to
the emergence of a shared Indian identity that could overcome the ethnic
divisions of the reservation era.

Fort Hall was one of the most important centers of Ghost Dance activism
in the 1890s. Bannocks and Shoshones were among the first peoples to
visit the new prophet and spread the word of his religion. Fort Hall
Bannocks attended the second dance, held in the early months of 1889,
and Mooney reported that the Bannocks, Shoshones, Gosiutes, and Utes
took up the dance "almost simultaneously" at that time.[71] Fort Hall
Bannocks were in attendance at many subsequent dances, including a
particularly large gathering in March 1890.[72] The reservation's strategic
location, combined with the linguistic affinity between Bannocks and
Northern Paiutes, also made Fort Hall an essential stopping place for pilgrims. As the message of the Ghost Dance spread onto the Great Plains,
numerous parties passed through Fort Hall, which is located at one of
the great crossroads of the West. The fast-growing town of Pocatello sat
at the junction of the Utah Northern and Oregon Short Line Railroads,
and the main line of the Union Pacific lay to the south at Ogden, Utah, a
short day's journey by rail. Just as important, delegations could receive
the latest news of the prophet and obtain Bannock interpreters at Fort
Hall. Mooney found that "almost every delegation from the tribes east of
the mountains" stopped at Fort Hall and concluded: "The Bannocks
and Shoshoni of Fort Hall reservation in Idaho have served as the chief
medium of the doctrine between the tribes west of the mountains and
those of the plains."[73]

The experiences of two famous eastern delegations illustrate the role
of Fort Hall Indians, particularly Bannocks, in supporting these pilgrim-
ages. In the fall of 1889, the Northern Cheyenne medicine man
Porcupine passed through Fort Hall with a group that also included the
Lakota apostles Short Bull and Kicking Bear. The agent invited the group
to stay at the agency, but, as the Cheyenne recalled, "the chief of the
Bannocks was there and took me to his camp nearby." After discussing
the state of Indian-white relations for ten days, during which time the
"Bannock Chief," probably Tyhee, counseled peace and cooperation,
Porcupine sought to continue his journey. Maintaining that he simply
wanted to see the country, he returned to the agency and requested passes
for "some Bannocks and Shoshones [who] wanted to go along." The
agent, presumably Fisher, issued passes "to the chiefs of the three parties." From Fort Hall, in the company of his Bannock and Shoshone

guides, Porcupine went south to a "town on a big lake," where he caught
a train heading west to his meeting with the "Indian Christ."[74] Nearly
two years later, the Arapaho and Cheyenne delegation from Oklahoma,
which included Casper Edson, made a remarkably similar visit to Fort
Hall. Lt. William Johnson reported that English-speaking Indians met the
group at the Pocatello station on 22 July 1891 and immediately conducted them to the home of Tyhee, "who claim[ed] to control the
Bannocks as their chief." The Arapahos stayed five days and seldom left
their tents "except to go in a roundabout way to Tighee's house."
Johnson found the visitors to be "very intelligent" and was greatly dis-
appointed that they "talked only with the wildest and most ignorant
Bannocks, avoiding the more progressive Shoshones." On 28 July the
Arapahos boarded a Montana-bound train to continue their "vacation,"
but later the same day Johnson spotted them riding south on a baggage
car "in the midst of a group of blanket Indians." When the lieutenant
spoke to them, they acted as if they did not recognize him. Because of
their strange behavior, Johnson questioned several Fort Hall Indians and
found that the delegation had discussed the "Indian Messiah" with
Tyhee and were now on their way to Walker River to meet with the
prophet in person.[75]

   In addition to assisting pilgrims, Fort Hall Indians actively missionized
neighboring peoples and served as the religion's most effective apostles
west of the Rockies. In fact, it was probably a series of events begun two
years earlier that brought the Edson delegation to Fort Hall. In the spring
of 1889, a Fort Hall Bannock visited the Wind River Reservation. He
told the Shoshones that he had just returned from Nevada and that
"messengers had told him that the dead people were coming back . . .
[and] had commanded him to go tell the tribes." Consequently five
Shoshones and one Arapaho set out from Wind River to investigate the
religion.[76] Washakie, the aging but still influential headman at Wind
River, remembered the arrival of the Ghost Dance missionary this way:
"When this Indian from Fort Hall came, he turned my head and pleased
my heart for he talked so nice about the dead and their coming [back] so
soon and many other things did he say, also we were to dance almost all
the time day and night."[77] It was from Wind River, initially through the
U.S. mail, that news of the Ghost Dance religion reached the Oklahoma
reservations. In effect, the Bannocks had passed the religion on to the
Arapahos, who became its most active proselytizers east of the Rockies.[78]
Fort Hall Indians were also active among tribes west of the mountains. A
former Paiute agent residing at Elko, Nevada, blamed the "uneasiness

and unusual number of dances" that occurred throughout 1890 among the Western Shoshones on "visiting delegations of Indians from several tribes, particularly Fort Hall."[79]

It is clear that Fort Hall Indians practiced the Ghost Dance religion and continued their roles as missionaries and interpreters well after the Wounded Knee massacre in December 1890, an event that many historians have viewed as the brutal conclusion of the Ghost Dance fervor. In August 1891, Agent Fisher reported that the "messiah craze" had subsided, "but is liable at any time to be revived by some weak-brained individual or medicine man."[80] Apparently interest in the dance had not waned as much as Fisher believed, for the Edson delegation had passed through Fort Hall just weeks earlier. Only one year later, shamans on the reservation were using the Ghost Dance doctrine to rally opposition to the Fort Hall school.

Even after the end of the century, Fort Hall remained a focus of the Ghost Dance movement. In 1900, the Northern Cheyenne shaman and Ghost Dance activist Porcupine was once again the center of turmoil, this time on the Tongue River Reservation in Montana. Porcupine and two disciples were preaching a far more militant version of the "Messiah doctrine" than he had related ten years earlier. He told the Cheyennes to ignore the agent, warning that "all those who did not listen . . . will surely die, that the resurrection is sure coming this summer, meaning that the Cheyennes who have died are all coming back, and that the whites will all be swept out of existence."[81] On 21 June Porcupine and six other "Messiah men" slipped off the reservation, intending to "consult with the Great Father who lived a long way off." Porcupine did not mean the president of the United States. He promised to return with "Medicine arrows and other charms which would prevent the whites from having any control over the Indians." He also allegedly claimed that he would have the "same power as the Messiah or Great Father." After visiting Wind River, the party passed "over the mountains to the Fort Hall reservation." It was there, in August, that Porcupine and his party were arrested among his old friends the Bannocks.[82]

What then were the meanings attached to the Ghost Dances at Fort Hall? Who participated? Who led them? Bannocks were apparently more active than Shoshones in the practice and propagation of the Ghost Dance. Although Mooney identified both Bannocks and Shoshones as Ghost Dance missionaries, he emphasized the role of the former people, especially as interpreters who regularly accompanied eastern delegations on their visits to Nevada, over that of the latter. He also identified the

Fort Hall Indian who brought the dance to Wind River in 1889 as a Bannock. Yet it seems obvious that the Bannocks associated with the religion need not have been Bannock speakers. When Fisher first reported Ghost Dance activity, he estimated that 90 percent of the "Bannock Indians" followed the religion. His use of quotation marks suggests that Fisher, who had lived for decades among the Shoshones and Bannocks and knew them better than any other agent, saw some ambiguity in the use of the term as it applied to the Ghost Dancers. Lt. Johnson's comment that visiting Ghost Dance delegations sought out the "wildest and most ignorant Bannocks," while avoiding the more "progressive Shoshones," indicates that his understanding of ethnicity at Fort Hall (and by extension Ghost Dance activism) hinged not on the language spoken but on an individual's reaction to government assimilation programs.[83] By the 1880s, in official correspondence *Bannock* meant the "nonprogressives" who opposed the government's assimilation programs. Thus, just as in the early 1870s, the Ghost Dance was again most closely identified with the Fort Hall Indians who resisted the reservation system.

But even if Bannocks were the principal Ghost Dancers, there was no single Bannock understanding of the dance. Individuals as well as groups could follow or represent different teachings. Contemporary observers identified both Tyhee and Pagwite as Ghost Dance leaders. Both were Bannocks, yet the two had very different personal histories, which suggest different interpretations of the Ghost Dance religion. Tyhee remained the most influential Bannock headman on the Fort Hall reservation through his generally cordial relations with the whites and his ability to balance their demands with the needs of his people. If one accepts Mooney's narrow definition of resistance, as opposition to the "further encroachment of whites," Tyhee cannot be characterized as a resister. He led the Bannock contingent of the Fort Hall delegation to Washington, D.C., in 1880, which negotiated the Marsh Valley cession. In 1887, he supported the sale of the Pocatello townsite.[84] In each case Tyhee believed the cessions were inevitable and that the Bannocks and Shoshones should get the best settlement possible for the benefit of future generations. Tyhee represented the anomaly of a "progressive" Bannock. Whereas the agents characterized the Bannocks as wild and uncontrollable, Tyhee cut his hair and took up farming. At the same time, he maintained a following among the nonprogressives, so much so that he was recognized as the Bannock chief at Fort Hall. He was an effective intermediary, yet he slowed or opposed many other cultural changes. He supported the school only briefly and resisted the agent's attempt to fix blame for the 1882 mill fire on his people.

This apparent contradiction in attitude may have been a product of divergent interpretations of cultural symbols. Symbols and actions that whites have interpreted as progressive have often been adopted and creatively reinterpreted by Indian peoples as a means of recreating persistent cultural forms.[85] Tyhee is identified as the Ghost Dance leader in Johnson's account of the Arapaho and Cheyenne delegation's 1891 visit. He was also the "Bannock Chief" who had spent days discussing the nature of Indian-white relations with Porcupine during his stay at Fort Hall one year earlier. Although Johnson feared the worst from these visits, it is quite likely that Tyhee advised all the visitors, as he did Porcupine, "We ought all to be friends with the whites and be at peace with them and with each other."[86] He may have sensed that the Ghost Dance was a way to strengthen Indian communities, his own as well as others. His involvement in the propagation of the Ghost Dance indicates that he had yet to give up the hope that his people could maintain independent lives.

Pagwite, on the other hand, had a long history of being a political outsider, a complete and vocal opponent of assimilation programs, and a Ghost Dance activist. He never assumed the status of "head chief" of the Bannocks but remained a band headman and a thorn in the government's side until his death in 1891. Shamans from his band had preached the Ghost Dance doctrine in 1872 and inspired the Wood River murder. Pagwite worked against the Fort Hall school from the beginning, as the leading accuser of Peter Matthews. He opposed the 1887 Pocatello cession but lost out to Tyhee's influence. He was identified as the Ghost Dance leader at Fort Hall in two separate official reports. In October 1890 E. R. Kellogg, the commander of Fort Washakie, charged that "Bannack Jim" [Pagwite] was the so-called "Indian Christ," and that the Mormons had instigated the entire affair.[87] A year and a half later, after Pagwite's death, Fisher branded the deceased headman the "foremost leader in the Ghost Dance." Judging by his personal history and reaction to government programs, it is much more probable that Pagwite interpreted and used the Ghost Dance as a more militant form of resistance to physical and cultural encroachment. The differing experiences of Tyhee and Pagwite illustrate how the Ghost Dances could be simultaneously interpreted and used in distinct ways: as a unifying force in an Indian community creating an identity and as the source of militant, sometimes physical, resistance to the whites. At

Fort Hall in the 1890s, both types of resistance came together in the struggle over the boarding school.

The school fight at Fort Hall was intense but certainly not unique. On many reservations compulsory school attendance became the flashpoint of the struggle between Indian and white ways. While the education offered was practical—mechanical and industrial training for boys, domestic skills for girls, and the three R's for both—white reformers also viewed the schools as potent tools for cultural reeducation. Agriculture might infuse "American" values of thrift and capitalism into the adults, but it would be the succeeding generations, reformers and officials believed, who would truly reap the benefits of the white man's world. Schools would train Indian children in the values and expectations of that world. "The Indian must be trained young to the ways of the white man," wrote Arden Smith, who visited Fort Hall in 1882, "or he cannot be trained at all."[88] Because Indian cultures were to be eliminated, it was also crucial to move the children as far as possible from their homes and native cultures. "One of the greatest drawbacks to this school," wrote J. M. Needham of the Lemhi day school in 1888, "is the children associating with their parents," who discouraged them from speaking English or in any way trying to "imitate the whites."[89] Boarding schools were seen as the answer because they isolated children from their families and cultures. At the national boarding schools, native languages were prohibited, hair was cut, and students were renamed. Although only a handful of students from each reservation could attend the famous institutions like Carlisle, reservation boarding schools sprang up across the West.[90] The cultural aggression inherent in the schools was obvious to Indian peoples. In many communities, including Fort Hall, shamans emerged as the principal critics of the schools and led the opposition to them. This should come as no surprise. Schools represented a direct assault on the religious customs and worldview of American Indian peoples. Indeed, the agents uniformly belittled Indian religions as mere superstitions, which proper education would eradicate.

In the effort to destroy the power of the "medicine men" and get the children into school, Euro-Americans employed a number of tactics, each of which was met by able Indian resistance. Christian missionaries represented the most direct challenge to the shamans but had little real influence at Fort Hall in the nineteenth century. After an underfunded Catholic mission closed in 1873, the Methodist Episcopal organization, which had once again been assigned Fort Hall, showed only sporadic interest in establishing a working mission.[91] A sustained missionary presence did not exist until July 1887, with the arrival of Amelia J. Frost of the Connecticut Indian Association. Her associate, Ella J. Stiles, came to Fort Hall in October, and together the two women began a dedicated and long-term mission to the Shoshones and Bannocks. Frost remained at Fort Hall for the rest of the century and was beloved for her ministrations to the sick and the needy. But there is no evidence that the mission had any real or lasting effect on the power of Fort Hall's shamans or their resistance to the school. In 1899, the agent C. A. Warner remarked that, except for Frost's school for girls, "no active missionary work has ever been carried on upon this reservation." The agent did acknowledge, however, that a mission begun by Presbyterian Nez Percés in 1896 had that year achieved some success.[92] In the end, the missionary efforts at Fort Hall in the nineteenth century were of limited importance in the cultural war of assimilation.

A second weapon in the culture war was the Indian police force. Along with the establishment of Courts of Indian Offenses, police forces were intended to demonstrate the justice of the white man's laws and operate as agents of assimilation.[93] Officers were expected to behave as white men and abstain from all types of customary religious and cultural practices, including "dancing."[94] But although white officials expected the Indian police to serve as the vanguard of a new order, the institution often functioned as a culturally conservative force. At Fort Hall, the ethnic division between Bannocks and Shoshones also shaped the organization and activities of the police. The agent E. A. Stone established the first police force in December 1881, and from the beginning it was obvious that the agent was never completely in charge. Tyhee and Pagwite escorted the eleven Bannock volunteers to the agency and told Stone that "they had selected the best young men of their tribe, in order to help Washington break up whiskey selling, horse stealing, and other crimes." None of the original volunteers were Shoshones. Reportedly the Shoshones were unconcerned with Bannock dominance, stating "their people do not steal and are law-abiding, and hence do not need any police."[95] Within two months, however, the Shoshones demanded equal representation on the force. The new agent, A. L. Cook, agreed that it would "avoid trouble" and asked to double the size of the police force.[96] Until the end of the century, Bannocks usually dominated the Fort Hall Indian police force, both numerically and in terms of leadership. Moreover, Bannock headmen such as Tyhee continued to select the men for the force, subverting the original intention of the force and illustrat-

ing how progressive symbols like policing could be adopted and reinterpreted by Indian peoples.[97] Whereas the agents viewed the police force as
an instrument of assimilation, which indeed it could be, the Indian officers were more likely to see participation as an avenue to status and prestige. In many ways it was a modified outlet for the warrior tradition, and
symbols of authority and distinction, such as uniforms and badges, were
important to the officers.[98] In the struggle over the Fort Hall school, the
limitations of the police as a weapon of assimilation became all too obvious. When ordered to round up children and bring them to the school,
the same officers who would willingly risk their lives in pursuit of dangerous criminals resigned en masse rather than act as truant officers.

Perhaps the greatest obstacle to education was the prevalence of disease, and for this reason the third weapon the agents employed in the culture war was the presence of medical doctors. In the reservation era,
American Indian peoples came to rely increasingly on white physicians
and their cures. Schools were a perfect medium for the transmission of
contagions. In the 1880s and 1890s epidemics of smallpox, measles,
typhoid fever, scarlet fever, influenza, whooping cough, and diphtheria
struck one or all of the schools at Fort Hall, Lemhi, and Duck Valley
with vicious regularity. Opposition to the schools was often rooted in
these epidemics. In 1888, for instance, Needham, the agent at Lemhi,
claimed that "as soon as one of the children becomes sick [the "medicine
men"] use their influence to have them taken from the school and the
care of the physician."[99] For many white Americans like Needham, physical illness and spiritual turmoil were two discrete categories. Yet it
would be a gross oversimplification to argue, as some agents did, that the
rising acceptance of Western scientific medicine marked the demise of
shamanism.[100]

Divisions between the physical and spiritual were never clear in Newe
belief systems, and the increasing acceptance of white medicine may have
in fact had its basis in shamanic belief. The old dichotomy between less
skilled shamans, whose abilities were based on practical knowledge, and
the powerful *bo'hagande,* or "singing doctors," who dealt with spirit loss
and object intrusion, paralleled a widespread Indian distinction between
"white" and "Indian" diseases. In 1892 M. A. Miller, the agency doctor
at Fort Hall, reported a dramatic increase in calls to Indian camps. Even
more interesting, he wrote: "When I first came it was a very rare thing
for an Indian to take internal treatment, but it is quite common now for
them to request something to take internally."[101] The willingness to
ingest medicines for certain diseases suggests that Indian peoples did not

link these conditions with object intrusion, one of the most common shamanic diagnoses. At the same time, the continued practice of powerful singing shamans indicates that belief in object intrusion remained strong. It was not necessary for Shoshones and Bannocks to reject their own healing methods wholesale in order to accept Western scientific cures for some ailments. The shamans remained the doctors of choice in serious cases of suspected soul loss or object intrusion. Only as succeeding generations were educated to believe in the Western scientific conception of medicine did physicians surpass shamans as the doctors of choice on the reservations. Agents, Christian missionaries, and medical doctors all did their part to destroy the shamans' power, but none achieved complete success. By adopting new beliefs, even those of their opponents, shamans retained an important influence over Shoshone and Bannock religious life. For this reason, shamans were often the focus of the struggle for cultural control at Fort Hall and numerous reservations across the West.

The Fort Hall boarding school opened in February 1880 and quickly became a battleground for identity and power. Surprisingly, Bannock children dominated the first enrollment. More than two-thirds of the twenty-seven pupils that first session were Bannocks. The agent John Wright believed that this was because the Bannocks were "naturally more intelligent than their neighbors, the Shoshones." He added that the Bannocks were "the leading Indians in agriculture, in stock-raising, in patronizing the school, and in every other enterprise connected with the reservation, as they were foremost in the war of 1878."[102] Wright's commentary is an anomaly in what is otherwise an unbroken string of reports, stretching from the reservation's founding into the twentieth century, citing the Bannocks as the intractable foes of progress. As his comment about the Bannock War suggests, Wright was obviously taken with the Bannocks' martial and domineering manner. But there was another factor at work here. It is probable that the Bannocks were using school attendance as a way of gaining the agent's favor and buttressing their claim to primacy at Fort Hall.[103] In fact, Wright acknowledged as much: "The jealousy between the Bannocks and Shoshones is rather an advantage in their government than otherwise, as it presents an opportunity of securing competition for the different favors conferred by the department in its regulation upon the most deserving, and their own observation keeps constantly before their minds the fact that those who do most to help themselves are the recipients of the greatest help from the agency."[104] It is likely that only a handful of Bannock families (Wright drew his conclusion, after all, from fewer than twenty children) supported the school, much as only a few Bannocks (most notably Tyhee) took up farming, in order to secure the government's favor and their position on the reservation. But whether because of the death of school-children, the influence of the shamans, or Wright's successors' favoring the Shoshones, the Bannock dominance of school enrollment was short-lived, and by the mid-1880s few Bannock children attended the school.

The subsequent history of the boarding school revealed that Wright's optimism was unfounded. In 1881, his successor complained "not one single Indian on this reservation can read a word."[105] Lack of funding and proper facilities were constant problems. Finding competent and committed teachers willing to live in sometimes harsh conditions also proved difficult. In September 1882, Agent Cook suggested that classes be postponed until a proper school building was constructed. Two months later the Rev. George B. Mead arrived at Fort Hall to open the school, proclaimed the buildings unfit, and promptly returned to his home in Massachusetts. Undeterred, Cook hired the Rev. M. B. Bristol to replace him, and the school began sessions in December.[106] Special Agent Smith, who was visiting Fort Hall, gave a glowing report of the events: "The well fed, well clothed children are out, cheery and happy, where their people can see them, this being ration day, and the effect on all interested is one of thorough satisfaction and confidence."[107] Clearly Smith knew that convincing the parents was the key to the school's success, but his account makes the children sound strangely like hostages being paraded before their loved ones. By February Bristol warned that new school facilities were a must.[108] The following year the school was moved from the decrepit building near the agency to the old military post on Lincoln Creek, some eighteen miles away. For a time the agents reported greater success, but by 1887 things had again fallen into disrepair. When he resigned as school superintendent in May, J. D. Everest (the eighth man to hold that post in a little over two years) complained that the buildings were filthy and run-down, with hundreds of broken window panes and inadequate cooking and laundry facilities. The children were exposed to the weather, with insufficient food and clothing, and the school employees showed little concern for the children's welfare.[109]

By the mid-1880s the shamans posed the most serious cultural threat to schooling. In 1884 Cook singled out Shoshone shamans as leaders of the opposition. They "told [the parents] that the school was 'bad medi-

cine,' that those who attend it would die." He believed, however, that he
had induced one of the "medicine men" to send his children to school,
and by the next year he claimed that the shamans' influence over the
parents was declining.[110] Yet why would Cook single out the Shoshone
shamans when Bannock opposition to the school was a constant and the
agent's frustration with the latter people was so great that he recommended their complete removal from the reservation the following year?
The answer is probably that very few Bannock children attended the
school; Shoshones and "half-breeds" dominated the enrollment by the
mid-1880s.[111] Thus, Cook viewed Shoshone children as the most likely
to enroll in the school and Shoshone shamans as its most dangerous
opponents.

Cook, like many of his contemporaries, saw "white man's medicine"
as a tool for breaking the shamans' power, but neither the Shoshones nor
the Bannocks seemed willing to give up on their curing traditions, even
when white doctors proved more successful. In 1885 Cook wrote: "The
pernicious influence and practices of the medicine men is still felt, rendering the efforts of the agency physician to place them under proper
medical treatment somewhat unavailing. In several instances when the
physician has been able to induce a few of them to place themselves
under treatment for these [venereal diseases and tuberculosis] and other
diseases, entire or partial cures have been effected and the result in its
influence has been beneficial."[112] Success bred acceptance, but only
slowly. The epidemics that constantly raked the reservation, and the
school in particular, may have led to a gradual acceptance of white medicine. Three years later Cook's replacement, Peter Gallagher, reported
that several epidemics had struck Fort Hall, causing a "fearful mortality"—a 50 percent increase over the previous year. Yet he noted that the
Bannocks and Shoshones still sought out their shamans first. "Their own
medicine men are still in the lead among the most intelligent of them,"
wrote Gallagher, "and not until a failure is made by their own, will they
call for the agency physician."[113]

It appears that political pressure may have been far more influential in
undermining resistance to the school. In 1887 Supt. Everest reported
that both Tyhee and Captain Jim had brought "scholars to the agency"
to be enrolled in the school. Tyhee's action in particular surprised
Everest, as the Bannock leader had "heretofore been against" the
school.[114] The explanation for this turnaround was closely tied to political concerns and the pending Pocatello townsite sale. Two years earlier,
Cook had threatened the reservation headmen that if they did not bring

children to the school, he would "not mention their names as chiefs to Washington or talk to them in council until they had made an effort to do so." Maintaining influence among white officials, and consequently access to their power, was critical to the political survival of Indian leaders during the reservation era. Visiting the nation's capital was a potent symbol of authority, as were the letters of good conduct that the commissioner furnished to delegation members and that they could use as tangible symbols of their influence with the whites. By linking the school issue with Washington, Cook had made it a matter of political urgency for the headmen, who again sought to manipulate the symbols of progress. After making his threat, Cook reported that some of the chiefs had tried to gather students but had been repelled by the children's club-wielding mothers.[115] By 1887, the chiefs had partially broken down parental resistance to the school. But support for the school was neither uniform nor long-lasting. Most parents still refused to send their children, and in his 1888 annual report the commissioner of Indian affairs issued this dictum: "The Indians must conform to the 'white man's' ways. Peaceably if they will, forcibly if they must."[116] The stage was set for the most prolonged battle in the cultural war at Fort Hall, a battle that the Ghost Dance doctrine was a principal tool of the resistance.

In 1889 Stanton Fisher took over the job of agent at Fort Hall, and with it he assumed the task of forcing parents to bring their children to school. Fisher doubted that cutting off rations would work and had serious reservations about using the Indian police. He took pride in knowing that his officers would not hesitate to pursue the most desperate and dangerous men, but forcing children to attend school was a very different matter. The officers regarded the children as "under the control of their parents only." And even if the police obeyed his order to retrieve truant children, Fisher feared a violent response by the parents.[117] Although he doubted the efficacy of these tactics, Fisher eventually resorted to both. In March 1890 he ordered each tribe to send ten children to the school within one week, or else their rations would be cut off. In addition to the heavy snows, Fisher cited the death of Pocatello John as a factor in declining enrollment. According to Fisher, Pocatello John was the only headman of consequence on the reservation who had influence among both Shoshones and Bannocks and also supported schooling. Many of the Indians apparently blamed Pocatello John's death on his close association to the school, as they did the deaths of schoolchildren. "They never attribute a death to natural causes," wrote Fisher. "It is either the school, or something equally as foolish."[118]

One month later Fisher was able to be far more specific as to the nature of the "superstition." Although he did not identify the Ghost Dance or "Messiah Craze" by name, he complained that the Indian parents who opposed the school "have become insolent and sullen, and through the secret influence of the so-called 'medicine-men' they are led to believe that all white men will soon die, and that all the *dead* Indians will be resurrected. Absurd as it is, $9/10$ of the 'Bannock Indians' firmly believe it" [emphasis his].[119] He felt that the doctrine on the reservation made keeping children in school impossible and suggested that the company of soldiers spending the summer at Fort Hall might "remove from their minds every consideration of an outbreak, and render them submissive to the education of their children." His request for troops in the summer of 1890 was ignored, and school enrollment peaked at one hundred that summer before falling to eighty-five by October.[120]

In the fall of 1890, as the Ghost Dance excitement was reaching its peak on the Lakota reservations to the east, scarlet fever struck the Fort Hall school. Both Fisher and the agency doctor were away, and the school superintendent, John Williams, was left to deal with the crisis alone. On 22 November he sent a panicked telegram advising the Indian bureau that he had hired a "prominent physician." Later that day he wrote: "The old Indians are very much excited. I need the agent badly." Within a week forty-seven children had fallen ill, and three had died. By Williams's report, the epidemic must have been a frightening thing to witness: "The children are nearly all delirious and have to be held in their beds."[121] But from the historical record it is impossible to determine the exact effects of the epidemic on the Ghost Dance or in reinforcing the message of the Ghost Dance prophet. What is clear is that the parental fear of losing children who were sent to school was once again tragically real, and the battle between the agent and the shamans was only beginning.

By December, Fisher's struggle with the shamans had spread beyond the school issue. The agent became frustrated with a "Mexican medicine man" practicing on the reservation. He had come from New Mexico a few months earlier and "only recently started in as an Indian medicine man." Though an outsider at Fort Hall, he practiced curing techniques that were clearly acceptable within the Great Basin shamanic tradition. Fisher reported that the man doctored on the "Indian principle, by contortions, howls, and lamentations." "His charges are $5 a call, and I understand that he is getting all the work he can attend to." Fisher also suggested that this new shaman strengthened his position by participating in the ceremonial life of the community; "I am told that he joins in all

their heathenish dances & c."[122] Presumably this meant the Ghost Dance
as well as other ceremonies. Fisher confronted the man in Pocatello and
ordered him to leave the reservation in twenty-four hours or be locked
up in the agency jail. What happened next, however, sorely aggravated
the agent. About fifty Fort Hall Indians called on Fisher and demanded
that the shaman be allowed to remain on the reservation. They asserted
that "he was the best medicine man that had ever been here." They also
argued that past agents had never interfered with their shamans and
called on Fisher to continue this de facto religious toleration. What upset
the agent most was the fact that policemen and headmen (he did not
report if they were Bannocks or Shoshones, or both) were "most loud in
their demands that he must stay."[123] The insistence of the Fort Hall
Indians put Fisher in a difficult position. He did not believe the shaman
would leave willingly, and he also felt that any attempt to arrest the man
would lead to violence. His hands were tied. The case of this mysterious
shaman's appearance during the height of the 1890 Ghost Dance excitement demonstrates the fluid nature of Shoshone and Bannock society
and the often easy incorporation of outsiders and their doctrines as well
as the centrality of shamanism in the religious lives of Fort Hall Indians.

Fisher lost one of his greatest opponents in the school fight in
December 1891, when Pagwite died at the hands of Baptiste "Bat"
Avery, the mixed-blood Salish who had served in Fisher's scout company
in 1877 and was, in 1891, employed as the agency butcher.[124] In the
intervening years Avery had married a Shoshone woman named Mary
and had been "put on the books of that tribe." Fisher praised his work
ethic and reported that Avery had the "best cultivated" farm at Fort Hall
as well as the friendship and respect of local whites and the "better class
of Indians." In other words, he was a progressive. Fisher, on the other
hand, vilified Pagwite as "one of the most quarrelsome and arrogant men
on this reservation . . . A man who with great persisting fought every
attempted advancement of his race, whose death removed a wall in the
line of civilization. A man who was the foremost leader in the 'Ghost
Dance,' as well as all like heathenish customs."[125] Fisher asserted that
Pagwite attacked Avery, who only acted in self-defense. Avery surrendered to civil authorities but was not indicted. An Indian department
inspector had told the enraged Bannocks at the time of the incident that
if Avery was not punished by the courts, they could still ban him from the
reservation. In March Fisher reported that Bat's "life is threatened by the
worst members of the Bannock tribe" who demanded that "he shall
either be killed or driven off."[126] But Avery neither fled nor was killed.

He lived out the remainder of his life on the reservation, raising three children with his wife.[127]

Over the next two years, Fisher came increasingly to blame the shamans for the problems at Fort Hall. He called them the "greatest drawback to their [people's] civilization." He complained that the "medicine-men's" influence had rendered the police force ineffective. "No Indian policeman can be induced to arrest one of them;" he wrote, "neither will any member of the tribe appear as a witness against one, believing as they do that a 'medicine man' has supernatural power."[128] Once again, Fisher repeated the basics of Ghost Dance doctrine as expressed by the Fort Hall shamans, "that all the dead Indians and game will soon be resurrected, and that the whole white race will soon die, but that in order to bring about this great event the Indians must adhere strictly to their old heathenish ways and customs."[129] While his account of the doctrine was accurate (if biased), his analysis of the shamans' motivations reflected the ethnocentric views of his age. It was possible that the shamans actually believed the doctrine, he admitted, but it was more likely they, "like the late Brigham Young," realized that "education and enlightenment would curtail their power, which would mean they would have to 'rustle' for a living like the balance."[130]

The school remained the symbolic and actual battleground of the struggle. In January 1892, after the captain of the Indian police, Rufus Timoke, failed to get parental cooperation, the Indian department ordered Fisher to personally recruit the children. Never one to shy away from a fight, he accepted the mission but sarcastically told the commissioner that the only obstacle to enrolling every child on the reservation was the "lack of about three hundred U.S. troops, with orders to take the children by force."[131] Without military support, and after his police again failed, he went personally into the camps and took the children with "considerable force." Several brawls with angry parents were the result. In one instance Fisher would have been badly beaten but for the intervention of Joe Rainey, the former Bannock scout and then Indian policeman. "As it was," Fisher wrote, "it became necessary for me to choke a so-called chief into subjection." Fisher and Rainey enrolled the man's children, but five Bannock policemen, who had promised their headmen that they would force no more children to attend school, resigned over the incident.[132] Fisher's assessment that "things are assuming a more serious aspect everyday" proved correct. The next day, the agent again called for troops after the "Bannocks and some of the Shoshones have stood off and threatened the lives of persons trying to recruit to the school." When the police again refused to take the children, Fisher fired virtually the entire force and demoted Timoke to the rank of private.[133]

With the situation at Fort Hall reaching a breaking point, the bureau dispatched Special Agent J. A. Leonard to investigate. Leonard visited many Indian camps, seeking to enroll children, only to be met with "positive refusal, accompanied with more or less insolence." He was amazed that Indian policemen who were "fearless when ordered to arrest even desperate criminals" would resign when asked to act as truant officers. And, like Fisher, he found the greatest foe of the school to be a "dozen nonprogressive medicine men and would be chiefs." These "nonprogressive disturbers," he argued, were motivated by a "religious fanaticism" manifest in "persistent dancing, peculiar ceremonies and the unusual amount of paint and charms displayed," all of which were grounded in the Ghost Dance doctrine. He wrote: "The medicine men predicted during the winter that great floods would destroy the whites, and curiously enough there have been unprecedented rains this spring, which has so emboldened the most fanatical that they are prepared to resist any efforts to stop the dances, extend farming operations, or put their children in school. The coming of the Indians' Messiah, according to the revelation of the medicine men, is conditioned upon firm resistance to the white man's ways."[134] Leonard felt certain that the medicine men dominated a majority of the Indians at Fort Hall, though he was unsure how many could be incited to violence.[135] Both Leonard and Fisher asked that troops be sent onto the reservation, but, with memories of Wounded Knee still fresh, President Benjamin Harrison felt the use of soldiers was too "extreme."[136]

Thomas B. Teter inherited the school fight in December 1894. School enrollment had risen from 65 to 140, but there was still great opposition. At first Teter blamed the rude treatment the students and their parents had received from school employees, rather than the influence of the shamans.[137] The agent's honeymoon at Fort Hall, however, was short-lived. By September 1895, the commissioner of Indian affairs received a letter written by a local white settler, Isaac Yandell, purportedly on behalf of William Penn, the captain of the Fort Hall Indian police, and a "delegation of Indians." The Indians claimed that if Teter persisted in forcing children to the school he was likely to get himself killed, and "then troops and white men would rush in here and massacre the innocent as well as the guilty." Penn believed that the best course was to go slow but admitted there were a "lot of old Bannacs" who were unlikely to ever voluntarily send their children to school. The letter concluded with a blast at Teter: "The man has neither education, experience, or brains. He will yet be the cause of serious trouble here."[138] How much of this complaint was a product of Yandell's dislike for Teter is hard to say. Within six months Jim Ballard, the emerging nonprogressive leader on the reservation and a coauthor of the letter to the Lakotas exhorting them to fight for their "Indian" ways, along with several other Bannocks, tried to kill the agent, in large part because of the school issue. This violence attests to the real anger of many Fort Hall Indians.

The conflict over the school reached its climax in the fall of 1897. Teter's replacement, F. G. Irwin, an army lieutenant, treated the situation with military resolve. When he sent the Indian police out for the annual roundup of students, one of the captured students was a recently married fourteen-year-old girl, whose husband took exception to her removal. Along with some friends, he attacked the police contingent, which was beaten, disarmed, and humiliated. In response to this "riot," Irwin called in the cavalry, a measure that had been suggested numerous times before. This time it had the desired effect. The Indian police began collecting children in unprecedented numbers. Seventy-five children were enrolled in ten days, forty in a single day. Many parents began to bring their children to the school voluntarily. Only "old Mc Kie, or Mack Macki, one of the "chief men of the Bannocks," objected, and he was "promptly" arrested. Irwin believed that the arrest and the presence of troops sent a message to the "turbulent element of the Bannocks which has long been beyond control" and marked an "important step . . . in the advancement of these Indians."[139]

Irwin also realized that enrolling children was not enough; the school must protect the children in attendance and convince their parents of its worth. His first concern was the startling number of deaths from disease among the schoolchildren. Many of the Indian parents viewed the school as a "charnel house, and many of them when they give up their children to school are firmly convinced that they will never return." Fear of losing a child cut across ethnic and progressive lines, and, unlike many of his predecessors, Irwin argued that this was not a "mere excuse" employed to keep children from school but a reality. He recommended that a completely new school complex be built and that, until it was ready, a doctor should be permanently assigned to the school. By the end of October the troops were gone, and physical resistance had ceased.[140]

The end of the school fight did not mean that the agents had won the war or that Bannocks and Shoshones fell in behind the assimilation program. If anything, the struggle was a shared experience that strengthened

Indian identity. Just six months after the soldiers had broken the physical resistance to the school, Irwin complained to the commissioner of a "small element of extremely unprogressive Indians, principally the young Bannocks" who remained an impediment to "civilization and improvement" at Fort Hall. Their principal tool of resistance was the "dance." According to Irwin it was a "grotesque" display of "their own and their tribe's valor" and served to "keep alive vicious practices." Most frustrating of all was that the dancing was not limited to the young Bannocks but appealed to nonprogressives and progressives alike. Irwin lamented: "Occasionally a former school boy can be seen among the dancers as hideously painted as the others, and many progressive Indians, especially the younger class are always in attendance."[141] This "dance," like the Ghost Dance, had become a statement of Indian identity in the face of aggressive assimilation programs. The fact that progressives were drawn to it reveals that, although they had chosen to follow a path which in some ways led them closer to the dominant society, they rejected that society's demand that they abandon their separate identity and dissolve into a sea of English-speaking, petty capitalist farmers.

By the mid-1890s the shared experiences of reservation life at Fort Hall had contributed to the development of a pan-Indian identity that could cut across the ethnic and tribal boundaries of Shoshone and Bannock and reach far beyond the physical boundaries of the reservation. The Ghost Dance religion was a part of this process at Fort Hall, and it was within this context that Jim Ballard and Joe Wheeler wrote to the Lakotas urging them not to give up on their "Indian" ways and beliefs.[142] The Ballard-Wheeler letter (reprinted in the introduction to this volume) is indicative of the complex negotiation of identity and power on the reservation. It illustrates how multiple categories—Bannock and Shoshone, progressive and nonprogressive—and issues of both ethnicity and race intersected in the ongoing process of identity formation.

Ballard and Wheeler identified themselves as "principal chief" and "chief justice," roles that seemingly represented the Indian and white worlds, respectively. But both positions were in fact complicated symbols that combined the new and the old, the progressive and the nonprogressive. The concept of a principal chief was meaningless to Shoshone and Bannock peoples before the treaty making and reservation eras. On the reservation, men like Tyhee combined an older ideal of leadership—the talkers who negotiated a group's access to resources and directed combined efforts like the buffalo hunt—with an understanding of the political limitations of the era to create a role as a reservation head chief. On the surface, the chief justice was more clearly an imposition of a foreign system of justice. There was no equivalent role in Newe society. Justice was the responsibility of the kin group, not the state. Moreover, the Courts of Indian Offenses were intended to punish crimes of assimilation. Punishing theft and homicide often took a back seat to enforcing prohibitions against alcohol and indigenous religious practices. Still, Indian judges, like Indian police officers, applied meaning to and often used their positions in ways that contradicted the assimilation program. The roles of principal chief and chief justice were not evidence of two different ways of life but rather indicative of the renegotiation of identity in the reservation context.

Ballard's and Wheeler's life stories are as telling as the offices by which they identified themselves. In 1897 Teter characterized Jim Ballard as a member of the "hunting, uncivilized, and nonprogressive element." The agent had no doubt developed this opinion a year earlier, when Ballard and twenty or so other Bannocks physically assaulted him during the continuing struggle over forced attendance at the Fort Hall school.[143] When the progressive Shoshone leader Billy George (who had ridden with Buffalo Horn during the Bannock War and only later chose the trail toward assimilation) was shot a few months later, Teter blamed the "Jim Ballard outfit."[144] Ballard's core followers consisted of about twenty Bannock and Shoshone families "bitterly opposed to any movement savoring of civilization and education." While usually identified as Bannock in official correspondence, Ballard and his followers were defined by their rejection of assimilation programs rather than by linguistic or cultural affinities. In fact, Jim Ballard was a Shoshone speaker.

In many ways Ballard was the successor to Pagwite. He enjoyed greater political support than the latter, perhaps because no leader had emerged to fill Tyhee's role as a conciliator and possibly because both Bannock and Shoshone speakers resented the interminable delays and broken promises that marked their dealings with the government. In the mid-1890s Ballard's message of staunch resistance to assimilation resonated with many on the Fort Hall reservation. The tone of the letter he signed in 1894, however, indicates a more subtle understanding of the political realities he faced as well as the effects of the shared experiences of reservation life.

Joe Wheeler seemed to be the direct opposite of Ballard. A few years earlier, Fisher had described him as an English-speaking, progressive, full-blood Shoshone, who had served on the Court of Indian Offenses ever since its inception at Fort Hall. "He has money in the bank," wrote the agent, and "is the wealthiest and one of the most influential Indians on the reservation. He dresses wholly in citizens' clothes, favors schools and civilization, and is a man of honesty and integrity."[145] Wheeler certainly exhibited the outward symbols of assimilation, but he had not become a white man. For instance, he remained married to two women throughout the 1890s, all the while serving as a justice.[146] Wheeler thus presents the enigma, like Tyhee, of a progressive who defended traditional ways. But he is an enigma only if one accepts the reformers' vision of assimilation as a transformative process that killed the Indian and left behind the man. He chose a path that often put him at odds with men like Ballard. His signature on the letter, however, suggests that no matter how far apart he and Ballard were on the issues such that defined identity, they shared a common understanding of themselves as Indians. Cutting his hair and becoming a successful farmer did not make Joe Wheeler any less Indian.

Jim Ballard and Joe Wheeler rose to leadership at a time when being Indian truly became salient. Their vision of Indianness was contested but ultimately unifying. Just as Ballard could not discount the American Indian present, Wheeler could not dismiss the past. Both men could envision the survival of their "customs of worship and dances" in a world where there was also a "time for work" according to the white man's system. At Fort Hall, the Ghost Dances provided one path from older belief systems to a unified Indian identity that explained reservation life and gave hope for the future. In 1894, both men felt their Lakota friends, as fellow "Indians," could also benefit from following that path.

Conclusion

Prophecy and American Identities

It soon became evident that there was more in the Ghost
dance than had been expected . . . as the dance still exists
and is developing new features at every performance.

James Mooney, 1896

On New Year's Day 1889 Jack Wilson died, and so began perhaps the
most famous and most studied American Indian religious movement of
the nineteenth century. When his spirit returned to his body, Wilson, who
was also known as Wovoka, began to preach to his people, the Northern
Paiutes, or Numu, of the Smith and Mason valleys of western Nevada.
He told them that if they practiced the rituals that had been revealed to
him and led honest, peaceful lives, they would be reunited with their
deceased friends and loved ones on a reborn earth. From its beginnings
on the Walker River Reservation, the doctrine spread far and wide, and
pilgrims from reservations across the West came to visit the prophet.
Some came from the Lakota reservations in South Dakota, where one of
the most tragic and symbolic events in the history of the American West
would take place. In the popular imagination, as in many histories,
Wovoka's religion leads inexorably to a cold December day, the report of
a Hotchkiss cannon, and a mass grave on a windswept hill in South
Dakota. The Ghost Dance and Wounded Knee have become synony-
mous. Yet the Ghost Dances did not necessarily lead to Wounded Knee,
nor did they die there. The religion was far more than a tragic coda to the
autonomous life that native peoples enjoyed before their dispossession.

Ghost Dances became part of a common process of identity formation
that took place at different times and in different ways in Indian communities across the United States. It may be a truism that a people cannot
survive as a people if they are utterly absorbed by another, but in

nineteenth-century America, indigenous peoples faced this very prospect. The destruction of their subsistence economies, warfare, epidemics, shrinking populations, and an aggressive assimilation program all seemed to seal the fate of the "vanishing Americans." Indian peoples, however, did not disappear: they adapted and survived. Whether living in a recognized indigenous community on a reservation or scattered within overwhelming white settlement, American Indians survived in part by asserting distinct social identities.

The construction of meaningful social identities, be they ethnic, tribal, racial, or otherwise, is always a reflective process. Identity formation does not take place in isolation; it is not dependent on exclusion of the Other. Rather, the process takes place in conversation and interaction with the Other. American Indian social identities emerged from the interplay of indigenous understandings (social, political, economic, and religious), external forces, and contingent events. For many American Indian groups, defining social identity meant asserting their existence as sovereign tribal nations alongside the United States of America. Moreover, for these tribal groups as well as for the many people of native descent who found themselves outside such defined communities, a shared sense of Indianness became an important means to assert their survival in the face of the policies and demands of white America.

American Indians were not alone in reshaping meaningful social identities. In an "imagined community" like the United States, the contest over national identity is one of the great themes of history.[1] The struggle to define what it meant to be an American raged in the nineteenth century, and it continues today. At various times in American history, economic and social elites have proposed rather narrow definitions of American. The Friends of the Indian, for instance, could not envision an American who practiced an indigenous religion or held communal values. For these influential citizens, evangelical Christianity and individualistic, competitive capitalism were the hallmarks of American identity. In the face of the dominant society's attempts to shape a national identity, marginalized groups countered with ideas of their own. African Americans, European immigrants, and American Indians all found it necessary to control their own identities, lest they be entirely absorbed or completely isolated in the dominant group's version of America. Although none of these groups could define their existence completely outside the dominant society, they could, and did, shape their relationship to the larger society by exerting control over their own social identities. The Ghost Dances were not the only means through which American Indian peoples expressed their identity and asserted their survival (nor was identity the only meaning that Indian peoples attached to the movement), but they must be understood as part of this process as well.

Native communities across the United States in the late nineteenth and early twentieth century engaged the dominant society in a sort of intercultural conversation about race, ethnicity, and identity. The one constant factor in the exchange was the attempts of white officials to remake native peoples into Americans. As evidenced by their belief in the transformative power of the federal assimilation program, these officials consistently looked past the great diversity of many native communities, assuming not only strong and innate tribal or ethnic identities but also a set of shared racial characteristics. Increasingly, white Americans defined Indian peoples as a separate race and questioned their fitness for full inclusion in American society and participation in the competitive capitalist economy (although this view did not slow the quest to incorporate native resources).[2] But Indian peoples were not all alike, any more than were the individuals supposedly encompassed by one tribe or ethnicity. The pressures of assimilation might be fairly uniform, but the responses of native peoples were not. Cultural factors as well as specific historical experiences shaped identity formation and could just as easily lead to factionalism and sharp divisions as to a unified vision of a people.

At White Earth in Minnesota, for instance, Anishinaabe bands with complex and variable histories of intermarriage and participation in the market economy settled on a single reservation. There, a contest over identity and rights ultimately led to the alienation of resources and dispossession. At first it was possible for the "mixed-blood" Métis and the "full-blood" Anishinaabeg to maintain relatively separate yet complementary ways of life. The former gravitated towards commerce and cash-crop agriculture on the western portion of the reserve, which held the best agricultural lands. The latter settled farther east and pursued a more traditional lifestyle, based on seasonal subsistence patterns supplemented by occasional wage labor. White Earth, according to the historian Melissa Meyer, was best understood as a "community of communities."[3] The impact of federal assimilation programs and rapacity of white interests destroyed this symbiosis and engendered a contest between emergent reservation ethnicities. When federal legislation restricted the sale of individual allotments by "full-bloods," outside financial interests, aided and abetted by the "mixed-bloods," worked to open the reservation to economic exploitation by defining nearly all reservation residents as being of mixed blood. This end was achieved by adopting a quasi-scientific measure of ethnicity: blood quantum. Since nearly all Anishinaabe had one or more non-Indian ancestors, the number of full-bloods on tribal rolls plummeted. For their part, the full-bloods organized their resistance around their newfound ethnic identity and tried unsuccessfully to remove many of the mixed-bloods from tribal rolls and prevent the alienation of reservation lands. Economic and political factionalism made emergent ethnic categories critically important within what had always been a multiethnic community.

Such interchanges over ethnicity, race, and identity were not limited to reservation communities like White Earth or Fort Hall. Native peoples who lived in small groups among the non-Indian majority also struggled to assert and maintain a distinct group identity. In her study of Indian identity around Puget Sound, Alexandra Harmon demonstrates that although the category of "Indian" has persisted, Indianness has been defined in many different ways and for different purposes, from kinship and trade relations to treaty councils, federal assimilation programs, BIA recognition, and treaty fishing rights. Before the arrival of Europeans and Euro-Americans, native peoples around Puget Sound identified themselves by the village in which they resided. Tribal, ethnic, or linguistic identities had little saliency, and the concept of an Indian was completely meaningless. An intricate web of kinship tied together peoples divided by linguistic difference and often vast distances. Into this world came British and American traders, who sought to make sense of native peoples by categorizing them in very different ways. Trade, treaties, warfare, and reservations not only made emergent ethnic identities meaningful but resulted in a new racial category: "Indians." Many Indians chose to forgo life on reservations and live among the rapidly growing white population along Puget Sound. Frequent intermarriage with non-Indians further complicated the ethnic and racial picture. How could people who refused to live on a reservation, and who lived, worked, intermarried, and often looked like whites, claim to be Indians? When rights and resources were at stake, the discussion could become heated. By the mid–twentieth century, Puget Sound Indians actively shaped their own identity, emphasizing their fishing culture and their rights to the catch under the Stevens Treaties of 1854 and 1855.[4]

The White Earth and Puget Sound examples illustrate the negotiated and contingent nature of ethnic and racial identity. Economic, political, and social relations with the dominant society exerted a profound influence over identity formation, yet native people's own cultural traditions and histories were just as important. The ethnic and racial identities that developed in native communities across the United States reflected the internal and external diversity of those communities as well as the shared experience of being Indians in the eyes of white America.

For many Indian peoples the Ghost Dances remained a powerful and malleable statement of identity and worldview well into the twentieth century. Writing six years after Wounded Knee, James Mooney certainly did not view the dances, which he witnessed in person on numerous occasions after 1890, as an obsolete fantasy. On the contrary, he found the Ghost Dance to be a vibrant religion "developing new features at every performance."[5] Wounded Knee had not struck a shattering blow to the faith even among the Lakotas. They continued to dance and prepare for the return of the buffalo for at least two years after the massacre.[6] Moreover, in 1902 one of the original Lakota apostles, Kicking Bear, again visited Wovoka. Later that year he brought the Ghost Dance to the Fort Peck Reservation in Montana, where an Assiniboine man named Fred Robinson heard his teachings. Robinson introduced his own interpretation of the doctrine to the Dakotas in Canada, where it became known as New Tidings.[7] The New Tidings religion among the Wahepton Sioux of Saskatchewan provides another example of a Ghost Dance survival that revitalized an Indian culture. The core of New Tidings was the 1890 Ghost Dance prophet's admonition to all Indian peoples to lead a "clean, honest life." Alice Beck Kehoe argues that this interpretation allowed the Sioux to prune "unobtainable or anachronistic elements" of their culture (bison hunting, for example) while permitting the revival of other cultural elements and drawing the community together in mutual support.[8]

In several other cases, American Indian peoples transformed the Ghost Dance. The partial revival of Pawnee culture through the Ghost Dance and hand game is just one example. By 1892 Pawnee life had become "barren" and "empty of cultural value" in the wake of "uncontrolled assimilation." The hand game, which had been a male-only gambling game, became an important part of the Pawnee Ghost Dance ritual performed by men, women, and children. It reintroduced the joy of play into Pawnee life and initiated a partial revival of Pawnee culture and identity that persisted long after the Ghost Dance era.[9] A lesser-known Kiowa revival of the religion lasted from 1894 to 1916. In the revised dance, the focus was on trances, which allowed participants to visit their relatives in heaven. It is possible that a horrendous infant mortality rate on the Kiowa-Comanche-Apache Reservation in the early 1890s led many grieving parents to adopt the dance. The retooled Kiowa Ghost Dance took two distinct ceremonial forms: outdoor round dances, which resembled the earlier movement, and indoor "sings," which functioned as practice sessions for the larger outdoor dances. In both cases syncretism was obvious. The outdoor dances were held every year on the Fourth of July and Christmas, and the "sings" took place on Sundays. Regardless of the syncretic American and Christian elements, however, the dance functioned as a statement of Kiowa and Indian identity. Dance leaders reportedly told the Christian missionary Isabel Crawford: "He gave the book to the white people . . . but he gave the Indians the dance road."[10]

For Shoshone- and Bannock-speaking peoples the *nazánga*—what the whites deemed the Ghost Dance—was an abiding part of their road as well as an expression of their identity as Indian peoples. The religion was enduring and meaningful not only because it emerged from deep cultural practice but also because of its syncretic, incorporative nature. The Ghost Dance religion was not a rigid, tradition-bound belief system. On the contrary, it provided a flexible doctrine that held the power to explain native peoples' current situation and prophesy their survival. It could be used to rally resistance to the cultural oppression of the assimilation program as well as draw together socially and politically diverse individuals in a reservation community. And it held the power to unite ethnically plural peoples as Indians.

Although white Americans did not follow the "dance road," they too found that prophecy held great power for "explaining" American identity. Prophecy, mission, and providence had always swirled around mythological understandings of the United States' origins, identity, and destiny. The definition of an American national identity and its ramifications for citizenship and inclusion in the republic is a central theme of nineteenth-century United States history. Early in the century contests over what it meant to be an American often evinced a regional character, as the Anglo residents of the Northeast, South, and Midwest staked their claims as the true heirs of the American Revolution. Using strongly nationalist language, each region claimed it was the most American and most clearly fulfilled the nation's promise.[11] Increasingly, religion became a defining feature of American identity. American evangelical Protestantism was infused with a millennial fervor. Although expectations of the actual Second Coming waned as the century passed, this fervor was rechanneled into other areas, most notably into beliefs in American innocence, righteousness, and Manifest Destiny.[12] By the post–Civil War era, the self-defined Americans who dominated government, business, and reform clearly and narrowly defined the American national identity as white, middle-class, native-born, and Protestant. This group, which included the Friends of the Indian, took it as their mission to Americanize others who did not fit this mold, including American Indians.[13]

Visions of millennial nationalism, however, also held great salience for those with other definitions of what it meant to be American. Born of the same social upheaval as evangelical Protestantism, utopian social experiments such as those at New Harmony and Oneida offered visions of cooperative communities starkly at odds with the emergent Christian individualism. At the same time, the millennial vision of conservative Christian movements, most notably Mormonism, questioned the emerging social and gender relations of the new evangelical Protestant order and its cult of domesticity, which elevated women to positions of moral authority. Using the shared millennial discourse of the age, Mormon prophets countered with a world of patriarchal communalism. The United States in the early nineteenth century was a nation in cultural tumult. As Euro-Americans struggled to define the political and ideological boundaries of nationhood, prophetic religion often provided a common language for the dominant and the marginalized.

American Indians took part in this process and utilized the shared discourse of prophecy to mark Indian difference. As native peoples experienced the effects of colonization, including epidemic disease, economic dependency, and the loss of land, a series of millennial religious movements arose that were premised upon a shared Indian identity. Like African American slaves who used religion to define themselves and their resistance to the master class, Indian peoples used religion to create an identity and resist white territorial and cultural encroachments. By 1761, the Delaware holy man Neolin had prophesied a pan-Indian spiritual renewal that echoed through American Indian millennial movements for the next century and a half. The "Master of Life" appeared to Neolin and showed him that the Europeans blocked the native's path to heaven. To clear the path, Indian peoples were to wean themselves from dependence on the British and their trade goods and cultivate older methods of accessing spiritual power. In the wake of the French and Indian War, the Ottawa leader Pontiac invoked Neolin's prophecy to unite hundreds of native warriors drawn from dozens of villages and peoples to make war on the British and stall their expansion into the Ohio country.[14] A half century later the Shawnee prophet Tenskwatawa experienced similar visions and again preached pan-Indian revival. Tecumseh, the prophet's brother, led the political and military resistance against white expansion that promised to unite native peoples from the Gulf of Mexico to the Great Lakes.[15] Scholarly studies of these movements have consistently cast the intertribal, prophetic nativism inherent in the respective religions as one aspect of an emerging American Indian nationalism, due in no small part to the direct ties between the religious prophecies and the political and military movements led by the iconic leaders Pontiac and Tecumseh.

The millennial and nativist movements that emerged farther west or later in the nineteenth century, however, have been explained not in terms of emergent identity but rather as narrower reactions to colonization and deprivation. The Prophet Dances, the Dreamer religion of the Wanapum prophet Smohalla, and the Ghost Dances all exhibited to one degree or another the unifying pan-Indian spirit of the earlier religions. Smohalla's doctrine inspired the "renegades" who rejected reservation life and held out in their traditional homes along the Columbia River. And, of course, the Ghost Dance was forever linked to Wounded Knee by both contemporary observers and later historians. Still, the lack of charismatic political leaders or a direct military challenge to the United States should not lead us to underestimate the Indian "nationalism" inherent in native prophecies in the West. These later movements occurred when the evangelical American identity was fully formed and dominant and at the very time that a shared American Indian identity emerged as meaningful. This was no accident of history. The Ghost Dances were a prophetic expression of an American Indian identity that countered American attempts to assert a particular national identity and to impose that vision on American Indians.

Why is it, then, that one vision of the Ghost Dance religion has come to dominate all others? In part this view has arisen from intellectual interpretations that have privileged material and universal explanations over the ideal and the particular. Scholarly treatments of the Ghost Dances and other millenarian socioreligious movements have produced valuable insights and theoretical approaches, but they have also steered the discussion toward deprivation theory. There is no doubt that the Ghost Dances emerged at a time of economic, political, and cultural devastation for nearly all American Indian peoples. The movements cannot be fully understood outside the context of these social stresses. The Ghost Dances were an appeal to spiritual power to overturn a world that was not of their making. Yet, as a consequence, explanations involving external motivation and material conditions have nearly always overshadowed the values of identity and cultural persistence that Indian peoples attached to the dances. What could be read as a tale of hope and survival has usually been cast as one of despair and death.

James Mooney, a self-trained anthropologist with the Bureau of American Ethnology (BAE), set the tone with his seminal study of the Ghost Dance religions. His report, published in 1896, is a classic of comparative history and ethnography shaped by the evolutionary theories then prevalent in American anthropology.[16] Mooney produced a sweeping study that placed both Ghost Dances (he was the first to identify the 1870 movement) within the larger contexts of American Indian prophetic movements and world traditions of prophecy and ecstatic religion. He did not suggest direct historical connections among all of these movements but rather asserted that each illustrated a common response to oppression. For Mooney, the motivation for ghost dancing was universal:

> And when the race lies crushed and groaning beneath an alien yoke, how natural is the dream of a redeemer, an Arthur, who shall return from exile or awake from some long sleep to drive out the usurper and win back for his people what they have lost. The hope becomes a faith and the faith becomes a creed of priests and prophets, until the hero is a god and the dream a religion, looking to some great miracle of nature for its culmination and accomplishment. The doctrines of the Hindu avatar, the Hebrew Messiah, the Christian millennium, and the Hesûnanin of the Indian Ghost Dance are essentially the same, and have their origin in a hope and longing common to all humanity.[17]

Mooney's cultural relativism was too much for the BAE director, John Wesley Powell, who cautioned in his introduction to the report against "comparing or contrasting religious movements among civilized people with such fantasies" as the Ghost Dance. Later anthropologists, however, adopted Mooney's emphasis on deprivation arising from colonization as the essential cause of the Ghost Dances and similar socioreligious movements.

Throughout the twentieth century, deprivation theory became increasingly sophisticated, as anthropologists sought to explain the origins, motivations and function of "revitalization" and "nativistic" movements. The work of Anthony F. C. Wallace and David Aberle has been particularly influential. A psychological anthropologist, Wallace defined revitalization movements as an "organized, conscious effort by members of a society to construct a more satisfying culture" and described a general pattern discernible in most cases. After prolonged and general stress or deprivation (economic distress, military defeat, epidemic disease, etc.), he claimed, cultural systems begin to break down, and the society enters a phase of "cultural distortion" marked by regressive behaviors such as alcoholism, intragroup violence, and depression. At this point revitalization begins, often through the vision of a charismatic leader who reformulates the cultural system and preaches renewal to the society. In time the new system becomes "routinized" and emerges as a new "steady state." Revitalization movements can be either secular or religious. They can seek the revival of older cultural patterns or, as with the Melanesian cargo cults, seek to import a foreign culture. Some revitalization movements were "nativistic" and sought to "expel the persons or customs of foreign invaders."[18] The concept of revitalization helps explain the long-standing individual and cultural effects of movements such as the Ghost Dance. Their persistence and power have never been tied to the actual fulfillment of a singular prophecy. Indeed, Christians have been waiting far longer for their millennium.

Aberle's study of Navajo peyotism also introduced important concepts for understanding the nature of deprivation and social movements. Aberle classified social movements into four categories, depending on the locus and amount of change sought. Some movements sought only partial change of the individual or community, and these Aberle labeled *alterative* and *reformative* respectively. *Transformative* movements worked at the community level and sought a total change in existence. *Redemptive* movements also sought total change, but at the individual level. Aberle was quick to point out that most movements cannot be contained within a single category and that "redemptive elements are common in transformative movements."[19] The Ghost Dance religion offers the classic example: the message of cataclysmic renewal of the earth was clearly transformative, but many Indian people used the redemptive aspects of Wovoka's prophecies—"do not fight, do always right"—to make sense of the massive changes in their lives.

Aberle also moved the theory of social movements away from a monolithic view of deprivation. Mooney's evolutionist approach assumed a uniformity in human experience that could not account for specific historical experience. Aberle adopted the more variable approach of "relative deprivation." Simply put, what might strike one as deprivation could easily be interpreted by another as a relative improvement in life and status. He explained through example: "A man who thinks he is suited to be a plant manager and is chained to a clerical job, experiences relative deprivation. A man who congratulates himself on achieving a clerical job in spite of deficiencies in his earlier training does not."[20] Deprivation, then, will be felt differently by different groups and even by individuals within the same group. At Fort Hall, for example, Bannocks and Shoshones were subject to same pressures (assimilation programs, lack of rations, and so on) but interpreted them differently within the context of their respective experiences.

Deprivation, then, is a powerful explanation for some of the external motivations of the Ghost Dances and other social movements, but it cannot fully explain their meanings and practice within a particular cultural or historical context. This was the central insight behind the work of Leslie Spier and Cora Du Bois. Spier dismissed deprivation and identified a motif of world destruction and renewal, common in Columbia Plateau cosmology and mythology, as the wellspring of the Prophet Dance and every other American Indian prophetic movement in the far West.[21] Du Bois reached similar conclusions concerning the Ghost Dance movement of 1870, but she situated these older beliefs directly within Northern Paiute culture.[22] The "cultural complex" argument was a needed corrective for the simplest forms of deprivation theory. The Indian peoples who practiced prophetic religions were embedded in living cultures and understood the world around them on their own terms. Unfortunately, the nearly complete dismissal of historical factors obscures more than it explains. There is no doubt that Plateau peoples interpreted events through the context of their own cultures, yet the world they lived in by 1790 (the date of the earliest Prophet Dances) could hardly be considered aboriginal. The indirect effects of Euro-American colonization—the acquisition of horses, shifting trade patterns, and epidemic diseases— had spurred great changes in Indian societies well before the first white fur traders set foot in the area.[23] Indian peoples understood the changes in their world on their own terms, certainly, but those terms were always changing.

A more reasonable approach is to seek to understand the interplay between culture and history, preexisting belief and deprivation, and internal order and external motivation. Culture and history are inextricably linked. Historical events are understood through the prism of culture; that is, they acquire their significance through culture. At the same time, cultures are a product of history. As the meanings that a culture applies to things, events, and people are put at risk in the material world, they are continually reevaluated and modified. Cultural change that is externally motivated is thus internally ordered.[24] In his 1982 study of the Lakota Ghost Dance, Raymond J. DeMallie chastises historians who have ignored Lakota culture and presented the Ghost Dances as either a narrow reaction to deprivation or the desperate fantasies of a dying culture. He argues that Ghost Dancers were neither "uncomprehending children" nor people "motivated by precisely the same political and economic drives as white men."[25] Nineteenth-century Lakotas held fundamentally different conceptions of spirituality and ecology. They did not, for instance, share the Western scientific concept of extinction, believing instead that whites or Indians had offended the buffalo, who had fled to an underground sanctuary. The Ghost Dance promised their return and was "completely consistent with the old Lakota system of cause and effect by which they comprehended the ecology." DeMallie thus calls for ethnohistorians to grant native peoples their "own legitimate perspective" and seriously consider the symbolic aspects of their cultures.[26] If one adopts this approach, the myriad meanings—including emergent identity—which Indian peoples attached to socioreligious movements like the Ghost Dances become far more visible.

This study presents an alternative explanation for the importance of the Ghost Dances, seeing them as one vehicle for the expression of ethnic and racial identities among American Indian peoples. In the nineteenth century, Shoshone- and Bannock-speaking peoples, like nearly all indigenous groups, underwent enormous social, economic, demographic, and religious change. For the Shoshones and Bannocks, the evolution of meaningful ethnic and tribal identities among closely related peoples was one of the most important manifestations of these changes. So, too, was the development of an shared sense of Indianness, which increasingly tied them to other native peoples with whom they may or may not have had contact before. Underlying specific Shoshone and Bannock responses to the Ghost Dance religion are ethnogenesis and the relative deprivation that each people felt in the postcontact era. Yet while ethnicity became increasingly salient and divided Shoshone from Bannock, the shared experience of reservation life gave meaning to Indianness, and thus the Ghost Dances were a prophetic expression of that shared identity at Fort Hall. In the pre-reservation period, Bannock and Shoshone ethnicity developed as a result of differing responses to white contact in an era of relative autonomy. Then, during the reservation era, the struggle to survive on the underfunded and undersupplied reservation led to intense political factionalism and a sharper definition of Shoshone and Bannock ethnicity and tribal identity. During this period of declining autonomy, a shared Indian identity became far more important in the face of the aggressive demands of white settlers and their government. The Ghost Dance was adopted and performed first and most intensely by the Bannocks—the mixed bands that wintered in the Fort Hall region—as a religion of resistance. Although initial reactions to the dance might be conditioned by ethnic identity, the effects of the religion helped to forge a shared racial identity as American Indians. Like earlier "nativistic" or "revitalization" movements, the religion was predicated on the existence of a distinct Indian identity.

For Shoshone and Bannock people, the *nazánga* could become a powerful statement of identity because it was rooted in deep cultural practice. Shamanism was at the heart of these understandings and created a remarkable flexible and incorporative religious worldview. Shamanism is based on the belief that a spiritual power—*bo'ha*—pervades the universe and that all human beings may seek out that power. As a result, in shamanic cultures spiritual knowledge is not the singular domain of priests and is not seen as having been revealed in a single place at a single time. Rather, *bo'ha* is a constant in everyone's lives, and spiritual knowledge is constantly being revealed. Shamanism was also the wellspring of the prophetic tradition among many American Indian peoples in the far West. As early as the 1850s, that tradition had emerged as a religion of identity and resistance that made sense of the massive changes wrought by colonization. Ghost Dances were acceptable and logical expressions of identity precisely because they emerged from long-standing religious beliefs, predicated on constant religious innovation, which allowed Shoshone and Bannock peoples to engage in a discourse with the colonizers—who appeared equally prophetic in their own expressions of identity.

That nineteenth-century Shoshone and Bannock peoples understood and expressed themselves and their histories in prophetic terms is evidenced by the practice of the Ghost Dance. The movements were not isolated events but part of a religious continuum. In 1890 Stanton G. Fisher asserted that Ghost Dances had been going on for at least twenty years at Fort Hall.[27] As an agency trader, captain of scouts, and finally agent, Fisher was a keen observer of Shoshone and Bannock life, and there is ample evidence to support his claim and extend it to much earlier in the century. James Mooney also heard evidence of the enduring nature of the Ghost Dance when Wind River Shoshones told him that the dance was a revival of one that had existed among them fifty years earlier.[28] For the most part, however, histories of the Ghost Dances have paid little attention to continuities such as the connections between the 1870 and 1890 manifestations of the religion.[29] This interpretation is partially due to the reliance on older anthropological sources, but, more important, it is the result of an uncritical acceptance of deprivation theory and a corresponding inability to accept the legitimate perspective of native peoples. If the Ghost Dances are seen as desperate fantasies, it is reasonable to interpret them only as discrete movements. Anthropologists have generally presented a more accurate historical picture, but, even so, the persistence of the religion has not been adequately explored. Mooney reported that Bannocks and Shoshones adopted both the 1870 and 1890 versions of the religion but did not suggest that the religion had survived in the interim. The studies of the 1870 Ghost Dance published in the 1920s and 1930s concentrated on the dance among the Northern Paiutes and its derivatives to the west and northwest, and so the Fort Hall dances were outside their scope. It was not until 1955 that J. A. Jones presented compelling primary historical evidence that the 1870 movement had spread as far east as Utah by way of the Shoshones and Bannocks. Joseph Jorgensen, who, like Jones, was primarily concerned with the Sun Dance religion, argues that this phase of the religion survived at least into the 1880s.[30] The evidence from Fort Hall suggests that continuities are even more important. The Ghost Dances were not two discrete movements but rather two periods of intense excitement in a continuing pattern of religious practice that stretched throughout the nineteenth century and survives to this day.

The Ghost Dances are also part of a pan-Indian religious continuum, which has included the Sun Dance and the Native American Church as significant expressions of Indian identity. Beginning in the 1880s, the Sun Dance underwent a major reordering and assumed new meanings for the Eastern Shoshones. What had been a ritual intended to bring success in hunting and warfare became one aimed at curing illness and maintaining a unified community. In 1901 a Shoshone shaman named Bear brought the modified Sun Dance to Fort Hall. After Bear had failed to cure a patient because his *bo'ha* was too weak, his spirit tutor told him to attempt the Sun Dance, which he had witnessed in his youth among the Eastern Shoshones. He induced his people to follow, and within a few years the ceremony was established at Fort Hall and spread to Lemhi.[31] Joseph Jorgensen has argued that the Sun Dance at that point effectively replaced the Ghost Dance as a regular part of religious life at Fort Hall.

He also suggests that the Sun Dance has persisted because its "redemptive" message of individual change takes clear precedence over the complete transformation of the social or natural order.[32] Notwithstanding the importance of the Sun Dance, the *nazága* remains an important part of Shoshone-Bannock spiritual life as a means of giving thanks for their lives, celebrating those who have passed on, and securing blessings for the coming year.[33]

The Fort Hall experience illustrates how the message of Ghost Dance prophets could be interpreted in different ways—ranging from militant resistance to measured accommodation—by different peoples and even by members of the same group. Ethnic, band, and political differences persist, just as they do in any community, Indian or non-Indian.[34] Moreover, identities are multilayered. Tribal members today commonly refer to themselves as Shoshone-Bannock or quite often simply as Sho-Ban. At the same time they retain a sense of ethnic, band, and geographic origin in addition to a well-developed sense of their Indianness that unites them with native peoples across the United States. Differing interpretations and multiple levels of identity notwithstanding, the ultimate message of the Ghost Dance religion was one of Indian unity and identity. It was a message that resonated among peoples who shared the experience of reservation life and faced an aggressive policy of assimilation which sought the complete elimination of their cultures. It is not a coincidence that the clearest statements of an American Indian racial identity coincided with attempts both to assert a national identity and to assimilate Indian peoples into that vision. American Indians, like other groups outside the dominant evangelical Protestant American identity in the nineteenth century, used common experiences and the common discourse of prophecy to declare and enact their survival as a people.

Notes

AG	Adjutant General
AAG	Assistant Adjutant General
ARCIA	U.S. Department of the Interior, *Annual Report of the Commissioner of Indian Affairs to the Secretary of the Interior*
ARSW	*Annual Report of the Secretary of War*
CIA	Commissioner of Indian Affairs
LR	*Letters Received, 1881–1907*
RG75	Record Group 75: Records of the Bureau of Indian Affairs
SC	Special Case
SI	Secretary of the Interior
Stat.	*Statutes at Large of the USA*
USNA	United States National Archives

INTRODUCTION

Epigraph: James Ballard and Joe Wheeler to Sioux Chiefs, 17 September 1894; included in Capt. Charles Penny to CIA, 22 November 1894, USNA, RG75, SC 188: *The Ghost Dance.*

    1. Robert M. Utley, *The Last Days of the Sioux Nation* (New Haven, CT: Yale University Press, 1963), 227–28; James Mooney, "The Ghost-Dance Religion and the Sioux Outbreak of 1890," *Fourteenth Annual Report of the Bureau*

of American Ethnology, part 2 (Washington, D.C.: Government Printing Office, 1896), 653; Jeffrey Ostler, *The Plains Sioux and U.S. Colonialism from Lewis and Clark to Wounded Knee* (New York: Cambridge University Press, 2004), 348–50. The officially reported death toll on the battlefield was 146. Seven Lakotas later died of their wounds. Many others escaped the battlefield to die of wounds later, and some corpses were carried away before the burial party arrived. Utley estimates that another 20 to 30 Lakotas died. Fifty more Lakotas were wounded. In all, two-thirds of Bigfoot's band were killed or wounded that day. Many of the soldiers died as a result of friendly fire. Ostler rightly argues that too much emphasis has been placed on who fired the first shot and that "the United States ultimately bears responsibility for the massacre" (350).

2. Capt. Charles Penny to CIA, 22 November 1894, USNA, SC 188. Penny described Kicking Bear as "one of the very conservative . . . Indians, belonging to this agency." Kicking Bear gave the letter to Penny.

3. Thomas B. Teter to CIA, 8 January 1897, USNA, RG75, LR.

4. ARCIA, 1890, 77.

5. Fort Hall Census, 1887–1897, USNA, Microcopy M595, Reel 138.

6. Joane Nagel, *American Indian Ethnic Renewal: Red Power and the Resurgence of Identity and Culture* (New York: Oxford University Press, 1996), 21.

7. John Hutchinson and Anthony D. Smith, eds., *Ethnicity* (New York: Oxford University Press, 1996), 5–7; Max Weber, "The Origins of Ethnic Groups," in ibid., 35.

8. William C. Sturtevant, "Creek into Seminole," in Eleanor Burke Leacock and Nancy Oestreich Lurie, eds., *North American Indians in Historical Perspective* (New York: Random House, 1971), 92, 105. See also James H. Merrell, *The Indians' New World: Catawbas and Their Neighbors from European Contact through the Era of Removal* (Chapel Hill: University of North Carolina Press, 1989); Joane Nagel and C. Matthew Snipp, "Ethnic Reorganization: American Indian Social, Economic, Political, and Cultural Strategies for Survival," *Ethnic and Racial Studies* 16 (April 1993): 203–35; Jonathan D. Hill, ed., *History, Power, and Identity: Ethnogenesis in the Americas, 1492–1992* (Iowa City: University of Iowa Press, 1996). Sturtevant defined ethnogenesis simply as the "establishment of group distinctness" in his exploration of the emergence of the Seminoles. In the Seminole case, as with many Indian groups, ethnogenesis was a postcontact phenomenon and a response to European settlement, epidemics, warfare, and depopulation. Sturtevant also argued that *ethnonymy,* "the naming of sociopolitical ('tribal' or 'ethnic') groups by their own members and by outsiders," is a crucial part of this process, but he did not develop the concept further. Other scholars refer to the same process as "ethnic renewal" and "ethnic reorganization."

9. Nagel, *American Indian Ethnic Renewal,* 21; Raymond D. Fogelson, "Perspectives in Native American Identity," in Russell Thornton, ed., *Studying Native America: Problems and Prospects* (Madison: University of Wisconsin Press, 1998), 41. My interest is in the creation and expression of ethnic and racial identity at the social and cultural levels rather than in the legal sense. Unlike any other minority group in American society, Indian peoples may also have a legal identity as members of sovereign nations. Legal "Indianness" is derived from the treaties

and agreements that tribes made with the United States and is defined by enrollment in a federally recognized tribe or community. Each tribe determines its own criteria for membership, with blood quantum being a very common standard. With rights and access to tribal and federal assistance programs at issue, legal identities can be hotly contested.

10. Fredrik Barth, *Ethnic Groups and Boundaries: The Social Organization of Culture Difference* (Boston: Little, Brown and Company, 1969), 9–10.

11. Alexandra Harmon, *Indians in the Making: Ethnic Relations and Indian Identities around Puget Sound* (Berkeley: University of California Press, 1998), 3.

12. See Kirsten Fischer, *Suspect Relations: Sex, Race, and Resistance in Colonial North Carolina* (Ithaca, NY: Cornell University Press, 2002); Reginald Horsman, *Race and Manifest Destiny: The Origins of American Racial Anglo-Saxonism* (Cambridge, MA: Harvard University Press, 1981).

13. Neil Foley, *The White Scourge: Mexicans, Blacks, and Poor Whites in the Texas Cotton Culture* (Berkeley: University of California Press, 1997).

14. Throughout this book, I refer to Indianness as a racial identity. Not all scholars accept this terminology. Nagel, in *American Indian Ethnic Renewal,* for instance, refers to Indianness as a "supratribal ethnicity."

15. Much of the scholarship concerning American Indian concepts of race has dealt with the Southeast, where native peoples were confronted by a system of racial slavery. See Nancy Shoemaker, "How Indians Got to Be Red," *American Historical Review* 102 (June 1997): 624–44; James Merrell, "The Racial Education of the Catawba Indians," *Journal of Southern History* 50 (August 1984): 363–84.

16. Hill, "Introduction," in *History, Power, and Identity,* 4.

17. Harmon, *Indians in the Making;* Frederick E. Hoxie, *Parading through History: The Making of the Crow Nation in America, 1805–1935* (New York: Cambridge University Press, 1995); Melissa L. Meyer, *The White Earth Tragedy: Ethnicity and Dispossession at a Minnesota Anishinaabe Reservation* (Lincoln: University of Nebraska Press, 1994); Nagel, *American Indian Ethnic Renewal;* Theda Perdue, *Cherokee Women: Gender and Culture Change, 1700–1835* (Lincoln: University of Nebraska Press, 1998).

18. Drusilla Gould and Christopher Loether, *An Introduction to the Shoshoni Language: Dammen Daigwape* (Salt Lake City: University of Utah Press, 2002); Drusilla Gould to Gregory E. Smoak, personal communication, 11 January 2005; Christopher Loether to Gregory E. Smoak, personal communication, 12 January 2005. In the Shoshone language, ai is a vowel pronounced roughly like the vowel in the English word *get.*

1. SNAKES AND DIGGERS

Epigraph: Nathaniel J. Wyeth to Henry R. Schoolcraft, 3 April 1848, reprinted in Henry R. Schoolcraft, *Information Respecting the History, Condition, and Prospects of the Indian Tribes of the United States,* part 1 (Philadelphia: Lippincott, Grambo & Co., 1851), 206.

1. Robert F. Murphy and Yolanda Murphy, *Shoshone-Bannock Subsistence and Society,* Anthropological Records vol. 16, no. 7 (Berkeley: University of Cal-

ifornia Press, 1960), 298, 315; Drusilla Gould and Christopher Loether, *An Introduction to the Shoshoni Language: Dammen Da̱igwape* (Salt Lake City: University of Utah Press, 2002), 5. Referring to Shoshones as "Snakes" originated in the Indian sign language of the Plains. The hand motion that Shoshone people used for themselves referred to salmon but meant *snake* to Plains groups.

2. Gould and Loether, *An Introduction to the Shoshoni Language,* 4–5; Drusilla Gould to Gregory E. Smoak, personal communication, 11 January 2005; Christopher Loether to Smoak, personal communication, 12 January 2005; Sven S. Liljeblad, "Indian Peoples in Idaho," manuscript, Idaho Museum of Natural History, Pocatello, 1957, 20–22, 23; Robert Murphy and Yolanda Murphy, "Northern Shoshone and Bannock," in *Handbook of North American Indians,* vol. 11, *Great Basin,* edited by Warren L. d'Azevedo (Washington, DC: Smithsonian Institution, 1986), 284, 305–6; Wick Miller, "Numic Languages," ibid., 98–106; Gary E. Moulton, ed., *The Journals of the Lewis and Clark Expedition,* vol. 5, *July 28–November 1, 1805* (Lincoln: University of Nebraska Press, 1988), 115. Portions of Liljeblad's important manuscript appeared under the same title in Merrill D. Beal and Merle W. Wells, *History of Idaho* (New York: Lewis Historical Publishing, 1959), 29–59. I have adopted the term *Newe* to refer generally to Shoshone- and Bannock-speaking peoples before the development of band organization. Liljeblad renders the term *néme* in Shoshone and *nemé* in Bannock. His writing system is not commonly used by linguists today.

3. Sydney M. Lamb, "Linguistic Prehistory in the Great Basin," *International Journal of American Linguistics* 24, no. 2 (1958): 95–100; James A. Goss, "Linguistic Tools for the Great Basin Prehistorian," in Don D. Fowler, ed., *Models and Great Basin Prehistory: A Symposium,* University of Nevada, Desert Research Institute Publications in the Social Sciences 12 (Reno: Desert Research Institute, 1977), 49–70; Miller, "Numic Languages," 98–16; David B. Madsen and David Rhode, eds., *Across the West: Human Population Movement and the Expansion of the Numa* (Salt Lake City: University of Utah Press, 1994).

4. Jesse D. Jennings, "Prehistory: Introduction," in *Handbook of North American Indians,* vol. 11, *Great Basin,* edited by Warren L. d'Azevedo (Washington, DC: Smithsonian Institution, 1986), 113–19; Earl H. Swanson Jr., *Birch Creek: Human Ecology in the Cool Desert of the Northern Rocky Mountains, 9000 B.C.–A.D. 1850* (Pocatello: Idaho State University Press, 1972); B. Robert Butler, *When Did the Shoshoni Begin to Occupy Southern Idaho? Essays on Late Prehistoric Cultural Remains from the Upper Snake and Salmon River Country,* Occasional Papers of the Idaho Museum of Natural History 32 (Pocatello: Idaho Museum of Natural History, 1981); B. Robert Butler, "Prehistory of the Snake and Salmon River Area," in *Handbook of North American Indians,* vol. 11, *Great Basin,* edited by Warren L. d'Azevedo (Washington, DC: Smithsonian Institution, 1986), 127–34. The Great Basin offers an interesting case in which ethnographic and linguistic analyses have long influenced archaeological interpretation. Jennings was the major proponent of the "desert culture" model, which posited a stable culture of great antiquity in the basin. He and others of this school were greatly influenced by the ethnologist Julian Steward. Since it was first proposed, Lamb's "Numic spread" theory has exerted the greatest influence

over archaeologists, leading to interpretations suggesting much more recent Numic occupation.

5. Julian H. Steward, *Basin-Plateau Aboriginal Sociopolitical Groups,* Bureau of American Ethnology Bulletin 120 (1938; reprint ed., Salt Lake City: University of Utah Press, 1970); Julian H. Steward, "The Foundations of Basin-Plateau Shoshonean Society," in Earl H. Swanson, ed., *Languages and Cultures of Western North America: Essays in Honor of Sven S. Liljeblad* (Pocatello: Idaho State University Press, 1970), 113–51; Liljeblad, "Indian Peoples in Idaho," 16–17, 34–35; Murphy and Murphy, *Shoshone-Bannock Subsistence and Society,* 316; Murphy and Murphy, "Northern Shoshone and Bannock," 292.

6. Steward, *Basin-Plateau Aboriginal Sociopolitical Groups,* 46.

7. Ibid., 235. Yet even in his later work Steward stood firmly behind environmental determinism and wrote: "The small family cluster based on bilateral principles was the inevitable response to areas of meager resources, low population density, and an annual cycle of nomadism." See Steward, "Foundations of Basin-Plateau Shoshonean Society," 115.

8. Thomas N. Layton, "Traders and Raiders: Aspects of Trans-Basin and California-Plateau Commerce, 1800–1830," *Journal of California and Great Basin Anthropology* 3 (1981): 127–37.

9. Fred Eggan, "Shoshone Kinship Structures and their Significance for Anthropological Theory," *Journal of the Steward Anthropological Society* 11 (Spring 1980): 175; Liljeblad, "Indian Peoples in Idaho," 34–35; Willie George, as told to Jack F. Contor, "Two Trails," *True West* 10 (January–February 1963): 8. George recalled, "The son-in-law was supposed to help his wife's parents with the hunting and other work for a while but by the time mother had her first baby they [moved to his parents' camp]. Maybe Father couldn't get along with his mother-in-law, I don't know."

10. Liljeblad, "Indian Peoples in Idaho," 16–17, 34–35; Murphy and Murphy, *Shoshone-Bannock Subsistence and Society,* 316; Murphy and Murphy, "Northern Shoshone and Bannock," 292; Steward, *Basin-Plateau Aboriginal Sociopolitical Groups,* 3.

11. Gould to Smoak, 11 January 2005; Liljeblad, "Indian Peoples in Idaho," 54–57. I have adopted the spelling provided by Gould, a native Shoshone speaker.

12. Beverly Crum and Jon Dayley, *Western Shoshone Grammar,* Occasional Papers and Monographs in Cultural Anthropology and Linguistics 1 (Boise, ID: Boise State University, 1993), 275; Liljeblad, "Indian Peoples in Idaho," 51–52; Gould to Smoak, 11 January 2005. See also Omer C. Stewart, "The Question of Bannock Territory," in Swanson, *Languages and Cultures of Western North America,* 201–31.

13. Francis Haines, "Where Did the Plains Indians Get Their Horses?" *American Anthropologist* 40 (1938): 112–17; Francis Haines, "The Northward Spread of Horses among the Plains Indians," *American Anthropologist* 40 (1938): 429–37; Demitri B. Shimkin, "The Introduction of the Horse," in *Handbook of North American Indians,* vol. 11, *Great Basin,* edited by Warren L. d'Azevedo (Washington, DC: Smithsonian Institution, 1986), 517–24.

14. John C. Ewers, *The Horse in Blackfoot Indian Culture*, Bureau of American Ethnology Bulletin 159 (1955; repr., Washington, DC: Smithsonian Institution Press, 1969), 6–7.

15. Shimkin, "Introduction of the Horse," 518. See also Pekka Hämäläinen, "The Western Comanche Trade Center: Rethinking the Plains Indian Trade System," *Western Historical Quarterly* 29 (Winter 1998): 485–513; and Pekka Hämäläinen, "The Rise and Fall of Plains Indian Horse Cultures," *Journal of American History* 90 (December 2003): 833–62.

16. Liljeblad, "Indian Peoples in Idaho," 34, 40; Murphy and Murphy, *Shoshone-Bannock Subsistence and Society*, 294–95.

17. Robert H. Lowie, *The Northern Shoshone*, Anthropological Papers of the American Museum of Natural History vol. 2, part 2 (New York: American Museum of Natural History, 1909), 179; Deward E. Walker, *Indians of Idaho* (Moscow: University of Idaho Press, 1978), 90–91. More recently there has been a greater recognition of the critical importance of fishing to Shoshone and Bannock peoples and their connection to Plateau culture. See Deward E. Walker, "The Shoshone-Bannock: An Anthropological Reassessment," *Northwest Anthropological Research Notes* 27, no. 2 (1993): 139–60; and Deward E. Walker, "Lemhi Shoshone-Bannock Reliance on Anadromous and Other Fish Resources," *Northwest Anthropological Research Notes* 27, no. 2 (1993): 215–50.

18. Liljeblad, "Indian Peoples in Idaho," 81–82.

19. Ibid., 62–63; Gould to Smoak, 11 January 2005.

20. Liljeblad, "Indian Peoples in Idaho," 81–85; George, "Two Trails," 6. George described his Boise Shoshone ancestors as "rich and happy" and as traveling in search of Bison.

21. George, "Two Trails," 22–23; Gould to Smoak, 11 January 2005; Alexander Ross, *The Fur Hunters of the Far West: A Narrative of Adventures in the Oregon and Rocky Mountains* (1855; repr., Norman: University of Oklahoma Press, 1956), 166.

22. Liljeblad, "Indian Peoples in Idaho," 57–58, 87–88; Murphy and Murphy, "Northern Shoshone and Bannock," 284. The Bannock term for their Shoshone counterparts, *wihínakwate*, also gives a clue as to the time frame for the origin of the mixed bands. *Wihi* means both "iron" and "knife" in both languages. Because flaked stone knives were common among both peoples, iron is probably the referent. Thus the arrival of the first Paiute-speaking immigrants must have postdated Shoshone access to European manufactures through intertribal trade. By this time, of course the Shoshones were also mounted, and it is a safe assumption that the Paiute immigrants came east to participate in the horse and bison economy.

23. L. J. Burpee, ed., *Journals and Letters of Pierre Gaultier de Varennes de la Vérendrye and His Sons* (Toronto: Champlain Society, 1927), quoted in Murphy and Murphy, *Shoshone-Bannock Subsistence and Society*, 294–95.

24. Murphy and Murphy, *Shoshone-Bannock Subsistence and Society*, 295.

25. David Thompson, *Travels in Western North America, 1784–1812*, edited by Victor G. Hopwood (Toronto: Macmillan of Canada, 1971), 192–93, 196; see also Frank Raymond Secoy, *Changing Military Patterns on the Great Plains (Seventeenth Century through Early Nineteenth Century)*, Monographs of

the American Ethnological Society 21 (Locust Valley, NY: J. J. Augustin, 1953), 33–38. Meriwether Lewis provided a detailed description of both the Newe stone *puk-a-mog-gan,* or war club, and the skin armor they wore into battle. See Moulton, *Journals of the Lewis and Clark Expedition,* vol. 5, 151.

26. Thompson, *Travels,* 193–95, 197.

27. Thompson, *Travels,* 198–201; L. J. Burpee, ed., *Journal of Larocque from the Assiniboine to the Yellowstone, 1805* (Ottawa: Government Printing Bureau, 1910), 72; Katherine M. Weist, "An Ethnohistorical Analysis of Crow Political Alliances," *Western Canadian Journal of Anthropology* 7 (1977): 34–54.

28. Moulton, *Journals of the Lewis and Clark Expedition,* vol. 5, 68–174; see also James P. Ronda, *Lewis and Clark among the Indians* (Lincoln: University of Nebraska Press, 1984), 133–62. On 7 April 1805, Lewis wrote Thomas Jefferson that "the circumstances of the Snake Indians possessing large quantities of horses is much in our favour as by means of horses, the transport of our baggage will be rendered easy and expeditious over land, from the Missouri, to the Columbia river." Quoted in Ronda, *Lewis and Clark,* 132.

29. Moulton, *Journals of the Lewis and Clark Expedition,* vol. 5, 119–23.

30. Carol Lynn MacGregor, ed., *The Journals of Patrick Gass, Member of the Lewis and Clark Expedition* (Missoula, MT: Mountain Press Publishing Company, 1997), 119–20.

31. Moulton, *Journals of the Lewis and Clark Expedition,* vol. 5, 92. Counting coup was the act of striking or touching an enemy in the midst of battle and escaping without sustaining injury. Among Plains groups it was the pinnacle of bravery and honor and more esteemed than killing an enemy.

32. Ibid., 137.

33. Ibid., 87.

34. Ibid., 96–97.

35. Ibid., 123.

36. Ibid., 149. There was indeed evidence of starvation in the Newe camp. Lewis saw that some families had an ample supply of meat while others did not. He asked Cameahwait why the well-off did not share with their tribesmen, as was the custom among most Indian peoples. Cameahwait responded that "meat was so scarce with them that the men who killed it reserved it for themselves and their own families."

37. Ibid., 123, 165–66.

38. Ibid., 149.

39. Liljeblad, "Indian Peoples in Idaho," 88–89; See also Layton, "Traders and Raiders"; 127–37; and John C. Ewers, "The Indian Trade of the Upper Missouri before Lewis and Clark," *Indian Life on the Upper Missouri* (Norman: University of Oklahoma Press, 1968), 14–33; William R. Swagerty, "Indian Trade in the Trans-Mississippi West to 1870," in *Handbook of North American Indians,* vol. 4, *History of Indian-White Relations,* edited by Wilcomb E. Washburn (Washington, DC: Smithsonian Institution, 1988), 351–74. Judging by the numerous historical references, it is very likely that a number of "trade fairs" took place across the Newe homeland at places like Green River, Bear Lake, the Great Camas Prairie, and *Sehewooki'.*

40. Moulton, *Journals of the Lewis and Clark Expedition,* vol. 5, 134–35, 140.

41. Ibid., 83, 91, 115, 160. Perhaps indicating the importance of guns, Cameahwait gave his war name as Too-et-te-con'l, or Black Gun. See also Ronda, *Lewis and Clark,* 147, 152; John C. Ewers, "The North West Trade Gun," *Indian Life on the Upper Missouri,* 34–44.

42. Moulton, *Journals of the Lewis and Clark Expedition,* vol. 5, 88–89.

43. K. G. Davies, ed., *Peter Skene Ogden's Snake Country Journal, 1826–27* (London: Hudson's Bay Record Society, 1961), 15. Ogden made this comment while traveling in eastern Oregon. The "Upper Snakes" who visited his camp spoke highly of the rivers to the east and were probably Newes from the Boise area.

44. Ross, *Fur Hunters,* 166–67.

45. Ibid., 167.

46. Warren Angus Ferris, *Life in the Rocky Mountains: A Diary of Wanderings on the Sources of the Rivers Missouri, Columbia, and Colorado, 1830–1835* (Denver, CO: Old West Publishing Company, 1983), 203–4. See also Steward, *Basin-Plateau Aboriginal Sociopolitical Groups,* 198; and Murphy and Murphy, *Shoshone-Bannock Subsistence and Society,* 298, 315. The historical record is filled with a multiplicity of confusing uses of the term *Bannock.* Steward noted that early-nineteenth-century travelers often placed the Bannocks in eastern Oregon, and he proposed four explanations: the Bannocks were actually located in Oregon in early historic times, Fort Hall Bannocks ranged as far west as Oregon, the Northern Paiutes of Oregon were also called Bannocks, and, finally, early observers were unable to distinguish the various peoples whom they encountered. Steward favored the last two explanations and found the first the least likely. In fact, all four explanations have some merit. Modern informants stated that the Paiute-speaking migration continued well into the reservation era, and genealogies support these claims. The same informants also reported that Fort Hall Bannocks recognized their close relationship to the Northern Paiutes of Oregon, whom they called Bannocks, and differentiated from themselves only with the phrase "They live in Burns [Oregon]." The mobility and immense range of the mounted groups doubtlessly contributed to their placement throughout the region in the early historic sources, and early observers did not recognize subtle cultural differences between peoples.

47. Ross, *Fur Hunters,* 166–67.

48. Elizabeth Vibert, *Traders' Tales: Narratives of Cultural Encounters in the Columbia Plateau, 1807–1846* (Norman: University of Oklahoma Press, 1997), 173–75, 245–73.

49. Frederick G. Young, ed., *The Correspondence and Journals of Captain Nathaniel J. Wyeth, 1831–1836: A Record of Two Expeditions for the Occupation of the Oregon Country* (1899; repr., New York: Arno Press, 1973), 163–70.

50. Ross, *Fur Hunters,* 169–71.

51. See also Omer C. Stewart, "Shoshoni History and Social Organization," *Idaho Yesterdays* 9 (Fall 1965): 2–5, 28. Stewart proposed that the apparent tripartite division in Newe society was actually the emergence of a "primitive democracy and a social system of three classes." On the top were the horse-own-

ing buffalo hunters; in the middle were the larger successful fishing groups; and in the "lower class" were the horseless foragers. These lifestyles were indeed evident in the literature, yet the use of the class concept obscures more than it explains. It suggests hard barriers that cannot explain the interrelationships and easy transfer of Newe peoples visible in the very same journals.

52. Ross, *Fur Hunters,* 254–55, 258–60.

53. Francis D. Haines, ed., *The Snake Country Expedition of 1830–1831: John Work's Field Journal* (Norman: University of Oklahoma Press, 1971), 11, 66, 71.

54. John Kirk Townsend, *Narrative of a Journey across the Rocky Mountains to the Columbia River* (Lincoln: University of Nebraska Press, 1978), 132; John C. Ewers, *The Blackfeet: Raiders on the Northwestern Plains* (Norman: University of Oklahoma Press, 1958), 124–44; Washington Irving, *The Adventures of Captain Bonneville, U.S.A., in the Rocky Mountains and the Far West* (Norman: University of Oklahoma Press, 1986), 50–51. Traveling hundreds of miles on foot was not uncommon for parties who intended to ride their plunder home.

55. Irving, *Adventures of Captain Bonneville,* 103–6; Young, *Correspondence and Journals of Wyeth,* 197–200; Townsend, *Narrative,* 122; Ross, *Fur Hunters,* 249. While traveling along the Snake River, Ross's party "came to a spot among the rocks where some Snakes had left in a hurry as the fire was still alive, and in the little bulrush hut we found six beaver skins and several other articles which they had abandoned through fear at our approach." Unable to find the inhabitants, Ross's party took the skins and left "articles of more value to them."

56. Ross, *Fur Hunters,* 151.

57. Ibid., 166.

58. Townsend, *Narrative,* 86. A typical example is Townsend's reference to the land between Ham's Fork and Snake River: "We have had an accession to our party of about thirty Indians; Flat-heads, Nez Percés, &c., with their wives, children, and dogs. Without these our camp would be small; they will probably travel with us until we arrive on Snake river, and pass over the country where the most danger is to be apprehended from their enemies the Black-feet."

59. Gould to Smoak, 11 January 2005; Loether to Smoak, 12 January 2005. I am indebted to Patricia C. Albers, director of the American Indian Studies Program at the University of Minnesota, for criticisms, suggestions, and ideas concerning the nature of Newe band formation and the role of the *dai'gwahni'* in treaty negotiations. See also Steward, *Basin-Plateau Aboriginal Sociopolitical Groups,* 170–71.

60. Moulton, *Journals of the Lewis and Clark Expedition,* vol. 5, 119–20.

61. Ross, *Fur Hunters,* 165, 168–69.

62. Ibid., 172.

63. Wyeth, "Indian Tribes," in Schoolcraft, *Information Respecting the History,* 207.

64. Young, *Correspondence and Journals of Wyeth,* 168.

65. Ferris, *Life in the Rocky Mountains,* 256.

66. Irving, *Adventures of Captain Bonneville,* 63, 88–89. Bonneville met

both a Nez Percé chief and several Pend d'Oreilles who were believed to be bulletproof. "Of these gifted beings marvelous anecdotes are related," wrote Irving, "which are most potently believed by their fellow savages, and sometimes almost credited by white hunters."

67. Ferris, *Life in the Rocky Mountains*, 256.

68. Willard Z. Park, "Paviotso Shamanism," *American Anthropologist*, n.s., 36 (1934): 98–113; Willard Z. Park, *Shamanism in Western North America: A Study in Cultural Relationships*, Northwestern University Studies in the Social Sciences 2 (Chicago: Northwestern University Press, 1938); Gould to Smoak, 11 January 2005.

69. Irving, *Adventures of Captain Bonneville*, 123–24.

70. Ferris, *Life in the Rocky Mountains*, 143–45.

71. F. Haines, *The Snake Country Expedition*, 64.

72. Ferris, *Life in the Rocky Mountains*, 255–57; Irving, *Adventures of Captain Bonneville*, 123–24; Aubrey L. Haines, ed., *Osborne Russell's Journal of a Trapper* (Lincoln: University of Nebraska Press, 1965), 37.

73. Irving, *Adventures of Captain Bonneville*, 123–24.

74. A. Haines, *Osborne Russell's Journal*, 36–37.

75. Ewers, *The Blackfeet*, 65–66.

76. A. Haines, *Osborne Russell's Journal*, 86–89.

77. Clifford Merrill Drury, ed., "Diary of Sarah White Smith," in *First White Women over the Rockies: Diaries, Letters, and Biographical Sketches of the Six Women of the Oregon Mission Who Made the Overland Journey in 1836 and 1838*, vol. 3 (Glendale, CA: Arthur H. Clark Company, 1966), 94.

78. Francis Haines, *The Buffalo: The Story of the American Bison and Their Hunters from Prehistoric Times to the Present* (1970; repr., Norman: University of Oklahoma Press, 1995), 13, 30–32; see also Dan Flores, "Bison Ecology and Bison Diplomacy: The Southern Plains from 1800 to 1850," *Journal of American History* 78 (September 1991): 465–85. Bison did best on the Great Plains, where grass could be found year-round. They also did well on the short-grass prairies. Some herds did "colonize" more marginal environments on the west slope of the Rockies and in the eastern woodlands, but in neither area could they reproduce fast enough to offset hunting pressures. Flores offers a more sophisticated environmental analysis of the Southern Plains and argues that, even there, the herds were not as large as often assumed. More important, a complex series of factors, including drought cycles, grazing pressure from horse herds, and Indian hunting had weakened the herds by the time white hide hunters arrived to obliterate the buffalo.

79. John Charles Frémont, *Narratives of Exploration and Adventure* (New York: Longmans, Green & Co., 1956), 266. Frémont made his comments in the vicinity of American Falls, where a dozen years earlier his equally famous guide Christopher "Kit" Carson had killed three bulls.

80. Murphy and Murphy, *Shoshone-Bannock Subsistence and Society*, 328–29; Steward, *Basin-Plateau Aboriginal Sociopolitical Groups*, 203–5. Informants in the 1950s told the Murphys that mostly Bannocks participated in the buffalo hunts but that numerous Fort Hall Shoshones also went along.

81. Steward, *Basin-Plateau Aboriginal Sociopolitical Groups*, 258; Murphy

and Murphy, "Northern Shoshone and Bannock," 291; Liljeblad, "Indian Peoples in Idaho," 43–45, 52–53.

82. A. Haines, *Osborne Russell's Journal,* 36.

83. Murphy and Murphy, "Northern Shoshone and Bannock," 328; Lowie, *The Northern Shoshone,* 184; Liljeblad, "Indian Peoples in Idaho," 64; Gould to Smoak, 11 January 2005. Liljeblad renders the name of the hunting ground as *kútsunambíhi,* or "buffalo heart." Every major ethnographic source describes the essentials of this subsistence cycle. See also Aubrey L. Haines, "The Bannock Indian Trails of Yellowstone National Park," *Archaeology in Montana* 4 (March 1962): 1–8; Harlow B. Mills, "The Bannocks in Yellowstone National Park," *Yellowstone Nature Notes* 5–6 (May–June 1935): 22–23.

84. Liljeblad, "Indian Peoples in Idaho," 82–83; Gould to Smoak, 11 January 2005. See also ARCIA, 1868, 657–58.

85. Liljeblad, "Indian Peoples in Idaho," 58–59, 84–85; Murphy and Murphy, *Shoshone-Bannock Subsistence and Society,* 327; Steward, *Basin-Plateau Aboriginal Sociopolitical Groups,* 200, 202–3, 207. Both Liljeblad and the Murphys collected genealogies which indicate that the Paiute migration lasted well into the nineteenth century. Because of their mobile lifestyle during the pre-reservation era, winter encampments have been used as the basis for judging the ethnic nature of Fort Hall bands. Julian Steward reported that there was "no segregation" of peoples in these encampments, and Liljeblad agreed. The Murphys, however, suggested that Bannock- and Shoshone-dominated groups camped in different portions of the Fort Hall region. All of these groups were "mixed," but the Bannock-dominated groups usually wintered along the Snake River bottom from Blackfoot to Rexburg, Idaho, whereas Shoshone groups favored the Portneuf River between Pocatello and McCammon, Idaho.

86. Liljeblad, "Indian Peoples in Idaho," 58–60, 90; Steward, *Basin-Plateau Aboriginal Sociopolitical Groups,* 297; Stewart, "The Question of Bannock Territory," 225. Stewart suggested that Bannock dominance actually represented the social differentiation brought about by the mounted lifestyle. Liljeblad remarked that both white and Indian observers agreed that the Paiute speakers were domineering wherever they settled among Shoshones. Liljeblad believed the Paiute speakers were more likely to "sacrifice their personal difference" to achieve a goal, whereas the Shoshones were "extreme individualists."

87. John D. Unruh, *The Plains Across: The Overland Emigrants and the Trans-Mississippi West, 1840–1860* (Urbana: University of Illinois Press, 1979), 119–20. Unruh's estimates are the most respected. He used newspapers, government accounts, and the emigrant registers at Fort Kearney and Fort Laramie to arrive at a final total of 253,397 emigrants over two decades.

88. U.S. Congress, House, *Report upon the Pacific Wagon Roads,* 35th Cong., 2d sess., Ex. Doc. 108, serial no. 1008, 1859, 55–56.

89. Charles Preuss, *Exploring with Frémont: The Private Diaries of Charles Preuss, Cartographer for John C. Frémont on His First, Second, and Fourth Expeditions to the Far West,* edited and translated by Erwin G. Guddle and Elisabeth K. Guddle (Norman: University of Oklahoma Press, 1958), 86.

90. Richard Grant to Sir George Simpson, 31 January 1851, Hudson's Bay

Company Archives. I thank Will Bagley, who has graciously allowed me to use his transcriptions of the Grant letters.

91. Brigham D. Madsen, *The Northern Shoshoni* (Caldwell, ID: Caxton Printers, 1980), 26–27. Madsen estimated 240,000 emigrants and 1.5 million head of stock passed through the Fort Hall area. If the Newes had charged 15 cents per head each night, as the Mormon settlers in northern Utah did at the time, the Indians would have recouped over $200,000, or $4,682,213 in current dollars.

92. Clarence B. Bagley, "Crossing the Plains," *Washington Historical Quarterly* 13 (July 1922): 166.

93. Clifford Merrill Drury, ed., "Diary of Mrs. Marcus Whitman," in *First White Women over the Rockies*, vol. 1, 75, 79; "Diary of Asahel Munger and Wife," *Quarterly of the Oregon Historical Society* 8 (1907): 397, 399. The Mungers, like the Whitmans, Spauldings, and Smiths before them, were part of the Oregon missionary effort. By 1839 it was commonly believed that the Blackfeet never raided below Fort Hall.

94. Unruh, *The Plains Across*. More whites than Indians died in 1845, 1847, 1856, 1859, and 1860.

95. Bagley, "Crossing the Plains," 174.

96. "Diary of Mrs. Marcus Whitman," 82; "Diary of Sarah White Smith," 104; "Diary of Asahel Munger and Wife," 401; Frémont, *Narratives of Exploration and Adventure*, 269–70; Charles H. Carey, ed., *The Journals of Theodore Talbot, 1843 and 1849–52* (Portland, OR: Metropolitan Press, 1931), 54; Preuss, *Exploring with Frémont*, 91; Bagley, "Crossing the Plains," 176.

97. "Diary of Mrs. Marcus Whitman," 82; "Diary of Sarah White Smith," 104.

98. Richard Grant to Sir George Simpson, 15 March 1844, 2 January 1846, and 1 April 1847, Hudson's Bay Company Archives. Grant considered the "Bonacks" his "life guards" against the sometimes troublesome emigrants who passed his post.

99. Carey, *Journals of Theodore Talbot*, 54. It is a bit to unfair the lump Talbot and the other members of the Frémont expedition with the emigrants. They were not just passing through but rather were charged with observing the country, its resources, and its people.

100. Brigham D. Madsen, *The Bannock of Idaho* (1958; repr., Moscow: University of Idaho Press, 1997), 73–74; Madsen, *The Shoshoni Frontier and the Bear River Massacre* (Salt Lake City: University of Utah, Press, 1985), 44–45; T. W. Davenport, "Recollections of an Indian Agent," *Quarterly of the Oregon Historical Society* 8 (1907): 363.

101. See Brigham D. Madsen, "Shoshoni-Bannock Marauders on the Oregon Trail, 1859–1863," *Utah Historical Quarterly* 35 (1967): 4–30.

102. U.S. Congress, *Report upon the Pacific Wagon Roads*, 7; Frederick W. Lander to CIA, 18 February 1860, USNA, RG 75, *Letters Received, 1824–1881*, Microcopy 234: *Utah Superintendency* [hereafter M234: *Utah*].

103. U.S. Congress, *Report upon the Pacific Wagon Roads*, 69.

104. Ibid., 8, 71. The final comment came from Albert H. Campbell, the general superintendent of the Pacific Wagon Road Office.

105. Lander to CIA, 18 February 1860, USNA, M234: *Utah.*

106. Ibid.

107. Ibid. The Newe bands, according to Lander, were the "Shoshonees or Eastern Snakes" (Washakie's Eastern Shoshones), the "Salmon River Snakes, Bannacks and Snakes and Sheep Eaters" (the mixed band of the Lemhi Valley), the "Western Snakes" (the Northwestern Shoshone bands, including Pocatello's), the "Bannacks, or Panackees or Pannacks" (the mixed buffalo-hunting bands of the Fort Hall region), "Bannacks of Fort Boise" (probably the mixed group that became known as the Boise Shoshones), the "Salt Lake Diggers, Lower or Southern Snakes" (the Northwestern Shoshone bands that lived among the Mormon settlements of northern Utah), and, finally, the "Warraricas, (in English 'Sun-Flower Seed Eaters,') or Diggers or Bannacks, Below Fort Boise, West of the Blue Mountains" (probably the Paiute speakers known as "Snakes" in Oregon).

108. Murphy and Murphy, "Northern Shoshone and Bannock," 288.

109. Murphy and Murphy, *Shoshone-Bannock Subsistence and Society,* 315.

2. SHAMANS, PROPHETS, AND MISSIONARIES

Epigraph: ARCIA, 1862, 213–14.

1. See Clifford Geertz, "Religion as a Cultural System," in *The Interpretation of Cultures* (New York: Basic Books, 1973), 87–125. Geertz defines religion as "(1) a system of symbols which acts to (2) establish powerful, pervasive, and long-lasting moods and motivations in men by (3) formulating conceptions of a general order of existence and (4) clothing these conceptions with such an aura of factuality that (5) the mood and motivations seem uniquely realistic" (90).

2. See Marshall Sahlins, *Islands of History* (Chicago: University of Chicago Press, 1985).

3. See Christopher L. Miller, *Prophetic Worlds: Indians and Whites on the Columbia Plateau* (New Brunswick, NJ: Rutgers University Press, 1985).

4. The literature on Shamanism is large. General studies include Mircea Eliade, *Shamanism: Archaic Techniques of Ecstasy* (Princeton, NJ: Princeton University Press, 1964); Spencer L. Rogers, *The Shaman: His Symbols and Healing Power* (Springfield, IL: Charles C. Thomas, 1982); and John A. Grim, *The Shaman: Patterns of Siberian and Ojibway Healing* (Norman: University of Oklahoma Press, 1983). Numic shamanism has also been the focus of much scholarship. The essential sources here include Willard Z. Park, "Paviotso Shamanism," *American Anthropologist,* n.s., 36 (1934): 98–113; Willard Z. Park, *Shamanism in Western North America: A Study in Cultural Relationships* (Chicago: Northwestern University Press, 1938); Beatrice Blyth Whiting, *Paiute Sorcery,* Viking Fund Publications in Anthropology 15 (New York: Wenner-Gren Foundation for Anthropological Research, 1950); Harold Olofson, "Northern Paiute Shamanism Revisited," *Anthropos* 74 (1979): 11–24; Jay Miller, "Basin Religion and Theology: A Comparative Study of Power (Puha)," *Journal of California and Great Basin Anthropology* 5 (1983): 66–86, and Jay Miller, "Numic Religion: An Overview of Power in the Great Basin of Native North America," *Anthropos* 78 (1983) 337–54.

5. Grim, *The Shaman,* 6; Rogers, *The Shaman,* 51.

6. Drusilla Gould to Gregory E. Smoak, personal communication, 11 January 2005.

7. J. Miller, "Basin Religion and Theology," 72–73, 81.

8. Ibid.; Park, *Shamanism*, 15–20, 79–80, 84; Julian Steward, *Culture Element Distribution: XXIII, Northern and Gosiute Shoshoni,* Anthropological Records vol. 8, no. 3 (Berkeley: University of California Press, 1943), 282, 286. Park found that the belief in ghosts as the source of power was strongest among the peoples of Northern California. Mountain dwarfs, like "water babies," are powerful mythical beings.

9. Park, *Shamanism*, 19.

10. Ibid., 8–10; Olofson, "Northern Paiute Shamanism Revisited," 13.

11. Aubrey L. Haines, ed., *Osborne Russell's Journal of a Trapper* (Lincoln: University of Nebraska Press, 1965), 143.

12. Park, *Shamanism*, 8–10.

13. Ibid., 14. The standard comparison might be with the religious systems of the Pueblos, with their scores of priesthoods, rituals, and extensive clan and moiety social order.

14. Steward, *Culture Element Distribution*, 281–82; Park, *Shamanism*, 14–15; Gould to Smoak, 11 January 2005.

15. John Wesley Powell, "Ute and Paiute Stories," Smithsonian Institution, National Anthropological Archives, Ms. 838. n.d.; Olofson, "Northern Paiute Shamanism Revisited," 15–16.

16. Park, *Shamanism*, 26–28.

17. Steward, *Culture Element Distribution*, 282. Steward renders the term for specialists as *numa'gunat*.

18. Ibid.

19. Park, *Shamanism*, 33–36.

20. Ibid., 48.

21. Haines, *Osborne Russell's Journal*, 143–44.

22. Park, *Shamanism*, 32–33; Whiting, *Paiute Sorcery*, 29–30.

23. Park, *Shamanism*, 23–26; Steward, *Culture Element Distribution*, 284.

24. Don D. Fowler and Catherine S. Fowler, eds., "Stephen Powers' 'The Life and Culture of the Washo and Paiutes,'" *Ethnohistory* 17 (1970): 131; Park, *Shamanism*, 51–52; Whiting, *Paiute Sorcery*, 39–40. Powers was somewhat taken aback by the fact that Ox Tom looked like any other Paiute, and even derided the doctor's "most unprofessional state of raggedness and filth."

25. ARCIA, 1886, 194–97.

26. Unfortunately, only brief, vague references to shamanic practice, such as Russell's, predate the reservation era. The major sources used in this composite are Powell, "Ute and Paiute Stories"; Fowler and Fowler, "Stephen Powers' 'Life and Culture'"; Park, *Shamanism*; Whiting, *Paiute Sorcery*; and Olofson, "Northern Paiute Shamanism Revisited." Stephen Powers witnessed an apparently typical healing ceremony during a visit to Nevada in 1875. His description, though brief, hints at the depth of emotion felt by Numic peoples at such rites. In his undated collection "Ute and Paiute Stories," Powell corroborated, summarized, and clarified the events in Powers's description. Further illumination is provided by anthropological studies. Park's work among the Northern Paiutes of Nevada

led to the seminal work on Basin shamanism. Whiting did her research among the Burns Paiutes of eastern Oregon (close relatives of Idaho Bannocks, who were sometimes also referred to as Bannocks), and produced a more narrowly drawn functionalist study that focused on shamanism and sorcery as mechanisms of social control.

27. Fowler and Fowler, "Stephen Powers' 'Life and Culture,'" 132; Powell, "Ute and Paiute Stories"; Park, *Shamanism,* 45–49. Park points out that in the initial discussion the shaman never inquires as to the patient's symptoms because his power is supposed to determine them.

28. Park, *Shamanism,* 48; Whiting, *Paiute Sorcery,* 38. In the 1930s the average fee on the Pyramid Lake and Walker River reservations was three to five dollars.

29. Park, *Shamanism,* 50–51; Powell, "Ute and Paiute Stories." Park stated that it must be completely dark for the rites to begin, and it was believed to be wrong to begin in the twilight. As a consequence, ceremonies during the summer usually did not start before 10 P.M. In emergencies, which included rattlesnake bites and gunshot wounds, the shaman was summoned and began work immediately.

30. Park, *Shamanism,* 46; Whiting, *Paiute Sorcery,* 39–40. The move indoors created a dilemma for the Paiutes of Burns, Oregon, who, like most Basin peoples, ritually destroyed the property of the deceased and abandoned the home where the person had died. This practice posed no problem while the people lived in brush wickiups, but one could not so easily leave the Bureau of Indian Affairs housing constructed in Burns in the twentieth century. As a result, particularly ill patients might be moved to a brush house, which could be quickly constructed and easily abandoned if the person died. Thus conditions mandated by a modern bureaucracy helped to preserve the traditional location of the healing ceremony.

31. Powell, "Ute and Paiute Stories."

32. Park, *Shamanism,* 52–53; Grim, *The Shaman,* 50. Grim writes, "The 'journey' to the source of the patient's illness cannot take place unless the shaman has undergone the initial trauma of his own dismemberment and the subsequent healing experience. This initial trauma establishes his relationship with certain helpful spirits. Thus the shaman evokes his spirits by reenacting his initial call."

33. Whiting, *Paiute Sorcery,* 42; Park, *Shamanism,* 52–53.

34. Park, *Shamanism,* 50; Olofson, "Northern Paiute Shamanism Revisited," 17–18. Park gave *poínabe,* the same term used for the leaders of communal activities such as piñon harvests, as the Northern Paiute word for "talker." Olofson recorded the word *tinnikwiikiadI.*

35. Fowler and Fowler, "Stephen Powers' 'Life and Culture,'" 131; Park, *Shamanism,* 50.

36. Park, *Shamanism,* 50; Olofson, "Northern Paiute Shamanism Revisited," 17–18. Park's informant told him that, in the old days, talkers were always men, but at the time of Park's research women served in this position as well. As for prayers, he stated that only a few of his informants agreed that talkers said prayers. The majority of informants reported that talkers only repeated the shaman's words. Olofson argues that the talkers were far more important than Park suggests.

37. Fowler and Fowler, "Stephen Powers' 'Life and Culture,' " 131; Park, *Shamanism*, 50–51. Park reported that older informants told him that there were fewer dancers in the past, but Powers's early account notes that "a couple of sympathizing women would now and then rise to their feet and set up a shuffling, swaying motion in harmony with the doctor's dance."

38. Park, *Shamanism*, 52–53.

39. Fowler and Fowler, "Stephen Powers' 'Life and Culture,' " 131; ARCIA, 1878, 104; Park, *Shamanism*, 52; Whiting, *Paiute Sorcery*, 39.

40. Park, *Shamanism*, 47, 55. The sale of property was a constant irritant to agents, who viewed shamanism as a superstition and waste of resources. See ARCIA, 1878, 104.

41. Park, *Shamanism*, 52–53.

42. Ibid., 39–40; Whiting, *Paiute Sorcery*, 35. See also Eliade, *Shamanism*, 259. Eliade writes: "The pre-eminently shamanic technique is the passage from one cosmic region to another."

43. Powell, "Ute and Paiute Stories."

44. Fowler and Fowler, "Stephen Powers' 'Life and Culture,' " 132.

45. Grim, *The Shaman*, 3.

46. Michael Hittman, "The 1870 Ghost Dance at Walker River Reservation: A Reconstruction," *Ethnohistory* 20 (1973): 247–78.

47. Park, *Shamanism*, 69–71; Michael Hittman, *Wovoka and the Ghost Dance* (Lincoln: University of Nebraska Press, 1997), 143.

48. James A. Teit, "Okanagon Tales," in, Franz Boas, ed., *Folk-Tales of the Salishan and Sahaptian Tribes* (Lancaster, PA: American Folk-Lore Society, 1917), 83.

49. Leslie Spier, *The Prophet Dance of the Northwest and Its Derivatives: The Source of the Ghost Dance*, American Anthropological Society General Series in Anthropology (Menasha, WI: George Banta, 1935), 5, 7–10. Spier writes: "The ultimate origin of the two Ghost Dance movements was not with the Paviotso but in the Northwest among the tribes of the interior Plateau area." He also argued that the Prophet Dance was the antecedent of Smohalla's Dreamer religion and probably influenced the development of the Indian Shaker Church as well.

50. Eugene Hunn and James Selam and family, *Nch'i-Wana, "The Big River": Middle Columbia Indians and Their Land* (Seattle: University of Washington Press, 1990), 250–51

51. Charles Wilkes, *Narrative of the United States Exploring Expeditions during the Years 1838–1842*, vol. 4 (Philadelphia: Lea and Blanchard, 1845), 439.

52. Walter Cline, "Religion and World View," in Leslie Spier, ed., *The Sinkaitek or Southern Okanagon of Washington* (Menasha, WI: George Banta Publishing Company, 1938), 172, 175; Spier, *Prophet Dance*, 55; Elizabeth Vibert, *Traders' Tales: Narratives of Cultural Encounters in the Columbia Plateau, 1807–1846* (Norman: University of Oklahoma Press, 1997), 68–71. Cline's informants, Lucy Joe and David Isaac, were both in their seventies when he interviewed them in 1930. Spier reports accounts of the "dry snow" dating to as early as 1770 and as late as 1800. He also asserted that the religion was of even greater antiquity.

53. David F. Aberle, "The Prophet Dance and Reactions to White Contact," *Southwestern Journal of Anthropology* 15 (1959): 74–88; Deward E. Walker, "New Light on the Prophet Dance Controversy," *Ethnohistory* 16 (1969): 245–55; Wayne Suttles, "The Plateau Prophet Dance among the Coast Salish," *Southwestern Journal of Anthropology* 13 (1957): 352–96.

54. Melburn D. Thurman, "The Shawnee Prophet's Movement and the Origins of the Prophet Dance," *Current Anthropology* 25 (1984): 530–31; Melburn D. Thurman to Gregory E. Smoak, personal communication, 30 April 1993. Thurman's article, originally slated for publication in *Ethnohistory* in the mid-1980s, has never appeared, and he is unwilling to share his research with other scholars until his book detailing the "mechanisms of the North American Prophetic movements" is published. He suggests that the "Kutenai manly-woman" was actually an Ojibwa who preached the Shawnee Prophet's religion.

55. Elizabeth Vibert, " 'The Natives Were Strong to Live': Reinterpreting Early Nineteenth-Century Movements in the Columbia Plateau," *Ethnohistory* 42 (1995): 204, 221. See also Sahlins, *Islands of History.*

56. James A. Teit, "Mythology of the Thompson Indians," in *The Jesup North Pacific Expedition: Memoirs of the American Museum of Natural History,* vol. 8, part 2 (New York: American Museum of Natural History), 416, quoted in Cole Harris, *The Resettlement of British Columbia: Essays on Colonialism and Geographic Change* (Vancouver: University of British Columbia Press, 1997), 103–4.

57. Quoted in Vibert, *Traders' Tales,* 69.

58. Barbara Belyea, ed., *Columbia Journals: David Thompson* (Montreal: McGill-Queen's University Press, 1994), 147.

59. C. Miller, *Prophetic Worlds,* 51–52, Vibert, *Traders' Tales,* 69; Hunn, *Nch'i-Wana,* 250–51.

60. Claude E. Schaeffer, "The Kutenai Female Berdache: Courier, Guide, Prophetess, and Warrior," *Ethnohistory* 12 (1965): 193–236; Hunn, *Nch'i-Wana,* 250–51; Vibert, *Traders' Tales,* 73–77, 240–41.

61. Schaeffer, "Kutenai Female Berdache," 195–97; David Thompson, *Travels in Western North America, 1784–1812* (Toronto: Macmillan of Canada, 1971), 302–3.

62. Belyea, *Columbia Journals,* 160; Thompson, *Travels,* 303.

63. Alexander Ross, *Adventures of the First Settlers on the Oregon or Columbia River: Being a Narrative of the Expedition Fitted Out by John Jacob Astor to Establish the Pacific Fur Company, with an Account of Some of the Indian Tribes on the Coast of the Pacific* (Lincoln: University of Nebraska Press, 1986), 153–54.

64. Schaeffer, "Kutenai Female Berdache," 212. Schaeffer argued that her new prophecy was "the second thoughts of a shrewd woman, who had learned that evil tidings are less safe than good among a strange people."

65. Vibert, *Traders' Tales,* 76–77.

66. Ross, *Adventures of the First Settlers,* 274–75.

67. Ibid., 273–74.

68. Quoted in Spier, *Prophet Dance,* 10. Spier's account comes from the unpublished field notes of Phileo Nash, who served as commissioner of Indian

affairs in the Kennedy and Johnson administrations. Nash did field work among the Modocs in 1934, and his principal informant on the Dream Dance and Ghost Dance was Mrs. George, "the aged widow of the Modoc leader of the Ghost Dance and herself a powerful force behind the Ghost Dance movement."

69. Alvin M. Josephy Jr., *The Nez Perce Indians and the Opening of the Northwest* (1965; repr., New York: Mariner Books, 1997), 54–55, 70, 81.

70. Alexander Ross, *The Fur Hunters of the Far West: A Narrative of Adventures in the Oregon and Rocky Mountains* (1855; repr., Kenneth A. Spaulding, ed., Norman: University of Oklahoma Press, 1956), 194–95.

71. Josephy, *Nez Perce Indians*, 124, 167–68, 666–67; C. Miller, *Prophetic Worlds*, 53; Robert M. Utley, *A Life Wild and Perilous: Mountain Men and the Paths to the Pacific* (New York: Owl Books, 1997), 167–68.

72. Quoted in Josephy, *Nez Perce Indians*, 124; C. Miller, *Prophetic Worlds*, 53; Lawrence B. Palladino, *Indian and White in the Northwest: A History of Catholicity in Montana, 1831–1891* (Lancaster, PA: Wickersham, 1922).

73. Spier, *Prophet Dance*, 31; C. Miller, *Prophetic Worlds*, 53; Palladino, *Indian and White*, 8–9. Palladino credits Old Ignace for the introduction of Catholicism. Miller writes, "This, no doubt, was very welcome to the millennium-anticipating Eastern Salish, who quickly adopted many of the rites and observances that Old Ignace showed them, applying, of course, their own significance to them. The new knowledge spread across the Plateau with the same rapidity as the prophet dance complex. In fact, Old Ignace's teachings were appended to that cult, forming a new and even more dynamic complex."

74. Josephy, *Nez Perce Indians*, 667; Dale L. Morgan, *Jedediah Smith and the Opening of the West* (Lincoln: University of Nebraska Press, 1964); Utley, *A Life Wild and Perilous*, 42, 66–67.

75. Josephy, *Nez Perce Indians*, 82–85; C. Miller, *Prophetic Worlds*, 57.

76. C. Miller, *Prophetic Worlds*, 56–59; Josephy, *Nez Perce Indians*, 83–90, 94–95.

77. W. S. Wallace, ed., *John McLean's Notes of a Twenty-Five Year Service in the Hudson's Bay Territory* (Toronto: Champlain Society, 1932), 159–60. Quoted in Josephy, *Nez Perce Indians*, 87.

78. Frederick G. Young, ed., *The Correspondence and Journals of Captain Nathaniel J. Wyeth, 1831–36: A Record of Two Expeditions for the Occupation of the Oregon Country* (1899; repr., New York: Arno Press, 1973), 192.

79. Ibid., 193–94.

80. Ibid., 196.

81. Ibid., 201.

82. John Kirk Townsend, *Narrative of a Journey across the Rocky Mountains to the Columbia River* (Lincoln: University of Nebraska Press, 1978), 116–17. It is impossible to recover the meanings of the words or ceremony, as Townsend spoke none of the Indian languages.

83. Washington Irving, *Adventures of Captain Bonneville, U.S.A., in the Rocky Mountains and the Far West* (Norman: University of Oklahoma Press, 1961), 356.

84. Dr. Gairdner, "Notes on the Geography of the Columbia River," *Journal*

of the Royal Geographical Society of London 11 (1841): 257, quoted in Spier, *Prophet Dance,* 33–34.

85. Josephy, *Nez Perce Indians,* 95–98; C. Miller, *Prophetic Worlds,* 59–62.

86. *Christian Advocate and Journal and Zion's Herald,* 22 March 1833, quoted in Josephy, *Nez Perce Indians,* 101.

87. See Clifford Merrill Drury, *Marcus and Narcissa Whitman, and the Opening of Old Oregon* (Glendale, CA: Arthur H. Clark Company, 1973); Julie Roy Jeffrey, *Converting the West: A Biography of Narcissa Whitman* (Norman: University of Oklahoma Press, 1991).

88. Clifford Merrill Drury, ed., *First White Women over the Rockies: Diaries, Letters, and Biographical Sketches of the Six Women of the Oregon Mission Who Made the Overland Journey in 1836 and 1838,* vol. 3 (Glendale, CA: Arthur H. Clark Company, 1966), 98.

89. See Leonard J. Arrington and Davis Bitton, *The Mormon Experience: A History of the Latter-Day Saints* (New York: Alfred A. Knopf, 1979); Richard Bushman, *Joseph Smith and the Beginnings of Mormonism* (Urbana: University of Illinois Press, 1984); Lawrence Foster, *Religion and Sexuality: The Shakers, the Mormons, and the Oneida Community* (Urbana: University of Illinois Press, 1984); Klaus J. Hansen, *Mormonism and the American Experience* (Chicago: University of Chicago Press, 1981).

90. Bushman, *Joseph Smith.*

91. See D. Michael Quinn, *Early Mormonism and the Magic World View* (Salt Lake City: Signature Books, 1987).

92. Brian M. Fagan, *Elusive Treasure: The Story of the Early Archaeologists in the Americas* (New York: Charles Scribner's Sons, 1977), 116–17; Robert Silverberg, *Moundbuilders of Ancient America: The Archaeology of a Myth* (Greenwich, CT: New York Graphic Society, 1968), 94. Sometime around 1809 the Rev. Solomon Spaulding published *The Manuscript Found,* which he claimed was the history of the continent's first inhabitants translated from twenty-eight pieces of parchment found in an Ohio earth mound. Critics have charged that Smith used Spaulding's work, or Ethan Smith's (no relation) *Views of the Hebrews: The Tribes of Israel in America,* published in 1823, as the basis of the Book of Mormon.

93. Ibid.; see also Nigel Davies, *Voyagers to the New World* (New York: William Morrow, 1979); and Dan Vogel, *Indian Origins and the Book of Mormon* (Salt Lake City: Signature Books, 1986).

94. The famous quote came in a message to the territorial legislature and appeared in the *Deseret News,* 14 December 1854: "I have uniformly pursued a friendly course towards them, feeling convinced that independent of the question of exercising humanity toward so degraded and ignorant a race of people, it was manifestly more economical and less expensive to feed and clothe them than to fight them."

95. See Howard A. Christy, "Open Hand and Mailed Fist: Mormon-Indian Relations in Utah, 1847–1852," *Utah Historical Quarterly* 46 (1978): 216–35; Lawrence G. Coates, "Brigham Young and Mormon Indian Policies," *Brigham Young University Studies* 18 (1978): 428–52; Beverly P. Smaby, "The Mormons

and the Indians: Conflicting Ecological Systems in the Great Basin," *American Studies* 16 (1975): 35–48.

96. The Book of Mormon, 2 Nephi 30. Here I am citing the 1961 edition of the Book of Mormon, which included the phrase "white and delightsome." In 1981 the church changed this phase to read "pure and delightsome."

97. Reginald Horsman, *Race and Manifest Destiny: The Origins of American Racial Anglo-Saxonism* (Cambridge, MA: Harvard University Press, 1981), 4–5.

98. John L. Brooke, *The Refiner's Fire: The Making of Mormon Cosmology, 1644–1844* (Cambridge: Cambridge University Press, 1994), 216–18.

99. David Moore, "Salmon River Mission Journal, Salt Lake City, LDS Church Archives, 22–24, quoted in Brigham D. Madsen, *The Bannock of Idaho* (1958; repr., Moscow: University of Idaho Press, 1997), 89.

100. Madsen, *Bannock of Idaho,* 84–110; Brigham D. Madsen, *The Lemhi: Sacajawea's People* (Caldwell, ID: Caxton Printers, 1990), 34–40.

101. George Washington Hill, "Cases of Miraculous Healing," *Juvenile Instructor* (1 February 1880): 45–46.

102. Richard White, *The Middle Ground: Indians, Empires, and Republics in the Great Lakes Region, 1650–1815* (New York: Cambridge University Press, 1991). For White the "middle ground" is less a set of measurable relationships than a series of creative cultural misunderstandings. Each side speaks to parts of the Other's culture which seem familiar yet which it cannot truly understand. This type of intercultural communication is only possible as long as neither side can forcibly impose its will on the other.

103. Hill, "Cases of Miraculous Healing," 45–46.

104. Journal of Dimick Baker Huntington, Salt Lake City, LDS Church Archives, Ms. 1419–2, entry dated 16 September 1857. The author is indebted to Will Bagley for making available a copy of his transcription of the Huntington journal.

105. See Juanita Brooks, *The Mountain Meadows Massacre* (1950; repr., Norman: University of Oklahoma Press, 1970); Will Bagley, *Blood of the Prophets* (Norman: University of Oklahoma Press, 2002).

106. The "Weber Utes" were actually a Northwestern Shoshone band that ranged along the east side of the Great Salt Lake between the modern sites of Ogden and Salt Lake City, Utah. In the primary literature they were often called Cumumbahs. See Warren L. d'Azevedo, ed., *Handbook of North American Indians,* vol. 11, *Great Basin* (Washington, DC: Smithsonian Institution, 1986), 282–83.

107. Huntington journal, 1 November 1857. For information on Simons, see Brigham D. Madsen, *The Shoshoni Frontier and the Bear River Massacre* (Salt Lake City: University of Utah Press, 1985), 67–68, 78.

108. George Washington Hill, "Message from an Indian Prophet," *Juvenile Instructor* 14 (15 April 1871): 91–92. Hill learned the Shoshone language at Lemhi and later led the Mormon mission to the Northwestern Shoshone bands in Utah.

109. Ibid., 91.

110. Ibid., 92.

111. William H. Hooper to Gov. Alfred Cumming, 13 April 1858, ARSW,

1858, 74; Madsen, *Bannock of Idaho,* 102. This official report suggests that soldiers who traveled from Fort Bridger to the Beaverhead Valley to buy stock animals had incited the Indians to drive off the Mormon stock and sell it to the army.

112. Huntington journal, 29 March 1858.

113. U.S. Congress, House, *Report upon the Pacific Wagon Roads,* 35th Cong., 2d sess., Ex. Doc. 108, serial no. 1008, 1859, 69–70.

114. Ibid., 70–71.

115. "Report of F. W. Lander, Superintendent, &c., to the Commissioner of Indian Affairs," 18 February 1860, in U.S. Congress, Senate, *Message of the President of the United States, Communicating, in Compliance with a Resolution of the Senate, Information in Relation to the Massacre at Mountain Meadows, and other Massacres in Utah Territory,* 36th Cong., 1st sess., Ex. Doc. 42, serial no. 1033, 1860, 138. Lander's report illustrates the confusion over group names among the Indian peoples of southern Idaho. Warrarica and its English translation, "Sun-Flower Seed Eaters," are food names, which must be used carefully. The name *Warrarica* first appears in the works of Alexander Ross, who led the Hudson's Bay Company's Snake River brigade in 1823 and 1824. See Ross, *Fur Hunters,* 166–67.

116. ARCIA, 1862, 213–14.

117. See Robert H. Ruby and John A. Brown, *Dreamer-Prophets of the Columbia Plateau: Smohalla and Skolaskin* (Norman: University of Oklahoma Press, 1989).

118. ARCIA, 1862, 265–68. The Oregon agent J. M. Kirkpatrick reported that he could not recruit an Indian runner from the Columbia or among the Umatilla to carry a message to the Snakes warning them away from the Powder River mines, because they were at war with the Snakes, and the messenger would surely be killed.

119. J. W. MacMurray, "The 'Dreamers' of the Columbia River Valley, in Washington Territory," *Transactions of the Albany Institute* 11 (1887): 247. MacMurray interviewed Smohalla in 1883.

120. James Mooney, "The Ghost-Dance Religion and the Sioux Outbreak of 1890," *Fourteenth Annual Report of the Bureau of American Ethnology,* part 2 (Washington, DC: Government Printing Office, 1896), 718–19; Ruby and Brown, *Dreamer-Prophets,* 26–27.

121. ARCIA, 1864, 145–46.

3. TREATY MAKING AND CONSOLIDATION

Epigraph: ARCIA, 1868, 658.

1. ARCIA, 1850, 128. Shoshone was the lingua franca of southern Idaho. See Nathaniel T. Hall to Thomas F. Meagher, 6 April 1866, USNA, RG 75, *Letters Received, 1824–1881: Montana Superintendency,* Microcopy 234 [hereafter M234: *Montana*]; ARCIA, 1867, 174.

2. Beverly Crum and John Dayley, *Western Shoshone Grammar,* Occasional Papers and Monographs in Cultural Anthropology and Linguistics 1 (Boise, ID: Boise State University, 1993), 275, 295; Sven S. Liljeblad, "Indian Peoples in Idaho," manuscript, Idaho Museum of Natural History, Pocatello, 1957, 51–52.

3. John Wesley Powell, "Indian Life," from "They Call Themselves Nu-mes," Smithsonian Institution, National Anthropological Archives, Ms. 798, ca. 1878, 8–9.

4. ARCIA, 1864, 174.

5. "Northwestern" Shoshones is an ethnographic convention meant to set the bands of northern Utah apart from the "Western" Shoshones of Nevada. The Newes themselves did not recognize such geographic labels in the nineteenth century. Today the descendants of these people identify themselves as the North-western Bands. Band identities have never completely disappeared, and many people on the Fort Hall Reservation today have a keen sense of where their families came from.

6. John Hailey, *The History of Idaho* (Boise, ID: Syms-York Company, 1910), 36–44; Leonard J. Arrington, *History of Idaho*, vol. 1 (Moscow: University of Idaho Press, 1994), 183–203.

7. Ibid.; see also Brigham D. Madsen, "The Northwestern Shoshoni in Cache Valley," in Douglas C. Alder, ed., *Cache Valley: Essays in Her Past and Her People* (Logan: Utah State University Press, 1976), 28–44; and John W. Heaton, " 'No Place to Pitch Their Teepees': Shoshone Adaptation to Mormon Settlers in Cache Valley, 1855–1870," *Utah Historical Quarterly* 63 (Spring 1995): 158–71.

8. ARCIA, 1862, 213–14. For an overview of this period, see Brigham D. Madsen, "Shoshoni-Bannock Marauders on the Oregon Trail, 1859–1863," *Utah Historical Quarterly* 35 (Winter 1967): 3–30; Brigham D. Madsen, *The Shoshoni Frontier and the Bear River Massacre* (Salt Lake City: University of Utah Press, 1985). See also John D. Unruh Jr., *The Plains Across: The Overland Emigrants and the Trans-Mississippi West, 1840–1860* (Urbana: University of Illinois Press, 1979). For a biography of Doty, see Alice E. Smith, *James Duane Doty: Frontier Promoter* (Madison: State Historical Society of Wisconsin, 1954).

9. For a biography of Connor, see Brigham D. Madsen, *Glory Hunter: A Biography of Patrick Edward Connor* (Salt Lake City: University of Utah Press, 1990).

10. Quoted in Madsen, *Shoshoni Frontier,* 167.

11. Ibid., 178.

12. Ibid., 190–92. After giving a detailed rundown of all the various casualty estimates, Madsen settles on 250 Shoshone deaths. Connor officially reported 224 bodies on the ground and as many as 50 more in the river.

13. ARCIA, 1863, 420.

14. ARCIA, 1864, 174–76; Treaty of Fort Bridger, 18 Stat. 685–88; Treaty of Box Elder, 13 Stat. 663–65; Treaty of Ruby Valley, 18 Stat. 689–92; Treaty of Tuilla [Tooele] Valley, 13 Stat. 681–84.

15. ARCIA, 1864, 176. By 1863, "Lander's Cutoff" carried the bulk of over-land traffic directly through the Fort Hall area, and there were several Snake River ferries in operation between Fort Hall and Eagle Rock.

16. The unratified treaty of 14 October 1863 is reprinted in Brigham D. Madsen, *The Bannock of Idaho* (Caldwell, ID: Caxton Printers, 1958), 326–27.

17. Brigham D. Madsen, *The Northern Shoshoni* (Caldwell, ID: Caxton

Printers, 1980), 37–38; Madsen, *The Bannock of Idaho,* 146–48; ARCIA, 1864, 174–76.

18. Madsen, *The Northern Shoshoni,* 37–38.

19. ARCIA, 1865, 143, 158.

20. ARCIA, 1866, 126–27.

21. A. B. Henderson, "Journal of the Yellowstone Expedition of 1866," Yellowstone National Park Archives. Both the Montana Historical Society and Yellowstone National Park hold typescript copies of the original from the collections of Yale University. Henderson's encounter with Taghee and Washakie occurred on 28–29 September 1866.

22. Merle W. Wells, "Caleb Lyon's Indian Policy," *Pacific Northwest Quarterly* (October 1970): 193–200; Arrington, *History of Idaho,* 220–23. A descendant of the Marquis de Montcalm, Lyon signed all of his correspondence "Caleb Lyon of Lyonsdale." When Lyon left Idaho in April 1866, he absconded with $46,000 belonging to the Nez Percés.

23. Caleb Lyon to SI, 20 October 1865, USNA, RG75, *Letters Received, 1824–1881: Idaho Superintendency,* Microcopy 234 [hereafter M234: *Idaho*]; *Idaho Statesman,* 11 October 1864. The other headmen present were Ahe-ten-tu, Pe-etse-cotose, Ship-it-see, and Sa-ra-ga.

24. *Idaho Statesman,* 13 October 1864.

25. SI to CIA, 22 September 1865, USNA, M234: *Idaho.* Reference to southern Idaho peoples as "Camas Indians" was common. Frederick W. Lander reported in 1859 that there were two major Shoshone groups in Idaho, the "Kammas Prairie and Fort Boise Pannacks." See Frederick W. Lander to CIA, 18 February 1860, USNA, RG 75, *Letters Received, 1824–1881: Utah Superintendency,* Microcopy 234 [hereafter M234: *Utah*].

26. Caleb Lyon to SI, 20 October 1865, M234: *Idaho;* ARCIA, 1865, 234. Like the secretary, Lyon suggested two reservations, a winter agency near the "Little Kammas Prairie" and a larger summertime reservation of some forty thousand acres along the "banks of the Malade [Big Wood] or Shoshonee [Snake] River." Lyon clearly recognized the seasonal nature of Shoshone-Bannock wild foods, yet he confused the times of year when the various foods were utilized. There are a number of "Camas Prairies" in Idaho. The "Great Camas Prairie" lies in modern Camas and Elmore counties, east of Boise and near the town of Fairfield. The "Little Kammas Prairie" is essentially a western adjunct to the latter. See Lalia Boone, *Idaho Place Names: A Geographical Dictionary* (Moscow: University of Idaho Press, 1988).

27. Caleb Lyon to SI, 17 February 1866, USNA, M234: *Idaho.* Lyon blamed much of the anti-Indian feeling on Senator James W. Nesmith of Oregon. Formerly Oregon superintendent of Indian affairs and Lyon's most vocal critic, Nesmith allegedly encouraged white settlers to "kill all Indians whenever they can be found." The Snake War lasted from 1864 to 1868.

28. Caleb Lyon to SI, 17 February 1866, USNA, M234: *Idaho.* Lyon enclosed the 17 February 1866 clipping from the *Owyhee Avalanche.*

29. Caleb Lyon to CIA, 1 March and 13 March 1866, USNA, M234: *Idaho.*

30. Unratified treaty with the Bruneau Shoshones, Lyon to SI, 12 April 1866, USNA, RG75, *Records of the Superintendencies and Agencies of the Office of*

Indian Affairs, Idaho, Microcopy 832 [hereafter M832]; reprinted as "Caleb Lyon's Bruneau Treaty," Reference Series 369 (Boise: Idaho Historical Society, 1968).

31. Ibid.

32. Ibid.

33. Madsen, *The Northern Shoshoni,* 45–47.

34. George C. Hough to CIA, 29 December 1865, USNA, M234: *Idaho.*

35. D. W. Ballard to George C. Hough, 18 September 1866; Hough to Ballard, 12 October 1866, USNA, M234: *Idaho.* The governor sent Hough to the Payette Valley to determine its suitability for a reservation.

36. D. W. Ballard to CIA, 18 November 1866, USNA, M234: *Idaho.*

37. Ibid.

38. ARCIA, 1867, 14.

39. Executive Order, 14 June 1867; ARCIA, 1867, 247–48; Madsen, *The Northern Shoshoni,* 49–51.

40. ARCIA, 1867, 247.

41. D. W. Ballard to CIA, 30 June 1867, USNA, M234: *Idaho;* ARCIA, 1867, 247–48.

42. Capt. C. F. Powell to D. W. Ballard, 15 July 1867, reprinted in ARCIA, 1867, 252.

43. ARCIA, 1868, 201–3.

44. Ibid.

45. ARCIA, 1868, 196–99.

46. Ibid., 197–98.

47. Ibid.

48. Ibid., 658.

49. Ibid.

50. U.S. Congress, Senate, *Condition of the Indian Tribes,* 39th Cong., 2nd sess., S. Rep. 156, serial no. 1279, 26 January 1867.

51. Robert M. Utley, *The Indian Frontier of the American West, 1846–1890* (Albuquerque: University of New Mexico Press, 1984), 104–7.

52. Paul Hutton, *Phil Sheridan and His Army* (Albuquerque: University of New Mexico Press, 1984), 122; Robert M. Utley, *Frontier Regulars: The United States Army and the Indian, 1866–1891* (Lincoln: University of Nebraska Press, 1973), 34. Augur graduated from West Point in 1843, served in the Mexican War, and fought in the campaign against the Yakamas in 1855. During the Civil War, he served as a corps commander, and he later headed the investigation into Lincoln's assassination.

53. C. C. Augur to president of the Indian Peace Commission, Omaha, Nebraska, 4 October 1868, USNA, RG75, *Irregular Sized Papers;* ARCIA, 1868, 156–58. The Fort Bridger agent Luther Mann reported that originally 800 Bannocks had come to the council grounds, but by the time Augur and the presents arrived, only 450 remained. They were greatly outnumbered by 1,350 of Washakie's Eastern Shoshones.

54. Ibid.

55. Ibid.

56. Treaty with the Shoshonees and Bannacks, 15 Stat. 673–78.

57. ARCIA, 1876, vii–viii; 1878, iv–vii.

58. For a good brief explanation of the theory and policy behind agricultural assimilation, see David Rich Lewis, *Neither Wolf nor Dog: American Indians, Environment, and Agrarian Change* (New York: Oxford University Press, 1994), 7–21.

59. D. W. Ballard to CIA, 10 April 1869 and 30 April 1869, USNA, M234: *Idaho;* ARCIA, 1869, 286–87.

60. Capt. C. F. Powell to D. W. Ballard, 30 May and 30 June 1869, USNA, M234: *Idaho.*

61. Col. DeLancey Floyd-Jones to CIA, 9 August and 26 August 1869, USNA, M234: *Idaho;* ARCIA, 1869, 276–77, 288.

62. Ely S. Parker to J. D. Cox, 23 July 1869; Parker to Col. DeLancey Floyd-Jones, 24 August 1869, USNA, M832; Executive Order, 30 July 1869, 2 Kappler 839.

63. Col. DeLancey Floyd-Jones to CIA, 2 September 1869, USNA, M234: *Idaho;* CIA to Floyd-Jones, 10 September 1869; Acting CIA to Floyd-Jones, 13 September 1869, USNA, M832.

64. ARCIA, 1872, 51.

65. Capt. C. F. Powell to D. W. Ballard, 30 June 1869, USNA, M234: *Idaho;* ARCIA, 1869, 271–72. The governor of Wyoming, J. A. Campbell, reported that the Wind River battle took place on April 20.

66. Capt. C. F. Powell to Col. DeLancey Floyd-Jones, 31 July 1869; W. H. Danilson to Floyd-Jones, 16 August 1869, USNA, M234: *Idaho;* ARCIA, 1869, 277, 286–87; 1870, 181, 187. Powell's first census found 300 Boises, 150 Bannocks, and 850 Bruneaus under his charge. His total population figures agree roughly with later counts, but his assessment of ethnic affiliation is far different. William H. Danilson, who had replaced Powell in July, found 600 Bannocks, 200 Boises, and only 100 Bruneaus, in addition to Pocatello's 200 Northwestern Shoshones. The following summer Danilson counted 520 Bannocks and only 256 "mixed" Shoshones. His early figures are more consistent and probably more accurate. He was also the first agent to lump all of the Shoshones together without regard to band affiliation.

67. ARCIA, 1869, 288; W. H. Danilson to CIA, 30 August 1869, U.S. Department of the Interior, Bureau of Indian Affairs, *Fort Hall Letter Book, 1869–1875,* Fort Hall, Idaho, 7.

68. ARCIA, 1869, 274–75.

69. ARCIA, 1869, 270–75.

70. Ibid.; ARCIA, 1870, 1175–67, 178–80; see also Loretta Fowler, *Arapaho Politics, 1851–1978: Symbols in Crises of Authority* (Lincoln: University of Nebraska Press, 1982), 39–48. The Arapahos' initial stay at Wind River was brief. After a series of raids blamed on the Arapahos, a large mob of whites attacked Black Bear's band in March 1870, killing him and ten others and taking the women and children as prisoners. The majority of the Arapahos then fled to their allies on the plains. They did not return to settle permanently at Wind River until 1878.

71. ARCIA, 1872, 270. The Wind River agent, James Irwin, also asked for the Bannock annuities to be sent to Fort Hall because he knew the Bannocks would come for them and probably stay the winter, endangering his reservation's meager food supply. As late as 1872, nearly two years after Taghee's death, the Bannocks' annuities were still being sent to Wind River.

72. See Loretta Fowler, *Shared Symbols, Contested Meanings: Gros Ventre Culture and History, 1778–1984* (Ithaca, NY: Cornell University Press, 1987). Fowler describes a similar process on the Fort Belknap Reservation in Montana. She argues that the Gros Ventres adopted the "progressive" symbol of stock raising as a means of maintaining primacy over the Assiniboines, with whom they shared the reservation.

73. W. H. Danilson to Col. DeLancey Floyd-Jones, 16 August 1869, USNA, M234: *Idaho;* ARCIA, 1869, 279. Floyd-Jones did not cite the source of the latter quote.

74. ARCIA, 1870, 188; W. H. Danilson to CIA, 23 November 1870; J. N. High to CIA, 118 April 1871, USNA, M234: *Idaho.*

75. Heaton, " 'No Place to Pitch Their Teepees,' " 158–71.

76. ARCIA, 1871, 539–40.

77. W. H. Danilson to CIA, 23 May 1870, USNA, M234: *Idaho;* ARCIA, 1870, 183, 188.

78. Col. DeLancey Floyd-Jones to CIA, 26 August 1869, USNA, M234: *Idaho.*

79. ARCIA, 1869, 279; 1870, 183.

80. Handwritten "Journal of a 1871 Trip to the Yellowstone Country," by Stanton G. Fisher. Stanton G. Fisher Collection, Idaho State Historical Society, Ms. 106. Fisher's recollections must be weighed carefully. He lived much of his life among the Shoshones and Bannocks, served as Fort Hall agent, and was generally the most accurate observer among the agents. This "journal," however, was written more than twenty years after the actual event.

81. M. P. Berry to CIA, 10 August 1871, USNA, M234: *Idaho;* Robert H. Lowie, *The Northern Shoshone,* Anthropological Papers of the American Museum of Natural History vol. 2, part 2 (1909): 208–9; Steward, *Basin-Plateau Aboriginal Sociopolitical Groups* (1938; repr., Salt Lake City: University of Utah Press, 1970), 209–11; Robert F. Murphy and Yolanda Murphy, *Shoshone–Bannock Subsistence and Society,* Anthropological Records vol. 16, no. 7 (Berkeley: University of California Press, 1959), 327, 333.

82. M. P. Berry to CIA, 8 July 1871, USNA, M234: *Idaho;* ARCIA, 1871, 540.

83. Col. DeLancey Floyd-Jones to CIA, 30 September 1869 and 12 February 1870, USNA, M234: *Idaho;* ARCIA, 1869, 279.

84. W. H. Danilson to Col. DeLancey Floyd-Jones, 13 September and 3 December 1869, USNA, M234: *Idaho.* See J. Wright to CIA, 6 February, 11 March, 13 March, and 24 March 1875, USNA, M234: *Idaho.*

85. ARCIA, 1871, 540; 1872, 273.

86. ARCIA, 1871, 544; *Fort Hall Letter Book,* 87.

87. M. P. Berry to CIA, 24 November 1871, USNA, M234: *Idaho.*

4. TWO TRAILS

Epigraph: Willie George, as told to Jack F. Contor, "Two Trails," *True West* 10 (1963): 8.

1. Although the first dances took place in 1869, the movement has been identified more often with the year 1870, when the doctrine became widely known and disseminated. Basic sources on the 1870 Ghost Dance include James Mooney, "The Ghost-Dance Religion and the Sioux Outbreak of 1890," *Fourteenth Annual Report of the Bureau of American Ethnology,* part 2 (Washington, DC: Government Printing Office, 1896); Leslie Spier, *The Ghost Dance of 1870 among the Klamath of Oregon,* University of Washington Publications in Anthropology no. 2 (Seattle: University of Washington, 1927), 39–56; A. H. Gayton, *The Ghost Dance of 1870 in South-Central California,* University of California Publications in American Archaeology and Ethnology vol. 28, no. 3 (Berkeley: University of California Press, 1930), 57–82; Cora Du Bois, *The 1870 Ghost Dance,* Anthropological Records vol. 3, no. 1 (Berkeley: University of California Press, 1939); Michael Hittman, "Ghost Dances, Disillusionment, and Opiate Addiction: An Ethnohistory of the Smith and Mason Valley Paiutes," Ph.D. diss., University of New Mexico, 1973; Michael Hittman, "The 1870 Ghost Dance at Walker River Reservation: A Reconstruction," *Ethnohistory* 20 (Summer 1973): 247–78; and Joseph Jorgensen, "Ghost Dance, Bear Dance, and Sun Dance," in *Handbook of North American Indians,* vol. 11, *Great Basin,* edited by Warren L. d'Azevedo (Washington, DC: Smithsonian Institution, 1986), 660–72. Only Jorgensen refers to the Ghost Dances by the actual years of their emergence, 1869 and 1889.

2. Mooney, "The Ghost-Dance Religion," 701–3, 764–65.

3. Du Bois, *The 1870 Ghost Dance,* 3–4.

4. Michael Hittman, *Wovoka and the Ghost Dance* (Lincoln: University of Nebraska Press, 1997), 29; Michael Hittman, *Corbett Mack: The Life of a Northern Paiute* (Lincoln: University of Nebraska Press, 1996), 49, 176, 352–53.

5. I have borrowed the term *transformative* from David Aberle, *The Peyote Religion among the Navaho* (1966; repr., Chicago: University of Chicago Press, 1982), 318–22. Aberle defines a transformative movement as one that "view[s] the process of change as cataclysmic, the time of change as imminent, the direction of change as teleologically guided, [and] the appropriate supervision of the movement as charismatic." Aberle's terms and his concept of "relative deprivation" have also been applied to the Ghost Dance and Sun Dance by Joseph Jorgensen in *The Sun Dance Religion: Power for the Powerless* (Chicago: University of Chicago Press, 1972). See also Hittman, "The 1870 Ghost Dance," 264–67.

6. Du Bois, *The 1870 Ghost Dance,* 130–31; Hittman, "The 1870 Ghost Dance," 263.

7. Jorgensen, "Ghost Dance, Bear Dance, and Sun Dance," 660.

8. Mooney, "The Ghost-Dance Religion," 657, 701; Leslie Spier, *The Prophet Dance of the Northwest and Its Derivatives: The Source of the Ghost Dance* (Menasha, WI: George Banta Publishing Company, 1935), 5, 13–16, 24; Du Bois, *The 1870 Ghost Dance,* 3.

9. Hittman, "The 1870 Ghost Dance," 256–66; Spier, *The Prophet Dance,*

13; Willard Z. Park, *Shamanism in Western North America: A Study in Cultural Relationships* (Chicago: Northwestern University Press, 1938), 69–71.

10. Du Bois, *The 1870 Ghost Dance,* 130; Spier, *The Ghost Dance of 1870 among the Klamath,* 45–46; Gayton, *The Ghost Dance of 1870 in South-Central California,* 60.

11. Du Bois, *The 1870 Ghost Dance,* 132–33; Gayton, *The Ghost Dance of 1870 in South-Central California,* 64–65; Spier, *The Ghost Dance of 1870 among the Klamath,* 45–46; see also Lowell John Bean and Sylvia Brakke Vane, "Cults and Their Transformations," *Handbook of North American Indians,* vol. 8, *California,* ed. Robert F. Heizer (Washington, DC: Smithsonian Institution, 1978), 662–72.

12. Hittman, "The 1870 Ghost Dance at Walker River," 269. One informant stated that Wodziwob no longer believed in his dream after a final visit to the land of the dead; all he found there were shadows, who would not respond to his calls, and an owl, an omen of misfortune among the Northern Paiutes.

13. Frank C. Miller, "Ghost Dance," in Howard R. Lamar, ed., *The New Encyclopedia of the American West* (New Haven, CT: Yale University Press, 1998), 426.

14. Jorgensen, *Sun Dance Religion,* 5; Jorgensen, "Ghost Dance, Bear Dance, and Sun Dance," 661; Charles A. Heidenreich, "A Review of the Ghost Dance Religion of 1889–90 among the North American Indians and Comparison of Eight Societies Which Accepted or Rejected the Dance," M.A. thesis, University of Oregon, 1967. Here, structural complexity is "measured by numbers and types of kinship organizations, annual and sporadic rituals, levels of jurisdictional hierarchy and the like." Heidenreich presents a simplistic picture of the ethnic makeup of Fort Hall, comparing "Western Shoshones" with "Bannocks." He assumes a uniform level of deprivation in all of the sample societies. Finally, he places the Bannocks on the "reject" side of a continuum of acceptance and rejection of the Ghost Dance.

15. Aberle, *The Peyote Religion,* 323.

16. M. J. Shelton to J. E. Tourtellotte, n.d. [May 1870], quoted in J. A. Jones, *The Sun Dance of the Northern Ute,* Anthropological Papers 47, Bureau of American Ethnology Bulletin 157 (Washington, DC: Government Printing Office, 1955), 239–40.

17. Ibid.

18. *Deseret Evening News,* 25 May 1870; *The Latter-Day Saints' Millennial Star,* 21 June 1870, 398.

19. Jones, *The Sun Dance of the Northern Ute,* 239; Jorgensen, *The Sun Dance Religion,* 39.

20. ARCIA 1872, 558.

21. Jorgensen, *The Sun Dance Religion,* 39.

22. Ibid., 39–40; ARCIA 1872, 288, 298.

23. J. M. Lee to James Mooney, n.d., quoted in Mooney, "The Ghost-Dance Religion," 701–2.

24. Frank Campbell to CIA, 19 November 1890, USNA, SC 188, reprinted in Mooney, "The Ghost-Dance Religion," 702–3.

25. Ibid.

26. *Idaho Statesman*, 2 July 1872; ARCIA 1871, 550–51.

27. ARCIA 1871, 542–43; J. N. High to CIA, 11 September 1872, USNA, M234: *Idaho.*

28. S. G. Fisher to J. N. High, 10 September 1872; High to CIA, 11 September 1872, USNA, M234: *Idaho.* The Bannocks also told Fisher that the man was killed to avenge the death of one of their own men during the previous fall's buffalo hunt in Montana.

29. J. N. High to CIA, 11 September 1872, USNA, M234: *Idaho.*

30. Ibid.; S. G. Fisher to J. N. High, 10 September 1872, USNA, M234: *Idaho.*

31. *Idaho Statesman*, 2 July 1872, p. 2; ARCIA 1872, 282.

32. *Idaho Statesman*, 2 July 1872, p. 2.

33. Ibid.

34. George W. Dodge to SI, 24 July 1872, USNA, M234: *Utah.*

35. Ibid.

36. ARCIA 1872, 294–95.

37. George Washington Hill, "My First Day's Work," *Juvenile Instructor* 10 (25 December 1875): 309. See also Scott R. Christensen, *Sagwitch: Shoshone Chieftain, Mormon Elder, 1822–1887* (Logan: Utah State University Press, 1999), 88–90.

38. Hill, "My First Day's Work."

39. George Washington Hill, "An Indian Vision," *Juvenile Instructor* 12 (1 January 1877): 11.

40. Ibid.

41. Richard White, *The Middle Ground: Indians, Empires, and Republics in the Great Lakes Region, 1650–1815* (New York: Cambridge University Press, 1991).

42. ARCIA 1872, 273.

43. *Idaho Statesman*, 26 April 1873.

44. *Idaho Statesman*, 17 October 1872; E. L. Applegate to SI, 15 February 1873; James H. Slater et al. to SI, 19 April 1873; Henry W. Reed to CIA, 4 January and 11 January 1873, USNA, M234: *Idaho.*

45. Thomas W. Bennett to SI, 15 February 1873, USNA, M234: *Idaho.*

46. Ibid.

47. SI to CIA, 26 March 1873, USNA, M234: *Idaho.*

48. Henry W. Reed to CIA, 23 April and 19 May 1873; J. P. C. Shanks, Thomas W. Bennett, and Henry W. Reed to CIA, 17 November 1873, USNA, M234: *Idaho*, reprinted in U.S. Congress, House, *Bannock and Other Indians in Southern Idaho*, 43d Cong., 1st sess., Ex. Doc. 129, serial no. 1608, 1874; Reed to CIA, 6 December 1873, *Fort Hall Letter Book*, 166.

49. Henry W. Reed to CIA, 30 July 1874, USNA, M234: *Idaho.* An Indian Department circular dated 17 July transmitted the act of Congress to the agents.

50. J. Wright to CIA, 30 December 1874, USNA, M234: *Idaho;* ARCIA 1873, 247–48; 1874, 284; 1875, 259.

51. ARCIA 1874, 284; Capt. J. L. Viven to Assistant Adjutant General [hereafter AAG], Department of California, 18 February 1875; J. M. Fisher to CIA, 1 July 1875, USNA, M234: *Idaho.*

52. Henry W. Reed to CIA, 20 February 1875, M234: *Idaho*.

53. W. H. Danilson to CIA, 24 February 1877; Peter O. Matthews to James A. Garfield, 10 May 1877, USNA, M234: *Idaho*.

54. ARCIA 1875, 258; 1876, 42.

55. Mooney, "The Ghost-Dance Religion," 703.

56. Ibid. Mooney believed that Wovoka's father, whose name he rendered as "Tavibo," or "White Man," was the 1870 prophet and seemed to suggest that this could account for the reference to the "beings with white skin."

57. Mooney, "The Ghost-Dance Religion," 703–4.

58. See Lawrence Coates, "The Mormons, the Ghost Dance Religion, and the Massacre at Wounded Knee," *Dialogue: A Journal of Mormon Thought* 18 (Winter 1985): 89–111; Gregory E. Smoak, "The Mormons and the Ghost Dance of 1890," *South Dakota History* 16 (Winter 1986): 269–94; Mooney, "The Ghost-Dance Religion," 772, 790–92.

59. ARCIA 1875, 342, 375–76.

60. Brigham D. Madsen, *The Northern Shoshoni* (Caldwell, ID: Caxton Printers, 1980), 95–97.

61. James Wright to CIA, 10 June 1875, USNA, M234: *Idaho*.

62. Ibid.

63. James Wright to CIA, 30 June 1875, *Fort Hall Letter Book*.

64. James Wright to CIA, 10 June 1875, USNA, M234: *Idaho*; ARCIA 1875, 258, 338–42, 375–76.

65. Madsen, *The Northern Shoshoni*, 97.

66. Bannock and Shoshone Chief and Headmen to CIA, 15 September 1875, USNA, M234: *Idaho*.

67. ARCIA 1876, 42–43; W. H. Danilson to CIA, 30 November 1875; SI to Danilson, 29 December 1875; Danilson to CIA, 24 January 1876, USNA, M234: *Idaho*.

68. Capt. J. L. Viven to AAG, Department of California, 18 February 1875, USNA, M234: *Idaho*.

69. Mason Brayman to secretary of war, 2 June 1877, USNA, M234: *Idaho*. Brayman dated his letter 2 June, but it is more likely he meant 2 July, as he included a hand-copied extract from the *Idaho Statesman* of 26 June 1877, which printed a transcript of the meeting.

70. Ibid.

71. Thomas H. Leforge, *Memoirs of a White Crow Indian* (New York: D. Appleton–Century Company, 1928), 262.

72. *Idaho Statesman*, 26 June 1877.

73. W. H. Danilson to Capt. A. H. Bainbridge, 21 June 1877, USNA, M234: *Idaho*.

74. Harrison Fuller to Capt. A. H. Bainbridge, 27 June 1877, USNA, M234: *Idaho*.

75. W. H. Danilson to CIA, 16 June, 21 July 1877, 7 August, and 7 November 1877, USNA, M234: *Idaho*.

76. W. H. Danilson to CIA, 9 August 1877, USNA, M234: *Idaho*.

77. Ibid.; ARCIA 1877, 79.

78. W. H. Danilson to CIA, 13 August 1877; secretary of war to SI, 22

August 1877, USNA, M234: *Idaho;* Special Orders No. 42, Capt. A. H. Bainbridge, 19 August 1877, Idaho State Historical Society, S. G. Fisher Collection, Ms. 106.

79. Ibid.; Diary of Stanton G. Fisher, S. G. Fisher Collection, Idaho Historical Society, Ms. 106, Folder 14; Fisher to CIA, 7 March 1892, USNA, RG75, *Letters Received, 1881–1907.* Fisher left three diaries covering the years 1875 and 1877. In the diary, Fisher spells Avery's name "Ouvrir," but in later official correspondence he settled on "Avery."

80. Fisher Diary, 19–21 August 1877.

81. Fisher Diary, 31 August 1877; Oliver O. Howard, *Nez Perce Joseph* (Boston: Lee and Shepard, 1881), 243–44.

82. Fisher Diary, 13 September 1877.

83. W. H. Danilson to CIA, 7 November 1877, USNA, M234: *Idaho.*

84. W. H. Danilson to CIA, 22 November 1877, USNA, M234: *Idaho.*

85. ARCIA 1878, 49.

86. Ibid.; W. H. Danilson to CIA, 27 November 1877, USNA, M234: *Idaho.*

87. ARCIA 1877, 79; 1878, 49; AAG to Gen. Philip H. Sheridan, 27 November 1877; W. H. Danilson to CIA, 28 November and 15 December 1877, USNA, M234: *Idaho.*

88. Col. John O. Smith to AAG, Department of the Platte, 25–26 December 1877, USNA, M234: *Idaho.*

89. Gen. George Crook to Gen. Philip H. Sheridan, 3 January 1878, USNA, M234: *Idaho.*

90. W. H. Danilson to CIA, 13 January 1878, USNA, M234: *Idaho.*

91. Joseph Skelton to George Shoup, 21 January 1878, George Shoup Papers, Idaho State University, Special Collections, MC 14; W. H. Danilson to CIA, 16 January 1878, USNA, M234: *Idaho;* ARCIA 1878, 49–50; *Idaho Statesman,* 11 June 1878; Brigham D. Madsen, *The Bannock of Idaho* (Caldwell, ID: Caxton Printers, 1958), 205, 212.

92. *Idaho Statesman,* 22 January 1878.

93. Frank J. Parker to Mason Brayman, 25 February 1878, USNA, M234: *Idaho.*

94. George Chapin to James Stout, 15 January 1878, reprinted in *Idaho Statesman,* 22 January 1878.

95. Mason Brayman to S. S. Fenn, 27 February 1878, USNA, M234: *Idaho.*

96. Levi A. Gheen to CIA, 27 May 1878, USNA, RG 75, *Letters Received, 1824–1881: Nevada Superintendency,* Microcopy 234 [hereafter M234: *Nevada*].

97. Steven J. Crum, *The Road on Which We Came (Po'i pentun tammen kimmappeh): A History of the Western Shoshone* (Salt Lake City: University of Utah Press, 1994), 35; Whitney McKinney, *A History of the Shoshone-Paiutes of the Duck Valley Indian Reservation* (Owyhee, NV: Duck Valley Shoshone-Paiute Tribal Council, 1983), 49–51.

98. Levi A. Gheen to CIA, 27 May 1878, USNA, M234: *Nevada.*

99. ARCIA 1878, 103.

100. Ibid.; Levi A. Gheen to CIA, 18 July 1878, USNA, M234: *Nevada.*

101. ARCIA 1872, 453.

102. Oliver O. Howard, *Famous Indian Chiefs I Have Known* (New York: Century Company, 1916), 264.

103. Sarah Winnemucca Hopkins, *Life among the Piutes: Their Wrongs and Claims* (1883; repr., Reno: University of Nevada Press, 1994), 140–46.

104. See John A. Ruby and Robert H. Brown, *Dreamer-Prophets of the Columbia Plateau: Smohalla and Skolaskin* (Norman: University of Oklahoma Press, 1989).

105. ARCIA 1878, 116.

106. Report of General O. O. Howard in ARSW, U.S. Congress, House, 45th Cong., 3d sess., Ex. Doc. 1, serial no. 1843, 1878, 211.

107. Howard, *Famous Indian Chiefs,* 265–66.

108. Ibid., 266–67.

109. Hopkins, *Life among the Paiutes,* 162–64.

110. ARCIA 1878, 119. The Malheur agent W. V. Rinehart reported that a Northern Paiute told him of the Bannock visit on 25 March 1878.

111. Ibid.

112. *Idaho Statesman,* 14 May 1878.

113. Ibid., 21 May 1878.

114. Ibid., 1 June 1878.

115. Ibid., 1 June 1878, 11 June 1878; Gen. Irwin McDowell to Gen. William T. Sherman, 7 June 1878, USNA, M234: *Idaho.* The *Idaho Statesman* was the voice of Brayman's political opposition, and it used his cordial reception of Buffalo Horn, and the permission note, in its campaign to unseat the governor. On 6 June Brayman defended his actions in a letter to Gen. McDowell, which was forwarded up the chain of command and is reprinted in ARSW, 1878, 136–37.

116. Brayman to Howard, 28 May 1878, quoted in George F. Brimlow, *The Bannock Indian War of 1878* (Caldwell, ID: Caxton Printers, 1938), 80.

117. *Idaho Statesman,* 1 June 1878, 13 June 1878. See also John Hailey, *The History of Idaho* (Boise, ID: Syms-York Company, 1910), 227–28. Hailey's history was based mostly on personal remembrances and is often mistaken in its details. He gave the names of the two Bannocks as Charley and Jim, but he also gave the wrong date for the war's outbreak.

118. Willie George, as told to Jack F. Contor, "Two Trails," *True West* 10 (January–February 1963): 9.

119. *Idaho Statesman,* 1 June 1878; 6 June 1878; 13 June 1878; C. N. Stowers to CIA, 20 June 1878, USNA, M234: *Idaho.* Major Jim reported that there were twelve lodges of "hostiles." Capt. Reuben Bernard found evidence of thirty-two or thirty-three lodges at the abandoned Bannock camp in the lava beds, suggesting that only one-third of the Bannocks chose war. In mid-June, the Lemhi agent Stowers wired that only ten "lodges of hostiles" had gone south to the Snake River.

120. ARCIA 1878, 119.

121. Ibid.

122. Eugene D. Genovese, *Roll, Jordan, Roll: The World the Slaves Made* (New York: Random House, 1972); Robert W. Blassingame, *The Slave Community: Plantation Life in the Antebellum South* (New York: Oxford University

Press, 1972); Albert J. Raboteau, *Slave Religion: The "Invisible Institution" in the Antebellum South* (New York: Oxford University Press, 1978); Roy Rosenzweig, *Eight Hours for What We Will: Workers and Leisure in an Industrial City, 1870–1920* (New York: Cambridge University Press, 1983).

123. E. E. McNeilly to Whom It May Concern, n.d., Bruneau John Collection, Idaho Historical Society, Ms. 2/49. The letter, received by the Idaho Historical Society in 1925, is the statement of Bruneau John's widow, Sallie, concerning her recollections of the Bannock War.

124. Mrs. Jefferson M. Waterhouse, "Indian's Paul Revere Ride to Save Bruneau Settlers," Bruneau John Collection, Idaho Historical Society, Ms. 2/49. The Bruneau Valley settlers lost a good deal of property, but only one man died, riding off in an ill-advised attempt to retrieve some horses.

125. ARSW, 1878, 142; Hopkins, *Life among the Piutes,* 148–49; *Idaho Statesman,* 20 June 1878. Military and government officials were unaware of Buffalo Horn's death for more than two weeks.

126. Interview with Oren George, Fort McDermitt, Nevada, July 1961, Sven Liljeblad Papers, 86–14, Field Notebook #1, 1961, Special Collections Department, University of Nevada, Reno.

127. Capt. E. F. Thompson to AAG, Department of California, 4 June 1878, reprinted in ARSW, 132.

128. ARCIA 1878, 120.

129. Howard, *Famous Indian Chiefs,* 276; Hopkins, *Life among the Piutes,* 157–63.

130. Howard, *Famous Indian Chiefs,* 276.

131. Report of Gen. Oliver O. Howard, in ARSW, 1878, 214; Hopkins, *Life among the Piutes,* 161–63; Brimlow, *The Bannock Indian War,* 101–6.

132. George, "Two Trails," 12. *Pasego* is the Shoshone word for camas, and this may have been one of many camas-gathering areas that Newe peoples visited.

133. "Wheaton's Letter," in ARSW, 1878, 218. The evidence was a letter from Governor Brayman of Idaho giving permission for three Bannocks to visit the Umatilla reservation to search for stolen horses. The letter's endorsement by the Umatilla agent N. A. Cornoyer indicates that Buffalo Horn and Egan had visited the reservation.

134. Gen. O. O. Howard to AAG, Division of the Pacific, 9 July 1878, ARSW, 1878, 170; Brimlow, *The Bannock Indian War,* 136–44; Robert H. Ruby and John A. Brown, *Indians of the Pacific Northwest* (Norman: University of Oklahoma Press, 1981), 251–52.

135. N. A. Cornoyer to CIA, 19 July 1878, *Letters Received, 1824–1881: Oregon Superintendency,* Microcopy 234 [hereafter M234: Oregon]; Ruby and Brown, *Indians of the Pacific Northwest,* 252; Report of Capt. Evan Miles, in ARSW, 1878, 224–26; Brimlow, *The Bannock Indian War,* 149–51.

136. Lt. J. A. Sladen to Adjutant General [hereafter AG], Division of the Pacific, 16 July 1878, in ARSW, 1878, 175; Col. Frank Wheaton to Maj. John Green, 18 July 1878, in ARSW, 1878, 177; Hailey, *History of Idaho,* 242–43; Ruby and Brown, *Indians of the Pacific Northwest,* 253.

137. Howard, *Famous Indian Chiefs,* 277.

138. Gen. O. O. Howard to AAG, 8 August and 13 August 1878, in ARSW, 1878, 184, 186.

139. *Idaho Statesman,* 2 September 1878; ARCIA 1879, 54; Col. Nelson A. Miles to Lt. Col. J. N. G. Whistler, 5 September 1878, reprinted in Brimlow, *The Bannock Indian War,* 224–25; Gen. Philip H. Sheridan to AG, 13 September 1878, USNA, M234: *Idaho.*

140. Col. Albert G. Brackett, "The Shoshonis, or Snake Indians, Their Religion, Superstitions, and Manners," *Annual Report of the Smithsonian Institution for the Year 1879* (Washington, DC: Government Printing Office, 1880), 332.

5. CULTURE WARS, INDIANNESS, AND THE 1890 GHOST DANCE

Epigraph: Stanton G. Fisher to CIA, 26 November 1890, USNA, RG 75, SC 188: *The Ghost Dance.*

1. On the Second Great Awakening, see William G. McLoughlin, *Revivals, Awakenings, and Reform* (Chicago: University of Chicago Press, 1978); Paul E. Johnson, *A Shopkeeper's Millennium: Society and Revivals in Rochester, New York, 1815–1827* (New York: Hill and Wang, 1978); Nathan O. Hatch, *The Democratization of American Christianity* (New Haven, CT: Yale University Press, 1989). On Indian policy in this era, see Francis Paul Prucha, *American Indian Policy in Crisis: Christian Reformers and the Indian, 1865–1900* (Norman: University of Oklahoma Press, 1976); Frederick E. Hoxie, *A Final Promise: The Campaign to Assimilate the Indians, 1880–1920* (Lincoln: University of Nebraska Press, 1984); David Rich Lewis, *Neither Wolf nor Dog: American Indians, Environment, and Agrarian Change* (New York: Oxford University Press, 1994).

2. Quoted in Francis Paul Prucha, *The Great Father: The United States Government and the American Indians* (Lincoln: University of Nebraska Press, 1984), 671. See also Frank Van Nuys, *Americanizing the West: Race, Immigrants, and Citizenship, 1890–1930* (Lawrence: University Press of Kansas, 2002). Van Nuys describes the ways in which reformers attempted to "Americanize" immigrants in the West and provides an instructive parallel to the approach to American Indian peoples.

3. ARCIA, 1872, 273; 1887, 67.

4. ARCIA, 1871, 540; 1887, 67.

5. A good example of the long-standing fear engendered by the Bannock War was a scare on the Great Camas Prairie in the summer of 1897. The Fort Hall agent Lt. F. G. Irwin investigated reports of over three hundred Bannocks on the prairie but found only a handful of Indians and assured the Indian bureau that there was "not a Bannock among them." SI to CIA, 30 June 1897; F. G. Irwin to CIA, 5 July 1897, USNA, RG 75.

6. William Parsons to CIA, 9 January 1886, USNA, RG 75, SC 72.

7. *Idaho News,* 18 April 1891; S. G. Fisher to CIA, 18 April 1891, USNA, RG75, *Letters Received, 1881–1907.*

8. Willie George, as told to Jack F. Contor, "Two Trails," *True West* 10 (January–February 1963), 9.

9. Arden R. Smith to CIA, 6 December 1882, USNA, RG 75.

10. A. L. Cook to CIA, 8 December 1882, USNA, RG 75. Cook rendered his name as *Prociberoo*. I have chosen to use the spelling *Pokibero*, which appears in the Fort Hall censuses throughout the 1880s and 1890s.

11. Ibid.; Arden R. Smith to CIA, 6 December 1882; ARCIA, 1882, 53–54. Cook reported that 950 of 1,085 Shoshones engaged in agriculture, while only 240 of 471 Bannocks did so.

12. Arden R. Smith to CIA, 19 December 1882, USNA, RG 75.

13. Ibid.; A. L. Cook to CIA, 8 December 1882, USNA, RG 75.

14. ARCIA, 1883, 54; Arden R. Smith to CIA, 19 December 1882, USNA, RG 75.

15. A. L. Cook to CIA, 8 December 1882, USNA, RG 75.

16. Arden R. Smith to CIA, 6 December and 19 December 1882, USNA, RG 75.

17. A. L. Cook to CIA, 19 December 1882, USNA, RG 75.

18. Arden R. Smith to CIA, 19 December 1882, USNA, RG 75.

19. A. L. Cook to CIA, 2 January 1883, USNA, RG 75.

20. Robert H. Lowie, *The Northern Shoshone*, Anthropological Papers of the American Museum of Natural History vol. 2, part 2 (New York: American Museum of Natural History, 1909), 209; see also Robert H. Lowie, *Notes on Shoshonean Ethnography*, Anthropological Papers of the American Museum of Natural History vol. 20, part 3 (New York: American Museum of Natural History, 1924), 284.

21. A. L. Cook to CIA, 15 January 1883, USNA, RG 75.

22. See Frederick E. Hoxie, *Parading through History: The Making of the Crow Nation in America, 1805–1935* (New York: Cambridge University Press, 1995). Hoxie's study of the Crow Nation provides a valuable model for understanding the evolution of political leadership in response to the growing power of the United States and the corresponding loss of autonomy for native peoples.

23. W. H. Danilson to CIA, 22 September and 23 October 1878, USNA, RG 75, M234: *Idaho;* SI to President Chester A. Arthur, 23 May 1881; SI to Sidney Dillon, 9 June 1881; Dillon to SI, 11 June 1881, USNA, RG 75; ARCIA, 1878, 50–51; Brigham D. Madsen, *The Northern Shoshoni* (Caldwell, ID: Caxton Printers, 1980), 109–11.

24. J. A. Wright to CIA, 22 March and 30 March 1880, USNA, M234: *Idaho.*

25. J. A. Wright to CIA, 19 April 1880, USNA, M234: *Idaho;* ARCIA, 1880, 62.

26. "Agreement with the Shoshones, Bannacks, and Sheepeaters, of Idaho," reprinted in ARCIA, 1880, 278.

27. George L. Shoup to CIA, 7 July 1880, USNA, M234: *Idaho;* ARCIA, 1880, xxx.

28. E. A. Stone to CIA, 19 May 1880, USNA, M234: *Idaho;* E. Nasholds to CIA, 1 May 1891, USNA, RG 75.

29. Joseph K. McCammon to CIA, 22 October 1881, USNA, RG 75, SC 99.

30. Ibid.; A. L. Cook to CIA, 4 April 1882, USNA, RG 75; Madsen, *The Northern Shoshoni*, 111.

31. E. A. Stone to CIA, 13 September and 30 September 1881; A. L. Cook to

CIA, 9 October and 11 November 1882; Arden R. Smith to CIA, 13 November 1882, USNA, RG 75.

32. Cyrus Beede to CIA, 26 January and 28 January 1884, USNA, RG75. The agreement also called for the Fort Hall Indians to share any benefits that came to the Duck Valley and Lemhi people in exchange for the surrender of their reservations.

33. Cyrus Beede to CIA, 6, February, 9 February, and 25 February 1884, USNA, RG 75.

34. Cyrus Beede to CIA, 3 March 1884; John S. Mayhugh to Rep. George W. Cassidy, 26 February 1884, USNA, RG 75; ARCIA, 1884, 128–30. The Western Shoshone agent John Mayhugh cited the Western Shoshones' desire to remain in the land of their birth, the number of whites near Fort Hall, and the presence of the Bannocks all as reasons to oppose their removal.

35. Cyrus Beede to CIA, 20 March 1884, USNA, RG 75.

36. Cyrus Beede to CIA, 21 March, 24 March, 31 March, and 1 April 1884, USNA, RG 75.

37. John Harries to CIA, 5 May 1884, USNA, RG 75; see also Brigham D. Madsen, *The Lemhi: Sacajawea's People* (Caldwell, ID: Caxton Printers, 1990), 126–29.

38. ARCIA, 1884, xxx; ARCIA, 1885, xxxiii–iv; ARCIA, 1886, xxxii–iii; S. Shellenbarger and J. Wilson to SI, 24 May 1886; SI to CIA, 7 August 1886; Peter Gallagher to CIA, 5 October and 6 October 1886; John Hailey to CIA, 20 October 1886; SI to CIA, 8 November 1886; Citizens of Idaho and Residents of Pocatello to SI, 18 November 1886; Jno. M. Evans to CIA, 22 March 1887; Gallagher to CIA, 28 March 1887; Liberty Hunt et al. to CIA, 22 April 1887; Gallagher to CIA, 20 May 1887, USNA, RG 75; U.S. Congress, Senate, *Utah and Northern Railroad,* 49th Cong., 1st sess., Ex. Doc. 20, 1886; Madsen, *The Northern Shoshoni,* 111–13. The November 1886 petition from the "Residents of Pocatello" was typical. It asked that they be allowed to stay in the "small dwelling houses" they had built to escape the "awful cold of the Idaho winter."

39. "Proceedings of a Council Held at Fort Hall Indian Agency, Idaho Territory, May 27th, 1887," included in Robert S. Gardiner and Peter Gallagher to CIA, 30 May 1887, USNA, RG 75.

40. Ibid. The "post" that Tyhee planted as a marker is reminiscent of the poles that Chief Joseph's father had planted in the Wallowa Valley of Oregon to mark off his people's land from the encroaching whites.

41. Ibid.

42. Ibid. The final cession consisted of 1,840 acres.

43. Peter Gallagher to CIA, 7 February, 27 February, 25 March, 4 May, 18 May, and 17 November 1888, USNA, RG 75; Madsen, *The Northern Shoshoni,* 117.

44. Basic sources on the 1890 movement include James Mooney, "The Ghost-Dance Religion and the Sioux Outbreak of 1890," *Fourteenth Annual Report of the Bureau of American Ethnology,* part 2 (Washington, DC: Government Printing Office, 1896); Michael Hittman, *Wovoka and the Ghost Dance,* 2d ed. (Lincoln: University of Nebraska Press, 1997); Michael Hittman, "The 1890 Ghost Dance in Nevada," *American Indian Culture and Research Journal*

16 (1992): 123–66; L. G. Moses, "'The Father Tells Me So!' Wovoka: The Ghost Dance Prophet," *American Indian Quarterly* 9 (1985): 335–51.

45. David F. Aberle, *The Peyote Religion among the Navaho* (1966; repr., Chicago: University of Chicago Press, 1982), 316–17.

46. See Alexander Lesser, *The Pawnee Ghost Dance Hand Game: Ghost Dance Revival and Ethnic Identity* (1933; repr., Lincoln: University of Nebraska Press, 1996); Alice Beck Kehoe, *The Ghost Dance: Ethnohistory and Revitalization* (Fort Worth, TX: Holt, Rinehart and Winston, 1989).

47. Hittman, "The 1890 Ghost Dance in Nevada," 158.

48. S. S. Sears to CIA, 17 November 1890; Maj. Henry Carroll to AAG, Division of the Missouri, 28 June 1890, USNA, SC 188. Sears identified Wovoka as "a peaceable, industrious, but lunatic Pah-Ute . . . Who proclaimed himself an aboriginal Jesus who was to redeem the Red Man."

49. E. A. Dyer Sr., "Wizardry," Manuscripts Division, Nevada Historical Society, Reno, n.d. The Dyer manuscript is also reprinted in Hittman, *Wovoka,* 247–55.

50. Hittman, "The 1890 Ghost Dance in Nevada," 158; Hittman, *Wovoka,* 61.

51. *New York Times,* 8 November 1890; Nelson A. Miles, "The Future of the Indian Question," *North American Review* 152 (January 1891): 9; ARSW, 1892, 141.

52. Maj. Henry Carroll to AAG, Division of the Missouri, 28 June 1890, USNA, SC 188.

53. E. R. Kellogg to AAG, Department of the Platte, 27 October 1890, SC 188; Lawrence Coates, "The Mormons, the Ghost Dance Religion, and the Massacre at Wounded Knee," *Dialogue: A Journal of Mormon Thought* 18 (1985): 96, 100–101. Coates searched church records but could find none indicating that Pagwite, or Bannack Jim, as he was identified in Kellogg's letter, was ever a member of the Mormon church.

54. See Gregory E. Smoak, "The Mormons and the Ghost Dance of 1890," *South Dakota History* 16 (Fall 1986): 269–94; Coates, "The Mormons, the Ghost Dance Religion, and the Massacre at Wounded Knee."

55. Quoted in Mooney, "The Ghost-Dance Religion," 792–93.

56. Ibid., 790–91.

57. Coates, "The Mormons, the Ghost Dance Religion, and the Massacre at Wounded Knee," 98–99. Coates points out that very few Indians went through the ceremony of endowment, a lengthy and important church initiation rite, in the years before the 1890 Ghost Dance.

58. Mooney, "The Ghost-Dance Religion," 777.

59. S. G. Fisher to CIA, 26 November 1890, USNA, SC 188.

60. Capt. J. M. Lee to AG, n.d., quoted in Mooney, "The Ghost-Dance Religion," 784.

61. Mooney, "The Ghost-Dance Religion," 797.

62. ARSW, 1891, 142–43, reprinted in Mooney, "The Ghost-Dance Religion," 789.

63. Maj. Henry Carroll to AAG, Division of the Missouri, 28 June 1890, USNA, SC 188.

64. A. I. Chapman to Gen. John Gibbon, 6 December 1890, in ARSW, 191–94, also reprinted in Hittman, *Wovoka*, 231–36.

65. Ibid.

66. Ibid.

67. Mooney, "The Ghost-Dance Religion," 780–81. Mooney gave a great deal of credit to educated Indians such as Edson: "The Ghost Dance could never have become so widespread, and would probably have died out within a year of its inception, had it not been for the efficient aid it received from the returned pupils of various eastern government schools, who conducted the sacred correspondence for their friends at the different agencies, acted as interpreters for the delegates to the messiah, and in various ways assumed the leadership and conduct of the dance" (820).

68. Mooney, "The Ghost-Dance Religion," 780–81.

69. Dyer, "Wizardry."

70. Mooney, "The Ghost-Dance Religion," 777.

71. Mooney, "The Ghost-Dance Religion," 785, 805.

72. A. I. Chapman to Gen. John Gibbon, 6 December 1890, in ARSW, 191–94.

73. Mooney, "The Ghost-Dance Religion," 807.

74. Maj. Henry Carroll to AAG, Division of the Missouri, 28 June 1890, SC 188. Lt. S. C. Robertson recorded Porcupine's statement and forwarded it through Maj. Carroll.

75. Lt. William H. Johnson to AAG, Department of the Platte, 13 August 1891, USNA, SC 188.

76. Ibid., 807.

77. Washakie and Oa-Tah to Wilford Woodruff, 7 July 1889, quoted in Coates, "The Mormons, the Ghost Dance Religion, and the Massacre at Wounded Knee," 102. Washakie wrote Woodruff, the Mormon church president, to tell him that he now believed that the "Indian from Fourt Hall has been giving Washakie and his people lies."

78. Mooney, "The Ghost-Dance Religion," 807, 820.

79. John S. Mayhugh to President Benjamin Harrison, 9 January 1891, USNA, SC 188.

80. ARCIA, 1891, 230.

81. O. C. Clifford to CIA, 5 May 1900, USNA, RG 75, *Letters Received, 1881–1907*.

82. O. C. Clifford to CIA, 5 May, 8 June, 27 June, 18 July, 1 August, and 10 October 1900; SI to CIA, 22 October 1900, USNA, RG 75.

83. S. G. Fisher to CIA, 11 April 1890, USNA, RG 75; Lt. William H. Johnson to AAG, Department of the Platte, 13 August 1891, USNA, SC 188.

84. Madsen, *The Northern Shoshoni*, 110–14.

85. Loretta Fowler, *Arapahoe Politics, 1851–1978: Symbols in Crises of Authority* (Lincoln: University of Nebraska Press, 1982); and Loretta Fowler, *Shared Symbols, Contested Meanings: Gros Ventre Culture and History, 1778–1984* (Ithaca, NY: Cornell University Press, 1987).

86. Mooney, "The Ghost-Dance Religion," 793–94. Although Porcupine did

not identify the Bannock Chief as Tyhee, the man told him he had been to Washington, D.C., to see the "Great Father." Tyhee led the Bannocks on the 1880 trip to Washington; Pagwite was not among the delegates.

87. E. R. Kellogg to AAG, Department of the Platte, 27 October 1890, SC 188.

88. Arden R. Smith to CIA, 16 December 1882, USNA, RG 75.

89. J. M. Needham to CIA, 6 April 1888, USNA, RG 75.

90. See David Wallace Adams, *Education for Extinction: American Indians and the Boarding School Experience* (Lawrence: University Press of Kansas, 1995), 57–58. Twenty-six off-reservation boarding schools opened between 1879 and 1902, compared with nearly 120 reservation boarding schools.

91. Madsen, *The Northern Shoshoni*, 195–96.

92. ARCIA, 1899, 181; Madsen, *The Northern Shoshoni*, 196–200.

93. See William T. Hagan, *Indian Police and Judges: Experiments in Acculturation and Control* (1966; repr., Lincoln: University of Nebraska Press, 1980); Prucha, *The Great Father*, 600–604.

94. C. A. Warner to CIA, 6 September 1898, USNA, RG 75. On this date Warner fired Nanas Teton from the Fort Hall police force for "dancing." The exact nature of the dance was not described.

95. Fred T. Dubois to CIA, 24 December 1881, USNA, RG 75.

96. A. L. Cook to CIA, 4 February 1882, USNA, RG 75.

97. Peter Gallagher to CIA, 4 December 1886, USNA, RG 75. Gallagher complained that the force in 1886 was entirely selected by the Bannock headmen and was in large part outside his control

98. S. G. Fisher to CIA, 6 December 1889, USNA, RG 75.

99. J. M. Needham to CIA, 6 April 1888, USNA, RG 75.

100. ARCIA, 1878, 104.

101. ARCIA, 1892, 235.

102. ARCIA, 1880, 62.

103. See L. Fowler, *Shared Symbols, Contested Meanings*. Fowler describes a very similar situation at Fort Belknap, Montana, where Gros Ventres and Assiniboines shared the same reservation. She argues that the Gros Ventres adopted and manipulated progressive symbols, such as stock raising, not as an acceptance of the white man's ways but as a means of maintaining their primacy over the Assiniboines.

104. Ibid.

105. ARCIA, 1881, 63.

106. A. L. Cook to CIA, 23 September, 24 November, and 11 December 1882, USNA, RG 75.

107. Arden R. Smith to CIA, 16 December 1882, USNA, RG 75.

108. M. B. Bristol to CIA, 13 February 1883, USNA, RG 75.

109. J. D. Everest to CIA, 7 May 1887, USNA, RG 75.

110. ARCIA, 1884, 64; ARSW, 1885, 65.

111. See Jon. W. Jones to CIA, 31 March 1886; George B. Porter to CIA, 30 June and 30 September 1886, USNA, RG 75.

112. ARCIA, 1885, 65.

113. ARCIA, 1888, 82.

114. J. D. Everest to CIA, 7 May 1887, USNA, RG 75.

115. A. L. Cook to CIA, 28 April 1885; Peter Gallagher to CIA, 14 April 1891, USNA, RG 75. Gallagher's letter illustrates the importance of symbols of authority for Indian leaders. He wrote to the commissioner at the behest of delegation members, who were anxious to receive the letters promised by the commissioner.

116. ARCIA, 1888, 3.

117. S. G. Fisher to CIA, 6 February 1890; John Y. Williams to CIA, 12 February 1890, USNA, RG 75.

118. S. G. Fisher to CIA, 3 March 1890, USNA, RG 75.

119. S. G. Fisher to CIA, 11 April 1890, USNA, RG 75.

120. Ibid.; John Y. Williams to CIA, 22 October 1890, USNA, RG 75; ARCIA, 1890, 76–78.

121. John Y. Williams to CIA, 22 November (telegram), 22 November (letter), and 28 November 1890, USNA, RG 75.

122. S. G. Fisher to CIA, 23 December 1890, USNA, RG 75.

123. Ibid.

124. S. G. Fisher to CIA, 2 December 1891, USNA, RG 75. After an argument over the beef issue, a fight broke out, and Avery hit Pagwite with a club.

125. S. G. Fisher to CIA, 7 March 1892, USNA, RG 75.

126. Ibid.

127. Fort Hall Census, 1887–97, USNA, Microcopy M595, Reel 138.

128. ARCIA, 1890, 77–78.

129. Ibid., 78.

130. Ibid.

131. S. G. Fisher to CIA, 2 January and 18 January 1892, USNA, RG 75; Madsen, *The Northern Shoshoni,* 185.

132. S. G. Fisher to CIA, 6 March 1892, USNA, RG 75; ARCIA, 1892, 151.

133. S. G. Fisher to CIA, 7 March 1892, USNA, RG 75.

134. J. A. Leonard to CIA, 7 May 1892, reprinted in ARCIA, 1892, 151–52.

135. Ibid.

136. ARCIA, 1892, 152; SI to CIA, 16 May 1892, USNA, RG 75.

137. Thomas B. Teter to CIA, 27 December 1894, USNA, RG 75.

138. Isaac I. Yandell to CIA, 11 September 1895, USNA, RG 75.

139. F. G. Irwin to CIA, 22 September and 5 October 1897; ARCIA, 1898, 144; Madsen, *The Northern Shoshoni,* 186.

140. F. G. Irwin to CIA, 6 October and 19 October 1897, USNA, RG 75.

141. F. G. Irwin to CIA, 28 March 1898, USNA, RG 75.

142. Capt. Charles Penny to CIA, 22 November 1894, USNA, SC 188.

143. Madsen, 121, 136.

144. Thomas B. Teter to CIA, 28 January and 16 April 1896, USNA, RG 75, SC 190; Madsen, *The Northern Shoshoni,* 135–36. Billy George was shot in an ambush. He survived, but his right leg was amputated above the knee.

145. ARCIA W, 1890, 77.

146. Fort Hall Census, 1887–1897, M595, Reel 138.

CONCLUSION

Epigraph: James Mooney, "The Ghost-Dance Religion and the Sioux Outbreak of 1890," *Fourteenth Annual Report of the Bureau of American Ethnology,* part 2 (Washington, DC: Government Printing Office, 1896), 653.

1. Benedict Anderson, *Imagined Communities: Reflections on the Origins and Spread of Nationalism* (London: Verso, 1983), 5–7. Anderson defines a nation as "an imagined political community—and imagined as both inherently limited and sovereign." He argues that nations are "imagined as a *community,* because, regardless of the actual inequality and exploitation that may prevail in each, the nation is always perceived as a deep, horizontal comradeship" (7).

2. The changing expectations attached to the boarding-school program illustrate this trend. At the inception of the Carlisle boarding school, Richard Henry Pratt expected education to utterly transform Indian children. By the beginning of the twentieth century, however, officials such as Francis Luepp, commissioner of Indian Affairs, believed that inherited "mental and moral" traits precluded the rapid assimilation of American Indians and a more gradual assimilation was all that could be hoped for. See David Wallace Adams, *Education for Extinction: American Indians and the Boarding School Experience, 1875–1928* (Lawrence: University Press of Kansas, 1995).

3. Melissa L. Meyer, *The White Earth Tragedy: Ethnicity and Dispossession at a Minnesota Anishinaabe Reservation* (Lincoln: University of Nebraska Press, 1994), 134.

4. Alexandra Harmon, *Indians in the Making: Ethnic Relations and Indian Identities around Puget Sound* (Berkeley: University of California Press, 1998).

5. Mooney, "The Ghost-Dance Religion," 653.

6. Richmond L. Clow, "The Lakota Ghost Dance after 1890," *South Dakota History* 20 (Winter 1990): 323–33; Robert M. Utley, *The Last Days of the Sioux Nation* (New Haven, CT: Yale University Press), 284. Clow provides primary evidence to refute Utley's interpretation that Wounded Knee dealt a death blow to the religion.

7. Alice Beck Kehoe, *The Ghost Dance: Ethnohistory and Revitalization* (Fort Worth, TX: Holt, Rinehart and Winston, 1989), 44.

8. Ibid., 47–48.

9. Alexander Lesser, *The Pawnee Ghost Dance Hand Game: Ghost Dance Revival and Ethnic Identity* (1933; repr., Lincoln: University of Nebraska Press, 1996).

10. Benjamin R. Kracht, "The Kiowa Ghost Dance, 1894–1916: An Unheralded Revitalization Movement," *Ethnohistory* 39 (Fall 1992): 463.

11. David Waldstreicher, *In the Midst of Perpetual Fetes: The Making of American Nationalism, 1776–1820* (Chapel Hill: University of North Carolina Press, 1997).

12. William G. McLoughlin, *Revivals, Awakenings, and Reform* (Chicago: University of Chicago Press, 1978); Paul E. Johnson, *A Shopkeeper's Millennium: Society and Revivals in Rochester, New York, 1815–1827* (New York: Hill and Wang, 1978); Nathan O. Hatch, *The Democratization of American Christianity* (New Haven, CT: Yale University Press, 1989).

13. Francis Paul Prucha, *American Indian Policy in Crisis: Christian Reformers and the Indian, 1865–1900* (Norman: University of Oklahoma Press, 1976); Frederick E. Hoxie, *A Final Promise: The Campaign to Assimilate the Indians, 1880–1920* (Lincoln: University of Nebraska Press, 1984); David Rich Lewis, *Neither Wolf nor Dog: American Indians, Environment, and Agrarian Change* (New York: Oxford University Press, 1994).

14. Gregory Evans Dowd, *War under Heaven: Pontiac, the Indian Nations, and the British Empire* (Baltimore, MD: Johns Hopkins University Press, 2002); Howard H. Peckham, *Pontiac and the Indian Uprising* (Princeton, NJ: Princeton University Press, 1947).

15. Gregory Evans Dowd, *A Spirited Resistance: The North American Indian Struggle for Unity, 1745–1815* (Baltimore, MD: Johns Hopkins University Press, 1992); Joel Martin, *Sacred Revolt: The Muskogees' Struggle for a New World* (Boston: Beacon Press, 1991); R. David Edmunds, *The Shawnee Prophet* (Lincoln: University of Nebraska Press, 1983).

16. For a biography of Mooney, see L. G. Moses, *The Indian Man: A Biography of James Mooney* (Urbana: University of Illinois Press, 1984); for the early history of the BAE and its anthropologists, see Curtis Hinsley, *Savages and Scientists: The Smithsonian Institution and the Development of American Anthropology, 1846–1910* (Washington, DC: Smithsonian Institution Press, 1981).

17. Mooney, "The Ghost-Dance Religion," 657.

18. Anthony F. C. Wallace, "Revitalization Movements: Some Theoretical Considerations for Their Comparative Study," *American Anthropologist,* n.s., 58 (1956): 264–81; Anthony F. C. Wallace, *The Death and Rebirth of the Seneca* (New York: Random House, 1969); see also Anthony F. C. Wallace, "Origins of the Longhouse Religion," in *Handbook of North American Indians,* vol. 15, *Northeast,* ed. Bruce G. Trigger (Washington, DC: Smithsonian Institution, 1978), 442–48.

19. David F. Aberle, *The Peyote Religion among the Navaho* (1966; repr. Chicago: University of Chicago Press, 1982), 316–17.

20. Ibid., 323.

21. Leslie Spier, *The Prophet Dance of the Northwest and Its Derivatives: The Source of the Ghost Dance* (Menasha, WI: George Banta Publishing Company, 1935).

22. Cora Du Bois, *The 1870 Ghost Dance,* Anthropological Records vol. 3, no. 1 (Berkeley: University of California Press, 1939).

23. David F. Aberle, "The Prophet Dance and Reactions to White Contact," *Southwestern Journal of Anthropology* 15 (1959): 74–88; Deward E. Walker, "New Light on the Prophet Dance Controversy," *Ethnohistory* 16 (1969): 245–55; Wayne Suttles, "The Plateau Prophet Dance among the Coast Salish," *Southwestern Journal of Anthropology* 13 (1957): 352–96.

24. See Marshall Sahlins, *Islands of History* (Chicago: University of Chicago Press, 1985).

25. Raymond J. DeMallie, "The Lakota Ghost Dance: An Ethnohistorical Account," *Pacific Historical Review* 51 (1982): 388–89.

26. Ibid., 390–91.

27. Fisher to CIA, 26 November 1890, USNA, RG 75, SC 188.

28. James Mooney, "The Ghost-Dance Religion," 791. The Shoshone name for the dance translates as "everybody dragging," in reference to the slow, clockwise shuffle of the ring dance.

29. See Utley, *The Last Days of the Sioux Nation*, 64. Utley devoted only a single paragraph to the existence of the 1870 prophet and his probable influence on Wovoka. To be fair to Utley, his interest lay elsewhere, but this perspective has carried over to most historical treatments.

30. J. A. Jones, *The Sun Dance of the Northern Ute*, Anthropological Papers 47, Bureau of American Ethnology Bulletin 157 (Washington, DC: Government Printing Office, 1955), 239–40; Joseph G. Jorgensen, *The Sun Dance Religion: Power for the Powerless* (Chicago: University of Chicago Press, 1972), 38–40; Joseph Jorgensen, "Ghost Dance, Bear Dance, and Sun Dance," in *Handbook of North American Indians*, vol. 11, *Great Basin*, edited by Warren L. d'Azevedo (Washington, DC: Smithsonian Institution, 1986), 661; Judith Vander, *Shoshone Ghost Dance Religion: Poetry Songs and Great Basin Context* (Urbana: University of Illinois Press, 1997), 8.

31. Jorgensen, *Sun Dance Religion*, 17–19; Jorgensen, "Ghost Dance, Bear Dance, and Sun Dance," 665–67; E. Adamson Hoebel, "The Sun Dance of the Hekandika Shoshone," *American Anthropologist* 37 (1935): 570–81. Community factionalism led to a split, and by the 1930s two separate Sun Dances were held at Fort Hall.

32. Jorgensen, *Sun Dance Religion*, 6–7, 18–19.

33. Gail Martin to Gregory E. Smoak, personal communication, 15 September 2004; Drusilla Gould to Smoak, personal communication, 11 January 2005.

34. John W. Heaton, "Power and Identity: The Emergence of a Shoshone-Bannock Community at Fort Hall, 1867–1939," Ph.D. diss., Arizona State University, 1999; Justina W. Parsons-Bernstein, " 'I Hope We Be a Prosperous People': Shoshone and Bannock Incorporation, Ethnic Reorganization, and the 'Indian Way of Living Through,' " Ph.D. diss., Rutgers University, 2001.

Selected Bibliography

PRIMARY SOURCES

Manuscript Sources

Bruneau, John. Collection. Idaho State Historical Society. Ms. 2/49. Boise, Idaho. N.d.

Dyer, E. A. "Wizardry." Nevada Historical Society, Manuscripts Division. Reno, Nevada. N.d.

Fisher, Stanton G. Collection. Idaho State Historical Society. Ms. 106. Boise, Idaho. 1875–77.

Henderson, A. B. "Journal of the Yellowstone Expedition of 1866." Yellowstone National Park Archives. Mammoth Hot Springs, Wyoming.

Huntington, Dimick Baker. Journal. LDS Church Archives. Ms. 1419–2. Salt Lake City, Utah. 1857.

Powell, John Wesley. "They Call Themselves Nu-mes." Smithsonian Institution, National Anthropological Archives. Ms. 798. Washington, D.C. Ca. 1878.

———. "Ute and Paiute Stories." Smithsonian Institution, National Anthropological Archives, Ms. 838. Washington, D.C. N.d.

Shoup, George. Papers. Idaho State University, Special Collections. MC 14. Pocatello, Idaho. N.d.

U.S. Department of the Interior. Bureau of Indian Affairs. *Fort Hall Letter Book, 1869–1875.* Fort Hall, Idaho.

———. *Letters Received, 1824–1881.* Record Group 75. U.S. National Archives. Microcopy M234: *Idaho Superintendency, 1863–1880.*

———. Microcopy M234: *Montana Superintendency, 1864–1880.*

———. Microcopy M234: *Nevada Superintendency, 1861–1880.*

———. Microcopy M234: *Utah Superintendency, 1849–1880.*

——. *Records of the Idaho Superintendency, 1863–1870.* Record Group 75. U.S. National Archives. Microcopy M832.

——. *Special Case 188: The Ghost Dance, 1890–1898.* Record Group 75. U.S. National Archives. Microcopy.

——. *Letters Received, 1881–1907.* Record Group 75. U.S. National Archives. Washington, D.C.

——. *Indian Census Rolls, 1885–1940.* Record Group 75. U.S. National Archives. Microcopy M595: *Fort Hall.*

Wheat, Margaret M. Papers, 1879–1981. "Series III: Nevada Indians, 1879–1971." University of Nevada, Special Collections. Reno, Nevada.

Newspapers

Deseret News
Idaho News
Idaho Statesman
Latter-Day Saints' Millennial Star
New York Times
Owyhee Avalanche
Pocatello Tribune

Printed Primary Sources

Bagley, Clarence B. "Crossing the Plains." *Washington Historical Quarterly* 13 (1922): 163–80.

Ball, John. *John Ball, Member of the Wyeth Expedition to the Pacific Northwest in 1832, and a Pioneer of the Old Northwest.* Glendale, CA: Arthur H. Clark Co., 1925.

Belyea, Barbara, ed. *Columbia Journals: David Thompson.* Montreal: McGill-Queen's University Press, 1994.

Brackett, Albert G. "The Shoshonis, or Snake Indians, Their Religion, Superstitions, and Manners." *Annual Report of the Smithsonian Institution for the Year 1879.* Washington, D.C.: Government Printing Office, 1880.

Burpee, L. J., ed. *Journal of Larocque from the Assiniboine to the Yellowstone, 1805.* Ottawa: Government Printing Bureau, 1910.

Carey, Charles H., ed. *The Journals of Theodore Talbot, 1843 and 1849–52.* Portland, OR: Metropolitan Press, 1931.

Davenport, T. W. "Recollections of an Indian Agent." *Quarterly of the Oregon Historical Society* 8 (1907): 353–74.

Davies, K. G., ed. *Peter Skene Ogden's Snake Country Journal, 1826–27.* London: Hudson's Bay Record Society, 1961.

"Diary of Asahel Munger and Wife." *Quarterly of the Oregon Historical Society* 8 (1907): 387–405.

Drury, Clifford Merrill, ed. *First White Women over the Rockies: Diaries, Letters, and Biographical Sketches of the Six Women of the Oregon Mission Who Made the Overland Journey in 1836 and 1838.* 3 vols. Glendale, CA: Arthur H. Clark Company, 1963–66.

Ferris, Warren Angus. *Life in the Rocky Mountains: A Diary of Wanderings on the Sources of the Rivers Missouri, Columbia, and Colorado, 1830–1835.* Denver, CO: Old West Publishing Company, 1983.

Fletcher, Alice C. "The Indian Messiah." *Journal of American Folklore* 4 (1891): 57–60.

Fowler, Don D., and Catherine S. Fowler, eds. "Stephen Powers' 'The Life and Culture of the Washo and Paiutes.'" *Ethnohistory* 17 (1970): 117–49.

———. *Anthropology of the Numa: John Wesley Powell's Manuscripts on the Numic Peoples of Western North America, 1868–1880.* Washington, D.C.: Smithsonian Institution Press, 1971.

Frémont, John Charles. *Narratives of Exploration and Adventure.* New York: Longmans, Green & Co., 1956.

Haines, Aubrey L., ed. *Osborne Russell's Journal of a Trapper.* Lincoln: University of Nebraska Press, 1965.

Haines, Francis D., ed. *The Snake Country Expedition of 1830–1831: John Work's Field Journal.* Norman: University of Oklahoma Press, 1971.

Hopkins, Sarah Winnemucca. *Life among the Piutes: Their Wrongs and Claims.* 1883. Repr., Reno: University of Nevada Press, 1994.

Howard, Oliver O. *Nez Perce Joseph.* Boston: Lee and Shepard Publishers, 1881.

———. "Indian War Papers: Causes of the Piute and Bannock War." *Overland Monthly* 9 (1887): 492–98.

———. *Famous Indian Chiefs I Have Known.* New York: Century Company, 1916.

Irving, Washington. *The Adventures of Captain Bonneville, U.S.A., in the Rocky Mountains and the Far West.* Norman: University of Oklahoma Press, 1961.

Kappler, Charles J. *Indian Affairs: Laws and Treaties, Compiled and Edited by Charles J. Kappler.* 7 vols. Washington, D.C.: Government Printing Office, 1904.

Leforge, Thomas H. *Memoirs of a White Crow Indian.* New York: D. Appleton–Century Company, 1928.

Leonard, Zenas. *Narrative of the Adventures of Zenas Leonard, a Native of Clearfield County, Pa. Who Spent Five Years in Trapping for Furs, Trading with the Indians, &c., &c., of the Rocky Mountains; Written by Himself.* Clearfield, PA: D. W. Moore, 1839.

MacGregor, Carol Lynn, ed. *The Journals of Patrick Gass, Member of the Lewis and Clark Expedition.* Missoula, MT: Mountain Press Publishing Company, 1997.

MacMurray, J. W. "The 'Dreamers' of the Columbia River Valley, in Washington Territory." *Transactions of the Albany Institute* 11 (1887): 240–48.

Miles, Nelson A. "The Future of the Indian Question." *North American Review* 152 (January 1891): 9.

Mooney, James. "The Ghost-Dance Religion and the Sioux Outbreak of 1890," *Fourteenth Annual Report of the Bureau of American Ethnology.* Part 2. Washington, D.C.: Government Printing Office, 1896.

Moulton, Gary E., ed. *The Journals of the Lewis and Clark Expedition.* Vol. 5, *July 28–November 1, 1805.* Lincoln: University of Nebraska Press, 1988.

Phister, Nathaniel P. "The Indian Messiah." *American Anthropologist* 4 (April 1891): 105–8.

Preuss, Charles. *Exploring with Frémont: The Private Diaries of Charles Preuss, Cartographer for John C. Frémont on His First, Second, and Fourth Expeditions to the Far West,* edited and translated by Erwin G. and Elisabeth K. Guddle. Norman: University of Oklahoma Press, 1958.

Ross, Alexander. *The Fur Hunters of the Far West: A Narrative of Adventures in the Oregon and Rocky Mountains.* 1855. Repr., edited by Kenneth A. Spaulding. Norman: University of Oklahoma Press, 1956.

———. *Adventures of the First Settlers on the Oregon or Columbia River: Being a Narrative of the Expedition Fitted Out by John Jacob Astor to Establish the Pacific Fur Company, with an Account of Some of the Indian Tribes on the Coast of the Pacific.* 1849. Repr., Lincoln: University of Nebraska Press, 1986.

Schoolcraft, Henry R. *Information Respecting the History, Condition, and Prospects of the Indian Tribes of the United States.* Philadelphia: Lippincott, Grambo & Co., 1851.

Stuart, Robert. *On the Oregon Trail: Robert Stuart's Journal of Discovery.* Edited by Kenneth A. Spaulding. Norman: University of Oklahoma Press, 1953.

Teit, James A. "Okanagon Tales." In Franz Boas, ed., *Folk-Tales of the Salishan and Sahaptian Tribes.* Lancaster, PA: American Folk-Lore Society, 1917.

Thompson, David. *Travels in Western North America, 1784–1812.* Edited by Victor G. Hopwood. Toronto: Macmillan of Canada, 1971.

Toponce, Alexander. *Reminiscences of Alexander Toponce.* 1923. Repr., Norman: University of Oklahoma Press, 1971.

Townsend, John Kirk. *Narrative of a Journey across the Rocky Mountains to the Columbia River.* 1839. Repr., Lincoln: University of Nebraska Press, 1978.

U.S. Congress. House. *Report upon the Pacific Wagon Roads.* 35th Cong., 2d sess. Ex. Doc. 108. Serial no. 1008. 1859.

———. *Report of the Negotiations and the Agreement Made with the Shoshone and Bannock Indians.* 42d Cong., 2d sess. Ex. Doc. 1. Serial no. 1560. 1872.

———. *Bannock and Other Indians in Southern Idaho.* 43d Cong., 1st sess. Ex. Doc. 129. Serial no. 1608. 1874.

U.S. Congress. Senate. *Message of the President of the United States, Communicating, in Compliance with a Resolution of the Senate, Information in Relation to the Massacre at Mountain Meadows, and other Massacres in Utah Territory.* 36th Cong., 1st sess. Ex. Doc. 42. Serial no. 1033. 1860.

———. *Condition of the Indian Tribes.* 39th Cong., 2nd sess. S. Rep. 156. Serial no. 1279. 1867.

———. *Report to Accompany S. 2612.* 52d Cong., 1st sess. S. Rep. 537. Serial no. 2913. 1892.

U.S. Department of the Interior. *Annual Reports of the Commissioner of Indian Affairs to the Secretary of the Interior.* Washington, D.C.: Government Printing Office, 1848–1900.

Wilkes, Charles. *Narrative of the United States Exploring Expeditions during the Years 1838–1842.* Philadelphia: Lea and Blanchard, 1845.

Wyeth, Nathaniel J. "Indian Tribes of the South Pass of the Rocky Mountains."
    In Henry R. Schoolcraft, *Respecting the History, Condition, and Prospects of
    the Indian Tribes of the United States.* Philadelphia: Lippincott, Grambo, and
    Co., 1851.
Young, Frederick G., ed. *The Correspondence and Journals of Captain Nathaniel
    J. Wyeth, 1831–1836: A Record of Two Expeditions for the Occupation of
    the Oregon Country.* 1899. Repr., New York: Arno Press, 1973.

SECONDARY SOURCES

Aberle, David F. "The Prophet Dance and Reactions to White Contact." *South-
    western Journal of Anthropology* 15 (1959): 74–88.
———. "A Note on Relative Deprivation Theory as Applied to Millenarian and
    Other Cult Movements." In Sylvia L. Thrupp, ed., *Millennial Dreams in
    Action: Studies in Revolutionary Religious Movements,* 209–14. New York:
    Schocken Books, 1970.
———. *The Peyote Religion among the Navaho.* 1966. Repr., Chicago: Univer-
    sity of Chicago Press, 1982.
Adams, David Wallace. *Education for Extinction: American Indians and the
    Boarding School Experience.* Lawrence: University Press of Kansas, 1995.
Albers, Patricia C. "Changing Patterns of Ethnicity in the Northeastern Plains."
    In Jonathan D. Hill, ed., *History, Power, and Identity: Ethnogenesis in the
    Americas, 1492–1992,* 90–118. Iowa City: University of Iowa Press, 1996.
Albers, Patricia, and Jeanne Kay. "Sharing the Land: A Study in American Indian
    Territoriality." In Thomas E. Ross and Tyrell G. Moore, eds., *A Cultural
    Geography of North American Indians,* 47–91. Boulder, CO: Westview Press,
    1987
Anastasio, Angelo. "The Southern Plateau: An Ecological Analysis of Intergroup
    Relations." *Northwest Anthropological Research Notes* 6 (Fall 1972): 109–
    229.
Anderson, Benedict. *Imagined Communities: Reflections on the Origins and
    Spread of Nationalism.* London: Verso, 1983.
Arrington, Leonard J. *History of Idaho.* Moscow: University of Idaho Press,
    1994.
Arrington, Leonard J., and Davis Bitton. *The Mormon Experience: A History of
    the Latter-Day Saints.* New York: Alfred A. Knopf, 1979.
Bagley, Will. *Blood of the Prophets: Brigham Young and the Massacre at Moun-
    tain Meadows.* Norman: University of Oklahoma Press, 2002.
Bailey, Paul. *Wovoka: The Indian Messiah.* Los Angeles: Westernlore Press, 1957.
Barber, Bernard. "A Socio-Cultural Interpretation of the Peyote Cult." *American
    Anthropologist,* n.s., 43 (1941): 673–75.
———. "Acculturation and Messianic Movements." In William A. Lessa and
    Evon Z. Vogt, eds., *Reader in Comparative Religion: An Anthropological
    Approach,* 474–78. Evanston, IL: Row, Peterson and Company, 1958.
Barrett, S. A. *Ceremonies of the Pomo Indians.* University of California Publica-
    tions in American Archaeology and Ethnology vol. 12, no. 10. Berkeley: Uni-
    versity of California Press, 1917.

Barth, Fredrik, ed. *Ethnic Groups and Boundaries: The Social Organization of Culture Difference.* Boston: Little, Brown and Company, 1969.

Beach, Margery Ann. "The Waptashi Prophet and the Feather Religion: Derivative of the Washani." *American Indian Quarterly* 9 (Summer 1985): 325–33.

Bean, Lowell John, and Sylvia Brakke Vane. "Cults and Their Transformations." In *Handbook of North American Indians.* Vol. 8, *California,* edited by Robert F. Heizer, 662–72. Washington: Smithsonian Institution, 1978.

Bowden, Henry Warner. *American Indians and Christian Missions: Studies in Cultural Conflict.* Chicago: University of Chicago Press, 1981.

Brimlow, George F. *The Bannock Indian War of 1878.* Caldwell, ID: Caxton Printers, 1938.

Brooke, John L. *The Refiner's Fire: The Making of Mormon Cosmology, 1644–1844.* Cambridge: Cambridge University Press, 1994.

Brooks, Juanita. *The Mountain Meadows Massacre.* 1950. Repr., Norman: University of Oklahoma Press, 1970.

Brown, W. C. "The Sheepeater Campaign, 1879." In *Tenth Biennial Report of the Idaho Historical Society.* Boise: Idaho Historical Society, 1926.

Brunton, Bill B. "Ceremonial Integration in the Plateau of Northwestern North America." *Northwest Anthropological Research Notes* 2 (Spring 1968): 1–28.

Burpee, Lawrence J. "La Verendrye: Pathfinder of the West." *Annals of Wyoming* 17 (1945): 107–11.

Bushman, Richard. *Joseph Smith and the Beginnings of Mormonism.* Urbana: University of Illinois Press, 1984.

Butler, B. Robert. *When Did the Shoshoni Begin to Occupy Southern Idaho?: Essays on Late Prehistoric Cultural Remains from the Upper Snake and Salmon River Country.* Occasional Papers of the Idaho Museum of Natural History 32. Pocatello: Idaho Museum of Natural History, 1981.

———. "Prehistory of the Snake and Salmon River Area." In *Handbook of North American Indians.* Vol. 11, *Great Basin,* edited by Warren L. d'Azevedo, 127–34. Washington, D.C.: Smithsonian Institution, 1986.

Carrey, Johnny, ed. *Sheepeater Indian Campaign: Chamberlain Basin Country.* Grangeville, ID: Idaho Country Free Press, 1968.

Carrey, Johnny, and Cort Conley. *The Middle Fork and the Sheepeater War.* Cambridge, ID: Backeddy Books, 1980.

Carroll, Michael P. "Revitalization Movements and Social Structure: Some Quantitative Tests." *American Sociological Review* 40 (June 1975): 389–401.

Champagne, Duane. "Social Structure, Revitalization Movements and State Building: Social Change in Four Native American Societies." *American Sociological Review* 48 (1983): 754–63.

Chance, David H. "Influences of the Hudson's Bay Company on the Native Cultures of the Colville District." *Northwest Anthropological Research Notes* 7 (Spring 1973): 1–166.

Christensen, Scott R. *Sagwitch: Shoshone Chieftain, Mormon Elder, 1822–1887.* Logan: Utah State University Press, 1999.

Christy, Howard A. "Open Hand and Mailed Fist: Mormon-Indian Relations in Utah, 1847–1852." *Utah Historical Quarterly* 46 (1978): 216–35.

Clastres, Pierre. *Society against the State: The Leader as Servant and the Humane Uses of Power among the Indians of the Americas.* New York: Urizen Books, 1977.

Cline, Walter. "Religion and World View." In Leslie Spier, ed., *The Sinkaitek or Southern Okanagon of Washington.* Menasha, WI: George Banta Publishing Company, 1938.

Coates, Lawrence G. "Mormons and Social Change among the Shoshoni, 1853–1900." *Idaho Yesterdays* 14 (Winter 1972): 3–11.

———. "Brigham Young and Mormon Indian Policies." *Brigham Young University Studies* 18 (1978): 428–52.

———. "The Mormons, the Ghost Dance Religion, and the Massacre at Wounded Knee." *Dialogue: A Journal of Mormon Thought* 18 (Winter 1985): 89–111.

Corless, Hank. *The Weiser Indians: Shoshoni Peacemakers.* Salt Lake City: University of Utah Press, 1990.

Crowder, David L. *Tendoy: Chief of the Lemhis.* Caldwell, ID: Caxton Printers, 1972.

Crum, Beverly, and John Dayley. *Western Shoshone Grammar.* Occasional Papers and Monographs in Cultural Anthropology and Linguistics 1. Boise, ID: Boise State University, 1993.

Crum, Steven J. *The Road on Which We Came (Po'i pentun tammen kimmappeh): A History of the Western Shoshone.* Salt Lake City: University of Utah Press, 1994.

D'Azevedo, Warren L., ed. *Handbook of North American Indians.* Vol. 11, *Great Basin.* Washington, D.C.: Smithsonian Institution, 1986.

Dangberg, Grace. *Letters to Jack Wilson, the Paiute Prophet, Written between 1908 and 1911.* Bureau of American Ethnology Bulletin 164. Washington, D.C.: Government Printing Office, 1957.

———. "Wovoka." *Nevada Historical Society Quarterly* 11 (Summer 1968): 5–53.

Davies, Nigel. *Voyagers to the New World.* New York: William Morrow and Company, 1979.

DeMallie, Raymond J. "The Lakota Ghost Dance: An Ethnohistorical Account." *Pacific Historical Review* 51 (November 1982): 385–405.

Dobyns, Henry F., and Robert C. Euler. *The Ghost Dance of 1889 among the Pai Indians of Northwestern Arizona.* Prescott, AZ: Prescott College Press, 1967.

Dowd, Gregory Evans. *A Spirited Resistance: The North American Indian Struggle for Unity, 1745–1815.* Baltimore, MD: Johns Hopkins University Press, 1992.

———. *War under Heaven: Pontiac, the Indian Nations, and the British Empire.* Baltimore, MD: Johns Hopkins University Press, 2002.

Downs, James F. *Washo Religion.* Anthropological Records vol. 16, no. 9. Berkeley: University of California Press, 1961.

Driver, Harold E. "Ethnological Interpretations." In Earl H. Swanson, ed., *Lan-*

guages and Cultures of Western North America: Essays in Honor of Sven S. Liljeblad, 265–76. Pocatello: Idaho State University Press, 1970.

Drury, Clifford Merrill. *Marcus and Narcissa Whitman, and the Opening of Old Oregon*. Glendale, CA: Arthur H. Clark Company, 1973.

Du Bois, Cora. *The 1870 Ghost Dance*. Anthropological Records vol. 3, no. 1. Berkeley: University of California Press, 1939.

Eliade, Mircea. *Shamanism: Archaic Techniques of Ecstasy*. Princeton, NJ: Princeton University Press, 1964.

Ewers, John C. *The Blackfeet: Raiders on the Northwestern Plains*. Norman: University of Oklahoma Press, 1958.

———. *Indian Life on the Upper Missouri*. Norman: University of Oklahoma Press, 1968.

———. *The Horse in Blackfoot Indian Culture*. Bureau of American Ethnology Bulletin 159. 1955. Repr., Washington, D.C.: Smithsonian Institution Press, 1980.

Fagan, Brian M. *Elusive Treasure: The Story of the Early Archaeologists in the Americas*. New York: Charles Scribner's Sons, 1977.

Flores, Dan. "Bison Ecology and Bison Diplomacy: The Southern Plains from 1800 to 1850." *Journal of American History* 78 (1991): 465–85.

Forbes, Jack D., ed. *Nevada Indians Speak*. Reno: University of Nevada Press, 1967.

Foster, Lawrence. *Religion and Sexuality: The Shakers, the Mormons, and the Oneida Community*. Urbana: University of Illinois Press, 1984.

Fowler, Catherine S., and Sven Liljeblad. "Northern Paiute." In *Handbook of North American Indians*. Vol. 11, *Great Basin*, edited by Warren L. d'Azevedo, 435–65. Washington, D.C.: Smithsonian Institution, 1986.

Fowler, Don D. "Great Basin Social Organization." In Warren L. d'Azevedo et al., eds., *The Current Status of Anthropological Research in the Great Basin: 1964*. Reno, NV: Desert Research Institute, 1966.

Fowler, Loretta. *Arapahoe Politics, 1851–1978: Symbols in Crises of Authority*. Lincoln: University of Nebraska Press, 1982.

———. *Shared Symbols, Contested Meanings: Gros Ventre Culture and History, 1778–1984*. Ithaca, NY: Cornell University Press, 1987.

Galbraith, John S. "Appeals to the Supernatural: African and New Zealand Comparisons with the Ghost Dance." *Pacific Historical Review* 51 (May 1982): 115–33.

Gayton, A. H. *The Ghost Dance of 1870 in South-Central California*. University of California Publications in American Archaeology and Ethnology vol. 28, no. 3. Berkeley: University of California Press, 1930.

Genovese, Eugene. *Roll, Jordan, Roll: The World the Slaves Made*. New York: Random House, 1972.

George, Willie, as told to Jack F. Contor. "Two Trails." *True West* 10 (January–February 1963): 6–12, 57–62.

Goss, James A. "Linguistic Tools for the Great Basin Prehistorian." In Don D. Fowler, ed., *Models and Great Basin Prehistory: A Symposium*, 49–70. University of Nevada, Desert Research Institute Publications in the Social Sciences. Reno: Desert Research Institute, 1977.

Gould, Drusilla, and Christopher Loether. *An Introduction to the Shoshoni Language: Dammen Daigwape.* Salt Lake City: University of Utah Press, 2002.

Greenway, John. "The Ghost Dance." *American West* 6 (July 1969): 42–47.

Grim, John A. *The Shaman: Patterns of Siberian and Ojibway Healing.* Norman: University of Oklahoma Press, 1983.

Gunnerson, James H. "Plateau Shoshonean Prehistory: A Suggested Reconstruction." *American Antiquity* 28 (July 1962): 41–45.

Hagan, William T. *Indian Police and Judges: Experiments in Acculturation and Control.* 1966. Repr., Lincoln: University of Nebraska Press, 1980.

Hailey, John. *The History of Idaho.* Boise, ID: Syms-York Company, 1910.

Haines, Aubrey L. "The Bannock Indian Trails of Yellowstone National Park." *Archaeology in Montana* 4 (1962): 1–8.

Haines, Francis. "Where did the Plains Indians Get Their Horses?" *American Anthropologist,* n.s., 40 (1938): 112–17.

———. "The Northward Spread of Horses among the Plains Indians." *American Anthropologist,* n.s., 40 (1938): 429–37.

———. *Indians of the Great Basin and Plateau.* New York: G. P. Putnam and Sons, 1970.

———. *The Buffalo: The Story of the American Bison and Their Hunters from Prehistoric Times to the Present.* New York: Crowell, 1970. Repr., Norman: University of Oklahoma Press, 1995.

Hansen, Klaus J. *Mormonism and the American Experience.* Chicago: University of Chicago Press, 1981.

Harmon, Alexandra. *Indians in the Making: Ethnic Relations and Indian Identities around Puget Sound.* Berkeley: University of California Press, 1998.

Harris, Cole . *The Resettlement of British Columbia: Essays on Colonialism and Geographic Change.* Vancouver: University of British Columbia Press, 1997.

Harris, Jack S. "The White Knife Shoshoni of Nevada." In Ralph Linton, ed., *Acculturation in Seven American Indian Tribes,* 39–116. New York: D. Appleton–Century Company, 1940.

Hatch, Nathan O. *The Democratization of American Christianity.* New Haven, CT: Yale University Press, 1989.

Heaton, John W. " 'No Place to Pitch Their Teepees': Shoshone Adaptation to Mormon Settlers in Cache Valley, 1855–1870." *Utah Historical Quarterly* 63 (Spring 1995): 158–71.

———. "Power and Identity: The Emergence of a Shoshone-Bannock Community at Fort Hall, 1867–1939." Ph.D. diss., Arizona State University, 1999.

Heidenreich, Charles A. "A Review of the Ghost Dance Religion of 1889–90 among the North American Indians and Comparison of Eight Societies Which Accepted or Rejected the Dance." M.A. thesis, University of Oregon, 1967.

Heizer, Robert F. "Ethnographic Notes on the Northern Paiute of Humboldt Sink, West Central Nevada." In Earl H. Swanson, ed., *Languages and Cultures of Western North America: Essays in Honor of Sven S. Liljeblad,* 232–45. Pocatello: Idaho State University Press, 1970.

Herzog, George. "Plains Ghost Dance and Great Basin Music." *American Anthropologist,* n.s., 37 (1935): 403–19.

Hill, Jonathan D., ed. *History, Power, and Identity: Ethnogenesis in the Americas, 1492–1992.* Iowa City: University of Iowa Press, 1996.

Hill, Willard W. "The Navajo Indians and the Ghost Dance of 1890." In William A. Lessa and Evon Z. Vogt, eds., *Reader in Comparative Religion: An Anthropological Approach,* 478–82. Evanston, IL: Row Peterson and Company, 1958.

Hinsley, Curtis. *Savages and Scientists: The Smithsonian Institution and the Development of American Anthropology.* Washington, D.C.: Smithsonian Institution Press, 1981.

Hittman, Michael. "The 1870 Ghost Dance at the Walker River Reservation: A Reconstruction." *Ethnohistory* 20 (Summer 1973): 247–78.

———. "Ghost Dances, Disillusionment, and Opiate Addiction: An Ethnohistory of Smith and Mason Valley Paiutes." Ph.D. diss., University of New Mexico, 1973.

———. "The 1890 Ghost Dance in Nevada." *American Indian Culture and Research Journal* 16 (1992): 123–66.

———. *Corbett Mack: The Life of a Northern Paiute.* Lincoln: University of Nebraska Press, 1996.

———. *Wovoka and the Ghost Dance,* 2d ed. Lincoln: University of Nebraska Press, 1997.

Hoebel, E. Adamson. "The Sun Dance of the Hekandika Shoshone." *American Anthropologist* 37 (1935): 570–81.

Horsman, Reginald. *Race and Manifest Destiny: The Origins of American Racial Anglo-Saxonism.* Cambridge, MA: Harvard University Press, 1981.

Hoxie, Frederick E. *A Final Promise: The Campaign to Assimilate the Indians, 1880–1920.* Lincoln: University of Nebraska Press, 1984.

———. *Parading through History: The Making of the Crow Nation in America, 1805–1935.* New York: Cambridge University Press, 1995.

Hulkrantz, Ake. "The Indians in Yellowstone Park." *Annals of Wyoming* 29 (1957).

———. "Tribal Divisions within the Eastern Shoshone of Wyoming." *Proceedings of the 32nd International Congress of Americanists, Stockholm* (1958): 148–54.

———. "The Shoshones of the Rocky Mountains Area." *Annals of Wyoming* 33 (1961): 19–41.

———. "The Ethnological Position of the Sheepeater Indians in Wyoming." *Folk* 8–9 (1966–1967): 156–63.

———. "The Source Literature on the 'Tukudika' Indians in Wyoming: Facts and Fancies." In Earl H. Swanson, ed., *Languages and Cultures of Western North America: Essays in Honor of Sven S. Liljeblad,* 246–64. Pocatello: Idaho State University Press, 1970.

———. *The Shoshones in the Rocky Mountain Area.* New York: Garland Publishing, 1974.

———. *The Religions of the American Indians.* Translated by Monica Setterwall. Berkeley: University of California Press, 1979.

———. *Native Religions of North America: The Power of Visions and Fertility.* New York: Harper Collins, 1987.

Hunn, Eugene, and James Selam and family. *Nch'i-Wana, "The Big River": Middle Columbia Indians and Their Land*. Seattle: University of Washington Press, 1990.

Hutton, Paul. *Phil Sheridan and His Army*. Albuquerque: University of New Mexico Press, 1984.

Jennings, Jesse D. "Prehistory: Introduction." In *Handbook of North American Indians*. Vol. 11, *Great Basin*, edited by Warren L. d'Azevedo, 113–19. Washington, D.C.: Smithsonian Institution, 1986.

Johnson, Edward C. *Walker River Paiutes: A Tribal History*. Salt Lake City: University of Utah Printing Service, 1975.

Johnson, Paul E. *A Shopkeeper's Millennium: Society and Revivals in Rochester, New York, 1815–1827*. New York: Hill and Wang, 1978.

Jones, J. A. "The Sun Dance of the Northern Ute." Anthropological Papers 47. Bureau of American Ethnology, Bulletin 157. Washington, D.C.: Government Printing Office, 1955.

Jorgensen, Joseph G. *The Sun Dance Religion: Power for the Powerless*. Chicago: University of Chicago Press, 1972.

———. "Ghost Dance, Bear Dance, and Sun Dance." In *Handbook of North American Indians*. Vol. 11. *Great Basin,* edited by Warren L. d'Azevedo. Washington, D.C.: Smithsonian Institution, 1986.

Josephy, Alvin M. *The Nez Perce Indians and the Opening of the Northwest*. 1965. Repr., New York: Mariner Books, 1997.

Kehoe, Alice Beck. *The Ghost Dance: Ethnohistory and Revitalization*. Fort Worth, TX: Holt, Rinehart and Winston, 1989.

———. "On McLoughlin's 'Ghost Dance Movements.'" *Ethnohistory* 38 (Winter 1991): 73–74.

Kelly, Isabel T. *Southern Paiute Shamanism*. Anthropological Records vol. 2, no. 4. Berkeley: University of California Press, 1939.

Knack, Martha C. "A Short Resource History of Pyramid Lake, Nevada." *Ethnohistory* 24 (Winter 1977): 47–63.

Knack, Martha C., and Omer C. Stewart. *As Long as the River Shall Run: An Economic Ethnohistory of the Pyramid Lake Indian Reservation*. Berkeley: University of California Press, 1984.

Kracht, Benjamin R. "The Kiowa Ghost Dance, 1894–1916: An Unheralded Revitalization Movement." *Ethnohistory* 39 (Fall 1992): 452–77.

Kroeber, A. L. "A Ghost Dance in California." *Journal of American Folklore* 17 (1904): 32–35.

LaBarre, Weston. *The Ghost Dance: The Origins of Religion*. New York: Doubleday & Company, 1970.

———. "Materials for a History of Studies of Crisis Cults: A Bibliographic Essay." *Current Anthropology* 12 (February 1971): 3–44.

Laidlaw, Sally Jean. *Federal Indian Land Policy and the Fort Hall Indians*. Occasional Papers of the Idaho State College Museum 3. Pocatello: Idaho State College Museum, 1960.

Lamb, Sydney M. "Linguistic Prehistory in the Great Basin." *International Journal of American Linguistics* 24, no. 2 (1958): 95–100.

Landsman, Gail. "The Ghost Dance and the Policy of Land Allotment." *American Sociological Review* 44 (February 1979): 162–66.

Lanternari, Vittorio. *The Religions of the Oppressed: A Study of Modern Messianic Cults*. London: MacGibbon & Kee, 1963.

Layton, Thomas N. "Traders and Raiders: Aspects of Trans-Basin and California-Plateau Commerce, 1800–1830." *Journal of California and Great Basin Anthropology* 3, no. 1 (1981): 127–37.

Leonhardy, Frank C., and David G. Rice "A Proposed Culture Typology for the Lower Snake River Region, Southeastern Washington." *Northwest Anthropological Research Notes* 4 (Spring 1970): 1–29.

Lesser, Alexander. "Cultural Significance of the Ghost Dance." *American Anthropologist*, n.s., 35 (1933): 108–15.

———. *The Pawnee Ghost Dance Hand Game: Ghost Dance Revival and Ethnic Identity*. 1933. Repr., Lincoln: University of Nebraska Press, 1996.

Lewis, David Rich. *Neither Wolf nor Dog: American Indians, Environment, and Agrarian Change*. New York: Oxford University Press, 1994.

Lewis, I. M. *Ecstatic Religion: A Study of Shamanism and Spirit Possession*. 2d ed. London: Routledge, 1989.

Liljeblad, Sven S. "Indian Peoples in Idaho." Unpublished manuscript, Idaho Museum of Natural History, Pocatello, 1957.

———. *The Idaho Indians in Transition, 1805–1960*. Pocatello: Idaho State University Museum, 1972.

———. "Some Observations on the Fort Hall Indian Reservation." *The Indian Historian* 7 (Fall 1974): 9–13.

Linton, Ralph. "Nativistic Movements." In William A. Lessa and Evon Z. Vogt, eds., *Reader in Comparative Religion: An Anthropological Approach*, 466–74. Evanston, IL: Row Peterson and Company, 1958.

Logan, Brad. "The Ghost Dance among the Paiute: An Ethnohistorical View of the Documentary Evidence, 1889–1893." *Ethnohistory* 27 (Summer 1980): 267–88.

Lowie, Robert H. *The Northern Shoshone*. Anthropological Papers of the American Museum of Natural History vol. 2, part 2. New York: American Museum of Natural History, 1909.

———. *Dances and Societies of the Plains Shoshones*. Anthropological Papers of the American Museum of Natural History vol. 11, part 10. New York: American Museum of Natural History, 1915.

———. *The Cultural Connections of Californian and Plateau Shoshonean Tribes*. University of California Publications in American Archaeology and Ethnology vol. 20, no. 9. Berkeley: University of California Press, 1923.

———. *Notes on Shoshonean Ethnography*. Anthropological Papers of the American Museum of Natural History vol. 20, part 3. New York: American Museum of Natural History, 1924.

———. "The Kinship Terminology of the Bannock Indians." *American Anthropologist*, n.s., 32 (1930): 294–99.

Madsen, Betty M., and Brigham D. Madsen. *North to Montana! Jehus, Bullwhackers, and Mule Skinners on the Montana Trail*. Salt Lake City: University of Utah Press, 1980.

Madsen, Brigham D. *The Bannock of Idaho.* Caldwell, ID: Caxton Printers, 1958.

———. "Shoshoni-Bannock Marauders on the Oregon Trail, 1859–1863." *Utah Historical Quarterly* 35 (Winter 1967): 4–30.

———. "The Northwestern Shoshoni in Cache Valley." In Douglas C. Alder, ed., *Cache Valley: Essays in Her Past and Her People,* 28–44. Logan: Utah State University Press, 1976.

———. *The Lemhi: Sacajawea's People.* Caldwell, ID: Caxton Printers, 1980.

———. *The Northern Shoshoni.* Caldwell, ID: Caxton Printers, 1980.

———. *The Shoshoni Frontier and the Bear River Massacre.* Salt Lake City: University of Utah Press, 1985.

———. *Glory Hunter: A Biography of Patrick Edward Connor.* Salt Lake City: University of Utah Press, 1990.

Madsen, David B., and David Rhode, eds. *Across the West: Human Population Movement and the Expansion of the Numa.* Salt Lake City: University of Utah Press, 1994.

Malouf, Carling. "Ethnohistory in the Great Basin." In Warren L. d'Azevedo et al., eds., *The Current Status of Anthropological Research in the Great Basin: 1964,* 1–38. Reno: Desert Research Institute, 1966.

Malouf, Carling I., and John Findlay. "Euro-American Impact before 1870." In *Handbook of North American Indians.* Vol. 11, *Great Basin,* edited by Warren L. d'Azevedo, 499–516. Washington, D.C.: Smithsonian Institution, 1986.

Martin, Joel. *Sacred Revolt: The Muskogees' Struggle for a New World.* Boston: Beacon Press, 1991.

McKinney, Whitney. *A History of the Shoshone-Paiute of the Duck Valley Indian Reservation.* Salt Lake City: Howe Brothers, 1983.

McLoughlin, William G. *Revivals, Awakenings, and Reform.* Chicago: University of Chicago Press, 1978.

———. "Ghost Dance Movements: Some Thoughts on Definition Based on Cherokee History." *Ethnohistory* 37 (Winter 1990): 25–44.

———. "Rejoinder to Kehoe." *Ethnohistory* 38 (Winter 1991): 74–75.

Meighan, Clement W., and Francis A. Riddell. *The Maru Cult of the Pomo Indians: A California Ghost Dance Survival.* Southwest Museum Papers 23. Los Angeles: Southwest Museum, 1972.

Meyer, Melissa L. *The White Earth Tragedy: Ethnicity and Dispossession at a Minnesota Anishinaabe Reservation.* Lincoln: University of Nebraska Press, 1994.

Miller, Christopher. *Prophetic Worlds: Indians and Whites on the Columbia Plateau.* New Brunswick, NJ: Rutgers University Press, 1985.

Miller, Frank C. "Ghost Dance." In Howard R. Lamar, ed., *The New Encyclopedia of the American West,* 426. New Haven, CT: Yale University Press, 1998.

Miller, Jay. "Basin Religion and Theology: A Comparative Study of Power (Puha)." *Journal of California and Great Basin Anthropology* 5 (1983): 66–86.

———. "Numic Religion: An Overview of Power in the Great Basin of Native North America." *Anthropos* 78 (1983): 337–54.

Miller, Wick. "Numic Languages." In *Handbook of North American Indians.* Vol. 11, *Great Basin,* edited by Warren L. d'Azevedo, 98–106. Washington, D.C.: Smithsonian Institution, 1986.

Mills, Harlow B. "The Bannocks in Yellowstone National Park." *Yellowstone Nature Notes* 5–6 (1935): 22–23.

Morgan, Dale L. *Jedediah Smith and the Opening of the West.* Lincoln: University of Nebraska Press, 1964.

Moses, L. G. "Jack Wilson and the Indian Service: The Response of the BIA to the Ghost Dance Prophet." *American Indian Quarterly* 5 (November 1979): 295–316.

———. "James Mooney and Wovoka: An Ethnologist's Visit with the Ghost Dance Prophet." *Nevada Historical Society Quarterly* 23 (Summer 1980): 71–86.

———. *The Indian Man: A Biography of James Mooney.* Urbana: University of Illinois Press, 1984.

———. "'The Father Tells Me So!' Wovoka: The Ghost Dance Prophet." *American Indian Quarterly* 9 (Summer 1985): 335–51.

Moses, L. G., and Margaret C. Szasz. "'My Father Have Pity On Me!': Indian Revitalization Movements of the Late Nineteenth Century." *Journal of the West* 23 (January 1984): 5–15.

Murphy, Robert F. "Basin Ethnography and Ecological Theory." In Earl H. Swanson, ed., *Languages and Cultures of Western North America: Essays in Honor of Sven S. Liljeblad,* 152–71. Pocatello: Idaho State University Press, 1970.

Murphy, Robert F., and Yolanda Murphy. *Shoshone-Bannock Subsistence and Society.* Anthropological Records vol. 16, no. 7. Berkeley: University of California Press, 1959.

———. "Northern Shoshone and Bannock." In *Handbook of North American Indians.* Vol. 11, *Great Basin,* edited by Warren L. d'Azevedo, 284–307. Washington, D.C.: Smithsonian Institution, 1986.

Nagel, Joane. *American Indian Ethnic Renewal: Red Power and the Resurgence of Identity and Culture.* New York: Oxford University Press, 1996.

Nagel, Joane, and C. Matthew Snipp. "Ethnic Reorganization: American Indian Social, Economic, Political, and Cultural Strategies for Survival." *Ethnic and Racial Studies* 16 (April 1993): 203–35.

Nybroten, Norman. *Economy and Conditions of the Fort Hall Indian Reservation.* Moscow: University of Idaho Press, 1964.

Olofson, Harold. "Northern Paiute Shamanism Revisited." *Anthropos* 74 (1979): 11–24.

Ostler, Jeffrey. "Conquest and the State: Why the United States Employed Massive Military Force to Suppress the Lakota Ghost Dance." *Pacific Historical Review* 65 (May 1996): 217–48.

———. *The Plains Sioux and U.S. Colonialism from Lewis and Clark to Wounded Knee.* New York: Cambridge University Press, 2004.

Overholt, Thomas W. "The Ghost Dance of 1890 and the Nature of the Prophetic Process." *Ethnohistory* 21 (Winter 1974): 37–63.

Palladino, Lawrence B. *Indian and White in the Northwest: A History of Catholicity in Montana, 1831–1891.* Lancaster, PA: Wickersham, 1922.

Park, Willard Z. "Paviotso Shamanism." *American Anthropologist,* n.s., 36 (1934): 98–113.

———. *Shamanism in Western North America: A Study in Cultural Relationships.* Northwestern University Studies in the Social Sciences 2. Chicago: Northwestern University, 1938.

———. "Cultural Succession in the Great Basin." In Leslie Spier, A. I. Hallowell, and Stanley S. Newman, eds., *Language, Culture, and Personality: Essays in the Memory of Edward Sapir,* 180–203. Menasha, WI: Sapir Memorial Publication Fund, 1941.

Park, Willard Z., et al. "Tribal Distributions in the Great Basin." *American Anthropologist,* n.s., 40 (1938): 622–38.

Parsons-Bernstein, Justina W. "'I Hope We Be a Prosperous People': Shoshone and Bannock Incorporation, Ethnic Reorganization, and the 'Indian Way of Living Through.'" Ph.D. diss., Rutgers University, 2001.

Peckham, Howard H. *Pontiac and the Indian Uprising.* Princeton, NJ: Princeton University Press, 1947.

Prucha, Francis Paul. *The Great Father: The United States Government and the American Indians.* Lincoln: University of Nebraska Press, 1984.

Raboteau, Albert J. *Slave Religion: The "Invisible Institution" in the Antebellum South.* New York: Oxford University Press, 1978.

Ray, Verne F. *The Sanpoil and the Nespelem: Salishan Peoples of Northeastern Washington.* University of Washington Publications in Anthropology 5. Seattle: University of Washington Press, 1933.

———. "The Kolaskin Cult: A Prophet Movement of 1870 in Northeastern Washington." *American Anthropologist,* n.s., 38 (1936): 67–75.

———. *Cultural Relations in the Plateau of Northwestern America.* Publications of the Frederick Webb Hodge Anniversary Publication Fund 3. Los Angeles: Southwest Museum, 1939.

———. *Culture Element Distributions: XXII, Plateau.* Anthropological Records vol. 8, no. 2. Berkeley: University of California Press, 1942.

———. "The Columbian Indian Confederacy: A League of Central Plateau Tribes." In Stanley Diamond, ed., *Culture in History: Essays in Honor of Paul Radin,* 771–89. New York: Columbia University Press, 1960.

Ray, Verne F., et al. "Tribal Distributions in Eastern Oregon and Adjacent Regions." *American Anthropologist,* n.s., 40 (1938): 384–415.

Rogers, Spencer L. *The Shaman: His Symbols and His Healing Power.* Springfield, IL: Charles C. Thomas, 1982.

Ronda, James P. *Lewis and Clark among the Indians.* Lincoln: University of Nebraska Press, 1984.

Rosenzweig, Roy. *Eight Hours for What We Will: Workers and Leisure in an Industrial City, 1870–1920.* New York: Cambridge University Press, 1983.

Ruby, Robert H., and John A. Brown. *Indians of the Pacific Northwest.* Norman: University of Oklahoma Press, 1981.

———. *Dreamer-Prophets of the Columbia Plateau: Smohalla and Skolaskin.* Norman: University of Oklahoma Press, 1989.

Sahlins, Marshall. *Islands of History.* Chicago: University of Chicago Press, 1985.

Schaeffer, Claude E. "The Kutenai Female Berdache: Courier, Guide, Prophetess, and Warrior." *Ethnohistory* 12 (1965): 193–236.

Schultz, John L. "Deprivation, Revitalization, and the Development of the Shaker Religion." *Northwest Anthropological Research Notes* 2 (Spring 1968): 92–119.

Secoy, Frank Raymond. *Changing Military Patterns on the Great Plains (Seventeenth Century through Early Nineteenth Century).* Monographs of the American Ethnological Society 21. Locust Valley, NY: J. J. Augustin, 1953.

Service, Elman R. *Primitive Social Organization: An Evolutionary Perspective.* New York: Random House, 1962.

Shapiro, Judith R. "Kinship." In *Handbook of North American Indians.* Vol. 11, *Great Basin,* edited by Warren L. d'Azevedo, 620–29. Washington, D.C.: Smithsonian Institution, 1986.

Shimkin, Demitri B. "Shoshone-Comanche Origins and Migrations." *Proceedings of the Sixth Pacific Science Congress,* vol. 4, 17–25. Berkeley: University of California Press, 1940.

———. *Wind River Shoshone Ethnogeography.* Anthropological Records vol. 5, no. 4. Berkeley: University of California Press, 1947.

———. "The Introduction of the Horse." In *Handbook of North American Indians.* Vol. 11, *Great Basin,* edited by Warren L. d'Azevedo, 517–24. Washington, D.C.: Smithsonian Institution, 1986.

Silverberg, Robert. *Moundbuilders of Ancient America: The Archaeology of a Myth.* Greenwich, CT: New York Graphic Society, 1968.

Siskin, Edgar E. *Washo Shamans and Peyotists: Religious Conflict in an American Indian Tribe.* Salt Lake City: University of Utah Press, 1983.

Smaby, Beverly P. "The Mormons and the Indians: Conflicting Ecological Systems in the Great Basin." *American Studies* 16 (1975): 35–48.

Smith, Alice E. *James Duane Doty: Frontier Promoter.* Madison: State Historical Society of Wisconsin, 1954.

Smoak, Gregory E. "The Mormons and the Ghost Dance of 1890." *South Dakota History* 16 (Fall 1986): 269–94.

———. "Ghost Dances and Identity: Ethnogenesis and Racial Identity among Shoshones and Bannocks in the Nineteenth Century." Ph.D. diss., University of Utah, 1999.

Spier, Leslie. *The Ghost Dance of 1870 among the Klamath of Oregon.* University of Washington Publications in Anthropology no. 2. Seattle: University of Washington Press, 1927.

———. *The Prophet Dance of the Northwest and Its Derivatives: The Source of the Ghost Dance.* American Anthropological Society General Series in Anthropology. Menasha, WI: George Banta Publishing Co., 1935.

Spier, Leslie, Wayne Suttles, and Melville J. Herskovits. "Comment on Aberle's Thesis of Deprivation." *Southwestern Journal of Anthropology* 15 (1959): 84–88.

Statham, Dawn Strain. "Camas and the Northern Shoshoni: A Biographic and Socioeconomic Analysis." Boise State University Archaeological Reports 10. Boise, ID: Boise State University, 1982.

Steward, Julian H. *Culture Element Distribution: XXIII, Northern and Gosiute Shoshoni.* Anthropological Records vol. 8, no. 3. Berkeley: University of California Press, 1943.

———. *Theory of Culture Change: The Methodology of Multilinear Evolution.* Urbana: University of Illinois Press, 1955.

———. *Basin-Plateau Aboriginal Sociopolitical Groups.* Bureau of American Ethnology Bulletin 120. 1938. Repr., Salt Lake City: University of Utah Press, 1970.

———. "The Foundations of Basin-Plateau Shoshonean Society." In Earl H. Swanson, ed., *Languages and Cultures of Western North America: Essays in Honor of Sven S. Liljeblad,* 113–51. Pocatello: Idaho State University, 1970.

Steward, Julian H., and Ermine Wheeler-Voegelin. *The Northern Paiute Indians.* New York: Garland Publishing, 1974.

Stewart, Omer C. *The Northern Paiute Bands.* Anthropological Records vol. 2, no. 3. Berkeley: University of California Press, 1939.

———. *Culture Element Distributions: XIV, Northern Paiute.* Anthropological Records vol. 4, no. 3. Berkeley: University of California Press, 1941.

———. *Washo–Northern Paiute Peyotism: A Study in Acculturation.* University of California Publications in Archaeology and Ethnology 40. Berkeley: University of California Press, 1944.

———. "Three Gods for Joe." *Tomorrow* 4 (1956): 71–76.

———. "The Shoshoni: Their History and Social Organization." *Idaho Yesterdays* 9 (Fall 1965): 2–5, 28.

———. "Tribal Distributions and Boundaries in the Great Basin." In Warren L. d'Azevedo et al., eds., *The Current Status of Anthropological Research in the Great Basin: 1964,* 167–237. Reno, NV: Desert Research Institute, 1966.

———. "The Question of Bannock Territory." In Earl H. Swanson, ed., *Languages and Cultures of Western North America: Essays in Honor of Sven S. Liljeblad,* 201–31. Pocatello: Idaho State University Press, 1970.

———. "Contemporary Document on Wovoka (Jack Wilson), Prophet of the Ghost Dance in 1890." *Ethnohistory* 24 (1977): 219–22.

———. "The Ghost Dance." In Raymond Wood and Margot Liberty, eds., *Anthropology on the Great Plains,* 179–87. Lincoln: University of Nebraska Press, 1980.

———. "Temoke Band of Shoshone and the Oasis Concept." *Nevada Historical Society Quarterly* 23 (1980): 246–61.

———. *Indians of the Great Basin: A Critical Bibliography.* Bloomington: Indiana University Press, 1982.

Sturtevant, William C. "Creek into Seminole." In Eleanor Burke Leacock and Nancy Oestreich Lurie, eds., *North American Indians in Historical Perspective,* 92–128. New York: Random House, 1971.

Suttles, Wayne. "The Plateau Prophet Dance among the Coast Salish." *Southwestern Journal of Anthropology* 13 (1957): 352–96.

Swanson, Earl H., Jr. *Birch Creek: Human Ecology in the Cool Desert of the*

Northern Rocky Mountains, 9000 B.C.–A.D. 1850. Pocatello: Idaho State University Press, 1972.

Swanson, Earl H., et al. "Cultural Relations between the Plateau and Great Basin." *Northwest Anthropological Research Notes* 4 (Spring 1970): 65–125.

Thomas, David Hurst. "An Empirical Test for Steward's Model of Great Basin Settlement Patterns." *American Antiquity* 38 (April 1973): 155–76.

Thornton, Russell. "Demographic Antecedents of a Revitalization Movement: Population Change, Population Size, and the 1890 Ghost Dance." *American Sociological Review* 46 (February 1981): 88–96.

———. "Demographic Antecedents of Tribal Participation in the 1870 Ghost Dance Movement." *American Indian Culture and Research Journal* 6 (1983): 79–90.

———. *We Shall Live Again.* Cambridge: Cambridge University Press, 1986.

Thurman, Melburn D. "The Shawnee Prophet's Movement and the Origins of the Prophet Dance." *Current Anthropology* 25 (1984): 530–31.

Trafzer, Clifford E., and Margery Ann Beach. "Smohalla, the Washani, and Religion as a Factor in Northwestern Indian History." *American Indian Quarterly* 9 (Summer 1985): 309–24.

Unruh, John D. *The Plains Across: The Overland Emigrants and the Trans-Mississippi West, 1840–1860.* Urbana: University of Illinois Press, 1979.

Utley, Robert M. *The Last Days of the Sioux Nation.* New Haven, CT: Yale University Press, 1963.

———. *A Life Wild and Perilous: Mountain Men and the Paths to the Pacific.* New York: Owl Books, 1997.

Vander, Judith. *Shoshone Ghost Dance Religion: Poetry Songs and Great Basin Context.* Urbana: University of Illinois Press, 1997.

Van Nuys, Frank. *Americanizing the West: Race, Immigrants, and Citizenship, 1890–1930.* Lawrence: University Press of Kansas, 2002.

Vibert, Elizabeth. " 'The Natives Were Strong to Live:' Reinterpreting Early-Nineteenth-Century Prophetic Movements in the Columbia Plateau." *Ethnohistory* 42 (1995): 197–229.

———. *Traders' Tales: Narratives of Cultural Encounters in the Columbia Plateau, 1807–1846.* Norman: University of Oklahoma Press, 1997.

Vogel, Dan. *Indian Origins and the Book of Mormon.* Salt Lake City: Signature Books, 1986.

Walker, Deward E., Jr. "New Light on the Prophet Dance Controversy." *Ethnohistory* 16 (1969): 245–55.

———. *Indians of Idaho.* Moscow: University of Idaho Press, 1978.

———. "Lemhi Shoshone-Bannock Reliance on Anadromous and Other Fish Resources." *Northwest Anthropological Research Notes* 27, no. 2 (1993): 215–50.

———. "The Shoshone-Bannock: An Anthropological Reassessment." *Northwest Anthropological Research Notes* 27, no. 2 (1993): 139–60.

———, ed. *Witchcraft and Sorcery of the American Native Peoples.* Moscow: University of Idaho Press, 1989.

Wallace, Anthony F. C. "Revitalization Movements: Some Theoretical Considerations for Their Comparative Study." *American Anthropologist*, n.s., 58 (1956): 264–81.

———. *The Death and Rebirth of the Seneca*. New York: Random House, 1969.

Weist, Katherine M. "An Ethnohistorical Analysis of Crow Political Alliances." *Western Canadian Journal of Anthropology* 7 (1977): 34–54.

Wells, Merle W. "Caleb Lyon's Indian Policy." *Pacific Northwest Quarterly* (October 1970): 193–200.

White, Richard. *The Middle Ground: Indians, Empires, and Republics in the Great Lakes Region, 1650–1815*. New York: Cambridge University Press, 1991.

Whiting, Beatrice Blyth. *Paiute Sorcery*. Viking Fund Publications in Anthropology 15. New York: Wenner-Gren Foundation for Anthropological Research, 1950.

Wissler, Clark. *General Discussion of Shamanistic and Dancing Societies*. Anthropological Papers of the American Museum of Natural History vol. 11, part 12. New York: American Museum of Natural History 1916.

Worsley, Peter. *The Trumpet Shall Sound: A Study of "Cargo" Cults in Melanesia*. London: MacGibbon & Kee, 1957.

Yeckel, Carl. "The Sheepeater Campaign." *Idaho Yesterdays* 15 (Summer 1971): 2–9.

Index

Italicized page numbers indicate maps.

Snake people *(continued)*
documented contact with, 25–26;
horses of, 213n28; use of term, 16,
209–10n1
Snake River: Bannock War raids along,
147–48; Christian beliefs spread via
trade along, 69–70; ferries across,
228n15; violence along, 44–45
Snake River Plain: buffalo extinction on,
39–40; as center of horse culture, 22;
Newe control of, 36–37
Snake War (1864–68), 93–94, 96, 143
social and economic differences: agent's
utilization of, 179–80; early historic
period changes among, 25–26;
emigration's impact on, 44–47;
ethnicity rooted in, 135; failed
treaties' effects on, 102; in fur-trade
era, 31–41; hardening of, 85–86,
134–39; horse ownership's impact
on, 20–25; increase of, 28–29,
31–32, 39–40, 85–86, 213n36;
in Indian police force, 177; as political, 108; as precursor to ethnic
identities, 47; reified but ignored in
treaty making, 86, 101–2; shared
identity in overcoming, 154–59;
trade's implications for, 28–29
social identities: complexity of, 4–5;
concept of, 5; construction of, 6–
9; control of, 192–93. *See also*
ethnicity and ethnic identities;
identity formation
social organization: diversity of, 18;
emigration's effects on, 46–47; Euro-
American vs. aboriginal concepts of,
8–10; flexibility in, 18–20, 39; war's
effects on, 25–29, 32–41. *See also*
band organization
Soda Springs treaty, 90–91, 96, 98
songs and singing: in Ghost Dances, 115,
168, 196; in healing rituals, 52–53,
54; in Mormon religious services, 74;
in Sabbath observances, 67–68; in
white religious services, 70–71
sorcery: as cause of sickness, 56
sosoni', 16. *See also* "Shoshone"
Spalding, Eliza, 70
Spalding, Henry Harmon, 70
Spaulding, Solomon, 225n92
Spencer, Frank (Weneyuga, Tsawenga,
Doctor Frank), 115–16, 130
Spier, Leslie: on cultural complex, 201; on
Dream Dances, 64; on "dry snow,"
222n52; on Prophet Dance, 58–59,
63, 222n49; on religious patterns,
115

spirit tutors/tutelary spirits: concept of,
36; healing ritual and, 53–57;
Moroni as, 71, 72; shamans'
relationship to, 51–52, 56
Standing Rock Reservation, 1–2
Stevens Treaties (1854 and 1855), 194
Steward, Julian H.: on buffalo extinction,
39; environmental determinism of,
17–18, 211n7; as influence, 210–
11n4; on Newe social organization,
17; on shamanic power, 52; on
winter camps, 217n85
Stewart, Omer C., 214–15n51, 217n86
Stone, E. A., 177
Stowers, C. N., 238n119
Sturtevant, William C., 208n8
subsistence practices: defense concerns
and, 26–27; diversity of, 18, 121–
22; extended range of, 39–40; Fort
Hall incorporated into, 107–8, 112.
See also buffalo hunting; Camas
Prairie (Great and Little); fishing
and fisheries
Sun Dances, 204–5, 249n31
Sun-Flower Seed Eaters, 78, 227n115. *See
also* War-are-ree-kas (Warraricas)
Surprise Valley Paiutes, 115–16

taboos: Bannock War and, 148; as causes
of sickness, 56; shamanic practice
and, 51, 53, 57–58
Taghee (Bannock headman): arrival and
status at Fort Hall, 104–5, 106;
death of, 109, 121; declining power
of, 91–92; demands of, 107–8; Horn
Chief as predecessor of, 36–37; as
leader, 85, 87–88, 96; treaty making
with, 91, 97–99, 100–101
Takona (Ute headman), 119
Talbot, Theodore, 43, 44
talkers *(poínabe)*: shaman assisted by, 54–
55, 57, 221n34
Tambiago (Bannock), 139–40
Tappan, Samuel F., 100
Tash-e-pah ("French Louis," headman),
46
Ta'vibo ("White Man"), 114
Taylor, Nathaniel G., 100
Tcho-wom-ba-ca ("Biting Bear," Bruneau
headman), 94
tebíwa (native land or homeland): concept of, 20, 86–87; negotiations to
preserve, 86, 99, 100–101, 164; of
Newe peoples, 12, 45–46, 71; reservations set on, 94, 98; in treaty
making, 92–93. *See also* land and
resources; subsistence practices

Text: 10/13 Sabon
Display: Sabon
Compositor: BookMatters, Berkeley
Printer and binder: Friesens Corporation
Index: Margie Towery